Exchange Rate, Monetary and Financial Issues and Policies in Asia

Exchange Rate, Monetary and Financial Issues and Policies in Asia

edited by

Ramkishen S Rajan
George Mason University, USA

Shandre Thangavelu
National University of Singapore, Singapore

Rasyad A Parinduri
University of Nottingham, Malaysia

NEW JERSEY • LONDON • SINGAPORE • BEIJING • SHANGHAI • HONG KONG • TAIPEI • CHENNAI

Published by

World Scientific Publishing Co. Pte. Ltd.
5 Toh Tuck Link, Singapore 596224
USA office: 27 Warren Street, Suite 401-402, Hackensack, NJ 07601
UK office: 57 Shelton Street, Covent Garden, London WC2H 9HE

Library of Congress Cataloging-in-Publication Data
Exchange rate, monetary and financial issues and policies in Asia / edited by
Ramkishen S Rajan, Shandre Thangavelu & Rasyad A Parinduri.
p. cm.
ISBN-13 978-981-283-457-7
ISBN-10 981-283-457-5
1. Monetary policy--Asia. 2. Foreign exchange rates--Asia. 3. Finance--Asia.
I. Rajan, Ramkishen S. II. Thangavelu, Shandre, 1969– III. Parinduri, Rasyad A., 1962–

HG1202 .E93 2009
332'.042095--dc22

2008047945

British Library Cataloguing-in-Publication Data
A catalogue record for this book is available from the British Library.

Typeset by Stallion Press
Email: enquiries@stallionpress.com

Printed in Singapore.

FOREWORD

The conference whose proceedings are collected in this volume is the latest event in a tradition of meetings that began four decades ago. Known then as the Claremont–Bologna International Monetary Conference, it was a biennial meeting alternating between the Bologna Center of Johns Hopkins University's Washington-based School for Advanced International Studies (SAIS) and the Claremont Graduate School (CGS), now known as Claremont Graduate University (CGU). It was initiated by Randall Hinshaw, a professor of economics at CGS and Robert Mundell, both of whom had served as visiting professors at the Bologna Center. Unlike the typical paper-focused academic conference, these biennial meetings brought together high-level experts for relatively unstructured conversations covering the major policy issues of the day in both international finance and open-economy macroeconomics. The discussions were unscripted but recorded, generating a transcript which Randall Hinshaw transformed into published monographs of elegant prose.

Over the years, these meetings enjoyed the regular participation of a number of Nobel Laureates and other well-known economists. Among the long-time players were Paul Samuelson, Robert Solow, James Tobin, and, of course, Robert Mundell, as well as Lionel Robbins, Richard Cooper, Max Corden, and Robert Solomon. Also involved were Milton Friedman, Franco Modigliani, James Meade, Nicholas Kaldor, Friedrich von Hayek, Roy Harrod, Fritz Machlup, Gottfried Haberler, Eric Roll, Robert Triffin, Ronald McKinnon, Thomas Willett, Barry Eichengreen, and Jeffrey Frankel. Lionel Robbins served for many years as the rapporteur of the proceedings, summarizing with great eloquence the essential conclusions of the discussions and doing so with a great deal of historical insight and humor.

As noted, the meetings alternated between Claremont and Bologna, but there were some exceptions, including two meetings in Germany and one in Mexico. A meeting in Frankfurt was co-sponsored by the Deutsche Bundesbank and attended by Karl Klasen, Otmar Emminger, and Helmut Schlesinger. The two other exceptions were meetings in Hamburg and in San Miguel de Allende, the latter including an appearance by presidential candidate Vicente Fox. There followed a hiatus, until Michael Plummer of the Bologna Center and Riccardo Rovelli of the University of Bologna raised the possibility of resuming the conference.

After extensive consultations, it was decided to revive the conference, but to include issues in trade policy and to shift the discussion format more toward prepared presentations. The first meeting of the Forum took place in Bologna in 2005 on the occasion of the 50th anniversary of the Bologna Center. Subsequently, Ramkishen Rajan suggested that the Forum needed to be broadened to include meetings in Asia. As it happened, the Singapore Centre for Applied and Policy Economics (SCAPE) at the National University of Singapore was ready to sponsor such a meeting. It took place in August 2007, with participants from all three regions. The Forum owes a special debt of gratitude to Shandre Thangavelu and Ramkishen Rajan for organizing the conference and for assembling this impressive volume of proceedings.

Sven W. Arndt
C.M. Stone Professor and Director
The Lowe Institute of Political Economy
Claremont McKenna College
Claremont, California

CONTENTS

BIOGRAPHY

BIOGRAPHIES OF EDITORS

Ramkishen S. Rajan is Associate Professor in the School of Public Policy, George Mason University, Virginia, a position he has held since January 2006. Prior to that he was on the faculty of the School of Economics, University of Adelaide for five years, where he continues to be a Visiting Associate Professor. Professor Rajan has also taught in the National University of Singapore and the Claremont McKenna College and has held visiting positions in various institutes in Asia including the Hong Kong Institute for Monetary Research. He specializes in international economic policy with particular reference to the emerging Asia-Pacific region. Professor Rajan has been a consultant with the Asian Development Bank, the World Bank, the UN-ESCAP, and other institutions.

Shandre Thangavelu is Associate Professor in the Department of Economics, National University of Singapore. His current research interests are on human capital development, technology transfer, government infrastructure investment, productivity, and economic growth. He has also worked on several international projects commissioned by the Asian Productivity Organization (APO) and the World Bank. Professor Thangavelu was the Director of SCAPE (Singapore Centre for Applied and Policy Economics) at the Department of Economics, National University of Singapore. He was also the Assistant Dean at the Faculty of Arts and Social Sciences from January 2004 to May 2006.

Rasyad A. Parinduri is Assistant Professor at the University of Nottingham, Malaysia Campus. He previously worked as a Senior Researcher at the Econit Advisory Group in Jakarta; a Visiting Lecturer at the Parahyangan Catholic University in Bandung, Indonesia; and a Research

Fellow at the Singapore Centre for Applied and Policy Economics. His research interests are in the fields of industrial organization, labor economics, and development economics. He has an M.A. in Economics from the University of Michigan and his Ph.D. in Economics from the National University of Singapore.

BIOGRAPHIES OF CONTRIBUTORS

Tony Cavoli is Lecturer in the School of Commerce and member of the Centre for Regulation and Market Analysis at the University of South Australia. He received his Ph.D. in Economics in 2005 from the University of Adelaide. His research interests span the areas of open-economy macroeconomics and international economic policy and include such topics as exchange rate regimes, monetary policies, trade and financial integration with particular reference to Asia.

Yin-Wong Cheung is Professor in the Economics Department at the University of California in Santa Cruz, a position he has held since 1990. He is also Professor at the University of Hong Kong, Research Fellow of the CESifo in Germany, board member of the Methods in International Finance Network in Europe, and Guest Professor of the Shandong University. He has published articles related to econometrics, applied econometrics, exchange rate dynamics, asset pricing, output fluctuation, and economic issues in Asian economies. Professor Cheung is listed among the top 1000 Economists and was the President of Chinese Economic Association in North America.

Barry Eichengreen is the George C. Pardee and Helen N. Pardee Professor of Economics and Professor of Political Science at the University of California, Berkeley, where he has taught since 1987. He is also Research Associate of the National Bureau of Economic Research and Research Fellow of the Centre for Economic Policy Research. In 1997–1998 he was a Senior Policy Advisor at the International Monetary Fund. He is a fellow of the American Academy of Arts and Sciences (class of 1997). He is the convener of the Bellagio Group of academics and economic officials. Professor Eichengreen has held Guggenheim and Fulbright Fellowships and has been a fellow of the Center for Advanced Study in the Behavioral Sciences (Palo

Alto) and the Institute for Advanced Study (Berlin). He was awarded the Economic History Association's Jonathan R.T. Hughes Prize for Excellence in Teaching in 2002 and the University of California at Berkeley Social Science Division's Distinguished Teaching Award in 2004. He is also the recipient of a *doctor honoris causa* from the American University in Paris.

Hans Genberg is Executive Director of Research at the Hong Kong Monetary Authority and Director of the Hong Kong Institute for Monetary Research, positions he has held since February 2005. He is on a leave from the Graduate Institute of International Studies in Geneva, Switzerland where he has been Professor of international economics since 1979. Until February he was also the Head of Executive Education at FAME (The International Center for Financial Asset Management and Engineering) in Geneva. A Swedish national, Mr. Genberg holds a Ph.D. degree in Economics from the University of Chicago. His teaching and research deals primarily with international finance, monetary economics and macroeconomics.

Dong He is Head of the Economic Research Division, the Hong Kong Monetary Authority (HKMA). Prior to joining the HKMA in August 2004 he was a Senior Economist in the International Monetary Fund. A Chinese national, he holds a Ph.D. degree in Economics from the University of Cambridge. Mr. He specializes in macroeconomics and financial sector issues, and has extensive operational experience in policy analysis and research.

Corrinne Ho is Senior Economist at the Bank for International Settlements (BIS). She joined the BIS in Basel in 2000 and served an appointment in its Representative Office in Hong Kong in 2003–2007. Before joining the BIS, she was a lecturer at Princeton University's Economics Department and Woodrow Wilson School.

Andrew Hughes Hallett is Professor of Economics and Public Policy in the School of Public Policy at George Mason University in Virginia, and Professor of Economics at the University of St. Andrews in Scotland. He is a graduate of the University of Warwick (UK), holds a Doctorate from Oxford University, and is a Research Fellow in the Centre for Economic Policy Research in London; a Fellow of the Royal Society of Edinburgh; and sits on the Council of the Economic Advisors to the Scottish Government. Professor Hughes Hallett's research interests are in the fields of international economic policy, the political economy of monetary integration, the theory of economic policy. He has given expert evidence to select committees of the Houses of Parliament, the World Bank, the IMF, the Federal Reserve Board, the European Commission, and various central banks.

Hiro Ito is Associate Professor in the Department of Economics at Portland State University, Oregon. His areas of focus are financial development, financial globalization, and macroeconomic interlinkages between countries. He has recently published in *Journal of Development Economics, Journal of International Money and Finance, and Review of International Economics.* Professor Ito received his Ph.D. in economics from University of California, Santa Cruz and M.A. in international relations from the Paul H. Nitze School of Advanced International Studies (SAIS) of Johns Hopkins University in Washington, D.C. Before joining PSU, he was a visiting instructor at Claremont McKenna College, California.

Alex Mandilaras is a full-time lecturer in economics at the University of Surrey, UK, where he also received his Ph.D. with a full scholarship in 2001. His research focuses on international finance with a special reference to emerging economies and his work has appeared in several refereed journals including World Development, North American Journal of Economics and Finance, Scottish Journal of Political Economy, Applied Economics Letters and the Manchester School. He has held a visiting lectureship at the University of Santa Clara and part-time teaching positions at New York University in London and elsewhere. He is associate director of the Surrey Centre for International Economic Studies.

Robert N. McCauley is Chief Representative at the BIS Representative Office for Asia and the Pacific in Hong Kong. He began his BIS career in Basel in 1994, after 13 years at the Federal Reserve Bank of New York and a teaching stint in 1992 at the University of Chicago's Graduate School of Business.

Eiji Ogawa is Professor in the Graduate School of Commerce and Management, Hitotsubashi University and also Faculty Fellow at the Research Institute of Economy, Trade, and Industry (REITI), both of which are based in Tokyo, Japan. He holds a Ph.D. in Commerce (International Finance) from Hitotsubashi University. Professor Ogawa has been a Visiting Scholar at the Department of Economics of Harvard University (September 1986–March 1988), the Department of Economics of University of California at

Berkeley (April 1992–March 1993), and the Research Department of the International Monetary Fund (September 2000).

Helen Popper is Associate Professor in the Department of Economics, Santa Clara University in California. Before joining Santa Clara, Professor Popper worked at the Federal Reserve Board in Washington, D.C. as an Economist in the Division of International Finance. She has received visiting research and teaching appointments at the Federal Reserve, the Bank of Mexico, the University of California at Berkeley, and the Hong Kong Institute for Monetary Research. She also has been a consultant for the World Bank, for the Federal Reserve, and in the private sector; and she has been Chair of Santa Clara University's economics department. Professor Popper holds a Ph.D. in Economics from the University of California at Berkeley. Her teaching and research deal primarily with international finance and open-economy macroeconomics.

Christian Richter is Lecturer in the Department of Economics at Loughborough University, UK, a position he has held since 2004. He is also chair of the International Network for Economic Research (INFER) since October 2007. Dr. Richter started his economic career at the University of Mainz where he graduated as Diplom-Volkswirt in 1994 and where he also started his Ph.D. In 1996 he joined the Scottish Doctoral Program for which he won the partnership scholarship of the University of Mainz. The Scottish Doctoral Programme was then based at Glasgow University, where he graduated in 1997 (M.Sc. in Economics). Continuing the Scottish Doctoral Program, he joined the University of Strathclyde in Glasgow and graduated in 2001. In 2002 he won a lectureship at Cardiff University. Mr. Richter's research areas are Macroeconomics, Financial Economics and Econometrics.

Dominick Salvatore is Distinguished Professor and Director of the Ph.D. Program in Economics at Fordham University. He is also the Fellow of the New York Academy of Sciences and was past Chairman of its Economics Section. He was the past President of the North American Economics and Finance Association, and the International Trade and Finance Association. He is Honorary Professor at Shanghai Finance University. He is a co-author of *Income Inequality* (Oxford University Press, 2006) and author of *International Economics* (9th ed., Wiley, 2007); and *Managerial Economics in a Global Economy* (6th ed., Oxford, 2007).

Willem Thorbecke is Associate Professor in the Department of Economics, George Mason University, Virginia and a Senior Fellow at the Research Institute of Economy, Trade, and Industry (REITI) in Tokyo, Japan. His principal fields are monetary and international economics. He has a Ph.D. from the University of California, Berkeley and over 50 publications in refereed journals, edited volumes, and public policy series. Professor Thorbecke is currently investigating how exchange rate changes in East Asia affect cross-border production networks and global imbalances.

INTRODUCTION

Ramkishen S. Rajan, Shandre Thangavelu and Rasyad A. Parinduri

This volume is a compilation of selected papers presented in the Claremont–Bologna–Singapore International Policy Forum held at the National University of Singapore on July 30–31, 2007.[1] The particular theme of the Forum was on exchange rate, monetary and financial issues and policies. The motivation for this theme was straightforward. It has been a decade since the Asian crisis of 1997–1998, which decimated many of the regional economies. While the crisis itself had severe economic and political consequences, one of its primary causes was an inappropriate mix of exchange rate, monetary and financial policies. In particular, one of the main reasons behind the crisis was the attempt by regional economies to maintain fairly rigid exchange rates (soft U.S. dollar pegs) as well as monetary policy autonomy in the presence of large-scale capital outflows. Part of the reason behind this obvious violation of Impossible Trinity Principle arose from the fact that the capital outflows had led to sever domestic liquidity crunch, which was threatening to lead to an outright financial collapse in many economies.

In the keynote address to the Forum by *Barry Eichengreen in Chapter 1*, he briefly outlines how the East Asian countries have fared since the crisis and also highlights the potential vulnerabilities and triggers for a future

[1]The funding support for the Forum was provided by the Faculty of Arts and Social Sciences, National University of Singapore.

financial crisis. He argues that the most likely place where a future crisis might emerge is in China, which has a combination of high corporate savings and investments, appreciated asset markets, weak banking system, and a rigid currency. Eichengreen suggests that a financial crisis in China could be triggered by a sharp fall in asset prices, which could set off a credit freeze and investment collapse. He goes on to draw parallels between China today and the U.S. in the 19th century when the U.S., like China today, experienced not only rapid investment-led growth, but also experienced a series of financial crises.

Apart from the need to strengthen domestic financial systems, an immediate lesson that many observers appear to have drawn from recent financial crises in emerging market economies in the 1990s is that the only viable exchange rate option boils down to one between flexibility, on the one hand, and "credible pegging", on the other. According to this view (which was dominant in the late 1990s and early 2000s but still has a number of followers), emerging economies have to gravitate to one of these two extremes. Any currency arrangements that lie in between these polar extremes or corners (i.e., those in the "middle") are viewed as being inherently unstable and crisis-prone. *Chapter 2 by Tony Cavoli and Ramkishen S. Rajan* compiles and discusses the *de jure* or official exchange rate regimes in the various Asian economies. Recognizing that countries do not always follow their policy pronouncements, the chapter also reviews the evidence regarding the *de facto* or actual exchange rate regimes in selected Asian countries, particularly Indonesia, Thailand, Korea, and the Philippines.

In one sense, it is apparent that many of the Asian economies continue to manage their currencies quite heavily, as evidenced by the rapid stockpiling of reserves since the 1997 crisis. The sharp switch from current account deficit to surplus for emerging Asia as a group has been well documented and is apparent from Table 1. The combination of current account surplus and renewed private capital inflows, along with active exchange rate management by the regional central banks, contributed to the rapid and significant reserve buildup in emerging Asia in recent years. Some have argued that the reserve growth in Asia is a by-product of a desire by regional central banks to smooth exchange rate movements. While concerns about "excessive" volatility of trade and foreign direct investment (FDI) may

Table 1. Sources of reserve accumulation in emerging Asia, 1995–2005 (U.S.$ billions).

	1995	1996	1997	1998	1999	2000	2001	2002	2003	2004	2005
Change in reserves	−42.6	−46.8	−35.8	−53.1	−88.2	−53.7	−90.2	−148.8	−226.5	−340.1	−281.9
Current account balance	−40.0	−40.1	14.0	114.0	106.0	85.0	88.4	127.5	166.3	183.5	240.8
Private capital flows, net	101.5	121.1	47.6	−53.8	3.1	6.5	19.6	20.8	63.5	120.3	53.8
Official capital flows, net	−4.7	−16.1	14.0	19.6	1.8	−11.7	−11.7	4.6	−17.6	1.8	5.0

Notes: Capital flows to "emerging Asia" is dominated by 10 economies, viz. the eight economies in this paper (India, Indonesia, Korea, Malaysia, Philippines, Singapore, Taiwan and, Thailand), as well as China and Hong Kong. It also includes a number of other countries categorized as "developing Asia" by the IMF.
Source: IMF, World Economic Outlook Database, April 2006.

be well founded (for instance, see Calvo and Reinhart (2002)), smoothing behavior by central banks should, over time, have no net impact on reserves.

The fact that reserves are continuously being built up suggests that intervention is largely asymmetric, i.e., sale of domestic currency during periods of upward pressure, but limited intervention on the downside. A far more plausible argument for Asia's reserve accumulation stems from its desire to maintain relatively stable and ultra-competitive exchange rates, so as to aggressively export their way out of the crisis and deep recession of 1997–1998.[2,3] In fact, Asian policymakers have chosen explicitly to amass reserves for precautionary or self-insurance motives against future financial crisis (Aizenman and Marion, 2003; Bird and Rajan, 2003).[4] Such large levels of "own liquidity" may be particularly necessary in the absence of the development of strong quasi-lender of last resort capabilities by the IMF and limited progress in monetary cooperation at the regional level (Bird and Rajan, 2002; Rajan, 2008).

Chapter 3 by Yin-Wong Cheung and Hiro Ito investigates the empirical determinants of the demand for international reserves in selected Asian and Latin American economies. They emphasize that different theories lead to quite different inferences about the appropriate level of international reserves. Their estimation highlights the importance of financial and institutional factors relative to conventional macroeconomic ones in determining demand for reserves in the post-Asian financial crisis period. The authors also find that deciphering whether Asia has been holding "excessive" reserves is a complex task, depending significantly on the choice

---

[2]In addition, part of the change in reserves in U.S. dollar terms arises from "revaluation gains" due to the depreciation of the U.S. dollar against the major currencies in which reserves might be held, especially the Euro.

[3]The World Bank (2005) has observed:

> Intervention was initially motivated by a desire to build up a buffer stock after the Asian crisis had depleted levels of reserves.... (H)owever (r)apid reserve accumulation ... continued through late 2004, as countries sought to limit the impact of heavy capital inflows on external competitiveness, at a time when domestic demand generally remained subdued (p. 29).

[4]There has been a growing body of literature exploring various aspects of the precautionary motive for reserve hoarding. See García and Soto (2004), Jeanne and Ranciere (2006), and Li and Rajan (2006).

of benchmark. They find evidence that Asian economies tend to hold more international reserves than their Latin American counterparts do. The difference in behavior may be a reflection of the difference in the empirical determinants found for the economies in these two regions.

Regardless of the rationale for the reserves, their buildup has contributed substantially to concerns about the creation of excessive global liquidity. How justified these concerns are depends heavily on the extent to which the reserve accumulating countries have been able to sterilize the effects on their domestic monetary aggregates. *Chapter 4 by Corrinne Ho and Robert N. McCauley* investigates the extent of monetary sterilization in Asia. They note that official international reserves in Asia have grown at an unparalleled scale since 2002. They find that regional monetary authorities have been sterilizing aggressively to mop up the liquidity consequences of their reserve accumulation.[5] It is often argued that sustained sterilization has significant fiscal and/or banking costs (for instance, see Calvo (1991)) and may not be sustainable. The authors, however, question the extent to which these concerns are relevant to Asia. They conclude that, with the exception of India "where a number of archetypal symptoms have emerged", many other Asian economies appear to have been able to sterilize without notable costs. They go on to argue that large-scale reserve accretion in Asia (except India) may be better viewed as being a consequence of economic slack due to the decline in national investment relative to savings as opposed to an independent policy *per se*.

While the region has experienced resurgence in net capital inflows since the crisis (see Table 1), Asia remains a *net* exporter of capital to the rest of the world as evidenced by its persistent reserve accumulation. Thus, while pre-crisis capital from developed countries financed the investment needs of emerging economies, currently the flows have reversed direction; capital from emerging economies has been financing the consumption needs for the developed world, most notably the U.S. economy.[6] What explains this "paradox of capital"[7] and, in particular, what determines capital flows in

[5]Also see Ouyang *et al.* (2007a) for the case of sterilization of China and Ouyang *et al.* (2007b) for the case of other emerging Asia.
[6]See Kharas *et al.* (2006).
[7]As noted by Prasad *et al.* (2007) and first brought up by Lucas (1990). Also see Gourinchas and Jeanne (2007).

Asia? Are they linked to macroeconomic developments within the country, among the other emerging market economies within the region, or to the macroeconomic conditions in the major industrialized countries outside Asia, the U.S. in particular? These issues are the focus of *Chapter 5 by Alex Mandilaras and Helen Popper.* They find that what matters the most are own country domestic financial market conditions, with domestic financial market capitalization consistently being the best predictor of the paradox. They also discuss some new research that suggests the role of macroeconomic conditions in the U.S. has also been limited; apparently the U.S. is not the key driver of the Asia-Pacific's capital flow behaviour.

While the Asian economies have bounced back from the crisis and are much healthier (in terms of macroeconomic fundamentals, corporate balance sheets, etc.), a financial crisis of sorts is now inflicting the U.S. in the form of the sub-prime malaise (discussed briefly in Chapter 1 by Barry Eichengreen). There is a danger that this crisis could lead to a prolonged slowdown in the U.S. What does this U.S. economic slowdown imply for Asia? Have Asian economies decoupled from the U.S. or are they still heavily dependent on the U.S. as an export market as well as via various financial channels. Will the U.S. slowdown derail Asian export and overall growth, or has regional demand in Asia grown sufficiently large (especially with the rise of China) to cushion the region from a recession in the U.S.?

The impact of the U.S. economy on Asia is a theme that is taken up in *Chapter 6 by Andrew Hughes Hallett and Christian Richter.* In particular, the chapter examines the hypothesis that the links in the Asia-Pacific region have altered over the past two decades (1987–2006), particularly with the economic rise of China as a major industrial power and the emergence of Japan as a major source of finance. The authors use time-varying spectral methods to decompose the linkages between China, Japan, four advanced Asian economies (Korea, Taiwan, Malaysia, and Singapore), and the U.S. In particular, they take the U.S., China, and Japan to be the potential leading economies ("economies of first resort" as they call them) in the Asia-Pacific area, and investigate the dynamics of the links among these three economies and between them and the other emerging economies in the region. The authors find evidence that regional links with the U.S. have been weakening since the 1980s with the rise of China. However, they also find that the U.S. is still able to shape the business cycles in Asia via the control of monetary conditions, though China and Japan influence the size of those cycles. With regard to exchange rates, the authors find little evidence of endogeneity of business cycle synchronization, i.e., pegged exchange rates *per se* will encourage economic convergence, and in fact, the reverse may be true.

While the region is still dependent on the U.S. market, has greater intra-regional trade and investment led to *de facto* macroeconomic convergence, and what in turn does this imply for regional exchange rate coordination? In *Chapter 7, Willem Thorbecke* focuses on the extent of intra-regional production and trade. He describes the production networks that have been established in Asia, whereby different parts of the production process of a good have been split into parts, components, and accessories (PCAs) and distributed across countries in the region. Thorbecke refers specifically to a triangular trading pattern, whereby firms located in Japan, Korea, Taiwan, and higher-income Southeast Asia economies (mainly Singapore, Malaysia, and Thailand) produce relatively sophisticated technology-intensive intermediate goods and capital goods and ship them to China and lower income Southeast Asian economies (including Indonesia, Vietnam, etc.) for final assembly. The ultimate buyers of the final products tend to be the U.S. and Europe. He notes that the export-oriented nature and fear of loss of price competitiveness of the Asian economies has given rise to a collective action problem, which has led many of countries to heavily manage their respective currencies. He argues that stable intra-regional exchange rates could facilitate the further development of regional production and distribution networks that has made East Asia a global manufacturing hub. Exchange rate stability in turn could, according to him, be facilitated if regional economies with less flexible exchange rates adopted more flexible regimes characterized by (1) multiple currencies basket-based reference rates instead of a dollar-based central rate, and (2) wider bands around the reference rate.

The need for regional exchange rate stability and the issue of regional exchange rate and monetary coordination is explored in more detail in *Chapter 8 by Eiji Ogawa*. He notes that the policymakers in ASEAN plus three (China, Japan, and Korea) have taken steps to strengthen regional exchange rate, monetary and financial cooperation since 2000. With regard to exchange rates coordination, the ASEAN plus three Financial Ministers Meeting has established a research group to examine the feasibility of an Asian Monetary Unit (AMU) for coordinated exchange rate policy. The chapter develops a measure to examine the degree of exchange rate divergence in the region (vis-à-vis a synthetic AMU). Using the so-called AMU Deviation Indictors, Ogawa argues that there is a growing deviation among the East Asian currencies. The author takes this to imply that there is a coordination failure in exchange rate policies in the region. He recommends the creation of an AMU in order to coordinate exchange rate policy among the monetary authorities of East Asian countries so as to facilitate the development of production networks and supply chains in the region.

In *Chapter 9, Hans Genberg and Dong He* revisit the issue of regional exchange rate regimes. As with Cavoli and Rajan in Chapter 2, they observe that there is a great degree of heterogeneity in the exchange rate regimes and monetary policy frameworks in the region. They note that, with the exceptions of China, Malaysia, and Hong Kong, the central banks in the region appear to have a mandate of domestic price stability as opposed to an explicit exchange rate objective. Under such circumstances — and in sharp contrast to the views of Thorbecke and Ogawa in Chapters 8 and 9, respectively — they argue that it would be in fact be undesirable to push for exchange rate policy coordination or any sort of regional cooperation on exchange rate policies. Attempting to do so, in their opinion, could create conflicts with domestic objectives that may lead to loss of central bank credibility and possibly even speculative attacks against the regional currencies. Instead of exchange rate and monetary policy coordination, they emphasize the need to focus on financial cooperation — developing more liquid financial markets in the region; harmonizing the objectives of monetary policy; and designing institutions that might become the foundation of deeper forms of cooperation in the long term.[8] While their focus on the development of financial markets is uncontroversial, clearly much greater work is needed on the issue of exchange rate coordination in Asia. Should the region attempt to go the European route over time?

In *Chapter 10, Dominick Salvatore* notes that Asia's interest in monetary and financial integration has been inspired in part by the apparent success of the European Monetary Union (EMU) in establishing a common central bank (the ECB) and a common currency (the euro). He examines the process

---

[8] Some of these issues are also explored in Rajan (2008).

of economic, monetary, and financial integration in Europe and goes on to evaluate the costs and benefits of the EMU and draws conclusions from Europe's experience for Asia, focusing on the feasibility and possible benefits that East Asia could derive from economic and monetary integration and the best way to achieve it. He notes that one of biggest concerns in East Asia is the seeming unwillingness by regional participants to establish the institutions necessary for monetary integration to work well. This stands in sharp contrast to Europe, which spent decades to build the institutions that were viewed as critical for the adoption of a monetary union. Clearly, Asia needs to start paying much more attention to the development of region-wide institutions prior to attempting more ambitious integration efforts.

References

Aizenman, J and N Marion (2003). The high demand for international reserves in the far east: What's going on? *Journal of Japanese and International Economics*, 17, 370–400.

Bird, G and RS Rajan (2002). *The Evolving Asian Financial Architecture*. Princeton Essays in International Economics No. 266. Princeton University.

Bird, G and RS Rajan (2003). Too good to be true?: The adequacy of international reserve holdings in an era of capital account crises. *The World Economy*, 26, 873–891.

Calvo, G (1991). The perils of sterilization. *IMF Staff Papers*, 38, 921–926.

Calvo, G and C Reinhart (2002). Fear of floating. *Quarterly Journal of Economics*, 117, 379–408.

Garcia, P and CG Soto (2004). Large hoarding of international reserves: Are they worth it? In *External Vulnerability and Preventive Policies*, Caballero, R, C Calderón and LF Céspedes (eds.) Central Bank of Chile.

Gourinchas, PO and O Jeanne (2007). Capital flows to developing countries: The Allocation puzzle. NBER Working Papers 13602.

International Monetary Fund (IMF) (2006). *Regional Economic Outlook: Asia and Pacific*, IMF, May.

Jeanne, O and R Ranciere (2006). The optimal level of international reserves for emerging market economies: Formulas and applications. IMF Working Paper No. 06/229.

Kharas, H, RS Rajan and E Vostroknutova (2006). Finance (in East Asia). In *An East Asian Renaissance: Ideas for Competitive Growth*, Kharas H and I Gill (eds.). Washington, DC: World Bank.

Li, J and RS Rajan (2006). Can high reserves offset weak fundamentals? A simple model of precautionary demand for reserves. *Economia Internazionale*, 59, 317–328.

Lucas, RE (1990). Why doesn't capital flows from rich to poor countries? *American Economic Review*, 80, 92–96.

Ouyang, A, RS Rajan and TD Willett (2007a). China as a reserve sink: The evidence from offset and sterilization coefficients. Hong Kong Institute for Monetary Research, Working Paper No. 10/2007.

Ouyang, A, RS Rajan and TD Willett (2007b). Managing the monetary consequences of reserve accumulation in emerging Asia. Hong Kong Institute for Monetary Research. Working Paper No. 20/2007.

Prasad, E, RG Prasad and A Subramanian (2007). The paradox of capital. *Finance and Development*, 44, March.

Rajan, RS (2008). Monetary and financial cooperation in Asia: Taking stock of recent on-goings. *International Relations of the Asia-Pacific*, 8, 31–45.

World Bank (2005). *Global Development Finance 2005*. New York: Oxford University Press.

PART I
OVERVIEW

CHAPTER 1

THE ASIAN CRISIS AFTER 10 YEARS[1]

Barry Eichengreen

1.1. Introduction

There is no shortage of conferences, commentaries, and even keynote addresses celebrating the 10th anniversary of the Asian crisis. "Celebrating" is, admittedly, an odd word to use in this context; recollections of a crisis are not typically being taken as an occasion for the popping of champagne corks. Yet, I use it consciously: 10 years after the crisis there are in fact important achievements. For one thing, Asia has not experienced further financial crises. For another, the region rebounded quickly, and now once again is the fastest growing part of the world. Some observers worry that investment rates in Emerging East Asia ex China have never recovered fully to pre-crisis levels, making for slower growth than in the first half of the 1990s.[2] However, less investment may, in this case, mean more efficient investment and, even if growth rates have slowed they are still impressive by the standards of the rest of the world.

Commentators on this experience faces two challenges. The first one is drawing inferences about the future from the past. The fact that Asia has not experienced another crisis is no guarantee against such problems in the future, just as the fact that Asia is now the world's fastest growing

[1] Keynote address to the Claremont-Bologna-Singapore Center for Applied and Policy Economics International Economic Policy Forum on "Capital Flows, Financial Markets and Economic Integration in Asia," 31 July 2007. This version has been slightly updated to reflect subsequent developments but still should be read in the context it was delivered.

[2] Readers seeking more detail on the decline in investment, its causes, and its implications for growth can find an extensive analysis in Asian Development Bank (2007).

region does not ensure that it will continue to outperform economically.[3] The second challenge is to approach these questions with a modicum of originality. I attempt both tasks in what follows.

1.2. Post-Crisis Changes

The big change from the pre-crisis period is the improvement in Asian current accounts. In Figure 1.1, countries are arrayed by the size of the

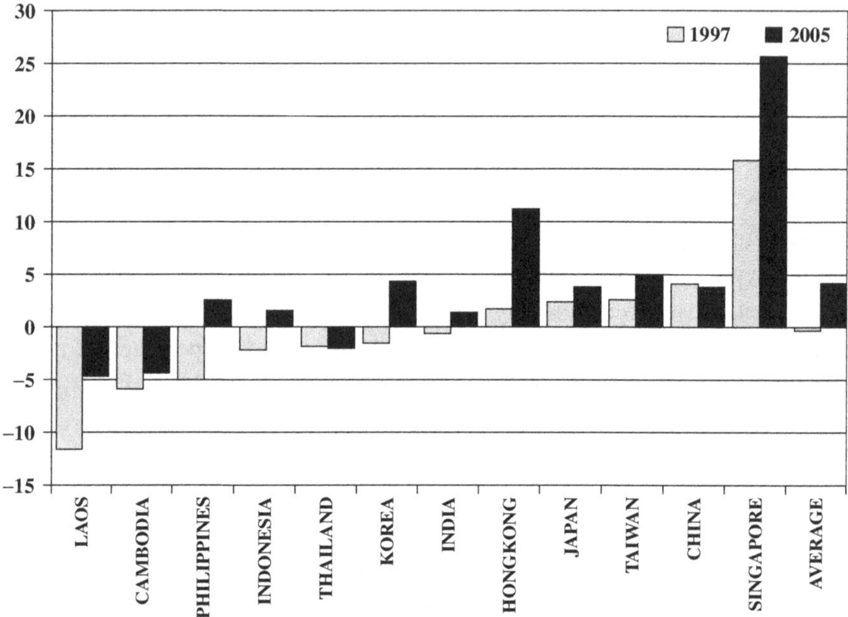

Fig. 1.1. Current account balance to GDP.
Source: World Bank World Development Indicators.

[3]Forecasting is risky business, especially when it involves the future, to paraphrase a comment traditionally attributed to Niels Bohr, the Danish physicist. An interesting letter to *The Economist* (21 June 2007) suggests that Bohr did not originate this quote but appropriated it to illustrate the difference between Danish and Swedish humor. (Mark Twain may have been the originator, but even this is uncertain.) Other quotes for which Bohr has clear patrimony are equally relevant to economics, however. "An expert is a man who has made all the mistakes, which can be made, in a very narrow field." "Never express yourself more clearly than you think." And "We all agree that your theory is crazy. The question that divides us is whether it is crazy enough."

current surplus, scaled by GDP, in 1997. Countries with substantial surpluses around the time of the crisis have maintained them, while a number of other countries have either shrunk their deficits (Laos, Cambodia) or moved from deficit to surplus (Philippines, Indonesia, Korea). Countries have used these surpluses to build their international reserves, keeping their currencies down and sterilizing some of the associated capital inflows (see Chapter 4 of this volume). Less widely appreciated is that while reserves are up dramatically as a share of short-term debt, they are up less dramatically relative to exports (Figure 1.2), where they have risen from 40 to 60 percent (most sharply in three countries that already had high reserves by this measure — Japan, India, and China — as well as in Korea), and they have risen not at all relative to the scale of the financial system as measured by M2 (Figure 1.3). Putting reserves up has been part and parcel with keeping currencies down. Mechanically applying the Reinhart–Rogoff criteria, it would appear that there is relatively little change in *de facto* exchange rate regimes; significant increases in flexibility are indicated only in Indonesia and Korea (Figure 1.4;

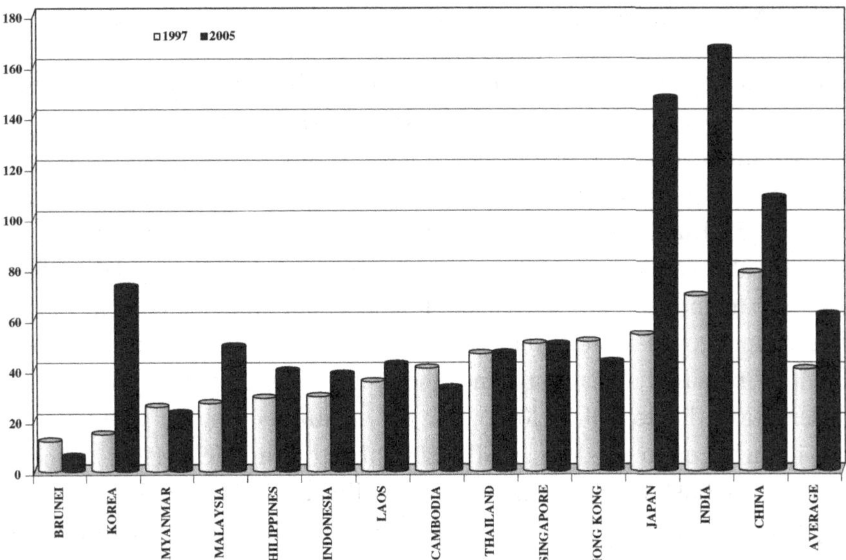

Fig. 1.2. Ratio of reserves to exports.
Note: Total reserves minus gold over goods exports (f.o.b.).
Source: IMF International Financial Statistics.

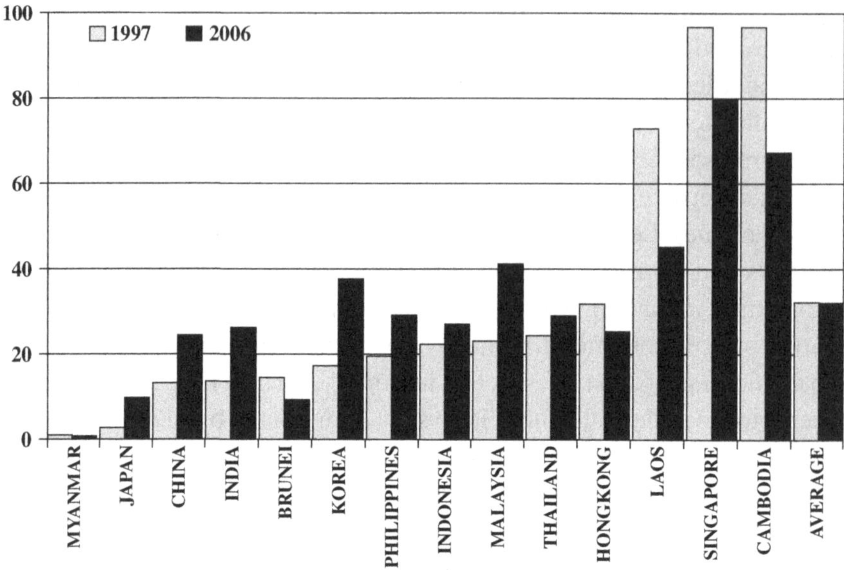

Fig. 1.3. Ratio of reserves to M2.
Note: Total reserves minus gold over money plus quasi-money.
Source: IMF International Financial Statistics.

also see Chapters 2 and 9 of this volume). This is a significant and not entirely reassuring development. I return to it below.

Arithmetically, current accounts have strengthened because investment rates have fallen while savings rates have been essentially flat (see Figure 1.5). But this observation just pushes the mystery back another step. Keeping the exchange rate low should boost not just exports but also profitability; the positive co-movement of exports and investment is one of the foundation stones of the Asian model. Some authors (e.g., Kramer, 2006) point to increased uncertainty since the Asian crisis. Countering this is the observation, due to Villar (2006), that the volatility of output and inflation has in fact been lower during 2001–2004 than during 1995–1999.[4] Others suggest that East Asian industry is being "hollowed out" by the rise of China, depressing investment. In practice, however, the impact of China's rise on its neighbors is mixed: China has had a positive impact on the exports and

[4]This contrast is presumably influenced by the fact that the first subperiod spans the Asian crisis. But my own calculations for the 1990–1995 period further support the point that volatility has declined in recent years.

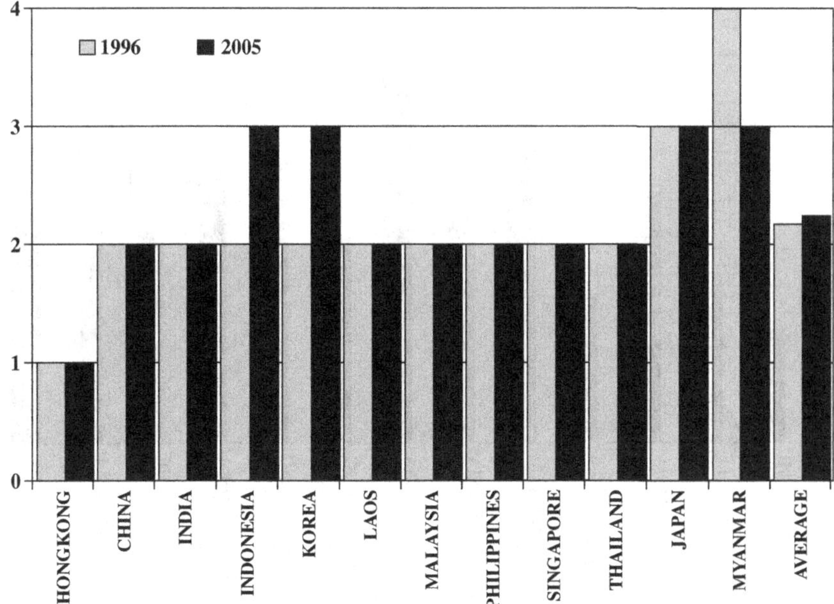

Fig. 1.4. Exchange rate regime.
Note: The exchange rate regime discrete variable takes the value of 1 if the exchange rate arrangement is a hard peg, 2 for intermediate regimes, 3 for freely floating, and 4 for freely falling.
Source: Reinhart and Rogoff (2004) natural classification (for 1996–2002) updated by Eichengreen and Razo-Garcia (2005) (for 2003–2005).

investment of producers of capital goods, components, and technology but a negative impact on countries that compete with it in assembly operations and the production of consumer goods (Eichengreen and Tong, 2006). Yet, with the exceptions of Cambodia, Vietnam, India, and of course China itself, investment rates have fallen across the board.

The explanation still standing is that budget constraints have hardened as financial systems have been reformed, governments have removed explicit investment subsidies and implicit guarantees, and corporate governance has been strengthened, discouraging empire building by managers and founding families. If so, one would think that Asian investment, while reduced in volume, has become more efficient.[5] But this has not shown up in a declining Incremental Capital Output Ratio (ICOR) or accelerating Total

[5]As alluded to in the introduction.

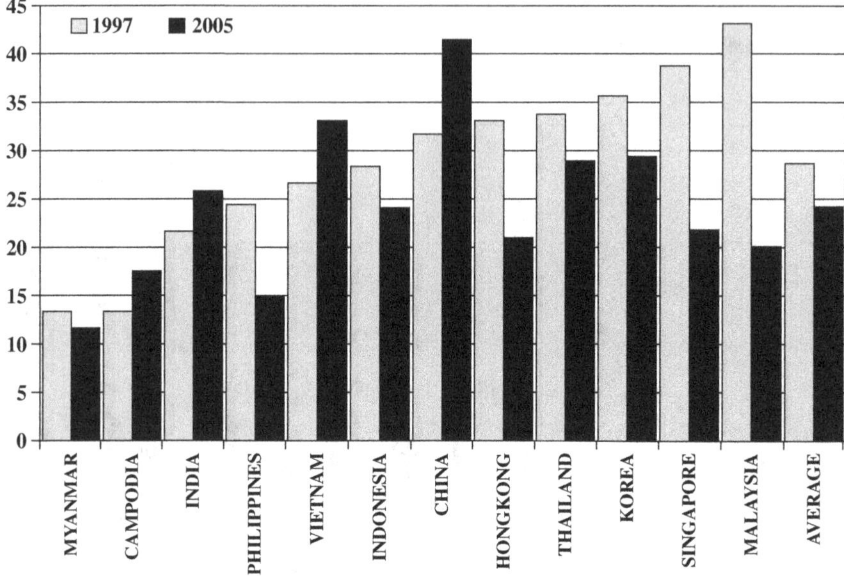

Fig. 1.5. Investment to GDP.
Note: Gross fixed capital formation over GDP.
Source: IMF International Financial Statistics.

Factor Productivity (TFP) growth. Rather, the decline in investment rates has been accompanied by a downward shift in growth rates (as emphasized by the Asian Development Bank in its 2007 *Asian Development Outlook*). It could be that more time will have to pass before more efficient investment translates into faster growth. We shall see.

Another big change is the composition of foreign finance (Figure 1.6). In Malaysia, Indonesia, and the Philippines, among other countries, dependence on borrowing from foreign commercial banks and other private creditors has been reduced, on net, while inward foreign direct and/or equity investment has increased. This is a more stable and reliable pattern of borrowing. Interestingly, Korea and Thailand do not fit the pattern in that net inflows remain large.[6] In the case of Korea it is also notable that net borrowing from foreign banks remains substantial, as local branches of foreign banks have taken advantage of low funding costs to invest heavily in higher-yielding Korean securities. I will have more to say about this shortly.

[6]Or at least they did, in the case of Thailand, prior to the coup last November.

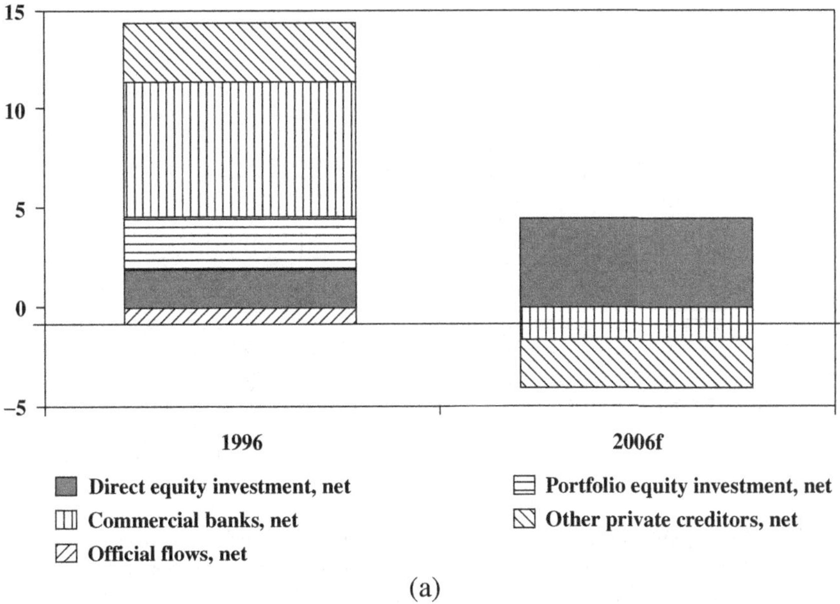

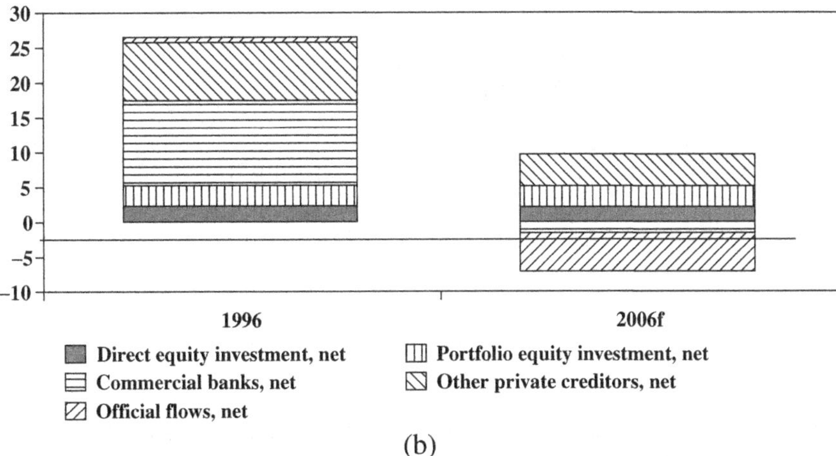

Fig. 1.6. External financing: (a) Malaysia, (b) Indonesia, (c) Philippines, (d) Korea, and (e) Thailand. (billions of U.S. dollars).
Source: Institute of International Finance.

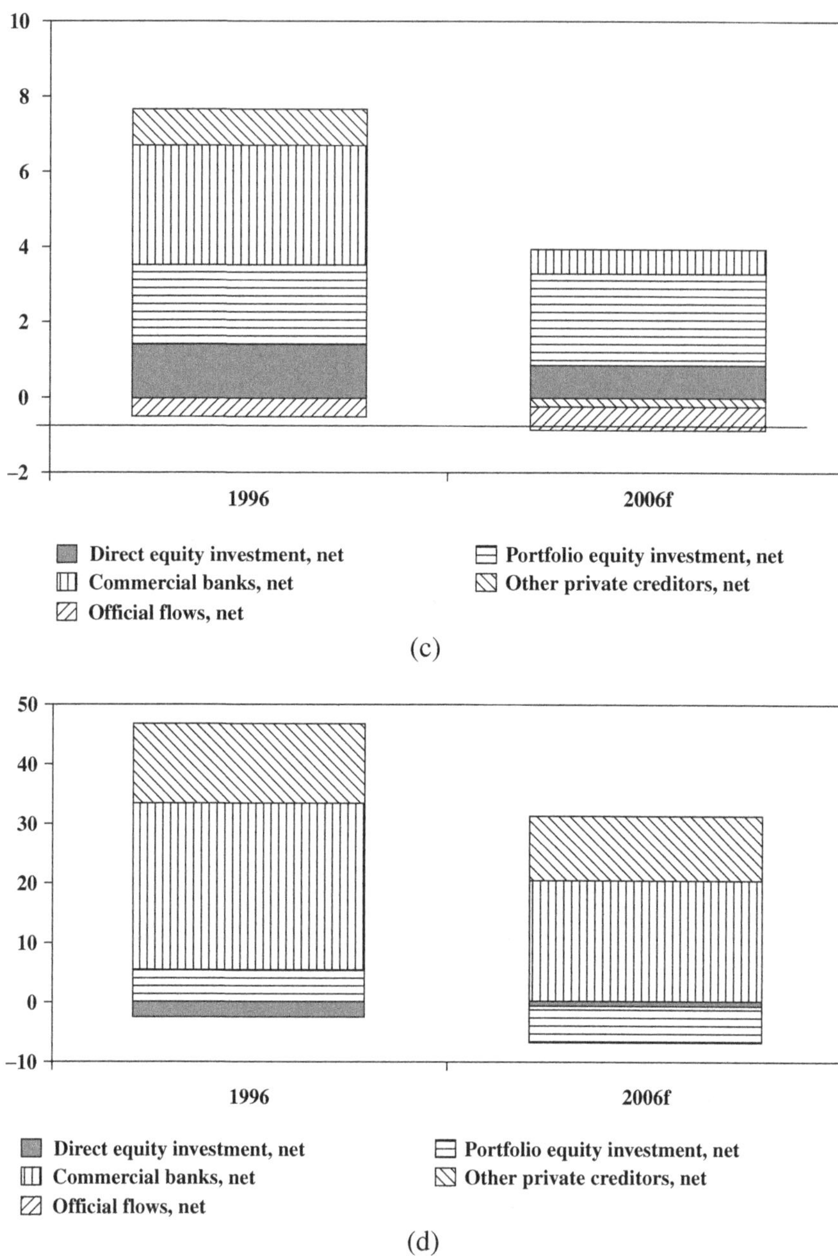

Fig. 1.6. (*Continued*)

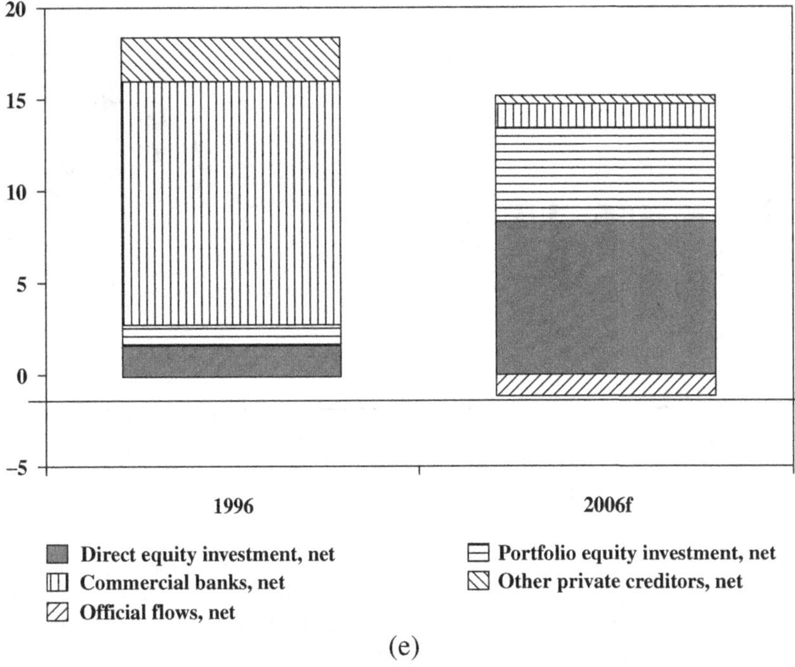

(e)

Fig. 1.6. *(Continued)*

What about Asia's much-vaunted institutional reforms? There has been little measured improvement in the rule of law (Figure 1.7) or government effectiveness (Figure 1.8), with the exception, in the case of the latter, of Korea, Malaysia, and Hong Kong.[7] Measures of regulatory quality are up only in Korea, Japan, Singapore, Taiwan, and Hong Kong, and down for the region as a whole (Figure 1.9). A less pessimistic perspective would emphasize that, adjusted for levels of economic development, Asia compared favorably with other regions in terms of these measures even before the crisis and that the absence of faster progress has not fundamentally transformed this picture. Figures 1.10–1.12 array countries according to their per capita incomes in U.S. dollars in 2006. Singapore, Malaysia, and to a lesser extent Hong Kong and Korea do visibly better than predicted on the basis of their development and incomes, while Japan does visibly worse.

[7]And, if countries with very low values are nonetheless accepted, Cambodia as well.

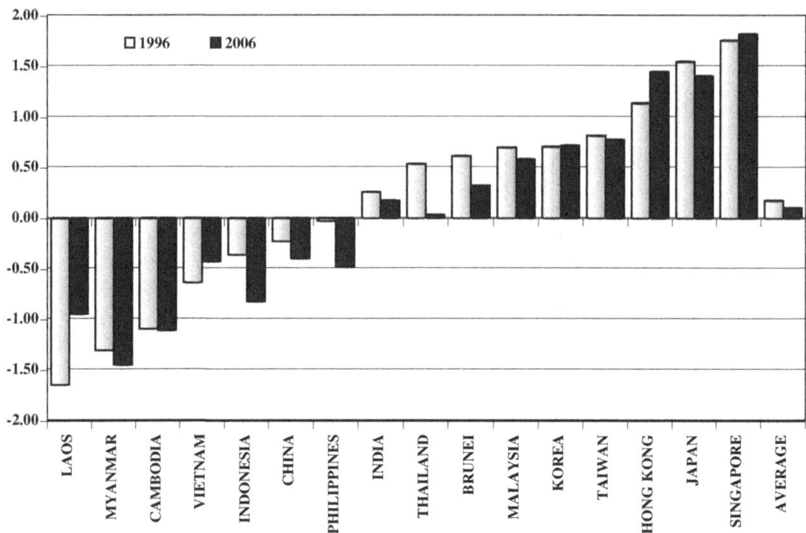

Fig. 1.7. Rule of law. (The rule of law index measures the extent to which the agents have confidence in and abide by the rules of society, and in particular the quality of contract enforcement, the police, and the courts, as well as the likelihood of crime and violence. A higher index is translated in a better rule of law.)
Source: World Bank Governance Indicators.

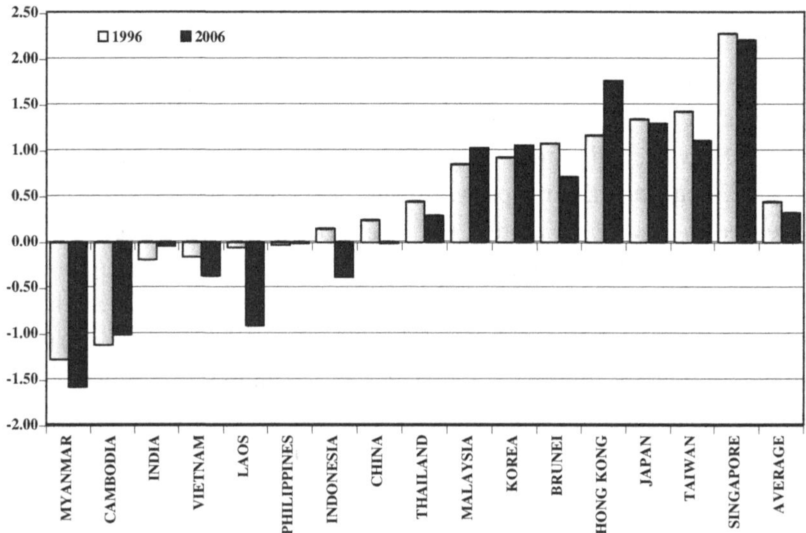

Fig. 1.8. Government effectiveness. (The government effectiveness index measures the quality of public services, the quality of the civil service and the degree of its independence from political pressures, the quality of policy formulation and implementation, and the credibility of the government's commitment to such policies. A higher index is translated in a more effective government.)
Source: World Bank Governance Indicators.

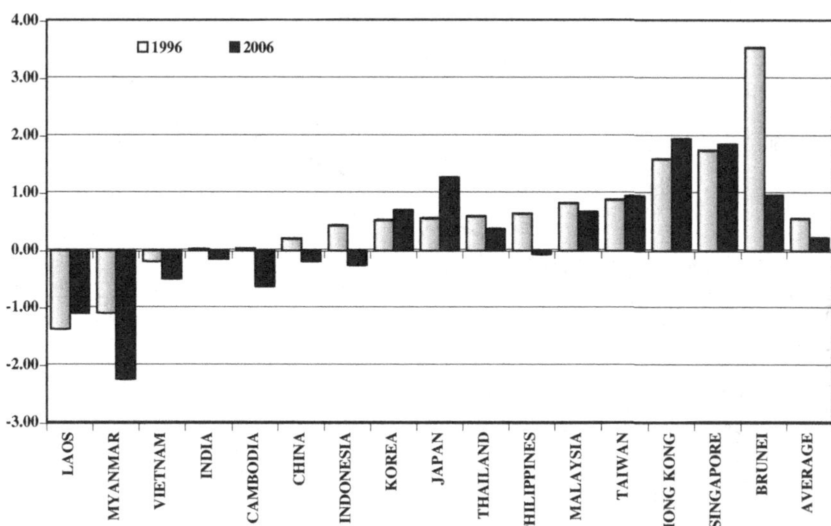

Fig. 1.9. Regulatory quality. (The regulatory quality index measures the ability of the government to formulate and implement sound policies and regulations that permit and promote private sector development. A higher index is translated in a higher regulatory quality.)
Source: World Bank Governance Indicators.

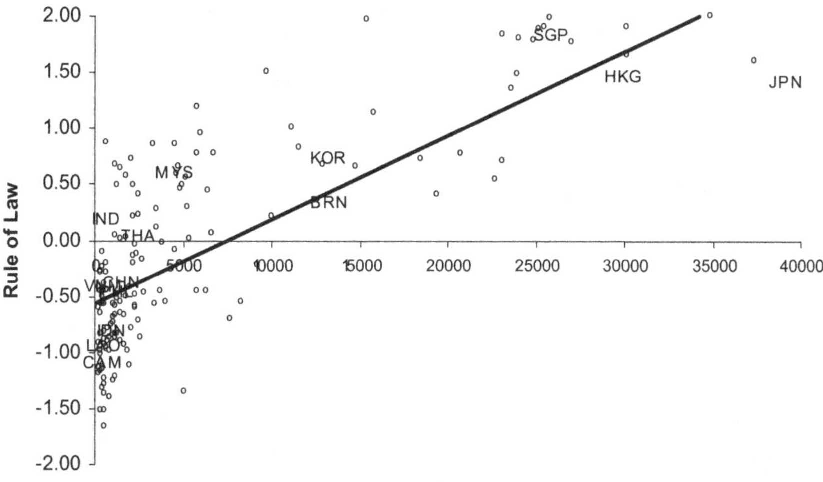

Fig. 1.10. Rule of law.
Source: World Bank, Governance Indicators and World Development Report.

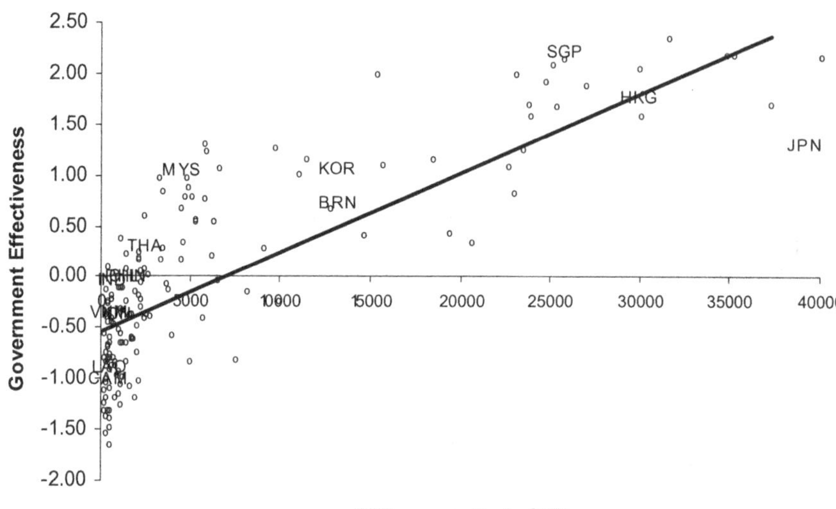

Fig. 1.11. Government effectiveness.
Source: World Bank, Governance Indicators and World Development Report.

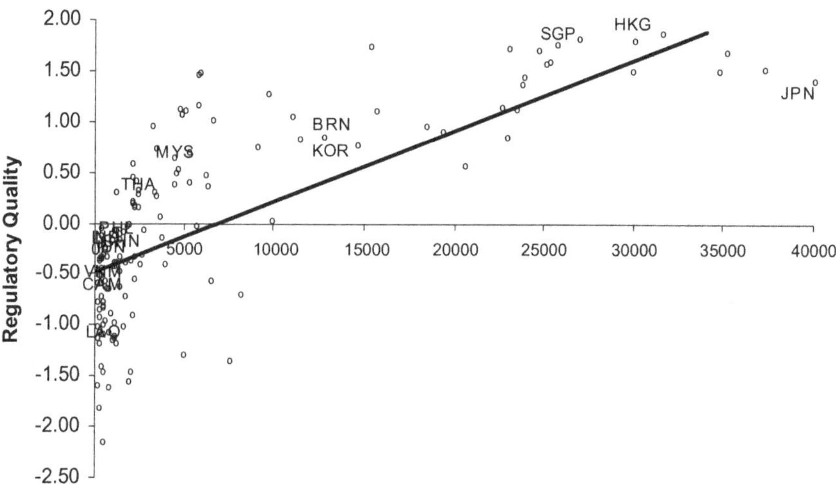

Fig. 1.12. Regulatory quality.
Source: World Bank, Governance Indicators and World Development Report.

Not surprisingly, then, Asia has made faster progress in changing policies than in changing institutions. The question raised by the contrast is whether policy reform not accompanied by commensurate institutional reform should be regarded as permanent.

1.3. Forecasting Is Risky, Especially When It Involves The Future

These changes in the economic and financial situation significantly complicate efforts to think about future financial prospects. At risk of oversimplification, I would place commentators in two broad camps. The first one is made up of those who argue that Asia has effectively bullet-proofed itself from financial crises. That short-term foreign-currency debt is less than in the 1990s and that it is now only a fraction of foreign reserves mean that, in the short run, crises will not resemble that in Korea in 1997, when foreign creditors' reluctance to renew maturing obligations pushed the banks and their implicit guarantor, the government, to the brink of default. Debt ratios have fallen, maturities have lengthened, and a growing share of debt to foreigners is denominated in local currencies. Even if a sudden reluctance on the part of foreign investors to renew their maturing claims creates problems for banks and firms, the national authorities can provide the resources needed for repayment, using their international reserves to pay off foreign currency-denominated obligations and printing money to supply the liquidity needed by banks and firms to meet their domestic currency-denominated obligations. To the extent that emerging markets have adopted more flexible currency regimes, the authorities are not prevented from engaging in lender-of-last-resort intervention by a commitment to defend a currency peg, and any associated weakening of the exchange rate will not be fatal to confidence. Because currency mismatches have been reduced, the fall in the exchange rate will not have such damaging balance-sheet effects. And if an isolated economy still requires emergency assistance, it can now obtain it from its regional neighbors, courtesy of the Chiang-Mai Initiative (see Chapter 9 of this volume).

Members of the second camp argue that less has in fact changed that meets the eye and that Asia could again experience financial instability not unlike that during 1997–1998 (Roubini, 2007). They observe that exchange rates are more flexible in theory than in practice, not least in the case of

China. In certain countries, South Korea for example, short-term foreign indebtedness is rising again (as noted in Section 1.1). While there has been progress in developing regional bond markets, the majority of bonds sold to foreign investors are still denominated in dollars, creating scope for currency mismatches (McCauley and Park, 2006). There are still weaknesses in Asian banking systems. While this is most obviously true of China, there are reasons to worry more generally that increased competition from foreign banks and nonbank financial intermediaries has led to the relaxation of lending standards and excessive compression of lending spreads.[8] Accounting transparency and shareholder rights may have been strengthened; yet by these and other measures the quality of corporate governance in Asia continues to lag behind that in the advanced industrial countries.[9] Past is prologue, in this view. It is impossible to rule out another crisis similar to that of 10 years ago.

My own view is that Asia is still at significant risk, but that any crisis is likely to take a different form than that in 1997–1998. The trigger this time would not be currency devaluation by a country facing difficulty in financing a large current account deficit but rather a sharp drop in asset valuations. I will suggest in the following Section 1.4 what could trigger such a reaction.

If asset valuations do crash, leveraged investors may be forced to sell into falling markets in order to meet margin calls and raise liquidity. Volatility having risen, banks and funds will be forced to liquidate positions to satisfy the prudential guidelines embedded in their value-at-risk models. Because they use positions in more liquid markets to hedge stakes in less liquid markets, an adverse shock to relatively illiquid markets may force them to sell their holdings of more liquid instruments to reduce the net loss from the portfolio. This creates a tendency for volatility to spill across countries, as we saw when tiny Iceland's problems spilled over to other countries in 2006.

---

[8]In addition, commentators worry that by extending interest-rate risk to their customers, including now households, in the form of variable-rate loans, the locus of maturity mismatches may have been changed without reducing the underlying risks. Contributors to Turner (2006) emphasize that much remains to be done in terms of changing the culture in supervisory agencies and the audit departments of banks in many countries in the region, and that many such agencies and banks suffer from shortages of adequately trained staff.

[9]As shown in the analyses of de Nicolo *et al.* (2005) and Ananchotikul and Eichengreen (2007).

The consequences will be rising liquidity preference and higher borrowing costs. Since much of their borrowing has been at variable rates, households may then find it difficult to keep current on their debts. Property prices will plummet as they hold off on purchases and even walk away from existing mortgages. The value of collateral will fall. Firms will find it hard to make interest payments, much less to issue bonds and roll over maturing obligations.[10] Depositors will grow uneasy, and banks will hesitate to lend. The interbank market may seize up as banks grow uncertain about the financial conditions of their potential counterparts. As a result of these events, the operation of the credit chain may be disrupted. The liquidity premium will skyrocket. This is what we mean by a financial crisis.

Two questions are then critical. First, would this sequence of events have major recessionary effects? Financial markets go up and down, and the declines can be abrupt and dramatic, but major recessionary effects need not follow. Second, speaking of Asia as a whole, as I have done to this point, conceals as much as it reveals. The second critical question is how the situation and associated risks will differ across countries.

Where they will most obviously differ is China. Unlike much of Emerging East Asia, China suffers from no shortage of investment. Investment rates have risen further since the late 1990s, to upward of 45 percent of GDP if the official statistics are to be believed. The country is attracting large amounts of FDI. Through late 2007, it experienced a dramatic stock market run-up.

But there are reasons to ask whether such a large increase in the capital stock, mobilized in short order, can be deployed efficiently. One can imagine a variety of economic, financial, and political shocks that could transform investors' positive views of this question. Asset valuations then would fall sharply. Investment would fall sharply. China's growth could fall sharply. These events would compound, and in turn be compounded by, problems in the banking and financial system.

There are obvious parallels with the situation in East Asia prior to 1997, which saw countries running high investment rates funded, directly or indirectly, by state-supported banks. Stock markets were furiously bid up in

[10]Here it is worth recalling that the average maturity of corporate bonds is still much shorter in Emerging Asia than in the advanced countries.

the first half of the 1990s.[11] Property prices rose strongly in Hong Kong, Singapore, Malaysia, and Thailand. This speculative activity was fueled by a sharp bank lending boom. These observations are more than enough to create a sense of *déjà vu*.

But I find more thought provoking a different parallel, namely that with my own country, the United States, before 1913. [Here, you will see, I am developing some ideas suggested by Larry Summers, albeit in a different context.] The U.S. then, like China now, was undergoing rapid growth. Previously a minor player, it was becoming a major force in the world economy. I think of this phase as extensive growth, where the availability of key resources to the modern sector was effectively unlimited. In the American case this meant unlimited land, which attracted capital and labor from abroad. In the Chinese case it means unlimited labor, which attracts capital.

The result in both cases was an investment-led boom. There is no question that these booms were grounded in fundamentals, abundant land and resources in America, abundant labor in China, and a supportive policy framework in both places, not the least consequential aspect of which was policy-makers' embrace of globalization. Both booms were fed by technological and organization revolutions: in the United States, the process of rail-roadization, the advent of the multidivisional corporate form, and modern mass production; in China, the commercialization of enterprise, export orientation, and abundant labor.

And[12] in neither case was a government budget deficit or a consumption binge at the root of events, as was the case in many episodes of rapid growth that culminated as in the crises in the final decades of the 20th century, especially in Latin America. Rather, these were investment-driven cycles.

While it is understandable that asset markets should have reacted favorably to such developments, it is also argued that they reacted excessively. The literature refers not just to the commercialization of rail transport but also to the railway mania. (The term "railway mania" actually comes from the railway-building boom in Britain in the 1840s — Carroll (1876) referred to it in *The Hunting of the Snark* — but it is applied to U.S. experience as well.) New technology and ample funding, against a backdrop of

[11] By some 65 percent between 1991 and the peak (typically in mid-1997) according to the data in Collyns and Senhadji (2003), p. 104.
[12] This being Summers' point.

excessive growth, combined to encourage surging investment and rapidly rising asset valuations. But in this environment of imperfect information and crony capitalism, what went up also could come down, with serious losses to investors. Scholars continue to debate whether the game was worth the candle. Realized returns on the bonds and stocks issued by early railways were often disappointing. But, some argue that there were positive externalities associated with investment in the railways, in the new generation of chemical technologies in the 1890s, and in electrification and the internal combustion engine at the turn of the century, above and beyond the returns captured by the initial investors. Carlota Perez, for example, argues that overinvestment and losses at what she calls the installation stage made possible high returns at the deployment stage, subsequently (Perez, 2002). (She makes the same argument about the "Nasdaq bubble" in the second half of the 1990s.) Karl Marx, writing about the British case, saw the losses consequent on the railway mania as integral to the process of primitive accumulation.[13] One is also reminded of the recent work of Ranciere *et al.* (2004) emphasizing the positive impact of bubbles and crises on growth.[14]

1.4. The Crisis Part of the Story

This brings me to the crisis part of the story. These investment-led booms in the U.S. were also associated with financial crises, in 1853, 1873, 1884, 1890, 1893, and 1907.[15] Accounts of these episodes make for colorful reading. Authors like Charles Kindleberger have earned generous royalties building on this fact.[16]

Why this particular environment should have been crisis-prone is not hard to see. Despite the development of various forms of market intelligence (rating agencies, investment banks, railway gazettes), information about the new investment opportunities was imperfect. Foreign investors were unfamiliar with the physical geography. (In China's case, one might similarly

---

[13]Marx refers to the railway mania in Volume 3 of *Capital*.

[14]See Ranciere, Tornell and Westermann (2004), where they argue that crises may ultimately have a positive impact on growth.

[15]Here I am adapting the chronology of Sprague (1910) in his classic book, *History of Financial Crises*, written for the commission that recommended creating the Federal Reserve System. An extension of Sprague's chronology is Bordo (2003).

[16]With particular success in Kindleberger (1978).

argue that they are unfamiliar with the economic and political geography.) In 19th century America, accounting and corporate-governance standards were lax. Mandatory disclosure of corporate information was successfully opposed by insiders until the 1930s. Most railroads did not publish annual reports until the 1890s, and those that did so were unaudited. Eventually, modern accounting practices were imported from Britain in the form of chartered accountants who traveled across the Atlantic, but getting to this point took time. Stock markets were lightly regulated, both by governments and their own members. The New York Stock Exchange made disclosure a requirement for listing, but there were many different ways and places to trade stocks in the United States, and when a company threatened to list elsewhere, the NYSE bent its rules. The U.S. banking system in this period was notoriously fragile.

Critically, a pegged exchange rate, which the U.S. again had after 1873, gave the authorities limited ability to lean against the wind. Interest rates were linked to those in the rest of the world. During the investment-led boom, price increases accelerated, making for lower real interest rates and encouraging yet additional investment. This was the familiar dilemma of the high-growth country enjoying lower real interest rates, in turn feeding its boom that we saw more recently in the context of the European Monetary System in the early 1990s and in the context of EMU at the beginning of the current decade.[17]

One can argue that these crises had an upside. They were part of the larger process that led to the deployment of new technologies. The larger process facilitated the integration of previously underutilized resources into the national and global economies. Disruptions at times of crisis did not prevent the U.S. from experiencing rapid economic growth. Among the consequences were the expansion of exports, the development of financial markets, and — above all — higher living standards. These very same disruptions prompted improvements in the institutional and policy environment, such as the founding of the Federal Reserve in 1914 and blue-sky laws requiring common carriers, utilities, and other public service corporations to disclose financial information, starting in Kansas in 1911.

[17]As emphasized by people like Alan Walters. On the so-called "Walters critique," see Miller and Sutherland (1990).

Still, it took the Depression of the 1930s to bring about real reform: the Fed's recognition of its responsibility to act as a lender of last resort, rationalization of the exchange rate regime, and the 1935 Federal Reserve Act, which consolidated decision-making authority at the Board. And that crisis, which had a number of elements in common with its pre-1913 predecessors, disrupted not just the U.S. economy but also the Western Hemisphere and the world. One worries that major problems in China could have equally dramatic effects. A sharp slowdown in China, in which growth falls by, say, half from its current levels, could trigger economic and financial problems elsewhere in the region.[18]

But would growth in fact fall so dramatically? This brings me to the other question, namely whether asset market busts in fact have recessionary effects. Here again it may be revealing to consider the U.S. experience in the 19th century, since weaknesses in financial markets were in some respects similar to those present in China today. Of the seven peacetime asset market busts in the U.S. in the century from 1815 to 1914, major recessions occurred in a bare majority of them — that is, four.[19] The average fall in output in these four episodes was 7 percent from peak to trough, a significant contraction by the standards of the Asian crisis. In contrast, in the 1873–1875 and 1881–1884 crises and the so-called Rich Man's Panic

[18]To be sure, there are important differences between the two cases. Where pre-1913 U.S. booms were fed by procyclical monetary and credit conditions resulting from the maintenance of a gold-standard peg, the Chinese authorities can ostensibly lean against the wind because the country has a flexible exchange rate. The problem, as I noted earlier, is that the currency is not very flexible in practice. China also has capital controls, which provide at least limited monetary autonomy. But those controls are increasingly porous, and absent exchange rate changes they afford the authorities only limited monetary control — witness their current difficulties in cooling off the economy. The problem in the banking system is of a different sort, although it is not clear whether, in comparison with the late-19th century America, problems in China today should be regarded as more or less severe. China also has extraordinarily high savings rates, which means that it is running current account surpluses rather than deficits even in the midst of an enormous investment boom. Those surpluses have allowed it to accumulate massive foreign reserves, whose existence limits the danger, compared to the U.S. a century ago, of China being pushed off its implicit peg by a run on the currency. So I do not want to exaggerate the similarities. Ok, maybe I do.

[19]The seven asset market busts commenced in 1835, 1853, 1875, 1881, 1892, 1902, and 1906. I put aside wartime busts (during the War of 1812, the American Civil War, and World War I), since war tends to be highly disruptive to output, and including these episodes would bias the conclusions toward finding recessionary effects.

of 1902–1904, equity markets fell by some 23 percent in real terms from peak to trough, but economic growth was barely disrupted.[20]

What was different about these episodes? In 1902–1904 there was no adverse impact on the banking system. In 1884 the banking and financial system in New York City was disrupted, but problems there were resolved quickly before they could spread to the rest of the country.[21] The year 1873 is a more difficult case. The New York banks and their country correspondents had essentially been engaging in a carry trade: country banks with low funding costs placed their deposits with New York banks, which paid them higher interest rates, and in turn "these deposits were to a great extent loaned upon stocks and bonds in Wall Street, payable "on call," with the confident belief that they were there earning more than the interest paid for securing them, and were available as promised."[22] Much of this money had been invested in railways, including a large stake in Canada Southern Railroad by Kenyon, Cox & Co., bad news about which set off the panic.[23] Once the panic spread to Jay Cooke & Co., which had a large position in the Northern Pacific Railroad, the country was engulfed.

If there is an explanation for why the real effects were not more disruptive, it is that the banks' difficulties were contained as a result of the issuance of clearinghouse certificates by the more conservative banks in

[20]According to the conventional historical statistics on GDP, activity fell by a bit less than 1/2 of 1 percent between 1873 and 1874 before recovering. There was no interruption of growth in the first half of the 1880s. Between 1903 and 1904 growth fell by 1 percent before recovering strongly. In a number of other cases, it can be argued that drop in output caused the banking crisis rather than the other way around (or at least that the banking crisis was not entirely responsible for the drop in output). This is another reason for caution in ascribing effects.

[21]First, the other New York banks formed a committee to inspect the books of main problem bank, the Metropolitan Bank, and finding its accounts in reasonable order provided it with financial support. The Comptroller of the Currency immediately sent in examiners who oversaw the rehabilitation of the Metropolitan bank and the financial system generally.

[22]From the 11 November 1873 report of the New York Clearinghouse, quoted in Sprague (1910), p. 93.

[23]In addition, 1873 in the United States had an element of international contagion: financial crises had broken out earlier in the year in Austria and Germany, and German investors in particular had invested heavily in American railroads; when crisis broke out in Berlin, they had to raise liquidity, causing them to liquidate their positions in the U.S., precipitating volatility there.

support of the larger system.[24] In addition, the fact that the U.S. was not yet back on the gold standard, which had been suspended in the Civil War, was important for removing a constraint on freedom of action. It is clearly better to avoid experiencing a banking panic in the first place. But the lesson of this history would appear to be that if you are going to have crisis, it is important to resolve it quickly.

This brings us to the key questions. How weak or strong are banking systems in China and the rest of Asia? And how much confidence should we have that, if a major financial bust implicates the banking system, resulting problems will be quickly resolved. It is not a controversial judgment that the condition of the Chinese banking system is poor. According to the official statistics, nonperforming loans came to 6.3 percent of total loans as of the middle of 2006. This ratio is down to barely a quarter of its level at the end of 2000, reflecting recapitalization and the rapid growth of the Chinese economy (high tides lift all boats).[25] But it is well known that loan-classification standards are lax. The cautious commentator's rule of thumb is to double official measures of NPLs. If one does this, then current problems in the Chinese banking system are comparable to those in Japan in 1998, Korea in 1999, and Taiwan in 2001.[26] In other words, they are highly worrisome.

Traditionally, problems in the China's banking system have been associated with loans to loss-making state enterprises. The question for the current discussion is whether a growing and worrisome share of loans and investments is now being devoted to real estate and is ending up in stock market speculation. Despite the incompleteness of the published statistic, we know that loans to households are the most rapidly growing component of the asset portfolios of the four big banks, and that mortgage loans are in turn the most rapidly growing (and single largest) component of loans to households.[27] Wang (2007) points out that the longer the stock market boom continues, the greater is the likelihood that loans will have been diverted to the stock market, either directly or indirectly. Allen *et al.* (2007) point

---

[24]This is the common explanation of Sprague (1910) and Friedman and Schwartz (1963).

[25]On the previous recapitalization initiatives, see Dobson and Kashyap (2007).

[26]Allen *et al.*, 2007, Table 3-A.

[27]Allen *et al.*, 2007, p. 16.

to the collapse of property prices in Shanghai and other major cities as the likely trigger of a Chinese banking and financial crisis. Roubini (2007) places more weight on a stock market collapse, fed by the panicked reaction of 100 million inexperienced Chinese day-traders. Either way, if a growth slowdown follows, the performance of the banks' outstanding loans to state-owned enterprises will be placed at risk.

How prevalent are such problems in other Asian countries? And if distress develops in the Chinese financial system, would there be spillovers to other Asian economies? Asian stock market returns being highly correlated, major asset price drops in China would all but certainly be accompanied by major drops elsewhere in the region. Less certain is whether banking systems in other Asian countries would be engulfed. Tarazi *et al.* (2007) look at co-movements in bank share prices across Southeast Asian countries: they find that proxies for bank fundamentals (the quality of bank assets, the structure of bank incomes) better explain cross-country bank contagion than within-country contagion.[28] This directs attention to the strength of fundamentals in other Asian countries to which China's difficulties might spread.

Here the only general statement is that circumstances differ. While nonperforming loans have fallen throughout the region, they remain in the double digits in the Philippines, Thailand, and Vietnam. The rebalancing of loan portfolios from corporate to consumer credit is no guarantee against problems, as the experiences of Korea, Hong Kong, and Taiwan all reveal. Internal controls, loan classification practices, and supervisory standards have been raised, but in many cases practice lags principle.[29] Fitch's indicator of the health of national banking systems as of March 2007 gives ratings of "low" (D on an A–E scale) to Indonesia, the Philippines, Taiwan, and Thailand, and only "adequate" (that is, C) to South Korea, and Malaysia.[30] In the first quarter of 2007, the prices of the shares of emerging Asian banks were up slightly, presumably reflecting revisions of investor

[28]Within countries, proxies for liquidity and opacity better explain the spread of difficulties, as if illiquidity is the major concern within national banking systems but fundamental solvency problems drive spillovers from one national system to another.

[29]Moody's (2007) describes the case of Indonesia, where owing to lax corporate governance of financial firms banks continue to lag their regional peers in terms of implementation of international standards, although the relevant standards are not obviously inferior to those of the neighboring countries.

expectations regarding the condition of the banks. Within the region, share prices were up in Thailand, Malaysia, the Philippines, South Korea, and China, but down in Indonesia, Hong Kong, and Taiwan.

If a crisis erupted, would the authorities be able to intervene quickly and forcefully to prevent it from spreading and protect the credit channel from being disrupted? In China's case, the authorities have upward $1.2 trillion in foreign currency reserves to draw on to recapitalize the banking system, as they have done in the past.[31] Compared to $1.2 trillion of reserves, $160 billion of nonperforming loans (the mid-2006 official figure) or even twice that level is not overwhelming.[32] And insofar as the foreign-currency-denominated liabilities of the banks are limited, the value of foreign exchange reserves is not the relevant metric; what are relevant are the central bank's ability to print money and the government's capacity to tax and borrow. In this sense, their scope for intervention is virtually unlimited.[33] The question is whether the authorities would be prepared to utilize that capacity freely, now that foreign financial institutions have taken stakes in the big banks. A public sector bailout of the banks would be a bailout or a subsidy to these foreign institutions, and the government might hesitate to use the hard-earned tax dollars of Chinese residents in this way. To be sure, the best course would be to provide the liquidity now and defer

[30]See Fitch Ratings (2007). Other sources flesh out this picture by analyzing national cases in detail. Thus, Nakornthab (2007) describes vulnerabilities in the Thai banking system associated with exposures to consumer credit and the property market. Pineda (2007) provides a detailed analysis of current weaknesses of the Korean banking system, citing its lending to other investors speculating in short-term securities its excessive extension of credit to the household sector — this time (in contrast to 2002, when it took the form of revolving credit) in the form of housing loans. Moody's (2007) describes how pre-election legislation may discourage timely debt repayment by consumers and extend consumer debt charge-offs from the banks' credit card books to their mortgage books.

[31]The government also has debt that should be subtracted from its assets, but explicit public debt is only on the order of 16 percent of GDP.

[32]It is not overwhelming from the perspective of capacity to maintain financial stability. On the other hand, previous recapitalizations have cost the Chinese taxpayer on the order of 10 percent of GDP (Ma, 2006), as interpreted by Dobson and Kashyap (2007).

[33]It can be argued that a large-scale injection of liquidity could destabilize the exchange rate and unleash flight from currency and the banks, feeding back on the banking system in destabilizing ways. Here the foreign exchange reserves of the authorities become relevant and provide reassurance against the development of this scenario.

questions of burden sharing to later. But there is an issue of whether the Chinese authorities will in fact respond in this fashion.

1.5. Concluding Remarks: The Credit Crisis and Asia's Reaction

After the first draft of this manuscript was delivered as a keynote address was delivered, the U.S. and Europe were engulfed in a credit crisis. The collapse of the prices of structured investments backed by residential mortgages caused major problems in Western credit markets starting in the second half of 2007. With banks providing guarantees and credit lines to special-purpose vehicles taking large positions in these securities, and with certain large financial institutions holding extensive positions in such securities themselves, U.S. and European banks suffered major losses. The incompleteness of information on the position of banks in the markets for these securities caused the interbank market to seize up. Superimposed on an ongoing decline in U.S. housing markets, the credit crisis sparked fears of recession in the advanced industrial countries.[34]

[34]Asian banks and nonbank financial intermediaries had only limited positions in Collateralized Debt Obligations (CDOs) and other structured investments backed by residential mortgages. According to Fitch (2008), the gross exposure of Asian banks' ex Japan to subprime residential-mortgage-backed securities and CDOs came to 2.1 per cent of their equity; adding in non-subprime Residential Mortgage-backed Securities (RMBs) and CDOs and the exposures of Structured Investment Vehicles (SIVs) and conduits brings total exposure to 5.6 per cent of regional bank equity. China was the largest investor in subprime and other structured products, with total exposures approaching 5 per cent of bank capital. While 5 per cent is not an inconsequential number, it pales in comparison with the problem of non-performing domestic loans to state-owned enterprises and others, which is a multiple of bank equity, notwithstanding recent recapitalization. Still, one might argue that, with non-performing loans so large, another 3 per cent may be the straw that breaks the camel's back. As shares of bank capital, the total exposures (subprime, other RMBS and CDOs, SIVs and other) of Taiwan and Hong Kong are largest, at 21 and 14 per cent. These countries have considerably stronger banking systems than China, of course, although cumulative losses have already reached 4 to 5 per cent of bank capital, a tolerable but not insignificant number. Subprime mortgage backed securities held by all Japanese banks, which include major banks, regional banks and cooperative financial institutions, as estimated by Japan's Financial Services Agency were relatively small — around $14 billion — and the total loss associated with these holdings was estimated to be less than $3 billion at the end of September 2007. See Financial Service Agency of Japan (2007). According to the Bank of Japan (2008), however, over the next three months the losses of the major banks rose to $6 billion, still

This credit stringency also prompted worries about sustainability of the finances and exchange rates of emerging markets in weak external positions. As a result, spreads on external debt issues shot up in late 2007 and early 2008. In the Philippines, sovereign spreads jumped by 200 basis points between August 2007 and February 2008. In the same period, spreads went up by 131 basis point in Indonesia, 93 basis points in Korea, and 70 basis points in China. Following the Bear Stearns rescue, these countries saw their spreads decline, reflecting the belief or at least hope that the worst of the credit crisis is over. There was no financial crisis in Asia in late 2007 and early 2008.

Indeed, there was little evidence of a slowdown in Asia in the first half of 2008. The explanation is straightforward enough: the Federal Reserve cut U.S. interest rates dramatically in response to deteriorating economic and financial conditions in the United States, and given the fact that Asian central banks continued to limit the flexibility of their exchange rates against the dollar, the Asian economies imported lower interest rates as well. While this meant that a slowdown was averted, it also meant inflation. One can debate whether Fed overdid it or whether it should have relied more on credit injections at penalty rates. But whatever one's view of the appropriateness of U.S. policy for U.S. conditions, it is indisputable that its policy was not appropriate for Asia. The Asian economy was growing full out in 2007. The last thing it needed was lower interest rates. But that's what it got, given the habit of limiting the fluctuation of Asian currencies against the dollar. Allowing Asian interest rates to rise more sharply against U.S. rates would have caused Asian currencies to appreciate against the dollar more strongly. And for all their talk of greater exchange rate flexibility, this was not something that Asian governments and central banks were prepared to countenance.

As a result, Asian economies that needed demand restraint got demand stimulus instead, what with the impact of central bank policies showing up first but slower growth in the U.S. and Europe taking time to develop and then feed through to other regions. There would have been more inflationary pressure in Asia in the first half of 2008, in other words, even without the

---

a small fraction of tier one capital of these banks which stood at $253 billion at the end of September 2007.

geopolitical uncertainty, oil-market speculation, bad weather and ethanol programs that garnered the headlines.

The obvious response for Asian central banks was to raise interest rates. There were some half-hearted efforts in this direction, but they did not do the job. As of April 2008, Indonesia's central bank rate stood at 8.5 per cent, but its inflation rate was above 10 per cent. The Philippines' central bank rate was 5.25 per cent, but its inflation rate was also 10 per cent. Vietnam's central bank rate was 14 per cent, but its inflation rate was 25 per cent. It made no sense when most Asian countries were growing at or near capacity that they should have had negative real interest rates. Negative real rates are an unhealthy subsidy for borrowing by households and firms. They encouraged inefficient investment and excessive leverage in Asia in the first half of the 1990s, and we all know what followed.

Critics of inflation targeting will say that central banks have a dual mandate not just to fight inflation but also to foster growth and that Asian central banks have no business raising rates in a deteriorating growth environment. But the fact of the matter is that the alternative to painful interest rate increases now was even more painful increases later.

Fortunately, there is another instrument for sustaining demand in these circumstances, namely fiscal policy. If higher interest rates push up the exchange rate and damp down inflation, then tax cuts and increases in public spending on locally-produced goods can be used to limit the contraction of aggregate demand. Insofar as these fiscal actions stimulate the demand for locally-produced goods, they tend push up the exchange rate still further, moderating the rise in import prices and further containing inflationary pressure.[35]

[35]Which Asian countries have scope for responding this way? In China, there is likely to be a high return on additional infrastructure investment, especially in the relatively underdeveloped west where producers still find it difficult to get goods to the market. There is the need for public spending on reconstruction in the wake of the earthquake. There is the need for increased public expenditure on health care, education and pensions. That the public sector is running a current surplus of 4 to 6 percent of GDP, depending on who is doing the measuring, points to the existence of maneuvering room. Elsewhere in Asia, tax cuts and public spending increases should be calibrated to the U.S. and global slowdown — in contrast to the case of China they should be explicitly temporary. Korea, Malaysia, Singapore, and Taiwan are at the top of my list of countries with room to expand public spending temporarily to offset the dampening effects of higher interest rates.

So there are two scenarios. One is where Asian central banks start tightening to fight inflation. They allow their currencies to rise in response to their tighter monetary policies and higher interest rates. They deploy fiscal policy to prevent demand and growth from slowing excessively.

The second scenario is one where Asian central banks and their political masters delay, attempting to preserve the stability of their currencies against the dollar. But, ultimately, they will get the same real appreciation without nominal appreciation and higher interest rates, in this case instead as a result of inflation. And the danger under this scenario is that inflation gains momentum and threatens to spiral out of control.

At that point, central banks will have no choice but to tighten, and sharply, like Paul Volcker in 1979 and Margaret Thatcher in 1981. This harsh reaction when it occurs may catch banks and other investors wrong footed. There could a sharp fall in asset valuations of the sort described in the previous section. At that point the crisis problem will be back.

References

Allen, F, J Qian and M Qian (2007). China's financial system: Past, present and future. Unpublished manuscript, University of Pennsylvania (March).

Ananchotikul, S and B Eichengreen (2007). Corporate governance reform in emerging markets: How much, why and with what effects? Unpublished manuscript, University of California, Berkeley (May).

Asian Development Bank (2007). *Asian Development Outlook 2007*. Manila: Asian Development Bank.

Bank of Japan (2008). Financial System Report, BOJ Reports and Research Papers, March.

Bordo, M (2003). A historical perspective on booms, busts, and recessions. *World Economic Outlook* (April). Washington, DC: International Monetary Fund, pp. 64–66.

Carroll, L (1876). *The Hunting of the Snark*. London: Macmillan.

Collyns, C and A Senhadji (2003). Lending booms, real estate bubbles, and the Asian crisis. In *Asset Price Bubbles: The Implications for Monetary, Regulatory and International Policies*, W Hunter, G Kaufman and M Pomerleano (eds.). Cambridge, Mass.: MIT Press.

de Nicolo, G, L Laeven and K Ueda (2005). Corporate governance quality: Trends and real effects. IMF Working Paper No. WP/06/293 (December).

Dobson, W and A Kashyap (2007). The contradiction in China's gradualist banking reforms. Institute on Global Financial Markets, University of Chicago Working Paper No. 4.

Eichengreen, B and YC Park (2006). Global imbalances and emerging markets. In *Global Imbalances and the U.S. Debt Problem*, JJ Teunissen and A Akkerman (eds.), pp. 14–44. The Hague: Fondad.

Eichengreen, B and R Razo-Garcia (2005). The international monetary system in the last and next 20 years. *Economic Policy*, 47, 393–442.

Eichengreen, B and H Tong (2006). How China is reorganizing the world economy. *Asian Economic Policy Review*, 1, 73–101.

Financial Service Agency of Japan (2007). Exposures of Japanese Deposit-taking Institutions to Subprime-related Products, Tokyo: FSA (30 November).

Fitch Ratings (2007). *Bank Systemic Risk Report*. New York: Fitch Ratings (March).

Fitch Ratings (2008). Banks in Asia Excluding Japan: Update on Exposure to Subprime and Structured Credit Products, Asia Special Report (21 April), www.fitchratings.com.

Friedman, M and A Schwartz (1963). *A Monetary History of the United States, 1867–1960*. Princeton: Princeton University Press.

Kindleberger, C (1978). *Mania, Panics and Crashes*. New York: Basic Books.

Kramer, C (2006). Asia's investment puzzle. *Finance and Development*, 43, www.imf.org (June).

Ma, G (2006). Sharing China's bank restructuring bill. *China and the World Economy*, 14, 19–37.

McCauley, R and YC Park (2006). Developing the bond market(s) of East Asia: Global regional or national? BIS Paper No. 30 (November).

Miller, M and A Sutherland (1990). The "Walters" critique of the EMS: A case of inconsistent expectations. CEPR Discussion Paper No. 480 (November).

Moody's (2007). *Asia's Banks — 10 Years Since the Crisis*. Moody's Banking Special Comment, Hong Kong: Moody's Investors Service (July).

Nakornthab, D (2007). Thai commercial banks one decade after the crisis: Assessment of risk to financial stability. Unpublished manuscript, Bank of Thailand (July).

Park, YC (2008). The subprime crisis and Asia. Unpublished manuscript, Seoul National University (January).

Perez, C (2002). *Technological Revolutions and Financial Capital: The Dynamics of Bubbles and Golden Ages.* Cheltenham and Northampton: Edward Elgar.

Pineda, M (2007). East Asian Bank sector reform since 1997. Unpublished manuscript, RGE Monitor (June).

Ranciere, R, A Tornell and F Westermann (2004). Crises and growth: A reevaluation. CESifo Working Paper No. 1160.

Reinhart, C and K Rogoff (2004). The modern history of exchange rate arrangements: A reinterpretation. *Quarterly Journal of Economics*, 119, 1–48.

Roubini, N (2007). Asia is learning the wrong lessons from its 1997–98 financial crisis. Unpublished manuscript, Roubini Global Economics (May).

Sprague, O (1910). *History of Financial Crises under the National Banking System.* Washington, DC: National Monetary Commission.

Tarazi, A, P Rous and C Bautista (2007). The determinants of domestic and cross border bank contagion in South-East Asia. Unpublished manuscript, University of the Philippines (February).

Turner, P (ed.) (2006). The banking system in emerging markets: How much progress? BIS Paper No. 28 (August).

Villar, A (2006). Is financial stability policy now better placed to prevent systemic banking crises? In *The Banking System in Emerging Markets: How Much Progress?* P Turner (ed.), pp. 106–122, BIS Paper No. 28 (August).

Wang, Q (2007). *An "Untimely" Question: What Could Go Wrong with the Economy?* Morgan Stanley Global Economic Forum, www.morganstanley.com (23 July).

PART II

EXCHANGE RATE REGIMES AND INTERNATIONAL RESERVES

CHAPTER 2

STILL SEARCHING FOR THE MIDDLE GROUND?: ASIAN EXCHANGE RATE REGIMES A DECADE SINCE THE 1997–1998 CRISIS[1]

Tony Cavoli and Ramkishen S. Rajan

2.1. Introduction

An immediate lesson that many observers appear to have drawn from the financial crises in emerging market economies in the 1990s is that the only viable exchange rate option boils down to one between flexibility on the one hand, and "credible pegging" on the other. According to this view (which was dominant in the late 1990s and early 2000s but still has a number of followers), emerging economies have to gravitate to one of these two extremes. Any currency arrangements that lie in between these polar extremes or corners (i.e., those in the "middle") are viewed as being inherently unstable and crisis-prone.

It used to be commonly believed that this so-called "Bipolar view" drew analytical support from the "Impossible Trinity" which essentially states that a country with an open capital account cannot simultaneously conduct a completely independent monetary policy and pursue a completely rigid or fixed exchange regime. However, the "Unholy Trinity" does *not* on its own imply that in an increasingly globalized world economy an intermediate regime is unviable, or that countries will be compelled to abandon the

[1]Jeff Kim, Alice Ouyang, and Nicola Virgill provided valuable research assistance on this chapter. The authors thank participants of the Claremont–Bologna–SCAPE International Economic Policy Forum in Singapore, 30–31 July 2007 for valuable comments and feedback on an earlier draft of this chapter. The usual disclaimer applies.

middle ground.[2] For instance, a country could choose to maintain an intermediate exchange rate regime while forsaking a degree of monetary policy autonomy. In other words, the analytical basis in support of the bipolar view is rather weak (particularly since some developing countries still maintain capital controls that are not entirely porous). Indeed, the only analytical support offered against intermediate regimes is their lack of verifiability of transparency: simple regimes are more verifiable by market participants than complicated ones (Frankel *et al.*, 2000). The other commonly repeated weakness of intermediate regimes is that they are more crisis-prone (Bubula and Ötker-Robe, 2003). However, a more careful examination of the links between *de facto* exchange rate regimes and currency crises suggests that there is no evidence that either of the two corners is necessarily less crisis-prone than intermediate regimes in general.[3]

The remainder of this chapter in organized as follows. The next section compiles and discusses the *de jure* or official exchange rate regimes in various Asian economies.[4] Recognizing that countries do not always follow their policy pronouncements, Section 3 presents some simple *de facto* exchange rate regime measures for selected Asian countries. Since different measures inevitably capture different dimensions of any regime, it is critical to use a number of methodologies to ensure robustness. To preview the main conclusions from Sections 2 and 3, it is evident that Asia is home to a wide array of exchange rate regimes, though there are signs of gradual movement toward somewhat greater exchange rate flexibility in many Asian countries. However, the propensity for foreign exchange intervention and exchange rate management among regional central banks remains fairly high in many instances. Section 4 concludes the chapter.

---

[2]Among the most recent and clearest statements on this, see Frankel (1999) and Willett (2002).

[3]For instance, see Angkinand *et al.* (2005). However, the authors find that adjustable parities (including conventional adjustable pegs and horizontal bands) appear to be the most crisis-prone of all.

[4]The focus of this chapter is on Asia defined to include North, South, and Southeast Asian economies. We do not consider West Asia, the Pacific island economies, Australia or New Zealand.

2.2. Official Exchange Rate Regimes in Asia

Until 1998 it was fairly easy to obtain *de jure* exchange rate classifications as this data was compiled from national sources by the IMF. Specifically, between 1975 and 1998 the IMF's *Annual Report on Exchange Arrangements and Exchange Restrictions* was based on self-reporting of national policies by various governments with revisions in 1977 and 1982. Since 1998 — and in response to criticisms that there can be significant divergences between *de facto* and *de jure* policies — the IMF's exchange rate classification methodology has shifted to compiling unofficial policies of countries as determined by Fund staff.[5] While the change in IMF exchange rate coding is welcome for many reasons (including the fact that the new set of categories is more detailed than the older one), the IMF is no longer compiling the *de jure* regimes. The only way this can be done is by referring to the web site of each central bank or other national sources individually and wading through relevant materials. The results of this detective work are summarized in Table 2.1. [6]

As is apparent, the *de jure* exchange rate regimes in Asia span a wide spectrum. A number of smaller Asian economies appear to prefer some form of single currency peg. This is true of Hong Kong SAR (whose currency board arrangement is pegged to the U.S. dollar), Brunei (pegged to the Singapore dollar), and Bhutan and Nepal (pegged to the Indian rupee). In contrast, Bangladesh, Sri Lanka, and the crisis-hit economies of Indonesia, Korea, the Philippines, and Thailand officially operate flexible exchange rate regimes. The flexible exchange rates in the four East Asian countries are accompanied by inflation-targeting frameworks (Table 2.2).

A number of other Asian countries have adopted a variety of intermediate regimes (currency baskets, crawling bands, adjustable pegs, and such). For instance, according to the Reserve Bank of India, India "monitors and manages the exchange rates with flexibility without a fixed target or a pre-announced target or a band, coupled with the ability to intervene if and when

[5]The data has since been applied retroactively to 1990.

[6]The descriptions in Table 2.1 are mostly direct quotes from the official sources and not paraphrased by the authors.

Table 2.1. *De jure* exchange rate regimes in Asia (As per country Central Bank Web sites unless otherwise stated).

Country	Official policy pronouncements (direct quotes)
Bangladesh	The exchange rates of the taka for inter-bank and customer transactions are set by the dealer banks themselves, based on demand–supply interaction. The Bangladesh Bank is not present in the market on a day-to-day basis and undertakes purchase or sale transactions with the dealer banks only as needed to maintain orderly market conditions.
Bhutan	Except for the Indian rupee to which the ngultrum is pegged at parity, and which circulates freely in Bhutan, paying or receiving payments in any other foreign currency for transactions in Bhutan is illegal.
	The Government may, by order, at any time, on the recommendation of the Board, declare an external value for the ngultrum, having due regard for the obligations which Bhutan has assumed in accordance with the provisions of any international monetary agreement to which it is a party, or to which it has adhered.
Brunei-Darussalam[1]	A currency interchangeability agreement was established between Singapore and Brunei Darussalam, which remains in effect till today and continues to play a central role in relations between the two countries. This agreement allows both countries to interchange their currencies at par without either country running the risk of currency exchange rate fluctuations which thus further facilitates trade and commerce between the two countries. The individual currencies are acceptable as customary tender when circulating in the country in which they are not legal tender.
Cambodia	N.A.
China, PRC	The PRC announced on 21 July 2005 the adoption of a managed floating exchange rate regime based on market supply and demand with reference to a basket of currencies. Since then, the new exchange rate system has operated stably, and the RMB exchange rate has been kept basically stable at an adaptive and equilibrium level. The exchange rate of the RMB against the U.S. dollar has been moving both upward and downward with greater flexibility.

(Continued)

Table 2.1. (*Continued*)

Country	Official policy pronouncements (direct quotes)
Hong Kong SAR	Since 1983 the Hong Kong dollar has been linked to the U.S. dollar at the rate of 7.8 HKD to 1 U.S. dollar. The link is maintained through the operation of a strict and robust Currency Board system which requires both the stock and the flow of the Monetary Base to be fully backed by foreign reserves. Any change in the size of the Monetary Base has to be fully matched by a corresponding change in the foreign reserves.
India	The exchange rate policy in recent years has been guided by the broad principles of careful monitoring and management of exchange rates with flexibility, without a fixed target or a pre-announced target or a band, coupled with the ability to intervene if and when necessary.
Indonesia	In July 2005, Bank Indonesia launched a new monetary policy framework known as the Inflation Targeting Framework, which has four basic elements as follows: (1) use of the BI rate as a reference rate in monetary control in replacement of the base money operational target, (2) forward looking monetary policymaking process, (3) more transparent communications strategy, and (4) strengthening of policy coordination with the Government.
	The rupiah exchange rate is determined wholly by market supply and demand. However, Bank Indonesia is able to take some actions to keep the rupiah from undergoing excessive fluctuation.
Korea	Inflation targeting is an operating framework of monetary policy in which the central bank announces an explicit inflation target and achieves its target directly. This is based on the recognition that to achieve sustainable economic growth, it is important above all else that inflation expectations, which have a great effect on wage and price decisions, should be stabilized. In this regard, inflation targeting places great emphasis on inducing inflation expectations to converge on the central bank's inflation target level by the prior public announcement and successful attainment of that target level.
	The exchange rate is, in principle, decided by the interplay of supply and demand in the foreign exchange markets. However, the Bank of Korea implements smoothing operations to deal with abrupt swings in the exchange rate caused by temporary imbalances between supply and demand, or radical changes in market sentiment.

(*Continued*)

Table 2.1. (*Continued*)

Country	Official policy pronouncements (direct quotes)
Lao, PDR	The Bank of the Lao PDR announces the exchange rate derived from the market, officially adjusted, based on the daily average trading rate of the inter-bank market to the commercial banks and the foreign exchange bureaus as a reference to determine their own daily trading rates. In case of necessity the Bank of the Lao PDR determines the exchange rate on its own for the commercial banks and foreign exchange bureaus for implementation.
Malaysia	On 21 July 2005, Malaysia shifted from a fixed exchange rate regime of U.S. dollar 1 = RM 3.80 to a managed float against a basket of currencies. Under the managed float system, the ringgit exchange rate is largely determined by ringgit demand and supply in the foreign exchange market. The Central Bank does not actively manage or maintain the exchange rate at any particular level — economic fundamentals and market conditions are the primary determinants of the level of the ringgit exchange rate. In this regard, the Central Bank intervenes only to minimize volatility, and to ensure that the exchange rate does not become fundamentally misaligned.
Myanmar	N.A.
Nepal	In the review year, the exchange rate of the Nepalese rupee vis-à-vis the Indian rupee remained constant, and NRB intervened 44 times in the foreign exchange market. Currently, Nepal is adopting a dual exchange rate arrangement. It is dual because the Nepali currency is pegged to the Indian currency (IC), whereas it floats with the convertible currencies. This system of exchange rate was introduced on 12 February 1993.
Pakistan[2]	Pakistan has adopted the floating inter-bank exchange rate as the preferred option since 2001. State Bank of Pakistan has attempted to maintain real effective exchange rate at a level that keeps the competitiveness of Pakistani exports intact. But, like other Central Banks, it does intervene from time to time to keep stability in the market and smooth excessive fluctuations. The current framework of monetary-cum-exchange rate policies and the underlying economic analysis in Pakistan can, thus, be broadly characterized as judgment- and discretion-based rather than model- or rule-based.

(*Continued*)

Table 2.1. (*Continued*)

Country	Official policy pronouncements (direct quotes)
Philippines	The primary objective of Bangko Sentral ng Pilipinas' monetary policy is to promote a low and stable inflation conducive to a balanced and sustainable economic growth. The adoption of inflation targeting framework for monetary policy in January 2002 is aimed at achieving this objective.
	The Monetary Board determines the exchange rate policy of the country, determines the rates at which the Bangko Sentral buys and sells spot exchange, and establishes deviation limits from the effective exchange rate or rates as it deems proper.
Singapore	Since 1981, monetary policy in Singapore has been centred on the management of the exchange rate. (1) The Singapore dollar is managed against a basket of currencies of its major trading partners and competitors. (2) The Monetary Authority of Singapore operates a managed float regime for the Singapore dollar. The trade-weighted exchange rate is allowed to fluctuate within an undisclosed policy band, rather than kept to a fixed value. (3) The exchange rate policy band is periodically reviewed to ensure that it remains consistent with the underlying fundamentals of the economy. (4) The choice of the exchange rate as the intermediate target of monetary policy implies that MAS gives up control over domestic interest rates (and money supply).
Sri Lanka	The Central Bank continues to conduct its monetary policy under an independently floating exchange rate regime within a framework of targeting monetary aggregates with reserve money (i.e., high powered money) as the operating target and broad money (M2b) as the intermediate target.
Taiwan	Prior to February 1979, management of foreign exchange in Taiwan was characterized by a central clearing and settlement system. Following the establishment of the Taipei Foreign Exchange Market in February 1979, a flexible exchange rate system was formally implemented. Since then, the NT dollar exchange rate has been determined by the market. However, when the market is disrupted by seasonal or irregular factors, the Bank will step in.

(*Continued*)

Table 2.1. (*Continued*)

Country	Official policy pronouncements (direct quotes)
Thailand	Since 2 July 1997, Thailand has adopted the managed-float exchange rate regime, in which the value of the baht is determined by market forces, namely demand and supply in both on-shore and off-shore foreign exchange market, to let the currency move in line with economic fundamentals. The Bank of Thailand will intervene in the market only when necessary, in order to prevent excessive volatilities and achieve economic policy targets.
	Under the inflation targeting framework, the Bank of Thailand implements its monetary policy by influencing short-term money market rates via the selected key policy rate, currently set at the 14-day repurchase rate.
Vietnam	Vietnam has adopted a crawling peg with the U.S. dollar for its exchange rate. The State Bank of Vietnam sets the official exchange rate daily, and commercial banks set their dealing rate within a trading band of plus or minus 0.25 percent. The State Bank of Vietnam tends to keep the dông depreciated against the U.S. dollar by keeping the exchange rate on an upward trend.

Notes: (1) Based on information available from Brunei Ministry of Finance. http://www.finance.gov.bn/bcb/bcb_index.htm.
(2) Based on speech by former Pakistan central bank Governor (Husain, 2005).
Source: Compiled by author with assistance of Nicola Virgill from web sites from various central banks and other official sources with minor modifications. Central Bank web sites available here: http://www.bis.org/cbanks.htm

necessary."[7] Vietnam officially maintains a crawling peg and band around the U.S. dollar. Singapore officially manages its currency against a basket of currencies, with the trade-weighted exchange rate used as an intermediate target to ensure that the inflation target is attained.[8] While Singapore's currency basket regime has a more strategic orientation, both China and

[7] See Cavoli and Rajan (2007a) and Shah and Patnaik (2005) for analyses of India's exchange rate policy.

[8] See Cavoli and Rajan (2007b), Khor *et al.* (2004), and McCallum (2005) for analyses of Singapore's exchange rate policy.

Table 2.2. Highlights of inflation targeting regimes in the five crisis-hit countries.

Country	Date	Target price index	Inflation target	Target horizon	Escape clauses	Accountability	Target set by	Publication and accountability
Indonesia	May 1999	Core CPI (excluding food and energy)	5–7 percent 3 percent	1–2 years Long-term	None	None, but parliament can request reports at any time	Central Bank	Quarterly inflation report, annual report to public
Philippines	Dec 2001	Core CPI (excluding food and energy)	4–5 percent	2 years	Yes, in the event of oil price shocks, food supply shocks	Public explanation of the nature of the breach and steps to address it	Central Bank	Quarterly inflation report, publication of monetary policy meetings
Thailand	Apr 2000	Core CPI (excluding food and energy)	0–3.5 percent	Indefinite	None	Public explanation of breach and steps taken to address it	Central Bank in consultation with Government	Inflation report, inflation forecasts, and publication of models used
Korea	Jan 1998	Core CPI (excluding non-cereal agricultural products and petroleum products)	2.5–3.5 percent 2.5 – 3.5 percent	1–2 years Indefinite	Changes caused by major force	None	Central Bank in consultation with Government	Inflation report and submission to parliament, publication of monetary policy meetings

Source: Compiled by authors from web sites from various central banks and other official sources.

Malaysia in July 2005 officially shifted to what may be best referred to as a more mechanical version of a currency basket regime (i.e., keeping the trade-weighted exchange rate within a certain band as a goal in and of itself). The remaining Asian economies in our sample, viz., Taiwan, Pakistan, and Laos, seem to operate rather *ad hoc* managed floats or adjustable pegs. Overall, it is readily apparent that "one-size does not necessarily fit all" when it comes to the choice of exchange rate regimes in Asia.

2.3. *De Facto* Exchange Rate Regimes in Crisis-hit Asia

2.3.1. *Existing Classifications*

As noted, the IMF has replaced its compilation of the *de jure* exchange rate regimes with the behavioral classification of exchange rates. The new IMF coding is based on various sources, including information from IMF staff, press reports, other relevant papers, as well as the behavior of bilateral nominal exchange rates and reserves.[9]

Table 2.3 summarizes the definitions of various IMF exchange rate classifications. As is apparent, the IMF has eight exchange rate categories. Table 2.4 categorizes Asian exchange rates based on the new IMF classifications as of July 2006.[10] A comparison of Tables 2.1 and 2.4 reveals no discrepancy between the *de jure* and *de facto* regimes of Bhutan, Brunei, Hong Kong SAR, and Nepal, all of which operate fixed exchange rates to a single currency. Similarly, India, Lao PDR, and Singapore are categorized as managed floaters, broadly consistent with their official pronouncements. Vietnam, which used to be in this category, has more recently been classified as having a conventional fixed peg regime in contrast to its official pronouncement of maintaining a crawling peg and band around the U.S. dollars. Bangladesh, Sri Lanka, and Thailand have been characterized as managed floaters (with no predetermined exchange rate path) despite their official declarations of being independent floaters. Pakistan is defined as operating conventional fixed peg arrangements (against a single currency) despite

[9]Also see Bubula and Ötker-Robe (2002), which appears to be the intellectual basis for the IMF *de facto* regimes.

[10]See Rajan (2006) for IMF specifications of Asian exchange rate regimes from 1998 to 2004. Taiwan is not included in Table 2.4 as it is not a member of the IMF.

Table 2.3. IMF descriptions of exchange rate regimes.

Type	Description
Exchange arrangements with no separate legal tender	The currency of another country circulates as the sole legal tender (formal dollarization), or the member belongs to a monetary or currency union in which the same legal tender is shared by members of the union. Adopting such regimes implies the complete surrender of the monetary authorities' independent control over domestic monetary policy.
Currency board arrangements	A monetary regime based on an explicit legislative commitment to exchange domestic currency for a specified foreign currency at a fixed exchange rate, combined with restrictions on the issuing authority to ensure the fulfilment of its legal obligation. This implies that the domestic currency will be issued only against foreign exchange and that it remains fully backed by foreign assets, eliminating traditional central bank functions, such as monetary control and lender-of-last-resort, and leaving little scope for discretionary monetary policy. Some flexibility may still be afforded, depending on how strict the banking rules of the currency board arrangement are.
Other conventional fixed peg arrangements	The country (formally or *de facto*) pegs its currency at a fixed rate to another currency or a basket of currencies, where the basket is formed from the currencies of major trading or financial partners and weights reflect the geographical distribution of trade, services, or capital flows. The currency composites can also be standardized, as in the case of the SDR. There is no commitment to keep the parity irrevocably. The exchange rate may fluctuate within narrow margins of less than ± 1 percent around a central rate, or the maximum and minimum value of the exchange rate may remain within a narrow margin of 2 percent for at least 3 months. The monetary authority stands ready to maintain the fixed parity through direct intervention (i.e., via sale/purchase of foreign exchange in the market) or indirect intervention (e.g., via aggressive use of interest rate policy, imposition of foreign exchange regulations, exercise of moral suasion that constrains foreign exchange

(*Continued*)

Table 2.3. (*Continued*)

Type	Description
	activity, or through intervention by other public institutions). Flexibility of monetary policy, though limited, is greater than in the case of exchange arrangements with no separate legal tender and currency boards because traditional central banking functions are still possible, and the monetary authority can adjust the level of the exchange rate, although relatively infrequently.
Pegged exchange rates within horizontal bands	The value of the currency is maintained within certain margins of fluctuation of at least ±1 percent around a fixed central rate or the margin between the maximum and minimum value of the exchange rate exceeds 2 percent. It also includes arrangements of countries in the exchange rate mechanism (ERM) of the European Monetary System (EMS) that was replaced with the ERM II on 1 January 1999. There is a limited degree of monetary policy discretion, depending on the bandwidth.
Crawling pegs	The currency is adjusted periodically in small amounts at a fixed rate or in response to changes in selective quantitative indicators, such as past inflation differentials vis-à-vis major trading partners, differentials between the inflation target and expected inflation in major trading partners, and so forth. The rate of crawl can be set to generate inflation-adjusted changes in the exchange rate (backward looking), or set at a pre-announced fixed rate and/or below the projected inflation differentials (forward looking). Maintaining a crawling peg imposes constraints on monetary policy in a manner similar to a fixed peg system.
Exchange rates within crawling bands	The currency is maintained within certain fluctuation margins of at least ±1 percent around a central rate — or the margin between the maximum and minimum value of the exchange rate exceeds 2 percent — and the central rate or margins are adjusted periodically at a fixed rate or in response to changes in selective quantitative indicators. The degree of exchange rate flexibility is a function of the bandwidth. Bands are either symmetric around a crawling

(*Continued*)

Table 2.3. (*Continued*)

Type	Description
	central parity or widen gradually with an asymmetric choice of the crawl of upper and lower bands (in the latter case, there may be no pre-announced central rate). The commitment to maintain the exchange rate within the band imposes constraints on monetary policy, with the degree of policy independence being a function of the bandwidth.
Managed floating with no predetermined path for the exchange rate	The monetary authority attempts to influence the exchange rate without having a specific exchange rate path or target. Indicators for managing the rate are broadly judgmental (e.g., balance of payments position, international reserves, parallel market developments), and adjustments may not be automatic. Intervention may be direct or indirect.
Independently floating	The exchange rate is market-determined, with any official foreign exchange market intervention aimed at moderating the rate of change and preventing undue fluctuations in the exchange rate, rather than at establishing a level for it.

Source: Taken directly from IMF web site on *Classification of Exchange Rate Arrangements and Monetary Frameworks*, http://www.imf.org/external/np/mfd/er/2006/eng/0706.htm.

proclaiming to be an independent floater. Japan, Korea, and the Philippines are characterized as independent floaters, consistent with their official assertions.[11] Contrary to the public pronouncement of the Chinese authorities that the currency is based on a currency basket, recent empirical studies suggest that the *de facto* regime appears to be a soft peg to the U.S. dollars with the IMF classifying China under "other conventional fixed peg arrangements."[12] The Malaysian ringgit since its official depegging is defined as being a managed floater with no predetermined path. This is consistent with

[11]We were not able to obtain official pronouncements of Cambodia's, Myanmar's and Timor Leste's exchange rate regimes. However, according to the IMF *de facto* classification, Cambodia and Myanmar both operate a managed float with no predetermined path while Timor Lester has adopted the U.S. dollar as its legal tender.

[12]See Shah *et al.* (2006) and Ogawa and Sakane (2006) for empirical validation.

Table 2.4. *De facto* IMF exchange rate classifications as of July 2006.

Country	As of July 2006
Bangladesh	Managed floating with no predetermined path.
Bhutan	Other conventional fixed peg arrangement (against a single currency).
Brunei Darussalam	Currency board arrangement.
Cambodia	Managed floating with no predetermined path.
China PRC	Other conventional fixed peg arrangements.
Hong Kong SAR	Currency board arrangement.
India	Managed floating with no predetermined path.
Indonesia	Independently floating.
Japan	Independently floating.
Korea	Independently floating.
Lao, P.D.R.	Managed floating with no predetermined path.
Malaysia	Managed floating with no predetermined path.
Myanmar	Managed floating with no predetermined path.
Nepal	Conventional pegged arrangement (against a single currency).
Pakistan	Other conventional fixed peg arrangements (against a single currency).
Philippines	Independently floating.
Singapore	Managed floating with no predetermined path.
Sri Lanka	Managed floating with no predetermined path.
Thailand	Managed floating with no predetermined path.
Vietnam	Other conventional fixed peg arrangements (against a single currency).

Source: IMF data on *Classification of Exchange Rate Arrangements and Monetary Frameworks*, http://www.imf.org/external/np/mfd/er/2006/eng/0706.htm.

the empirical analysis which suggests that the ringgit closely tracks a trade-weighted basket since its depegging in July 2005, not unlike the Singapore dollar.

In their seminal paper, Reinhart and Rogoff (2004) developed a so-called "natural classification" based on market information such as black market or parallel rates (rather than official rate), the statistical behavior of exchange rate, reserves, and interest rates as well as country chronologies using a five-year window (to prevent sporadic exchange rate changes).

Reinhart and Rogoff apply the methodology to 153 countries from 1946 to 2001 and find, among other things, that nearly half of the "official pegs" are better characterized as managed or freely floating arrangements or of limited flexibility.[13] More generally, once one uses *de facto* classifications, the bipolar view on exchange rate regimes which was based largely on *de jure* exchange rate classification is no longer obvious. This is also borne out in the case of *de facto* IMF coding for Asia. Referring to Figure 2.1, while

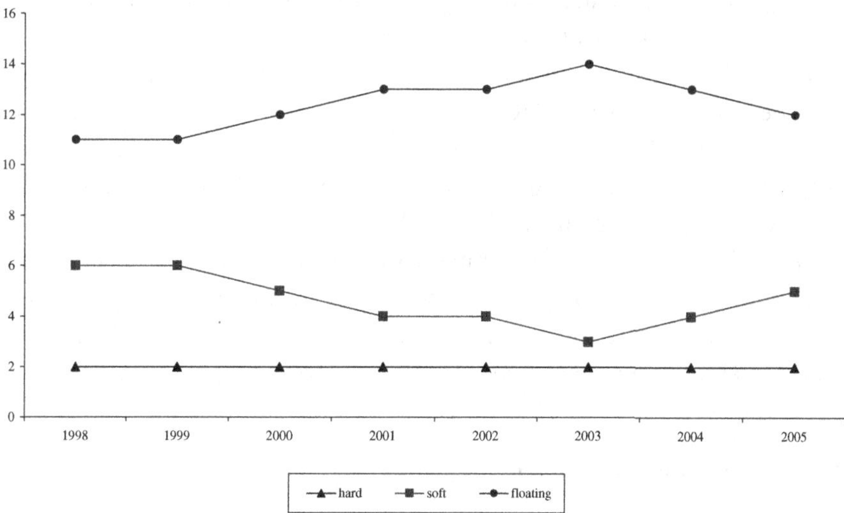

Fig. 2.1. Trends in exchange rate regimes among Asian countries using IMF classifications, 1998–2005. (Hard pegs refer to exchange arrangements with no separate legal tender (includes dollarization, currency unions) and currency boards. Soft pegs refer to conventional fixed pegs, horizontal band, crawling peg, and crawling band. Floating regimes refer to independent floats and managed floats. These definitions are based on using IMF *de facto* classifications (see Table 2.3) recategorized based on Bleaney and Francisco (2005). Data based on 19 Asian countries. Since the exchange rate categories are from the IMF, no distinction is made between freely falling and freely floating *a la* Reinhart–Rogoff as discussed in the text.). *Source*: Compiled based on IMF data on *Classification of Exchange Rate Arrangements and Monetary Frameworks* with the assistance of Jeff Kim.

[13]There are two other notable *de facto* exchange rate classifications. One is by Levy-Yeyati Sturzenegger (2003, 2005) who use rather broad exchange rate categories, viz., fixed, floating, and intermediate using cluster analysis. The second is by Shambaugh (2004) who closely follows Reinhart–Rogoff, except that he uses a one-year window while the latter uses a five-year window. Also see discussion by Genberg and Swoboda (2005).

there has been a discernible trend toward greater exchange rate flexibility from 1998 to 2003, there was a slight reversion to soft dollar pegs in the last 2 years.[14]

Unlike the new IMF classification, Reinhart and Rogoff were careful to distinguish between a flexible exchange rate regime and one that is freely falling rate *per se*. They define the latter as episodes in which the 12-month rate of inflation equals or exceeds 40 percent unless there is some type of pre-announced or narrow band. The authors also define the six-month period immediately after a crisis as being freely falling if there is a sudden transition from a fixed or quasi-fixed to more flexible exchange rate regime. Thus, in 1998, while the IMF codes Indonesia, Korea, and Thailand as "independently floating," Reinhart–Rogoff more accurately characterize them as "freely falling.[15] Notwithstanding this difference, by and large, the IMF and Reinhart–Rogoff reach the same conclusion regarding the Asian currency arrangements. While the more detailed classifications of Reinhart–Rogoff make it preferable to the IMF coding, the latter is far more frequently updated than the former.[16] Somewhat surprisingly, both the IMF and Reinhart–Rogoff coding characterize Japan and Korea as independently floating despite the sharp reserve buildup in both countries (Willett *et al.*, 2005).

2.3.2. *Some Simple De Facto Measures*

Clearly, there are a number of different ways of measuring *de facto* exchange rate regime — each offering different perspectives on the regime choices made by central banks but each possessing shortcomings in capturing all the essential characteristics of the regime as adopted by various countries. This section presents the results of two commonly used methods of measuring exchange rate regimes. The first is the Frankel–Wei (FW) method (Frankel and Wei, 1994). Here, we present the time-invariant results to the FW tests

[14]Needless to say, this statement should be interpreted with caution in view of the small sample size (19 economies).

[15]One needs to refer to the earlier NBER working paper version by Reinhart and Rogoff (2004) for country-specific exchange rate arrangements.

[16]However, neither classification is able to capture the most recent changes in exchange rate regimes in China and Malaysia. Hakura (2005) briefly compares the IMF *de facto* classification with the Reinhart–Rogoff one.

and we augment these results by reporting time-varying coefficients through recursive least squares. The second measure is an exchange rate flexibility index based on exchange market pressure (EMP) models.[17]

With regard to data, we use a time series of monthly observations from 1985:1 to 2006:12 for most of the regressions except in the case of the euro where the sample is 1999:1 to 2004:12. This sub-period allows us to examine the particular significance of the euro as a major currency since it actually came into existence. Data is from the *IMF International Financial Statistics* (IFS). Exchange rates are taken from line RF (RH for the pound sterling) and the cross rates for the local currency against the yen, pound, deutschmark (DEM), euro, and Swiss franc are calculated from the quoted bilateral exchange rates. The DEM/U.S. dollars and euro/U.S. dollars rate are taken from the *Pacific Exchange Rate Service.*[18] The countries examined are Bangladesh, Cambodia, mainland China, India, Indonesia, Korea, Laos, Malaysia, Nepal, Pakistan, the Philippines, Singapore, Sri Lanka, Thailand, and Vietnam.[19]

2.3.3. *Frankel–Wei Tests: Static Estimates*

This section examines the degree of influence between the target currencies and a vector of major currencies that includes the U.S. dollars, the Japanese yen, the UK pound, and the euro. We do this by employing the well-known Frankel–Wei regressions as shown in Eq. (1) below[20]:

$$\begin{aligned}\Delta e_{it} = \alpha_0 + \alpha_1 \Delta US_t + \alpha_2 \Delta JP_t + \alpha_3 \Delta UK_t + \alpha_4 \Delta EU_t \\ + \alpha_5 \Delta DEM_t + \mu_t,\end{aligned} \tag{2.1}$$

[17]There are clearly some weaknesses with the EMP models (which is why we do not use them in isolation). For a critical analysis of the EMP models, see Willett *et al.* (2005) who have developed a methodology for classifying exchange rate regimes based on the degree of foreign exchange intervention.

[18]http://fx.sauder.ubc.ca. The reason for this is that the service contains a sample for the euro/U.S. dollar from 1993. The data are no different from that available from the IFS.

[19]Compared to the list of countries in Table 2.1 we have left out Hong Kong, Bhutan, and Brunei, both of which maintain currency board arrangements vis-à-vis the U.S. dollar and the Singapore dollar, respectively. We also excluded Myanmar, which effectively operates a dual currency regime.

[20]Such regressions have recently been used in several subsequent studies such as Kawai (2002), McKinnon (2001), and Cavoli and Rajan (2006, 2007a,b) to name but a few.

where e_i refers to the local currency i and we estimate the effect of the DEM from 1985 to 1997 and the effect of the euro from 1999 to 2006 (i.e., $\alpha_4 = 0$ for 1985–1997 and $\alpha_5 = 0$ for 1999–2006). All currencies are expressed in logs and the numeraire currency used is the Swiss franc.[21] This method essentially involves conducting an OLS test of the local currency on other currencies that are considered to influence the former.

The higher the values of α coefficient corresponding to each major currency, the larger is the degree of influence of that currency on the local currency. As such, a coefficient provides some information about the possible degree of fixity of the local currency to the major currency.[22] However, a large coefficient value does not automatically imply a pegged exchange rate; it may merely reflect naturally occurring market-driven correlations between two currencies. In this context the standard deviation of the coefficient value may provide additional useful information in that a small standard deviation is more likely to imply an attempt to systematically maintain the correlation between two currencies by way of intervention (Baig, 2001).

The results of the Frankel–Wei tests are presented in Table 2.5. Two sets of results are presented — the first for the pre-crisis sample, 1985.1 to 1997.3, which presents the DEM as one of the currencies of influence, and the second is the post-crisis (and indeed post-euro) sample, 1999.1 to 2006.12. It is clear from the results that the U.S. dollar remains the currency with the most influence over the local currency, though in some cases, the yen, pound, or DEM/euro sustain some secondary influence. If one observes the relationship between the pre- and post-crisis results, it is clear that the U.S. dollar has been the sole influence over the Bangladeshi taka and the Chinese yuan over both time periods under consideration. Also noteworthy is the influence of the U.S. dollar. In the case of Bangladesh, China, India,

---

[21] In constructing the Frankel–Wei equation, we acknowledge the effect cross rates may have in influencing the currency pair we wish to examine. By estimating the equation in first differences and adding a constant we are assuming that the effect of the cross rates are fixed over the estimation period.

[22] The term "degree of influence" is used for these tests as an alternative — more general — interpretation to the coefficients being seen as "weights" in the currency basket. The basket weights story can only be valid under this method if the right-hand-side (RHS) variables are uncorrelated. Unfortunately, this cannot be assured here.

Table 2.5. Frankel–Wei regression results.

Dep variable	Bangladesh		Cambodia		China	
	Pre-crisis	Post-crisis	Pre-crisis	Post-crisis	Pre-crisis	Post-crisis
Constant	0.002	0.004	0.03	0.001	0.01	−0.0003
	(3.69)*	(2.94)*	(2.53)*	(1.83)	(1.71)	(−2.60)*
U.S.$	1.02	1.02	0.54	0.98	1.09	0.99
	(18.91)*	(22.41)*	0.54	(35.35)*	(3.55)*	(109.67)*
JPY	0.04	−0.08	0.23	0.02	0.07	−0.002
	(1.18)	(−1.91)	(0.47)	(0.46)	(0.67)	(−0.66)
DEM	0.04	—	−0.61	—	0.11	—
	(0.79)		(−0.55)		(0.27)	
EUR	—	−0.03	—	−0.04	—	0.04
		(−0.22)		(−0.50)		(1.88)
Other	—	—	—	—	—	—
Adj R^2	0.96	0.83	0.08	0.96	0.43	0.99
DW	2.20	1.67	1.60	1.75	1.95	2.03
Obs	145	95	86	90	145	95

Dep variable	India		Indonesia		Korea	
	Pre-crisis	Post-crisis	Pre-crisis	Post-crisis	Pre-crisis	Post-crisis
Constant	0.01	0.003	0.003	0.002	0.001	−0.002
	(3.41)*	(0.36)	(1.94)	(0.42)	(1.24)	(−1.02)
U.S.$	0.89	0.88	0.88	0.55	0.93	0.56
	(6.03)*	(20.48)*	(6.06)*	(2.25)*	(21.69)*	(6.84)*
JPY	−0.09	0.09	0.06	0.06	0.07	0.52
	(−0.78)	(1.86)	(1.05)	(0.28)	(3.04)*	(6.27)*
DEM	−0.04	—	−0.05	—	0.02	—
	(−0.24)		(−0.46)		(0.36)	
EUR	—	0.22	—	1.84	—	0.13
		(1.72)		(3.78)*		(0.56)
Other	—	—	—	—	—	—
Adj R^2	0.55	0.89	0.70	0.28	0.97	0.73
DW	2.03	2.07	1.86	1.96	2.13	1.90
Obs	145	95	145	95	145	95

(*Continued*)

Table 2.5. (*Continued*)

Dep variable	Laos		Malaysia		Myanmar	
	Pre-crisis	Post-crisis	Pre-crisis	Post-crisis	Pre-crisis	Post-crisis
Constant	0.02	0.01	0.0004	−0.001	0.0002	−0.0004
	(2.11)*	(1.68)	(0.54)	(−0.99)	(1.46)	(−0.64)
U.S.$	0.94	0.60	1.04	0.95	0.71	0.49
	(2.79)*	(3.33)*	(12.38)*	(31.87)*	(37.05)*	(24.02)*
JPY	−0.14	0.33	0.08	0.02	0.19	0.21
	(−0.46)	(1.04)	(1.77)	(1.30)	(20.71)*	(7.52)*
DEM	−0.04	—	0.21	—	0.31	—
	(−0.06)		(2.06)*		(16.80)*	
EUR	—	−0.59	—	−0.04	—	0.16
		(−1.42)		(−0.64)		(0.97)
Other	—	—	—	—	0.11	—
					(11.24)*	
Adj R^2	0.02	0.33	0.90	0.95	0.99	0.83
DW	2.03	2.09	1.96	2.15	1.51	2.18
Obs	146	86	145	95	145	94

Dep variable	Nepal		Pakistan		Philipping	
	Pre-crisis	Post-crisis	Pre-crisis	Post-crisis	Pre-crisis	Post-crisis
Constant	0.01	0.0003	0.004	0.002	0.001	0.002
	(4.21)*	(0.41)	(4.73)*	(1.45)	(1.47)	(1.44)
U.S.$	0.43	1.02	0.95	0.91	1.16	0.91
	(1.37)	(21.76)*	(10.74)*	(20.74)*	(9.78)*	(10.52)*
JPY	−0.06	0.01	−0.01	0.03	−0.06	0.09
	(−0.82)	(0.21)	(−0.30)	(0.42)	(−0.98)	(1.14)
DEM	−0.52	—	0.05	—	0.07	—
	(−1.50)		(0.49)		(0.65)	
EUR	—	0.05	—	0.48	—	0.41
		(0.46)		(1.76)		(1.50)
Other	0.22	—	—	—	—	—
	(2.07)*					
Adj R^2	0.63	0.91	0.89	0.76	0.87	0.75
DW	2.05	1.95	1.93	1.87	1.95	1.93
Obs	145	94	145	94	145	94

(*Continued*)

Table 2.5. (*Continued*)

Dep variable	Singapore		Sri Lanka		Thailand	
	Pre-crisis	Post-crisis	Pre-crisis	Post-crisis	Pre-crisis	Post-crisis
Constant	−0.001	−0.0004	0.01	0.004	0.001	0.00
	(−1.90)	(−0.58)	(4.88)*	(3.29)*	(2.21)*	(0.07)
U.S.$	0.84	0.61	0.88	1.07	0.81	0.59
	(14.04)*	(13.67)*	(8.38)*	(13.48)*	(19.46)*	(7.39)*
JPY	0.12	0.18	0.11	0.02	0.11	0.15
	(4.19)*	(3.58)*	(2.05)*	(0.30)	(11.06)*	(1.43)
DEM	0.13	—	−0.06	—	0.01	—
	(2.04)		(−0.49)		(0.22)	
EUR	—	0.37	—	−0.02	—	0.59
		(3.03)*		(−0.11)		(3.29)*
Other	0.04	—	−0.10	—	0.05	—
	(1.86)		(−2.25)*		(2.73)*	
Adj R^2	0.94	0.85	0.83	0.84	0.99	0.68
DW	1.99	1.96	2.00	2.04	1.89	1.82
Obs	145	95	145	94	146	95

Dep variable	Vietnam	
	Pre-crisis[d]	Post-crisis
Constant	0.01	0.002
	(2.37)*	(2.27)*
U.S. $	1.55	0.98
	(4.57)*	(29.40)*
JPY	−0.30	0.04
	(−1.22)	(1.34)
DEM	0.42	—
	(1.27)	
EUR	—	−0.22
		(−0.66)
Other	−0.21	—
	(−1.74)	
Adj R^2	0.51	0.88
DW	1.94	2.37
Obs	87	79

Notes: (*) represents significance at 5 percent. The terms in parenthesis are *t*-statistics. The analysis involved OLS estimation of each as an Autorgressive Distributed Lag (ARDL) model. The rationale behind this is to ensure that there is no omitted variable bias due to serial correlation that often results from the exclusion of lagged dependent variables and regressors. Details of the lagged variables that were included in each specification are available upon request.

Malaysia, and Pakistan, the U.S. dollar coefficient has remained quite stable between samples. There is, however, a significant increase in the degree of influence of the U.S. dollar post-crisis for Cambodia, Nepal, and Sri Lanka, and a marked decrease in the case of Indonesia, Korea, the Philippines, Thailand (all of which have adopted inflation-targeting frameworks as noted previously), as well as Singapore, Vietnam, and Laos.

In the post-crisis sample, the euro appears to have some influence over the yuan, Indian rupee, rupiah, Pakistan rupee, Singapore dollar, and Thai baht. The results for the Japanese yen are quite mixed but appear to have been moderately influential over both the periods for the Korean won and the Singapore dollar.

The post-crisis results for the Korean won, Singapore dollar, and Thai baht merit special mention. While the U.S. dollar has remained a major influence over these currencies, it appears as if the other major currencies play a significant role — partially at the expense of the U.S. dollar, as mentioned above. In the case of the won and the baht, the inclusion of the other major currencies results in significant parameter values but from the adjusted R^2, the overall fit of the model is weaker.[23] The results for Singapore also indicate that several currencies share the degree of influence. While care must be exercised in interpreting these results, it is broadly suggestive of the possibility of a basket peg arrangement in those currencies.

2.3.4. *Frankel–Wei Tests: Dynamic Estimates*

While the above results offer some insight, they fail to provide any information as to whether there has been a change in the degree of influence of the U.S. dollar or other major currencies over time. In view of this we expand the Frankel–Wei analysis by re-estimating Eq. (1) using recursive least squares estimates. Recursive least squares simply involves the equation being estimated repeatedly using subsets of the sample data that are increased by one observation at each iteration.[24] Such recursive estimates allow us to track

[23]This statement is supported by the observation of both Akaike information criteria (AIC) and Schwarz criteria. In fact, this phenomenon occurred for almost all currencies tested.

[24]We estimated the initial regression using the same number of observations as there are coefficients to be estimated in the α vector for each country. (Thus, the first few values are volatile and ignored given the low degrees of freedom — we removed the first 18 months from the pre-crisis period and the first 12 months from the post-crisis period.) We obtained largely

the evolution of the α coefficients over time. It thus allows us to ascertain whether one of the major currencies is becoming more influential compared to another. As with the standard errors in the time-invariant regressions, the variation of the degree of influence is important in extracting information about the possibility of exchange rate movements being policy-driven. For example, if the coefficient value for a particular currency on the local currency is high but relatively stable, this may be suggestive of sustained intervention by the central bank to manage the value of that particular currency pair. If the estimated value is high but variable, the correlation might possibly be market-driven rather than with conscious central bank intervention.

Results of the recursive regressions for post-crisis sample are presented in Figure 2.2.[25] The figure contains the dynamic properties of the coefficients for the U.S. dollar, the Japanese yen, the pound, and the euro. Generally speaking, the results are supportive of the static Frankel–Wei results. Two observations stand out.

First, the U.S. dollar generally remains the strongest influence over local currencies post-crisis, but the introduction of the euro does substitute for the influence of the U.S. dollar in some cases. Cases where the U.S. dollar remains strong throughout the sample include Bangladesh, China, India, Malaysia, Nepal, Pakistan, the Philippines, Sri Lanka, and Vietnam. One should note further that the stability of the U.S. dollar for Bangladesh, Cambodia, India, China, Malaysia, and Sri Lanka might be indicative of a desire to peg to the U.S. dollar.

Second, in the case of Korea, Thailand, Laos, Singapore, and Thailand, there is evidence of even and stable influences of multiple currencies. This is suggestive of management vis-à-vis a currency basket. (The basket hypothesis will be explored in the following section.)

---

similar results using a Kalman Filter test. Results are broadly unchanged and therefore not reported here.

[25]There are a number of rationales for presenting the post-crisis results. First, the pre-crisis period is characterized by a domination of the U.S. dollar as the currency of influence. Second, due to the change from DEM to euro and also to the fact that the crisis period is removed (owing to high parameter volatility), the time path of the recursive estimates is broken. Pre-crisis (1985–1987) recursive estimates are available from the authors on request.

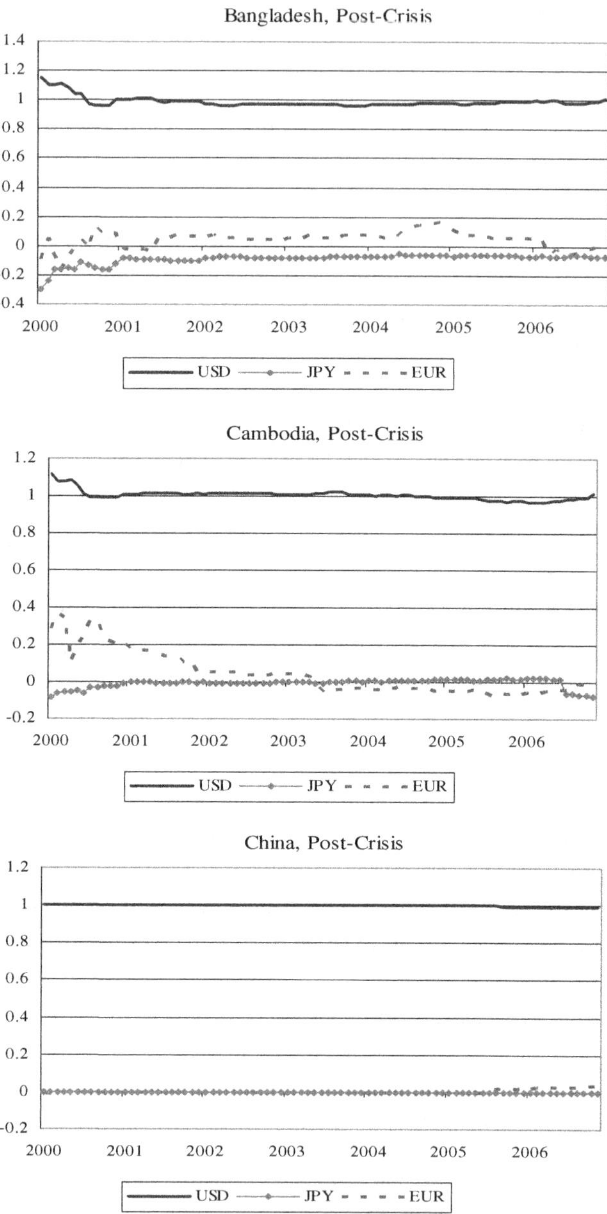

Fig. 2.2. Recursive least squares estimates, post-crisis.

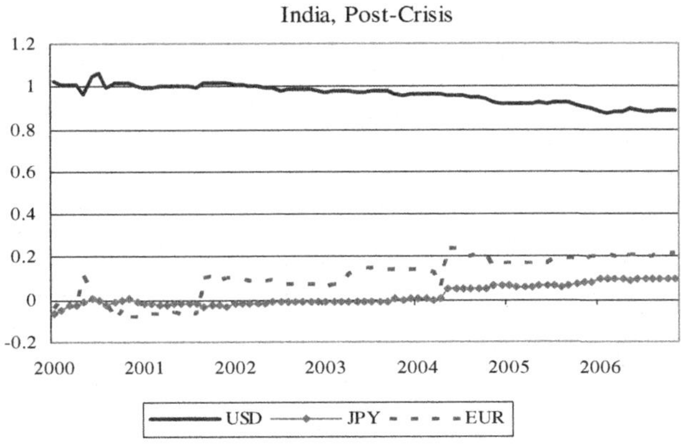

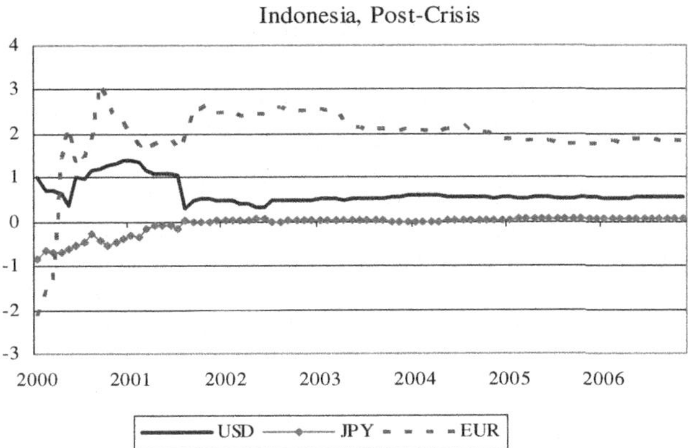

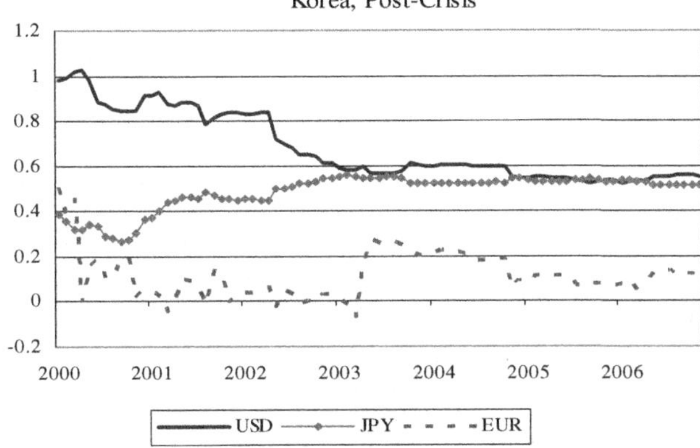

Fig. 2.2. *(Continued)*

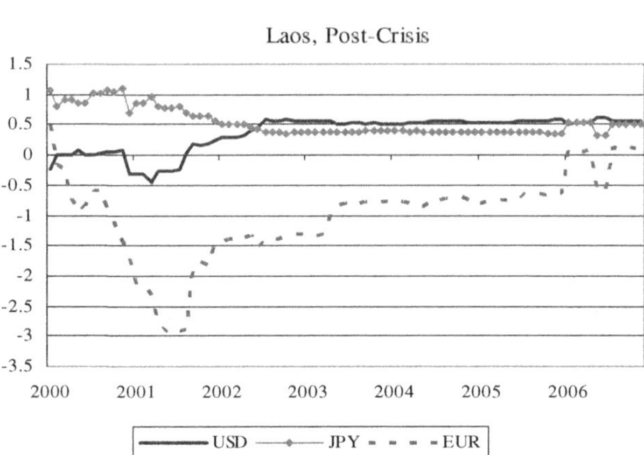

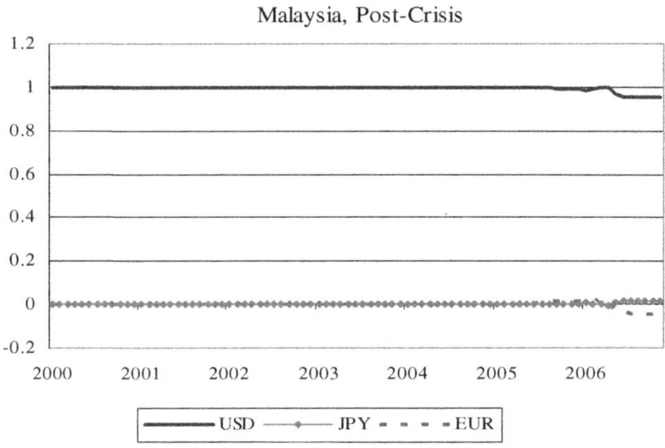

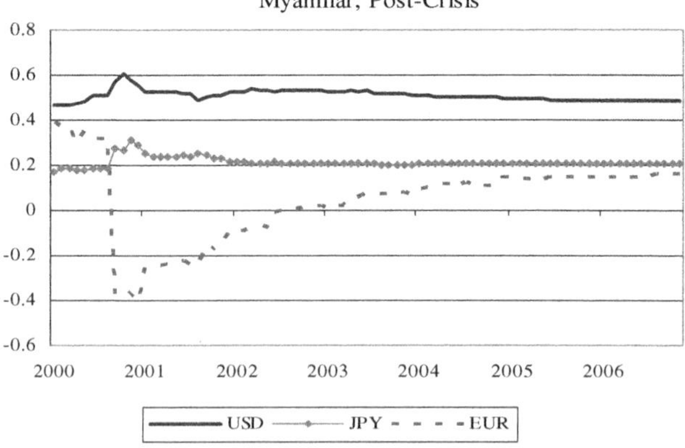

Fig. 2.2. *(Continued)*

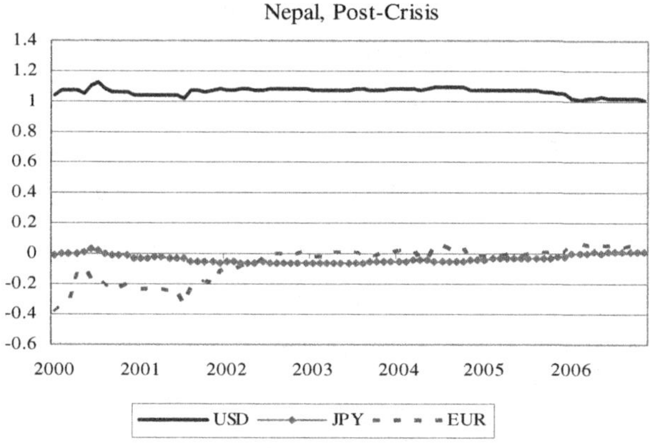

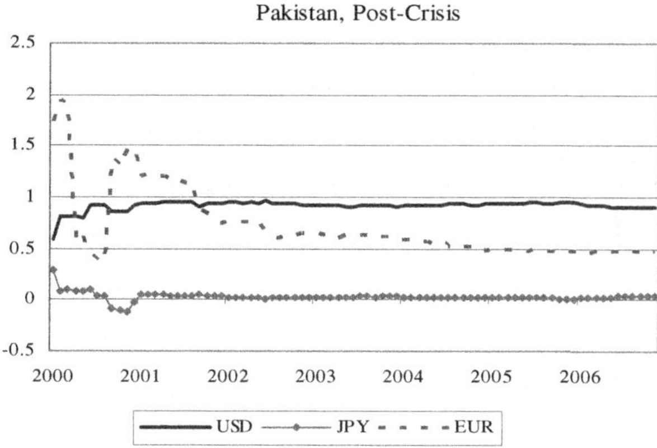

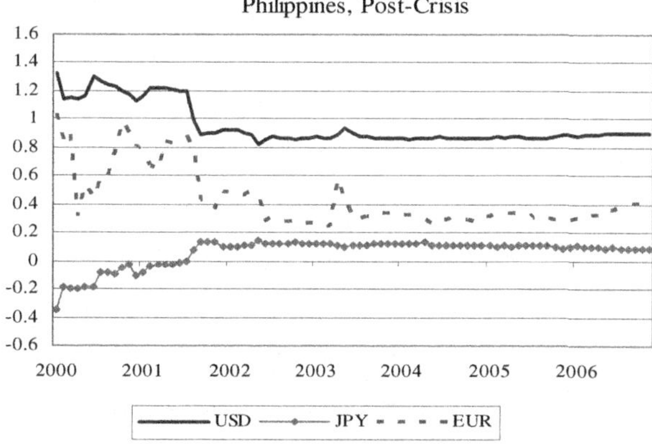

Fig. 2.2. *(Continued)*

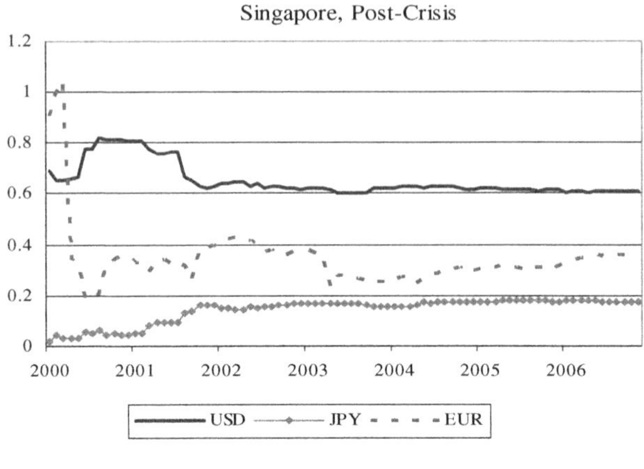

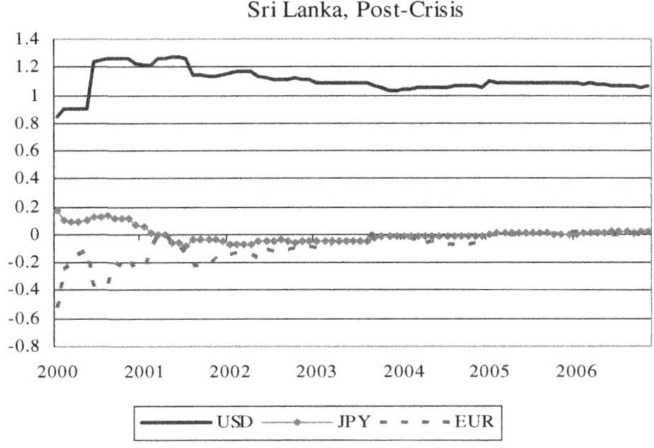

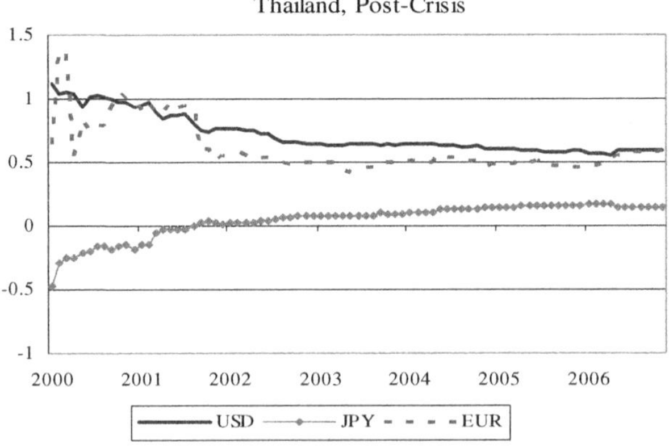

Fig. 2.2. *(Continued)*

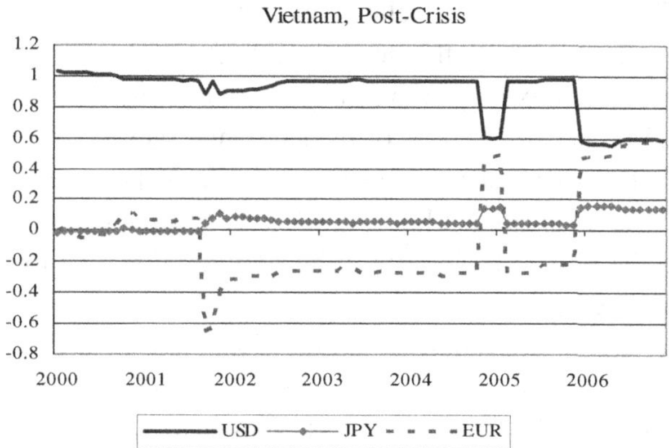

Fig. 2.2. *(Continued)*

2.3.5. *Exchange Rate Flexibility Index*

The second measure of exchange rate behavior adopted in this chapter is the exchange rate flexibility index. There are a variety of indices based on the idea of exchange market pressure (EMP). The theoretical foundation for EMP stems from a basic monetary model incorporating the demand for money, its supply, and relative PPP (Tanner, 2002 and Pentecost *et al.*, 2001). From these foundations, we can construct a measure of exchange rate flexibility such as the following:

$$Index = \Delta e/(\Delta e + \Delta f), \tag{2.2}$$

where Δe is as calculated in the previous section and Δf is change in net foreign assets (IFS line 11 – line 16c) scaled by lagged money base (line 14). We take the 12 monthly mean of Δe and Δf to form non-overlapping annual mean absolute deviations of each series. The index is deliberately constructed in this manner such that it returns a value between 0 and 1.[26] This

[26]Note that $1 - \Delta e/(\Delta e + \Delta f) = \Delta f/(\Delta e + \Delta f)$ is defined as a measure of exchange rate intervention. An index such as index 2 can also be constructed using standard deviations, e.g. $\sigma_{\Delta e}/\sigma_{\Delta e} + \sigma_{\Delta f}$. Baig (2001) and Calvo and Reinhart (2002) use variances. The index values using standard deviations are broadly similar to those for index 2 and are not reported here but are available on request. The nominal interest rate is often included in EMP measures but is excluded here due to the unavailability of market interest rates for all countries. It should be noted that part of the exchange rate change (and, indeed, interest rates) could

offers a scaling device for the relative exchange rate volatility; the closer the index is to 1 ($\Delta f \rightarrow 0$), the more flexible the exchange rate regime is, and the closer the index is to zero ($\Delta e \rightarrow 0$), the more fixed the regime is.

Figure 2.3 reports the results of the exchange rate flexibility index for the same selection of countries as the Frankel–Wei tests for the same period, 1985–2006. The index is calculated for the local currency vs the U.S. dollar, the yen, and the euro. The index for the nominal effective exchange rate (NEER) is also reported.

Two observations warrant highlighting. First, it is clear that for most of the countries examined, the index containing the U.S. dollar is lower than the other currency pairs and the NEER. This is suggestive that the local currency is more likely to be pegged to the U.S. dollar than to the others. This is most easily seen in the case of China — where the index value for the U.S. dollar is very near 0 for the sample of data collected, and for Malaysia — where the index value is 0 for the post-crisis period until mid-July 2005. An exception to this is Singapore where all currencies examined had very low index values (< 0.3) but where no single currency appeared to be significantly less flexible than the others. Is this a possible indication of a basket peg?

The second observation relates to the transition of exchange rate flexibility over time. We would expect that the crisis-affected economies of Korea, Indonesia, Thailand, and the Philippines would show an increase in flexibility after the crisis following the formal adoption of inflation-targeting regimes. Somewhat surprisingly this is not universally the case. We observe an increase in flexibility for Indonesia and Thailand, and the degree of flexibility has not altered materially for the Philippines. However, it would appear that the index value has diminished since the crisis for Korea (aside from a brief jump in flexibility in the immediate aftermath of the crisis). This is indicative of a possible reversion to a U.S. dollar (and yen) peg for Korea, though it may also reflect greater use of interest rates as a stabilization instrument.[27]

---

be valuation effects rather than adjustment because of foreign exchange intervention. The interest rate was added to the denominator to selection of countries as a robustness exercise and the results were very similar. Also see Cavoli and Rajan (2006) for more on this.

[27]Recall that the EMP we are using does not include interest rates.

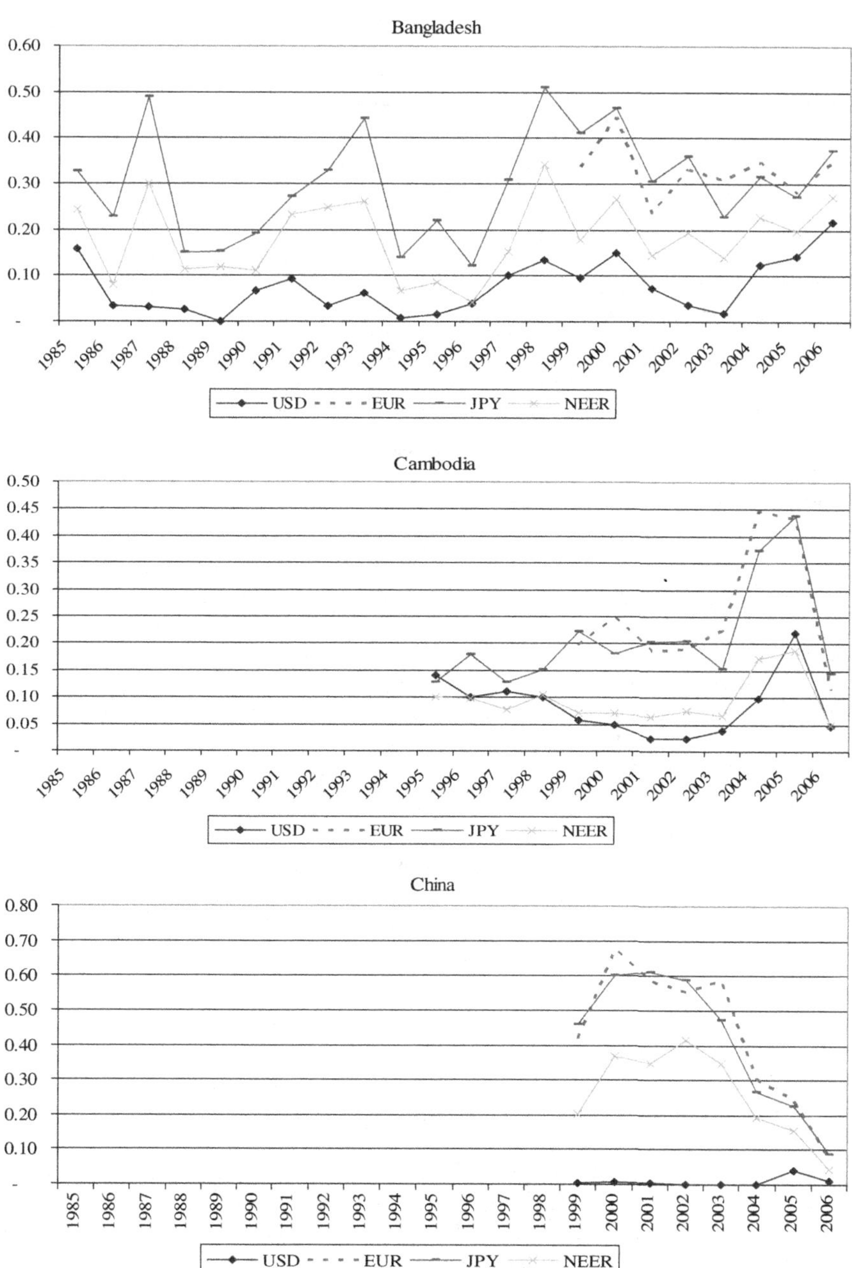

Fig. 2.3. Exchange rate flexibility indices, 1985–2006.

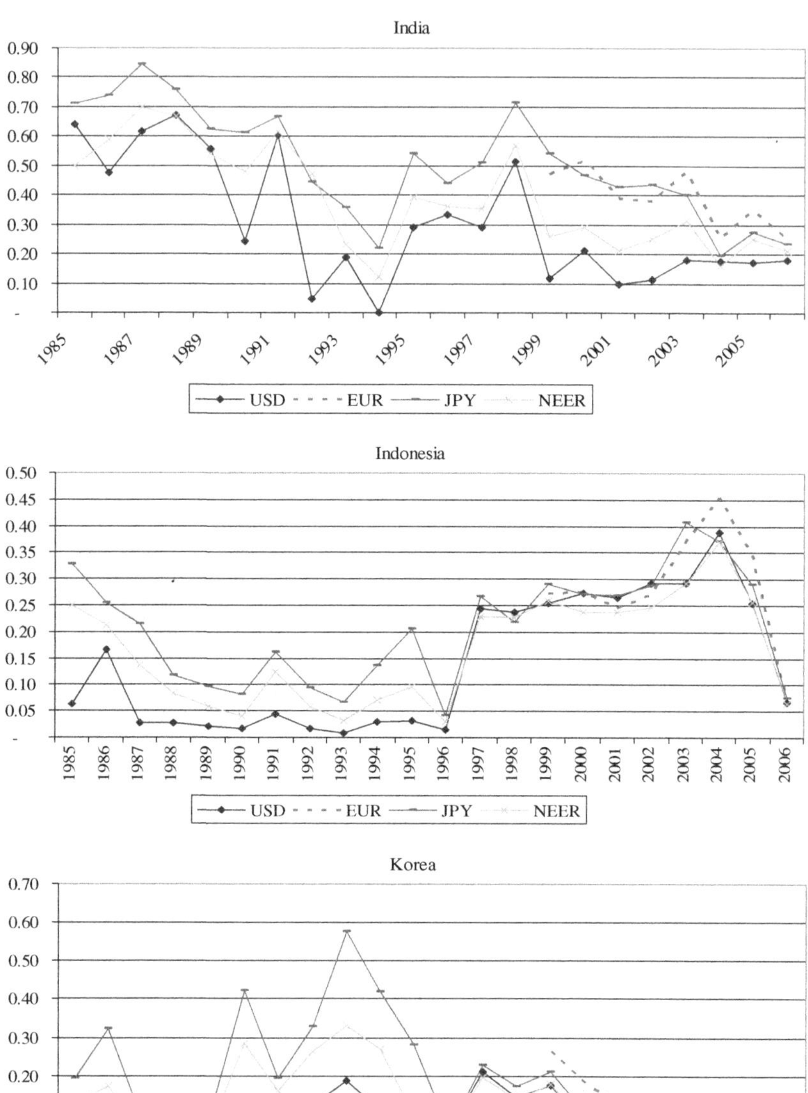

Fig. 2.3. (*Continued*)

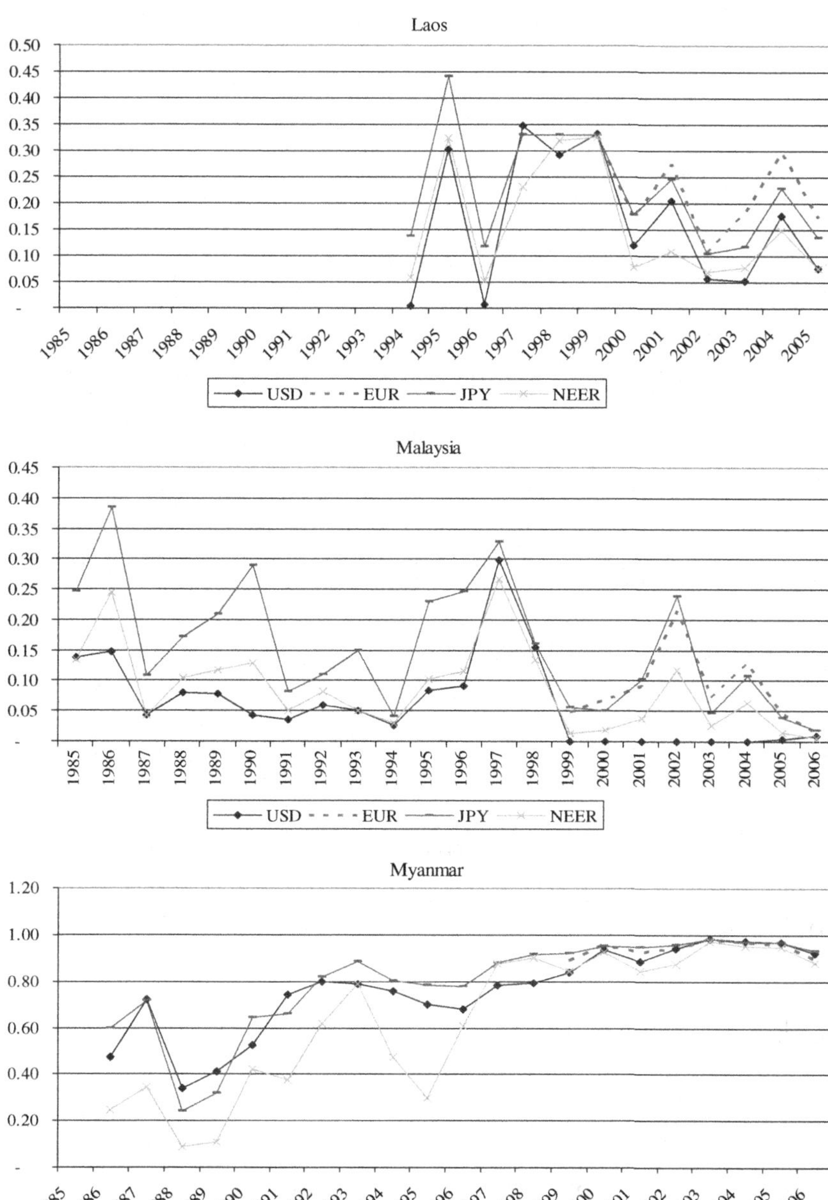

Fig. 2.3. *(Continued)*

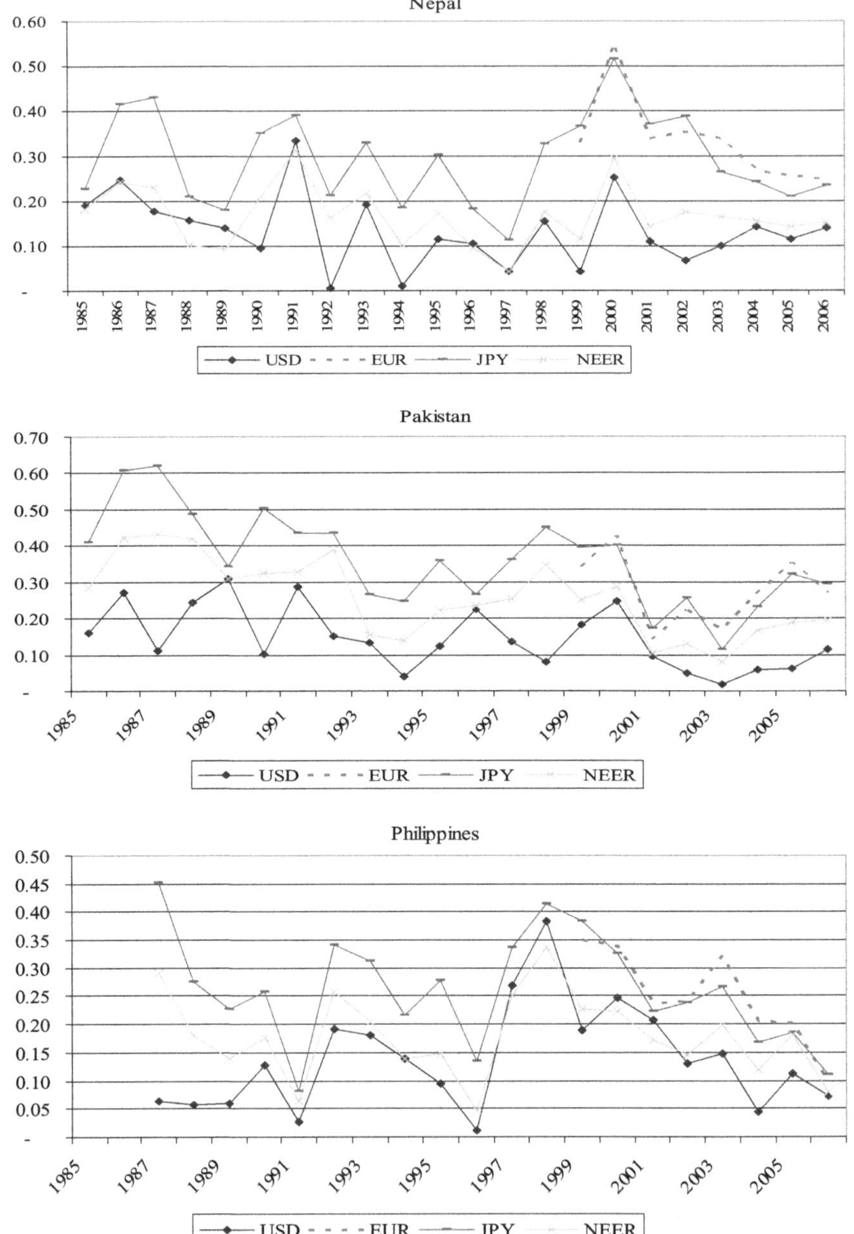

Fig. 2.3. *(Continued)*

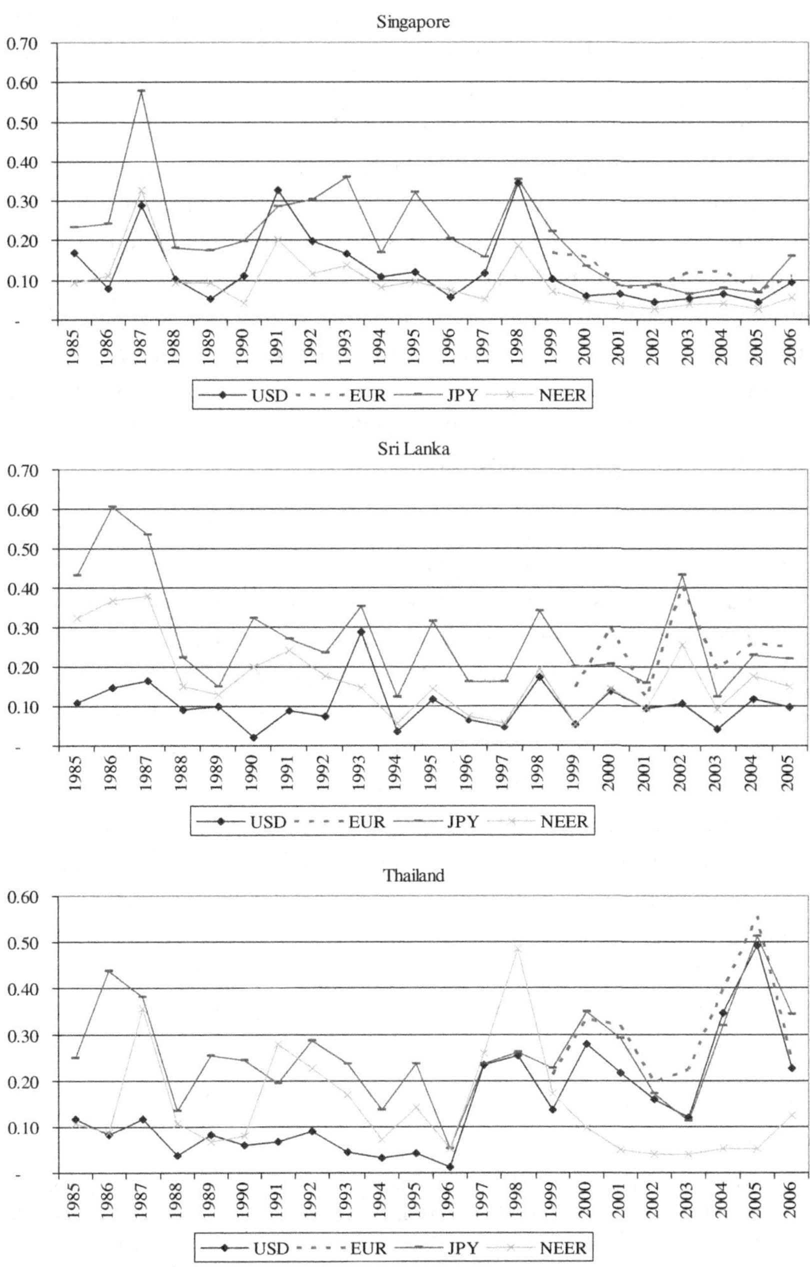

Fig. 2.3. (*Continued*)

Interestingly, if one observes the more recent index values for the crisis-affected countries (Thailand being the exception), there appears to be a trend toward a basket peg as the index values are very low for all currency pairs and they are all very close together. However, even if one concludes that the respective monetary authorities have consciously tried to stabilize the effective exchange rates, does this indicate a movement toward managing the currencies against a basket (i.e., trade-weighted exchange rate management), or is it a consequence of an open economy, inflation-targeting framework in which effective exchange rate fluctuations are taken into account in some manner (given their impact on trade, growth, and inflation, among other things)?[28] In an early review of the experiences of selected emerging economies, which included the four Asian economies noted above, Ho and McCauley (2003) note:

> While inflation targeting may be a framework that is typically free from formal exchange rate commitments, it is nonetheless not free from exchange rate considerations....(W)e find that, in practice, policymakers in inflation targeting countries do react to the exchange rate above and beyond its impact on inflation.... Notwithstanding the explicit concern and active response in some countries to exchange rate movements, there is as yet no clear evidence that any of them has acted in contradiction to the announced inflation target. Nonetheless, the line between responding to the exchange rate within the bounds of inflation targeting, and managing the exchange rate as a goal *per se*, can be quite thin at times. The onus is on the policymaker to explain to the public the difference, if any, between the two types of actions and the rationale for the policy decisions actually taken. Effective communication of policy intentions with respect to the role of the exchange rate will be crucial for the credibility of the policy regimes (pp. 35–36).[29]

[28]This issue is explored analytically by Cavoli and Rajan (2007c). Also see Genberg and He (Chapter 9 of this volume), Edwards (2006), Eichengreen (2002), and Ho and McCauley (2003). Eichengreen (2004) examines the issue with specific reference to Korea.

[29]Effective communication is especially critical going forward with the re-emergence of inflation globally and possible persistence of adverse supply shocks (energy prices, for instance).

2.4. Concluding Remarks

Overall, there appears to be a general trend toward somewhat greater exchange rate flexibility in Asia, though not complete flexibility. Unease clearly persists about allowing a completely free float. This is further apparent from the massive stockpiling of reserves in many Asian economies (for instance, see Ouyang *et al.*, 2007b). Many observers have pointed out that the export-oriented nature of the Asian economies — especially those in East Asia — has given rise to a collective action problem (the so-called "prisoner's dilemma") whereby the fear of losing competitiveness leads each of them to heavily manage their respective currencies, particularly in view of the limited flexibility of the Chinese currency. This in turn is contributing partly to large and growing global macroeconomic imbalances and global liquidity (Park, 2006).[30] The reserve stockpiling has also given rise to concerns about the creation of excessive liquidity buildup within the Asian economies themselves.[31] Eventually pegging the exchange rate always constrains monetary independence, and the loss of monetary-policy autonomy can have significant costs.[32] This monetary dilemma has been

---

[30]We do not broach the much-debated issue of the reasons behind the reserve buildup (i.e., insurance versus export-stimulus), except to note the following — quite reasonable observation — by the World Bank (2005):

> Intervention was initially motivated by a desire to build up a buffer stock after the Asian crisis had depleted levels of reserves....(H)owever (r)apid reserve accumulation continued through late 2004, as countries sought to limit the impact of heavy capital inflows on external competitiveness, at a time when domestic demand generally remained subdued (p. 29).

Also see Chapter 3 of this volume.

[31]How justified these concerns are depends heavily on the extent to which the reserve-accumulating countries have been able to sterilize the effects on their domestic monetary aggregates. Empirical analyses by Ouyang *et al.* (2007a,b) reveal that China and other Asian economies have sterilized very aggressively in the last few years (also see Chapter 4 of this volume).

[32]It is often noted that some recent empirical evidence casts doubt on the extent to which floating regimes in emerging economies provide insulation from foreign interest rate shocks (for instance, see Frankel *et al.*, 2004 and Hausman *et al.*, 2001). However, a more recent study using *de facto* exchange rates for 100 developing and industrial countries between 1973 and 2000 finds that the interest rates of the countries that operated pegged regimes followed the base country far more closely than non-pegs (Shambaugh, 2004). A closely

very apparent in many emerging Asian economies including China, India, Korea, and Thailand.

References

Angkinand, A, EMP Chiu and TD Willett (2005). *Testing the Unstable Middle and Two Corners Hypotheses*. Claremont Graduate University: Mimeo.

Baig, T (2001). Characterizing exchange rate regimes post-crisis East Asia. IMF Working Paper No. 01/152.

Bleaney, M and M Francisco (2005). Exchange rate regimes and inflation — only hard pegs make difference. *Canadian Journal of Economics*, 38, 1453–1471.

Bubula, A and I Ötker-Robe (2002). The evolution of exchange rate regimes since 1990: Evidence from de facto policies. IMF Working Paper No. 02/155.

Bubula, A and I Ötker-Robe (2003). Are pegged and intermediate exchange rate regimes more crisis prone? IMF Working Paper No. 03/22.

Calvo, G and C Reinhart (2002). Fear of floating. *Quarterly Journal of Economics*, 117, 379–408.

Cavoli, T and RS Rajan (2006). Have exchange rate regimes in asia become more flexible post crisis? Re-visiting the evidence. George Mason University and Queensland University of Technology: Mimeo.

Cavoli, T and RS Rajan (2007a). The extent of exchange rate flexibility in India: Basket pegger or closet U.S. dollar pegger? *India Macroeconomics Annual* 2007, pp. 125–140.

Cavoli, T and RS Rajan (2007b). Managing in the middle: Characterizing Singapore's exchange rate policy. *Asian Economic Journal*, 21, 321–342.

Cavoli, T and RS Rajan (2007c). Inflation targeting arrangements in Asia: Exploring the role of the exchange rate. *Briefing Notes in Economics*, No.74, September–October.

Di Giovanni, A and J Shambaugh (2005). The impact of foreign interest rates on the economy: The role of the exchange rate regime. IMF Working Paper No. 06/37.

Edwards, S (2006). The relationship between exchange rates and inflation targeting revisited. NBER Working Paper No. 12163.

---

related paper finds that small countries with fixed exchange rates are most directly affected by interest rate changes in large countries (Di Giovanni and Shambaugh, 2005). Of course, if unrestrained monetary policy has been a facet of a country's past, imposing exchange rate fixity may be an advantage as it constrains the active use of monetary policy.

Eichengreen, B (2002). Can emerging markets float? Should they inflation target? Banco Central Do Brasil Working Paper No. 36.

Eichengreen, B (2004). Monetary and exchange rate policy in Korea: Assessments and policy issues. Prepared for a Symposium at the Bank of Korea, Seoul, Korea.

Frankel, J (1999). No single currency regime is right for all countries or at all times. *Essays in International Finance* No. 215, Princeton University.

Frankel, J, S Schmukler and L Serven (2000). Verifiability and the vanishing intermediate exchange rate regime. In *Brookings Trade Forum 2000*, S Collins and D Rodrik (eds.), pp. 59–108.

Frankel, J, S Schmukler and L Serven (2004). Global transmission of interest rates: Monetary independence and currency regime. *Journal of International Money and Finance*, 23, 701–733.

Frankel, J and SJ Wei (1994). Yen bloc or dollar bloc? Exchange rate in the East Asian economies. In *Macroeconomic Linkage: Savings, Exchange Rates, and Capital Flows*, T Ito and A Krueger (eds.). Chicago: University of Chicago Press.

Genberg, H and AK Swoboda (2005). Exchange-rate regimes: Does what countries say matter? *IMF Staff Papers*, 52, 129–141.

Hakura, DS (2005). Are emerging market countries learning to float? IMF Working Paper No. WP/05/98.

Hausman, R, U Panizza and E Stein (2001). Why do countries float the way they float? *Journal of Development Economics*, 66, 387–414.

Ho, C and RN McCauley (2003). Living with flexible exchange rates: Issues and recent experience in inflation targeting emerging market economies. BIS Working Papers No. 130.

Husain, I (2005). Monetary-cum-exchange rate regime: What works best for emerging market economies? http://www.sbp.org.pk/about/speech/economic_management_policies/2005/Monetary-cum-Exchange-Rate-Regime.pdf

Kawai, M (2002). Exchange rate arrangements in East Asia: Lessons from the 1997–98 currency crisis. IMES Discussion Paper Series 2002-E-17, Institute for Monetary and Economic Studies, Bank of Japan, September.

Khor, HE, E Robinson and J Lee (2004). Managed floating and intermediate exchange rate systems: The Singapore experience. Staff Paper No.37, Monetary Authority of Singapore (MAS).

Levy-Yeyati, E and F Sturzenegger (2003). To Float or to fix: Evidence on the impact of exchange rate regimes on growth. *American Economic Review*, 93, 1173–1193.

Levy-Yeyati, E and F Sturzenegger (2005). Classifying exchange rate regimes: Deeds vs. words. *European Economic Review*, 49, 1603–1635.

McCallum, BT (2005). Is Singapore the model for China's new exchange rate policy? Rochester University: Mimeo.

McKinnon, RI (2001). After the crisis, the East Asian dollar standard resurrected: An interpretation of high-frequency exchange-rate pegging. In *Rethinking the East Asian Miracle*, J Stiglitz and S Yusuf (eds.). World Bank and Oxford University Press.

Ogawa, E and M Sakane (2006). The Chinese Yuan after the Chinese exchange rate system reform. REITI Working Paper No. 06-E-019.

Ouyang, AY, RS Rajan and TD Willett (2007a). China as a reserve sink: The evidence from offset and sterilization coefficients. Hong Kong Institute for Monetary Research Working Paper No. 10/2007.

Ouyang, A, RS Rajan and TD Willett (2007b). Managing the monetary consequences of reserve accumulation in Asia. Hong Kong Institute for Monetary Research: Mimeo.

Park, YC (2006). Global imbalances and East Asia's policy adjustments. Mimeo, Seoul National University, Korea.

Pentecost, EJ, C Van Hooydonk and A Van Poeck (2001). Measuring and estimating exchange market pressure in the EU. *Journal of International Money and Finance*, 20, 401–418.

Rajan, RS (2006). Asian currencies since the 1997–98 crisis. Mimeo. Paper prepared in conjunction with the World Bank–IMF Program of Seminars in Singapore.

Reinhart, CM and KS Rogoff (2004). The modern history of exchange rate arrangements: A reinterpretation. *Quarterly Journal of Economics*, 119, 1–48. (More country-specific information is available in the Working Paper version (NBER Working Paper No.8963)).

Shah, A and I Patnaik (2005). India's experience with capital flows: The elusive quest for a sustainable current account deficit. NBER Working Paper No. 11387.

Shah, A, A Zeileis and I Patnaik (2006). What is the new Chinese currency regime? Mimeo.

Shambaugh, J (2004). The effects of fixed exchange rates on monetary policy. *Quarterly Journal of Economics*, 119, 300–351.

Tanner, E (2002). Exchange market pressure, currency crises, and monetary policy: Additional evidence from emerging markets. IMF working Paper WP/02/14.

Willett, TD (2002). Fear of floating need not imply fixed exchange rates. Presented at the *Fordham CEPR Conference on Dollarization and Euroization*. Revised version published in *Open Economies Review* (2003), 14, 71–91.

Willett, TD, J Kim and I Nitithanprapas (2005). Some methodological issues in classifying exchange rate regimes. Claremont Graduate University: Mimeo.

World Bank (2005). *Global Development Finance 2005*. New York: Oxford University Press.

CHAPTER 3

HOARDING OF INTERNATIONAL RESERVES: A COMPARISON OF THE ASIAN AND LATIN AMERICAN EXPERIENCES[1]

Yin-Wong Cheung and Hiro Ito

3.1. Introduction

The Asian financial crisis of 1997–1998 is quite different from some previous crises including the 1982 Mexican debt crisis and the 1994 Tequila crisis. Prior to the Asian financial crisis, the so-called "First Generation" and "Second Generation" crisis models were developed to offer some insight into the earlier crises. While the First Generation models focus on the inconsistency between fundamentals and a pre-assigned fixed exchange rate, the Second Generation models highlight the role of public information, the self-fulfilling crisis, and the trade-off between credibility and flexibility when devaluation entails a fixed cost (Flood and Garber, 1984; Flood and Marion, 1999; Krugman, 1979; Obstfeld, 1995, 1996). While these models offer a

[1]We thank Menzie Chinn, Joseph Gruber, Jie Li, Helen Popper, Cedlic Tille, and participants of the 2006 APEA conference and the 2007 Claremont–Bologna–Singapore Centre for Applied and Policy Economics (SCAPE) International Economic Policy Forum for their helpful comments and suggestions on an earlier version of the paper, Dickson Tam for compiling some of the data, and Philip Lane and Gian Maria Milesi-Ferreti for making their data on external financial wealth available online. Cheung acknowledges the financial support of faculty research funds of the University of California, Santa Cruz. Ito acknowledges the financial support of faculty research funds of Portland State University and the Japan Foundation.

useful interpretation of crises observed in Latin America in the 1970s–1980s and other crises, the 1997–1998 crisis in East Asia has led to the "Third Generation" models that focus on the role of balance sheet factors and financial sector weaknesses, as well as the possibility of bailouts by international financial institutions, central banks, and governments (Krugman, 1999; Corsetti *et al.*, 1999; Chang and Velasco, 1999; Dooley, 1997).

An astonishing development in the aftermath of the 1997–1998 Asian financial crisis is the large-scale buildup of international reserves among Asian economies — even among those who were not inflicted by the crisis. China, perhaps, is the one of the most dramatic cases, since its holding of international reserves increased by more than five times between 2000 and 2006. Japan, the developed economy in the region, saw its international reserves ascended by more than 1.5 times during the same period. Indeed, in 1996 the list of top 10 global international reserve holders had five Asian economies but the 2006 list had eight. As of 2006, the eight Asian economies on the top 10 list accounted for almost three-fifths of the world's total international reserves.

While there may be a number of precautionary reasons for holding international reserves, the recent steep increase in holdings of international reserves has raised concerns in both policy and academic circles. This is so as excessive accumulation of international reserves can distort both global and domestic balances, and thus, can be a serious threat to the stability of the world economy. It is perceived that some economies are holding international reserves at a level that is difficult to be rationalized by conventional factors (Jeanne and Ranciere, 2006; Rodrik, 2006). One commonly used yardstick of international reserve adequacy is the reserves-to-imports ratio. The oft-used rule of thumb is to maintain international reserves worth 3 months of imports. At the end of 2006, the Asian economies of China, Taiwan, Japan, India, Malaysia, and Korea, for example, held international reserves that could cover 16.2, 15.8, 11.7, 15.0, 7.5, and 7.4 months of their respective imports.

In contrast, we do not observe such an upsurge of international reserve holdings after the financial crises in Latin America. Figure 3.1 compares the amounts of international reserves held by East Asian and Latin American economies. It is apparent that, during the last 20 years, the Asian economies have tended to hold more international reserves than the Latin American

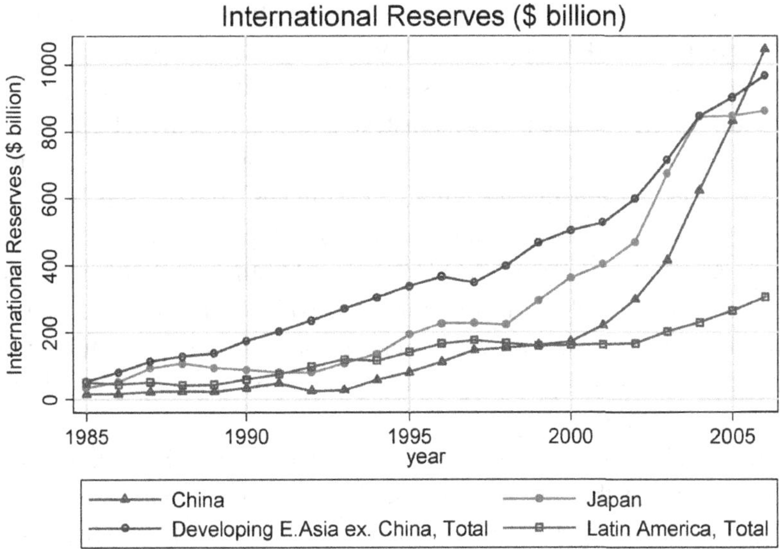

Fig. 3.1. Holdings of international reserves — East Asia vs Latin America.

economies. Although Latin American economies have been increasing their holdings of international reserves in the last few years — possibly due to the increase in commodity prices — the gap between the two regions appears to be widening. Indeed, at the end of 2006, the Latin American region had an average reserves-to-imports ratio of 5.0, while the Asian region has an average ratio of 6.9.[2]

Against this backdrop, a natural set of questions to ask is: "Why do economies in these two regions display such dissimilar international reserve holding behaviors?" and "Is the observed difference driven by the differences in their economic conditions?" The theme of our chapter is to empirically assess the determinants of the demand for international reserves and to compare the Asian and Latin American economies' holdings of international reserves in the post-Asian financial period. The choice of the sample period is motivated by the fact that, after the Asian crisis, these economies show dramatic discrepancies in their holdings of international reserves.

[2]The top five largest Latin American holders of international reserves are Bolivia, Brazil, Venezuela, Peru, and Argentina, and their reserves-to-imports ratio are, respectively, 11.3, 10.7, 9.4, 7.8, and 7.4.

Our approach in the chapter is as follows. First, we will provide an empirical framework for evaluating holdings of international reserves. The existing literature, however, offers a few alternative specifications of the demand for international reserves. Instead of selecting a model *a priori*, we opt to conduct the comparison based on a few commonly used specifications. Further, we generate the empirical estimates from two sets of data — one comprises data from developed and developing economies and the other consists of data from selected Asian and Latin American economies. Second, we use the alternative empirical specifications obtained from different theories and from different samples of economies to compare and contrast the international reserve holding behaviors of the Asian and Latin American economies.

The remainder of the chapter is organized as follows. Section 3.2 offers a brief review of the literature on the demand for international reserves. Section 3.3 presents the basic empirical equations and the related estimation results. The comparison exercise is reported in Section 3.4. Some concluding remarks are given in Section 3.5.

3.2. A Brief Review on the Determinants of International Reserves

The theoretical reasons for holding international reserves range from transaction demand, precautionary motives, collaterals, and mercantilist behavior. Although numerous studies have attempted to unravel the relevance of these factors, the debate on the determinants of international reserves is far from settled. The difficulty of explicating international reserve holding behavior may be attributed to the anecdotal view that the role and functionality of international reserves have evolved along with developments in global financial markets. For instance, the holding of international reserves is now increasingly susceptible to capital account transactions because of the continuing financial globalization and innovative advancements in international capital markets. The recent financial crisis also signified the importance of expectations, policy credibility, and institutional structures in determining the adequate level of international reserves.

In the following exercise, we group the determinants of international reserves into three categories: traditional macroeconomic variables, financial variables, and institutional variables. The group of traditional macrovariables consists of the propensity to import, volatility of real export receipts, international reserve volatility, the opportunity cost of holding international reserves, real per capita GDP, and population. These variables have been commonly considered as determinants since the 1960s. In the early stages the demand for international reserves was mainly attributed to the need for accommodating imbalances arising from trade account transactions, which was the main type of balance of payments transactions before the era of the modern international capital market.

Heller (1966) argues that the demand for international reserves should be negatively related to the marginal propensity to import because a higher propensity to import (m) implies a smaller marginal cost of balance of payments adjustment (i.e., $1/m$), implying a lower demand for international reserves. However, most empirical exercises — including Heller (1966) himself — use the average, and not the marginal, propensity to import. Frenkel (1974a) points out that the average propensity to import, i.e., the imports-to-GDP ratio, measures trade openness and, therefore, should have a positive effect on the demand for international reserves because of the precautionary holding to accommodate external shocks through trade channels.

The role of international reserve volatility is illustrated by the buffer stock model of international reserves. Extending the model for cash holding, Frenkel and Jovanovic (1981) illustrated the effect of international reserve volatility in a stochastic inventory control setting. In some studies, the volatility of real export receipts is used as an alternative proxy for the uncertainty of balance of payments (Kelly, 1970).

The opportunity cost of holding international reserves, which is commonly measured by the difference between the local interest rate and the U.S. interest rate, has been included in models to compare the costs and benefits of holding international reserves (Heller, 1966; Frenkel and Jovanovic, 1981). The effect of the opportunity cost is quite inconspicuous in the empirical literature because of the difficulty in assigning a single interest rate for international reserve assets while accounting for their risks.[3]

[3]Due to data availability, we use the differentials between the U.S. Treasury bill rates and domestic lending rates.

Following Aizenman and Marion (2003), Edison (2003), and Lane and Burke (2001), real per capita GDP and population are included to capture the size effect on international reserve holding. In view of the Baumol (1952) square-root rule for transaction demand, we expect these size variables to have a negative coefficient.

The second group of explanatory variables includes money supply, external debts, and capital flows. The use of money in explaining the hoarding of international reserves can be dated back to the 1950s. Courchene and Youssef (1967), for example, appeal to the monetarist model of balance of payments to justify the use of money in their international reserve regression (Johnson, 1958).[4] More recently, de Beaufort Wijnholds and Kapteyn (2001) argue that money stock in an economy is a proxy for potential capital flight by domestic residents and, therefore, can be a measure of the intensity of the "internal drain."[5]

The implications of external debts and capital flows on the holding of international reserves have received considerable attention after the Asian financial crisis. While capital inflows can enhance economic growth by supplementing domestic savings and/or financial intermediaries and improving the efficiency of domestic financial markets, a sudden capital flow reversal can devastate an economy, trigger a crisis, and cause significant output losses.[6] Generally, developing economies with inefficient and immature financial sectors are vulnerable to the adverse effect of capital reversals. Thus, it is conceived that economies with a high level of exposure to external financing, whether they are debts, FDI, or portfolio flows, should hold a high level of international reserves to reduce its vulnerability to financial

---

[4]One version of the "global monetarism" argues that an increase in international reserves is driven by an excess demand for money, which implies a balance of payments surplus whereas a fall in international reserve holding is caused by an excess supply of money, which implies a balance of payments deficit.

[5]De Beaufort Wijnholds and Kapteyn (2001) refer to the research on the Early Warning System and argue that the international reserves-to-$M2$ ratio is a reasonable measure of international reserve adequacy.

[6]Edwards (2004) analyzes the sudden stop of capital inflows and current account performance in the last three decades. Caballero and Panageas (2004) suggest that international reserve accumulation is not the best insurance against sudden stops.

crises and to boost confidence in their currencies (Aizenman *et al.*, 2007; Feldstein, 1999).[7]

Dooley *et al.* (2005) offer an alternative view on the link between capital flows and international reserves. These authors argue that under the current international financial architecture (the "Bretton Woods II system"), emerging market economies accumulate international reserves to secure FDI inflows from the "center" country (not clear what is a center country), i.e., the U.S. In other words, the economies in the "periphery" hold international reserves to ensure importation of financial intermediaries from abroad. According to this view, capital inflows are positively correlated with holdings of international reserves.

The effect of capital flows on international reserve accumulation, however, is not unambiguous. Besides the insurance motive, international reserves can be viewed as a substitute for external financing. In this case, an economy may hold a lower level of international reserves if it has secured access to international capital markets and, thus, the correlation between the two variables is negative. However, Lane and Milesi-Ferretti (2006) note that the types, volumes, and directions of capital flows have changed over time. Hence, the use of an aggregate variable may not capture the differential effects of different types of capital flows. In the following, we examine the individual effects of net external liabilities (i.e., external liabilities minus assets) in debt financing, portfolio equity financing, and FDI, as well as their growth rates.

The third group of explanatory variables is institutional variables. It has been argued that institutional characteristics like corruption, political stability, and capital controls affect the holding of international reserves. Aizenman and Marion (2003, 2004) and Alfaro *et al.* (2003), for example, show that holdings of international reserves are influenced by political uncertainty and corruption. Our empirical exercise includes a selected group of institutional variables pertaining to financial openness and political/social conditions.

---

[7] In general, it is suggested to cover one year amortized value of various types of liabilities over a wide range of possible outcomes. The role of short-term external debts is brought to the center stage by the popular Greenspan–Guidotti-rule (Greenspan, 1999).

3.3. Demand for International Reserves

In this section, we estimate the demand for international reserves. The explanatory variable we considered is a scaled measure of international reserves given by $r_{i,t} = R_{i,t}/\text{GDP}_{i,t}$, where $R_{i,t}$ is a generic notation of economy i's holding of international reserves and $\text{GDP}_{i,t}$ is economy i's gross domestic product at time t. Both variables are measured in U.S. dollars. Scaling international reserves facilitates comparison across countries of different sizes. For brevity, we call the ratio $r_{i,t}$ international reserves. The sample period covers 1999–2005. The choice of the post-Asian financial crisis period is motivated by the sharp difference between the Asian and Latin American economies' behaviors noted in Section 3.1. Further, there is evidence that the demand for international reserves changes after the crisis and, thus, the focus on the post-crisis period is relevant to the current discussion (Cheung and Ito, 2007).

3.3.1. *Model Specifications*

Following the discussion in the previous section, we consider three groups of explanatory variables. They are denoted by $X_{i,t}(= \{x_{i,k,t}; k = 1, \ldots, N_x\})$ that contains the traditional macrovariables, $Y_{i,t}(= \{y_{i,k,t}; k = 1, \ldots, N_y\})$ the financial variables, and $Z_{i,t}(= \{z_{i,k,t}; k = 1, \ldots, N_z\})$ the institutional variables.

In addition to these variables, we include some dummy variables to account for other characteristics of an economy. The first type is the exchange rate regime dummy variable. The common wisdom suggests that economies with fixed exchange rates and crawling pegs have incentives to hold international reserves to fight against exchange rate market pressures. The second type is a geographic dummy variable. Its inclusion is motivated by the folklore that economies in certain geographic regions such as East Asia tend to hoard high levels of international reserves especially after the Asian financial crisis. The third type is the crisis dummy variable. The variable is meant to capture the effects of a currency crisis, a banking crisis, or a twin crisis on hoarding of international reserves. The fourth type is a dummy variable that assumes a value of one if the economy is located in a region which is inflicted by a crisis. This dummy variable is included to evaluate the possible contagion effect of crises on international reserve accumulation. The dummy variables that capture other characteristics of the economies are collected under $D_{i,t}(= \{d_{i,k,t}; k = 1, \ldots, N_d\})$.

The effects of these variables on hoarding of international reserves are studied using the following cross-sectional regression equations:

$$r_i = c + X_i'\alpha + \varepsilon_i, \tag{3.1}$$

$$r_i = c + X_i'\alpha + D_i'\delta + \varepsilon_i, \tag{3.2}$$

$$r_i = c + X_i'\alpha + Y_i'\beta + D_i'\delta + \varepsilon_i, \quad \text{and} \tag{3.3}$$

$$r_i = c + X_i'\alpha + Y_i'\beta + Z_i'\gamma + D_i'\delta + \varepsilon_i. \tag{3.4}$$

The variables r_i, X_i, Y_i, Z_i, and D_i are, respectively, the period averages of $r_{i,t}$, $X_{i,t}$, $Y_{i,t}$, $Z_{i,t}$, and $D_{i,t}$. The use of period averages allows us to avoid complexity that arises from unknown and, possibly varying, dynamics and focus on the (time-) average behavioral relationship. The coefficient vectors α, β, γ, and δ are conformable to their associated explanatory variables. The intercept and disturbance term are given by c and ε_i, respectively.

Specification (3.1) is an international reserve demand equation of the 1970's vintage. The economy characteristic dummy variables are included in specification (3.2). Specification (3.3) includes the financial variables (Y_i) that are often referred to in the recent discussion on the demand for international reserves. The effects of institutional factors (Z_i) are examined in specification (3.4). These four specifications allow us to gauge the relative contributions of these different groups of explanatory variables.

3.3.2. *Estimation Results*

Note that we have a quite a large group of explanatory variables under consideration. Table 3.A.1 in the Appendix lists these variables, their definitions, and their sources. Some summary statistics are given in Table 3.A.2. As expected, not all of these variables show up significant in the regression analyses. We adopted a general to specific approach to investigate the determinants of international reserves. Starting with all the candidate variables, we dropped those insignificant ones and kept only the significant estimates.

In anticipation of their different types of demand behaviors, we estimated the international reserve demand equations separately for developed and developing economies (Frenkel, 1974b). Table 3.1 presents the estimation

Table 3.1. Demand for international reserves, 1999–2005.

	Developed economies				Developing economies			
	(1)	(2)	(3)	(4)	(1)	(2)	(3)	(4)
Population (in log)	−0.02	−0.017	−0.017	−0.026				
	[0.007]***	[0.006]**	[0.007]**	[0.004]***				
International reserve volatility	0.009	0.007	0.007	0.01				
	[0.004]*	[0.004]*	[0.004]$^{11\%}$	[0.003]***				
Opportunity cost					−0.394	−0.364	−0.111	−0.117
					[0.142]***	[0.127]***	[0.044]**	[0.047]**
Crawling peg regime		0.131	0.136	0.122				
		[0.011]***	[0.010]***	[0.008]***				
Fixed/pegged regime						−0.021	−0.037	−0.05
						[0.047]	[0.024]	[0.027]*
Latin America						-0.091	−0.073	−0.077
						[0.029]***	[0.022]***	[0.023]***
Net portfolio liabilities			−0.018	−0.029			−0.701	−0.717
			[0.015]	[0.012]**			[0.045]***	[0.049]***

(Continued)

Table 3.1. (*Continued*)

	Developed economies				Developing economies			
	(1)	(2)	(3)	(4)	(1)	(2)	(3)	(4)
*M*2/GDP							0.203 [0.029]***	0.201 [0.029]***
De jure capital acct. openness (Chinn–Ito index)				0.055 [0.016]***				
Leftist government								−0.065 [0.027]**
Number of observations	22	22	22	22	76	76	76	76
Adj. R-squares	0.28	0.65	0.65	0.83	0.1	0.13	0.61	0.63

Notes: Robust standard errors are given in brackets. *, **, and *** indicate significance at the 10, 5, and 1 percent levels, respectively. The column headings (1), (2), (3), and (4) correspond to the model specifications (1), (2), (3), and (4) in the text. Constant terms are omitted for brevity.

results from 22 developed and from 76 developing economies. The estimation results pertaining to the regression equations (3.1)–(3.4) are given under the columns labeled (1)–(4). Henceforth, we use the terms equations (3.1)–(3.4), specifications (3.1)–(3.4), and models (1)–(4) interchangeably. It is quite evident that the developed and developing economies have different patterns of demand for international reserves.

For developed economies, the traditional macroeconomic variables population and international reserve volatility are found to be significant. The population variable captures the size effect. The negative estimates are suggestive of the economies of scale effect — the larger the population size is, the smaller the (per capita) demand for international reserves will be. The positive effect of international reserve volatility is consistent with the precautionary motive. A larger amount of international reserves is held when an economy is facing a higher level of uncertainty represented by the variability of its international reserves (Frenkel and Jovanovic, 1981).[8]

Interestingly, economies with crawling peg exchange rate regimes tend to hold more international reserves.[9] The result corroborates the "unstable middle" hypothesis, which suggests crawling peg regimes are more prone to currency crises than flexible or fixed exchange rate regimes (Willett, 2003). With a weak credibility of maintaining a crawling peg, an economy has to hold a large amount of international reserves to pre-empt speculative attacks. The finding is supportive of the notion of precautionary holdings.

Among the financial variables, the net value of portfolio liabilities is a significantly negative determinant. The negative sign suggests that these economies regard international reserves and portfolio flows as substitutes. The substitutability effect appears to be a debtor economy's phenomenon because the dummy variable for the creditor economies, those which provide portfolio financing, is not found to be statistically significant.

---

[8]A dummy variable was constructed for Japan's international reserve volatility, which is an extreme outlier.

[9]The Reinhart–Rogoff (2002) index is used to construct the exchange rate regime dummy variable. Originally, their index ranges from 1 "no separate legal tender" to 14 "freely falling" (with increasing flexibility of exchange rate movement) and is a *de facto* index in contrast to IMF's *de jure* exchange rate regime classification. In this chapter, we excluded the "freely falling" category from the Reinhart–Rogoff classification and aggregated the remaining 13 into three categories, namely "floating," "crawling peg," and "fixed/pegged."

The relevance of financial openness is confirmed by the significance of the Chinn–Ito index reported in column (4).[10] Its positive coefficient estimate underlines the precautionary motive to guard against adverse capital flows under an open capital account regime. The finding appears to be consistent with the recent trend of financial globalization.

The results of the developing economies presented in the last four columns contrast quite starkly with those of the developed economies. For developing economies, the opportunity cost of holding international reserves is the only significant macroeconomic variable that affects the demand for international reserves. Specifically, a high opportunity cost deters hoarding of international reserves. The result is in accordance with the observation that, in recent years, the developing economies increase their holdings of international reserves when their opportunity costs of holding reserves decrease as a result of their domestic bond yields declining at a pace faster than the U.S. interest rate.

Apparently, developing economies with a fixed/pegged exchange rate arrangement tend to hold less international reserves. The result does not seem intuitive. On the other hand, if economies with a crawling peg hold more international reserves — the so-called "unstable middle" hypothesis — than those with a fixed one may appear to hold less. Among the regional dummy variables, the one for the Latin American economies is statistically significant, while the one for the East Asian economies is insignificant and therefore not reported in the Table. Thus, at least from a statistical perspective, among the developing economies in the sample, the Latin American economies tend to hold lower levels of international reserves.

Among the financial variables, the ratio of net portfolio liabilities and the $M2$ variable are significant. The estimated effect of net portfolio liabilities is qualitatively similar to the one for developed economies but is larger in magnitude. The result suggests that external equity financing for developing economies has a larger effect than for developed ones. The significant money

[10]A larger value of this measure means a higher level of capital account openness. The index is a reciprocal of regulatory restrictions on cross-border financial transactions and is based upon the IMF's categorical enumeration reported in *Annual Report on Exchange Arrangements and Exchange Restrictions* (*AREAER*). See Chinn and Ito (2006) for a detailed discussion. The index is viewed as a *de jure* index on capital account openness.

effect ($M2$/GDP) is in accordance with the monetary interpretation of the balance of payments and also with the view that money supply is a proxy for internal drains of international reserves (de Beaufort Wijnholds and Kapteyn, 2001). Given the increasing degree of global financial integration, the result lends support to the interlinks between domestic money supply and international reserve holdings.

The only significant institutional variable for the data of developing economies is the dummy variable that is a proxy for the presence of a leftist government. It is found that an economy with a leftist government, on average, holds fewer international reserves. The result collaborates the observation that developing economies with a leftist government tend to spend more and incur current account deficits and, thus, hold a lower level of international reserves (Roubini and Sachs, 1989).

A few observations are noteworthy. First, our results attest the differences between the developed and developing economies. Indeed, Cheung and Ito (2007) show that these two groups of economies have different demand functions of international reserves in the current sample period and other historical periods. Further, these demand functions exhibit a considerable degree of variability across history periods.

Second, the different vintages of the international reserve demand equation have different explanatory powers. The earliest vintage represented by specification (1) that focuses on macroeconomic variables offers the least explanatory power. For developed economies, the group of macroeconomic variables explains 28 percent of variability of their international reserves. For the developing economies, the group only explains 10 percent. Interestingly, despite the widespread use of the reserves-to-imports ratio, the trade openness variable is insignificant for both developed and developing economies.

Third, the more recent vintages represented by specifications (2), (3), and (4) offer a substantial improvement in explaining international reserves. For developed economies, including either the exchange rate regime or the capital account openness variable offers a noticeable increase in the adjusted R-squares estimate of the regression. For developing economies, the inclusion of financial variables increases the adjusted R-squares estimate from 13 percent to 61 percent. The large incremental improvement attests the relevance of these financial variables in explaining international reserves of these developing economies.

As was discussed in Section 3.2, the modeling of international reserve holding behavior evolves with the changing role and functionality of international reserves. When trade is the main channel through which the economies interact with each other, macroeconomic variables including trade openness are perceived to be the main factors determining the demand for international reserves. With globalization and advances in the world financial market, capital account transactions play an increasing role in determining the holding of international reserves. Our empirical results show that the effects of financial and institutional factors outweigh those of the macroeconomic variables in the new millennium.

Since the developed and developing economies behave differently, is it possible that the Asian and Latin American economies have different international reserve demand equations? To address the question, we consider the sample of Asian economies and Latin American economies separately. The results of fitting model (4) to each of the two groups are given in Table 3.2.

Table 3.2. The Asian and Latin American economies' international reserve demand equations, 1999–2005.

	Asia	Latin America
Import propensity	0.251	
	[0.033]***	
Industrial country dummy	−0.126	
	[0.029]***	
Dummy for crawling peg		0.035
Exch. rate regime		[0.021]*
$M2$ as a ratio to GDP	0.107	0.072
	[0.018]***	[0.020]***
Constant	0.025	0.077
	[0.039]	[0.018]***
Number of observations	25	28
Adjusted R-squares	0.75	0.54

Notes: Robust standard errors are given in brackets. *, **, and *** indicate statistical significance at the 10, 5, and 1 percent levels, respectively. Because of their extreme values, dummy variables for Singapore and Guyana were included in the regression.

Again, only significant estimates are reported. A caveat is in order — the sample sizes are quite small and, thus, the results should be interpreted with caution.[11]

The fitted models for these two groups of economies are quite different. The only common explanatory variable is the $M2$ variables. In both cases, the estimate coefficients of the $M2$/GDP ratio is significantly positive. Interestingly, the significant variables in Table 3.2 are quite different from those in Table 3.1. For the Asian economies, the import propensity variable is significantly positive — a result in accordance with the theory. The developed Asian economies tend to hold a lower level of international reserves. For the Latin American economies, the crawling peg dummy variable is the other significant explanatory variable in the regression.

3.4. Comparison Between Asia and Latin America

The results in the previous section clearly show that different vintages of the model of international reserves perform differently. Even for a given set of explanatory variables, the fitted international reserve demand equations are quite different across different types of economies. The fitted models for developed economies are different from the corresponding ones for developing economies. The Asian and Latin American economies also have different fitted equations of the demand for international reserves. Given these different specifications, which one is the proper benchmark for assessing the question of whether an economy holds an excessive amount of international reserves? Conceivably, different benchmarks can lead to different inferences about an economy's holding. In the following subsections, we discuss the implications of using a few benchmarks for assessing the Asian and Latin American economies' holdings of international reserves.

3.4.1. *Developed or Developing Economies*

In our sample, most of the Asian and Latin American economies are members of the group of developing economies. It is natural to use the

[11] The economies included in the Asian and Latin American samples are given in Table 3.A.3 of Appendix A.

specification for the developing economies to compare the holdings of international reserves. Suppose the estimated demand for international reserves of developing economies is given by

$$r_{i,dp} = \hat{c}_{dp} + W'_{i,dp}\hat{\alpha}_{dp} + \hat{\varepsilon}_{i,dp} \equiv \hat{r}_{i,dp} + \hat{\varepsilon}_{i,dp}, \quad i = 1, 2, 3, \text{ and } 4, \qquad (3.5)$$

where the subscribe i indicates that the equation is based on model 1, 2, 3, or 4 given in Section 3.3.1, the subscribe dp indicates that it is a demand equation of the developing economies, $W_{i,dp}$ contains the significant variables, $\hat{\alpha}_{dp}$ contains the corresponding estimates, and $\hat{r}_{i,dp}$ is the predicted level of international reserves.

Alternatively, the comparison can be based on the specification for the developed economies. Suppose the estimated demand for international reserves of developed economies is given by

$$r_{i,dd} = \hat{c}_{dd} + W'_{i,dd}\hat{\alpha}_{dd} + \hat{\varepsilon}_{i,dd}, \qquad (3.6)$$

where the subscribe dd indicates that it is a demand equation of the developed economies and the vectors $W_{i,dd}$ and $\hat{\alpha}_{dd}$ contain the significant variables and their coefficient estimates. To generate a predicted value for a developing economy, we apply this economy's data to (3.6). We label this predicted value $\tilde{r}_{i,dp}$. The variable $\tilde{r}_{i,dp}$ allows us to assess the level of international reserves that a developing economy is expected to hold if it behaves like a developed economy.

For each developing economy in the Asian and Latin American sample, we have three different international reserve variables: (a) $r_{i,dp}$, the actual value, (b) $\hat{r}_{i,dp}$, the predicted value obtained from (3.5), and (c) $\tilde{r}_{i,dp}$, the predicted value obtained from (3.6). By comparing these three variables we can assess an economy's holding of international reserves relative to other economies, and the implication of an economy is being viewed as a developing or a developed economy. For convenience, we label $\hat{r}_{i,dp}$ the simple prediction and $\tilde{r}_{i,dp}$ the cross prediction.

We generate the two predicted values based on models (1)–(4) for the Latin American economies and plot them in panels A to D of Figure 3.2. In each panel, we also include the actual holdings of international reserves. These figures include economies that have data to generate both simple and cross-predicted values. The economies are arranged in descending order

A. Model (1)

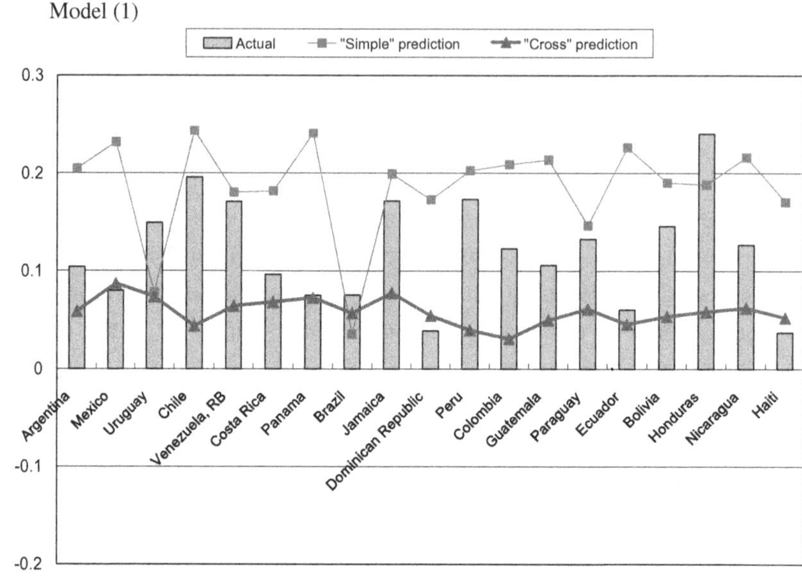

B. Model (2)

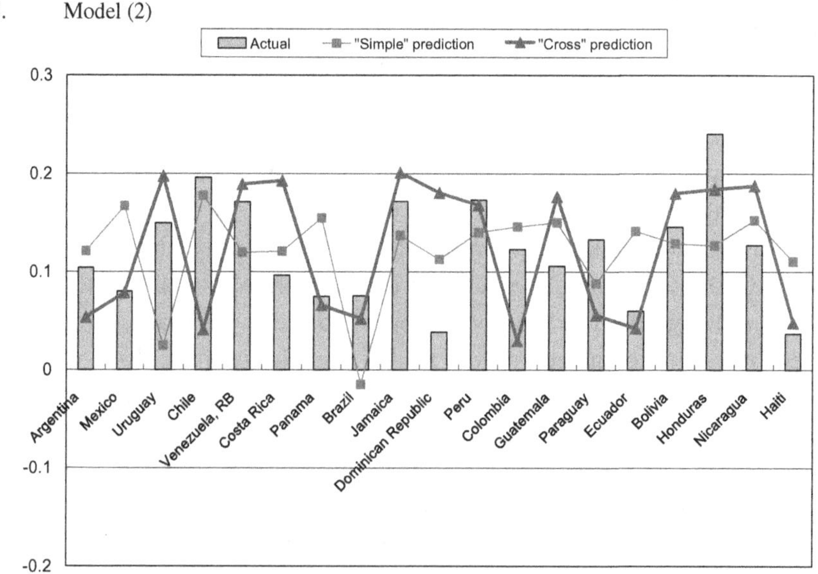

Fig. 3.2. The Latin American economies' international reserves — actual holdings, simple predicted values, and cross-predicted values, averages of 1999–2005.

C. Model (3)

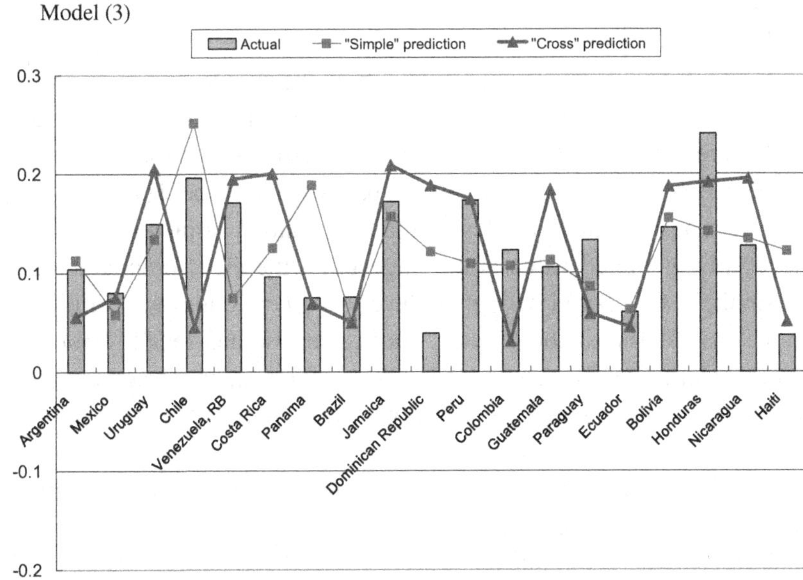

D. Model (4)

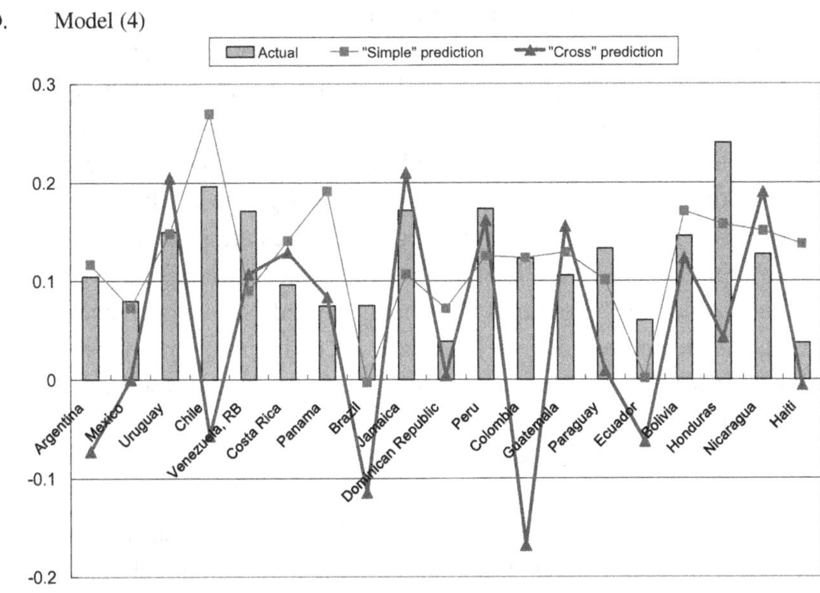

Fig. 3.2. (*Continued*)

(from the left to the right on the x-axis) according to their real per capita GDP in U.S. dollars.

For each Latin American economy, both the simple and cross-predicted values of international reserves vary quite substantially across the four model specifications. Panel A of Figure 3.2 shows that the three international reserve variables show a distinct pattern under model (1) that includes only macroeconomic variables as the explanatory variables. On average, the simple predicted value is the largest and the cross-predicted value is the smallest. Compared with other developing economies with similar economic characteristics, these Latin American economies tend to hold a lower level of international reserves. However, the Latin American economies tend to hold a higher level of international reserves compared with the developed economies.

Did the Latin American economies hold too much or too few international reserves? The answer depends on whether they are compared with other developing economies or with developed economies. Panels 2 and 3 suggest that the simple and cross-predicted values from models (2) and (3) are quite comparable with the actual values. Visually, it is quite difficult to discern the differences between these three international reserve variables.

The predicted values from model (4) that includes all four types of explanatory variables display an unusual pattern (Panel D, Figure 3.2). While both simple and cross-predicted values are quite variable, the intricate result is that a few economies actually have negative predicted levels of international reserves. Indeed, the negative values are mostly from the set of cross-predicted values. That is, given their economic characteristics, if the Latin American economies were being treated as developed economies, they are expected to hold a very low level of international reserves, and even a negative one — that is, to "lend" out international reserves. While a negative level of international reserves is a highly impossible situation, the result suggests that there is a cost for being a developing Latin American economy in terms of holding international reserves.

To offer a precise comparison of the three international reserve variables ($r_{i,dp}$, $\hat{r}_{i,dp}$, and $\tilde{r}_{i,dp}$), Table 3.3 presents their numerical values from all four model specifications. Recall that the international reserve variable is defined as a ratio of international reserves to GDP. The numbers confirm that, on average, the Latin American economies are deemed to hold a deficient amount of international reserves compared with other developing economies but an excessive amount compared with the developed economies according to model (1). The difference between the predicted and actual values ranges from a few percentage points to 20 percentage points.

Table 3.3. The Latin American economies' international reserves — actual holdings, simple predicted values, and cross-predicted values, averages of 1999–2005.

		Model (1)				Model (2)			
	r_i (%)	$\hat{r}_i$ (%)	$r_i - \hat{r}_i$ (%)	$\tilde{r}_i$ (%)	$r_i - \tilde{r}_i$ (%)	$\hat{r}_i$ (%)	$r_i - \hat{r}_i$ (%)	$\tilde{r}_i$ (%)	$r_i - \tilde{r}_i$ (%)
Argentina	10.4	20.5	−10.1	5.9	4.6	12.1	−1.7	5.4	5.0
Bolivia	14.6	19.0	−4.5	5.3	9.2	12.9	1.7	18.0	−3.4
Brazil	7.5	3.5	4.0	5.7	1.9	−1.5	9.0	5.2	2.3
Chile	19.6	24.3	−4.7	4.4	15.2	17.8	1.8	4.1	15.5
Colombia	12.3	20.9	−8.6	3.1	9.2	14.6	−2.3	2.9	9.3
Costa Rica	9.6	18.2	−8.6	6.8	2.8	12.1	−2.4	19.3	−9.6
Dominican Republic	3.9	17.3	−13.4	5.4	−1.6	11.3	−7.4	18.1	−14.2
Ecuador	6.0	22.6	−16.6	4.6	1.5	14.1	−8.1	4.3	1.8
Guatemala	10.6	21.4	−10.8	5.0	5.6	15.0	−4.4	17.7	−7.1
Haiti	3.7	17.1	−13.4	5.2	−1.5	11.0	−7.3	4.8	−1.1
Honduras	24.0	18.8	5.2	5.8	18.2	12.7	11.4	18.4	5.6
Jamaica	17.2	19.9	−2.7	7.8	9.4	13.7	3.5	20.1	−2.9
Mexico	8.0	23.2	−15.2	8.7	−0.7	16.7	−8.7	7.9	0.1
Nicaragua	12.7	21.6	−8.9	6.2	6.5	15.2	−2.5	18.8	−6.1
Panama	7.5	24.1	−16.6	7.3	0.2	15.4	−8.0	6.6	0.9
Paraguay	13.3	14.6	−1.4	6.1	7.2	8.8	4.5	5.6	7.7
Peru	17.3	20.3	−2.9	3.9	13.4	14.0	3.3	16.8	0.5
Uruguay	15.0	7.8	7.2	7.4	7.6	2.5	12.5	19.7	−4.8
Venezuela, RB	17.1	18.0	−1.0	6.4	10.7	12.0	5.1	18.9	−1.8
Average	9.8	16.3	−6.5	6.5	3.3	10.0	−0.2	7.9	1.9

(Continued)

Table 3.3. (*Continued*)

		Model (3)				Model (4)			
	r_i (%)	$\hat{r}_i$ (%)	$r_i - \hat{r}_i$ (%)	$\tilde{r}_i$ (%)	$r_i - \tilde{r}_i$ (%)	$\hat{r}_i$ (%)	$r_i - \hat{r}_i$ (%)	$\tilde{r}_i$ (%)	$r_i - \tilde{r}_i$ (%)
Argentina	10.4	11.3	−0.8	5.5	4.9	11.7	−1.3	−7.3	17.7
Bolivia	14.6	15.5	−1.0	18.7	−4.2	17.1	−2.5	12.3	2.2
Brazil	7.5	5.0	2.5	5.0	2.6	−0.3	7.8	−11.5	19.0
Chile	19.6	25.1	−5.5	4.5	15.1	26.9	−7.3	−5.7	25.3
Colombia	12.3	10.7	1.6	3.1	9.2	12.3	−0.1	−16.8	29.1
Costa Rica	9.6	12.5	−2.9	20.0	−10.4	14.1	−4.4	12.9	−3.3
Dominican Republic	3.9	12.1	−8.3	18.8	−15.0	7.2	−3.3	0.5	3.4
Ecuador	6.0	6.2	−0.2	4.5	1.5	0.1	5.9	−6.3	12.3
Guatemala	10.6	11.3	−0.7	18.4	−7.8	12.9	−2.3	15.5	−5.0
Haiti	3.7	12.2	−8.5	5.1	−1.4	13.7	−10.0	−0.5	4.2
Honduras	24.0	14.2	9.8	19.2	4.9	15.8	8.3	4.3	19.8
Jamaica	17.2	15.6	1.5	20.9	−3.7	10.7	6.5	21.0	−3.8
Mexico	8.0	5.8	2.2	7.5	0.5	7.3	0.7	0.0	8.0
Nicaragua	12.7	13.5	−0.8	19.5	−6.8	15.1	−2.4	19.0	−6.3
Panama	7.5	18.8	−11.4	6.9	0.6	19.1	−11.6	8.4	−0.9
Paraguay	13.3	8.6	4.7	5.9	7.4	10.1	3.2	0.9	12.4
Peru	17.3	10.9	6.4	17.5	−0.1	12.5	4.8	16.2	1.2
Uruguay	15.0	13.4	1.5	20.5	−5.5	14.8	0.2	20.5	−5.5
Venezuela, RB	17.1	7.4	9.7	19.5	−2.4	9.0	8.1	10.7	6.4
Average	9.8	8.0	1.9	7.8	2.0	7.2	2.6	−3.4	13.2

Notes: The table presents, for each developing Latin American economy, the actual average level of international reserves over the period 1999–2005 under the column labeled r_i. The simple predicted values and the cross-predicted values are given under the columns labeled $\hat{r}_i$ and $\tilde{r}_i$, respectively. See the text for the definitions of these variables. A positive entry in the column either labeled "$r_i - \hat{r}_i$" or "$r_i - \tilde{r}_i$" implies overhoarding while a negative implies underhoarding. The real U.S. dollar GDP weighted averages are reported in the row "average."

As indicated by the figures, the predicted and actual values are quite similar for models (2) and (3). Indeed, under these two model specifications, the average values of these three international reserve variables are quite close to each other even though the cross-predicted value is always the smallest.

The difference between the actual and cross-predicted values exhibits a large variation under model (4). There are seven economies that have a difference larger than 10 percent and two of these seven economies have a difference larger than 20 percent. According to both the simple and cross-predicted values, these Latin American economies tend to hold too much international reserves. Indeed, the average cross-predicted value suggests that these economies as a group should hold a negative level of international reserves.

Figure 3.3 contains the figures of the three international reserve variables for Asian economies. The format is the same as the ones in Figure 3.2 — only economies with data to generate both simple and cross-predicted values are reported and they are arranged in descending order (from the left to the right on the *x*-axis) according to their real per capita GDP in U.S. dollars. Similarly, Table 3.4 contains the numerical values of these three variables.

It is quite apparent that the pattern of actual, simple predicted and cross-predicted values of international reserves in each panel of Figure 3.3 is quite different from the pattern in the corresponding panel of Figure 3.2. A closer examination reveals some peculiar behavior displayed by Hong Kong, Singapore, and China. Both Hong Kong and Singapore, the two renowned small open economies in Asia, hold a very high level of international reserves — Hong Kong's holding of international reserves is more than 60 percent of its GDP and Singapore's is over 90 percent! Under models (1) and (2), both the simple and cross-predicted values suggest that these two economies hold an excessive amount of international reserves (Panels A and B, Figure 3.3). Interestingly, in Panels C and D, only the cross-predicted value indicates that Hong Kong and Singapore hold too much international reserves.

The case of China is quite unexpected. In all four cases under consideration, China is deemed to hold too few international reserves by both the simple and cross-predicted values. The degree of underhoarding implied by the simple predicted value is quite moderate but the one implied by the cross-predicted value is very substantial. The results suggest that China's actual holding of international reserves is slightly lower than developing economies that have similar economic conditions. However, when the

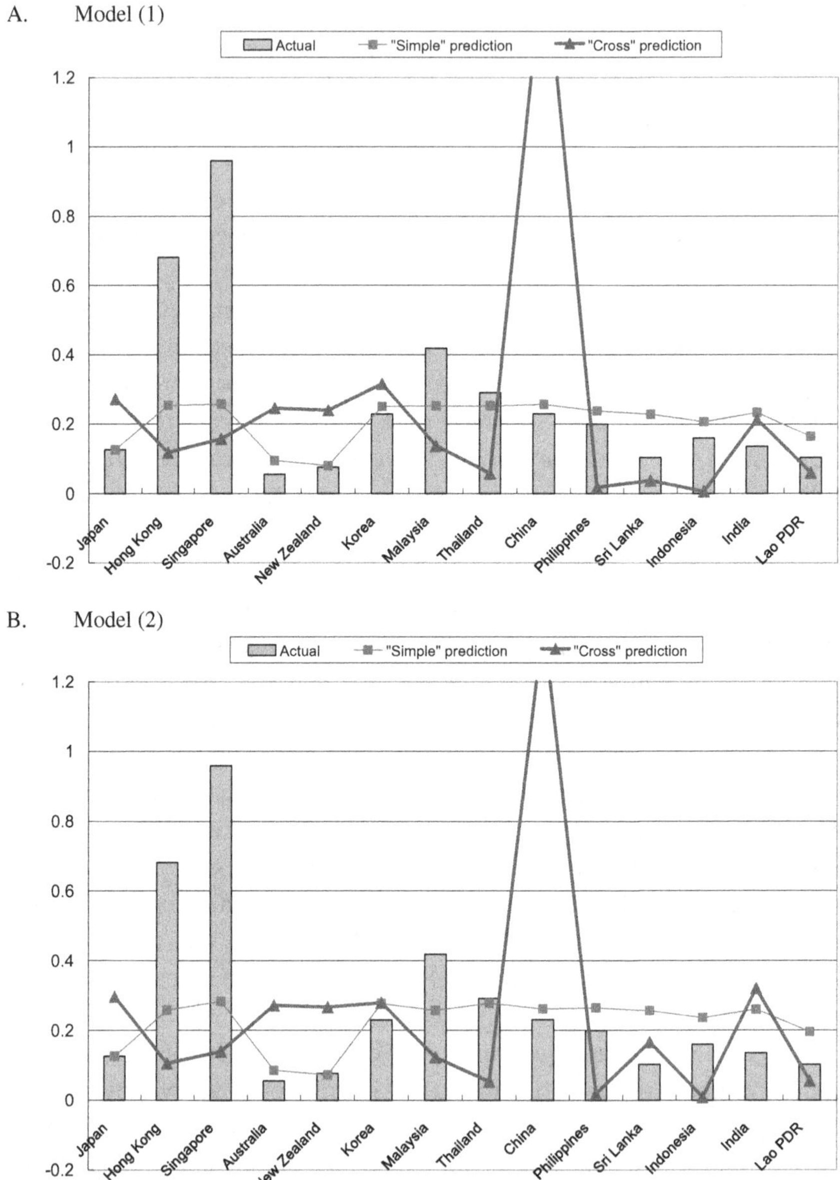

Fig. 3.3. The Asian economies' international reserves — actual holdings, simple predicted values, and cross-predicted values, averages of 1999–2005.

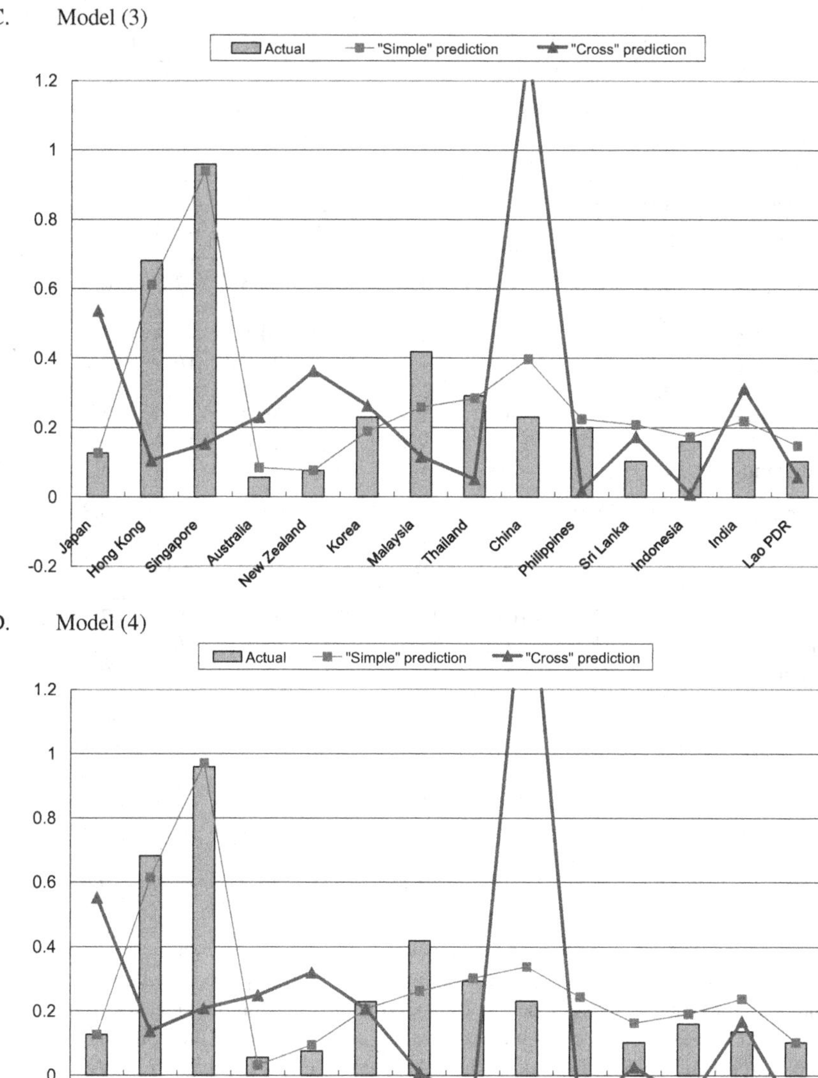

Fig. 3.3. *(Continued)*

Table 3.4. The Asian economies' international reserves — actual holdings, simple predicted values, and cross-predicted values, averages of 1999–2005.

	r_i (%)	Model (1) $\hat{r}_i$ (%)	Model (1) $r_i - \hat{r}_i$ (%)	Model (1) $\tilde{r}_i$ (%)	Model (1) $r_i - \tilde{r}_i$ (%)	Model (2) $\hat{r}_i$ (%)	Model (2) $r_i - \hat{r}_i$ (%)	Model (2) $\tilde{r}_i$ (%)	Model (2) $r_i - \tilde{r}_i$ (%)
China	23.0	25.8	−2.8	157.2	−134.2	26.2	−3.1	137.2	−114.1
Hong Kong	68.1	25.4	42.7	11.8	56.3	25.8	42.3	10.5	57.6
India	13.6	23.4	−9.8	21.4	−7.8	26.0	−12.4	32.0	−18.4
Indonesia	16.0	20.8	−4.8	0.6	15.4	23.6	−7.6	0.8	15.2
Korea	22.9	25.2	−2.2	31.7	−8.7	27.7	−4.7	27.9	−4.9
Lao PDR	10.3	16.4	−6.1	6.0	4.3	19.6	−9.3	5.5	4.8
Malaysia	41.9	25.3	16.6	13.7	28.1	25.7	16.2	12.2	29.6
Philippines	20.0	23.8	−3.9	1.8	18.2	26.4	−6.5	1.8	18.1
Singapore	95.9	25.8	70.0	15.7	80.1	28.3	67.6	14.0	81.9
Sri Lanka	10.3	22.9	−12.7	3.8	6.5	25.6	−15.3	16.6	−6.4
Thailand	29.2	25.3	3.9	5.8	23.4	27.8	1.4	5.3	23.8
Average	26.3	24.9	1.4	75.5	−49.2	26.4	0.0	68.3	−42.0

	r_i (%)	Model (3) $\hat{r}_i$ (%)	Model (3) $r_i - \hat{r}_i$ (%)	Model (3) $\tilde{r}_i$ (%)	Model (3) $r_i - \tilde{r}_i$ (%)	Model (4) $\hat{r}_i$ (%)	Model (4) $r_i - \hat{r}_i$ (%)	Model (4) $\tilde{r}_i$ (%)	Model (4) $r_i - \tilde{r}_i$ (%)
China	23.0	39.7	−16.7	129.3	−106.3	33.7	−10.7	167.8	−144.7
Hong Kong	68.1	61.1	7.0	10.6	57.6	61.5	6.7	13.8	54.4
India	13.6	21.8	−8.3	31.3	−17.7	23.8	−10.2	16.8	−3.2
Indonesia	16.0	17.2	−1.2	0.8	15.2	19.1	−3.1	−8.0	24.0
Korea	22.9	18.8	4.1	26.4	−3.4	20.6	2.3	20.7	2.3
Lao PDR	10.3	14.7	−4.5	5.8	4.5	10.3	0.0	−12.5	22.8
Malaysia	41.9	25.8	16.0	11.7	30.2	26.1	15.7	0.9	41.0
Philippines	20.0	22.4	−2.5	1.9	18.0	24.4	−4.4	−12.3	32.3
Singapore	95.9	93.9	1.9	15.2	80.6	97.1	−1.2	20.8	75.0
Sri Lanka	10.3	20.8	−10.5	17.4	−7.1	16.3	−6.0	2.7	7.5
Thailand	29.2	28.4	0.7	5.1	24.0	30.2	−1.0	−9.0	38.1
Average	26.3	33.0	−6.7	64.7	−38.4	26.3	31.6	−5.2	75.4

Notes: The table presents, for each developing Asian economy, the actual average level of international reserves over the period 1999–2005 under the column labeled r_i. The simple predicted values and the cross-predicted values are given under the columns labeled $\hat{r}_i$ and $\tilde{r}_i$, respectively. See the text for the definitions of these variables. A positive entry in the column either labeled "$r_i - \hat{r}_i$" or "$r_i - \tilde{r}_i$" implies overhoarding while a negative implies underhoarding. The real U.S. dollar GDP weighted averages are reported in the row "average."

developed economies are used as a benchmark, China's holding is far less than what it is supposed to be.[12]

Besides the three noted economies, the behavior of the other Asian economies is comparable to that of the Latin American economies. Specifically, the simple predicted values track the actual holdings quite well even though the actual holdings are usually less than the corresponding predicted values. The cross-predicted values, on the other hand, tend to indicate these economies are holding too much international reserves. Similar to the case of Latin American economies, some Asian economies have a cross-predicted value that is negative.

The numerical values of the actual holdings and the two predicted international reserve values in Table 3.4 underscore the unique behavior of Hong Kong, Singapore, and China. Specifically, Hong Kong and Singapore are quite often judged to hold excessive international reserves. China's actual holdings are quite small compared with the predicted values. Note that these three economies — especially China, have a substantial impact on the average value of the Asian economies' degree of over- and underhoarding.

In sum, with the exception of Hong Kong, Singapore, and China, the international reserve holdings of developing Latin American and Asian economies are quite comparable to those of other developing economies. However, compared to developed economies with similar economic conditions, the models suggest that these economies tend to hold too much international reserves.

3.4.2. *An Asian Phenomenon?*

Compared with some previous crises, the buildup of international reserves observed after the 1997–1998 Asian financial crisis is quite phenomenal. Since the Latin American economies are involved in a few previous crises including the 1982 Mexican debt crisis and the 1994 Tequila crisis, it would be interesting to directly compare the behavior of the Asian and Latin American economies. To this end, we modify the framework in the previous

[12]A quick check on the data reveals that the underhoarding inference is mainly driven by China's volatile international reserve holdings.

subsection and assess the consequences of treating an Asian economy as a Latin American economy and vice versa.

For each developing Asian economy, we generate the simple and cross-predicted values of the holding of international reserves from the two specifications reported in Table 3.2. In this case, the simple predicted value is from the Asian economies' estimated demand for international reserves. The cross-predicted value is from the equation fitted to Latin American data. Similarly, for each Latin American economy, we construct its simple and cross-predicted values from the fitted equations for the Latin American and Asian samples, respectively.

For each Latin American or Asian economy, Figure 3.4 presents its actual holding of international reserves, the simple predicted value, and the cross-predicted value subject to data availability. Table 3.5 presents the numerical values of these three variables. A few observations are in order.

First, the differences between the actual international reserve holdings and their simple predicted values are quite small — indicating that the demand for international reserves equations fitted to the Asian and Latin American economies perform quite well.

Second, the cross-predicted values indicate that the Latin American economies, compared with the Asian economies, tend to hold too few international reserves. The level of deficiency can be as high as 20 percent of an economy's GDP (Antigua, Barbuda, and Panama). If these Latin American economies behave like an average Asian economy, then 9 of the 28 economies have a level of international reserves that is lower than the level they are expected to hold by 10 percent or more.

Third, the cross-predicted values suggest that the Asian economies are holding "too much" international reserves. Five Asian economies — namely Singapore, Hong Kong, Malaysia, Thailand, and Korea — "overhoard" international reserves by an amount that is larger than 10 percent of their respective GDPs. Among these five economies, Singapore and Hong Kong are not directly impacted by the Asian financial crisis while the other three are. The extreme case is Singapore — the economy's overhoarding is close to 80 percent of its GDP. The next one is Hong Kong; its level of excessive holding equals 43 percent of its GDP. The amount of excessive international reserves held by China, compared with the hype in the media, is relatively moderate at the 4.5 percent level.

A. Latin America

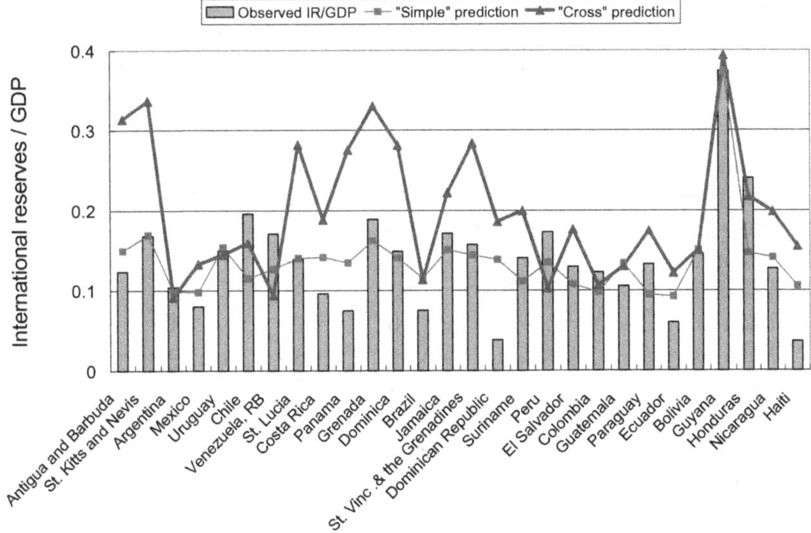

B. Asia

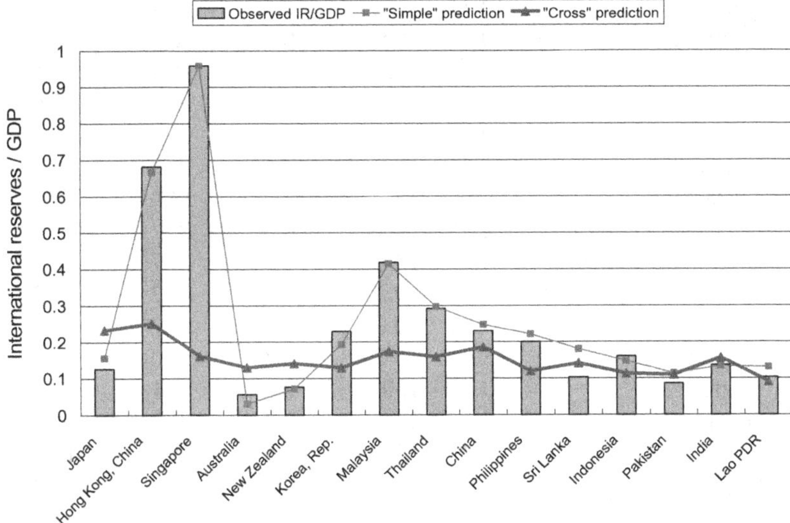

Fig. 3.4. The actual holdings of international reserves and their predicted values generated from results in Table 3.2.

Table 3.5. The actual holdings of international reserves and their predicted values generated from results in Table 2.

	$r_i(\%)$	$\hat{r}_i(\%)$	$r_i - \hat{r}_i(\%)$	$\tilde{r}_i(\%)$	$r_i - \tilde{r}_i(\%)$
Asia					
China	23.0	24.8	−1.7	18.6	4.5
Hong Kong	68.1	66.7	1.5	25.1	43.0
India	13.6	13.3	0.3	15.6	−2.0
Indonesia	16.0	14.7	1.3	11.3	4.7
Korea, Rep.	22.9	19.3	3.6	12.9	10.1
Lao PDR	10.3	13.0	−2.7	9.0	1.3
Malaysia	41.9	41.5	0.4	17.4	24.5
Pakistan	8.6	11.4	−2.8	10.9	−2.4
Philippines	20.0	22.0	−2.1	11.9	8.0
Singapore	95.9	95.9	0.0	16.1	79.7
Sri Lanka	10.3	18.0	−7.7	14.1	−3.9
Thailand	29.2	29.7	−0.6	15.9	13.3
Latin America					
Antigua and Barbuda	12.3	15.0	−2.6	31.4	−19.0
Argentina	10.4	9.9	0.5	9.2	1.2
Bolivia	14.6	15.1	−0.5	15.1	−0.6
Brazil	7.5	11.5	−4.0	11.4	−3.9
Chile	19.6	11.5	8.1	15.9	3.7
Colombia	12.3	9.8	2.5	10.7	1.6
Costa Rica	9.6	14.2	−4.5	18.9	−9.3
Dominica	14.9	14.1	0.8	28.2	−13.3
Dominican Republic	3.9	13.9	−10.0	18.7	−14.8
Ecuador	6.0	9.3	−3.2	12.2	−6.2
El Salvador	13.0	10.8	2.1	17.7	−4.7
Grenada	18.9	16.2	2.7	33.0	−14.1
Guatemala	10.6	13.4	−2.8	13.1	−2.5
Guyana	37.4	37.4	0.0	39.4	−2.0
Haiti	3.7	10.6	−6.9	15.5	−11.8
Honduras	24.0	14.7	9.4	21.8	2.3
Jamaica	17.2	15.1	2.1	22.2	−5.1
Mexico	8.0	9.8	−1.8	13.3	−5.3
Nicaragua	12.7	14.1	−1.4	19.9	−7.2
Panama	7.5	13.5	−6.0	27.6	−20.1

(*Continued*)

Table 3.5. (*Continued*)

	$r_i(\%)$	$\hat{r}_i(\%)$	$r_i - \hat{r}_i(\%)$	$\tilde{r}_i(\%)$	$r_i - \tilde{r}_i(\%)$
Paraguay	13.3	9.5	3.8	17.5	−4.2
Peru	17.3	13.5	3.8	10.3	7.0
St Kitts and Nevis	16.9	17.0	−0.1	33.7	−16.9
St Lucia	13.9	14.0	−0.1	28.2	−14.3
St Vincent and Grenadines	15.7	14.4	1.3	28.4	−12.7
Suriname	14.0	11.2	2.9	20.0	−5.9
Uruguay	15.0	15.4	−0.5	14.5	0.5
Venezuela, RB	17.1	12.7	4.4	9.4	7.7

Notes: The table presents, for each developing economy, the actual average level of international reserves over the period 1999–2005 under the column labeled r_i. The simple predicted values and the cross-predicted values computed from results in Table 3.2 are given under the columns labeled $\hat{r}_i$ and $\tilde{r}_i$, respectively. See the text for the definitions of these variables. A positive entry in the column either labeled "$r_i - \hat{r}_i$" or "$r_i - \tilde{r}_i$" implies overhoarding while a negative implies underhoarding.

All in all, the results in Figure 3.4 and Table 3.5 are supportive of the view that, compared to Latin American economies with similar economic characteristics, Asian economies tend to hold a higher level of international reserves. It is worth noting that the overhoarding phenomenon is quite prominent for a few economies including Singapore and Hong Kong.

3.5. Concluding Remarks

Against the backdrop of the unprecedented growth of global international reserves and the recent advances in modeling the demand for international reserves, we examined the empirical determinants of international reserve holdings. In addition to the specifications for developed and developing economies, we considered the demand for international reserves in the Asian and Latin American regions. While both regions have experienced an increase in their holdings of international reserves after the 1997–1998 Asian financial crisis, some Asian economies are perceived to have accumulated international reserves at a scale much larger than that of the Latin American economies.

Our exercise has highlighted the complexity of modeling the demand for international reserves. We find that the demand for international reserves seems to be quite different for developed versus developing economies. Further, the Asian economies and the Latin American economies have different empirical determinants of the demand for international reserves. In general, the estimation results underscore the importance of financial and institution factors in the post-Asian financial crisis period. The macroeconomic factors, including trade openness, play a relatively limited role in explaining the holding of international reserves in the new millennium.

The comparison of international reserve accumulation behaviors depends on the choice of a benchmark specification. Indeed, our results show that the inference about whether an economy is holding an excessive or deficient level of international reserves can be heavily affected by the choice of a benchmark model. For either Asian or Latin American economies, their degrees of over- or under-hoarding are quite moderate when the benchmark is the general specification for developing economies. However, if the benchmark is the demand for international reserves of developed economies, then economies in both regions tend to have held too much international reserves. Three Asian economies, namely Singapore, Hong Kong, and China are the exceptions to these general results. Singapore and Hong Kong, the two open economies in Asia, are quite often found to be holding an excessive amount of international reserves. The results for China do not support the often-made claim that the country holds "too much" international reserves. Indeed, in most specifications considered in the exercise, China is deemed to have held a deficient level of international reserves.

A direct comparison shows that the Asian economies and the Latin American economies have a region-specific empirical demand function of international reserves. Furthermore, our empirical results confirm the perception that the Asian economies tend to hold more international reserves than the Latin American economies. That is, on average, a Latin American economy is expected to hold more international reserves if it behaves like an Asian economy that has similar economic characteristics. On the other hand, Asian economies are likely to hold less international reserves if they act as a typical Latin American economy.

The difference in the accumulation of international reserves in the two regions warrants further investigation in the future. For instance, what are the factors, besides those considered in the current study, that explain the difference in the accumulation behavior? Does the difference in the holdings of international reserves have implications for the stability of these economies? While these questions are beyond the scope of the current study, the answers should shed some useful insight on the international reserve accumulation mechanism and the related policy discussions.

Appendix A

Table 3.A.1 Definitions and sources.

Variables	Definitions	Sources
1. *Dependent variables*		
R_GDP	total international reserves (including gold)/current GDP	WDI
2. *Variables in "X" — "Macrovariables"*		
RYPC_US	per capita GDP in constant U.S. dollars	WDI
POP	population	WDI
PIMP	propensity to import	IFS
RES_VOL	international reserve volatility	IFS
EXP_VOL	volatility of export receipts	IFS
DIFINT	opportunity cost of holding international reserves	WDI, IFS
3. *Variables in "Y" — "Financial variables"*		
M2Y	*M*2 to current GDP	WDI, IFS
NET_DEBT	net debt liabilities/current GDP	LM
NET_FDI	net FDI liabilities/current GDP	LM
NET_PORTFOLIO	net portfolio equity liabilities/current GDP	LM
D_DEBT_LIAB	growth rate of net debt liabilities/current GDP	LM
D_FDI_LIAB	growth rate of net FDI liabilities/current GDP	LM
D_PORTFOLIO_LIAB	growth rate of net portfolio liabilities/current GDP	LM

(*Continued*)

Table 3.A.1 (*Continued*)

Variables	Definitions	Sources
4. *Variables in "Z" — "Institutional variables"*		
KAOPEN	capital account openness	CI
DEFACTO_FININT	*de facto* financial openness = (Total external assets + liabilities)/current GDP	LM
CORRUPT	corruption [0, 6]	ICRG
BQ	bureaucratic quality [0, 6]	ICRG
LAO	law and order [0, 6]	ICRG
LEFT	dummy variable for left-wing government	DPI2004
PLURAL	dummy variable for parliament with plural electoral system	DPI2004
5. *Dummies ("D")*		
ER_CRAWL	dummy variable for the crawling peg exchange rate regime	RR
ER_FIX	dummy variable for the fixed exchange rate regime	RR
CRISIS	dummy variable for a currency crisis	Authors' calculations
BANKCRISIS	dummy variable for a banking crisis	CK
OIL	dummy variable for oil-exporting countries	Authors' calculations

Notes: The source codes are: BDL: Beck, Demirgüc-Kunt, and Levine (2001, updated in later years); CI: Chinn and Ito (2006); CK: Caprio and Klingebiel (2003); DPI2004: *Database of Political Institutions*, Beck *et al.* (2001); ICRG: *International Country Risk Guide*; IFS: IMF's *International Financial Statistics*; IMF: Other IMF databases; LM: Lane and Milesi-Ferretti (2006); RR: Reinhart and Rogoff (2002); and WDI: *World Development Indicators*.

Table 3.A.2 Summary statistics: 1999–2005.

	Developed	Developing	Asia	Latin America
International reserves/GDP	0.07	0.13	0.26	0.19
X (macroeconomic) variables				
Population in millions	38.42	23.52	186.65	44.76
International reserve volatility[a]	0.06	0.08	0.14	0.01
Real per capita GDP (in log U.S. dollars)	10.05	7.82	7.31	7.29
Propensity to import	0.35	0.34	0.51	0.42
Opportunity cost	0.03	0.20	0.08	0.17
Y (financial) variables				
*M*2/GDP	0.89	0.41	0.81	0.47
Net portfolio liabilities/GDP[b]	0.08	0.00	−0.01	−0.02
Net debt liabilities/GDP[b]	0.14	0.33	0.24	0.37
Net FDI liabilities/GDP[b]	−0.02	0.33	0.22	0.26
Z (institutional) variables				
Leftist government (0/1)[c]	0.45	0.19	0.25	0.23
Parliament/plural elect. sys. (0/1)[c]	0.55	0.52	0.80	0.69
Corruption index [0, 6][d]	4.45	2.55	2.33	2.35
Democracy index [0, 1][e]	5.47	2.76	3.48	3.44
Govt fractionalization [0, 1][f]	3.80	1.97	2.56	1.92
De jure KA-openness (Chinn and Ito)[g]	0.76	0.51	0.44	0.44
De facto KA-openness (Lane and Milesi-Ferretti)	0.28	0.19	0.29	0.25

Notes:
[a]International reserve volatility and export volatility are normalized by the period average of international reserves and exports, respectively.
[b]"Net liabilities" = (liabilities minus assets) of an external financial asset per GDP.
[c]The variables for leftist government and parliament with plural electoral system are zero–one dummy variables.
[d]For political/societal variables: anticorruption, law and order, and bureaucratic quality, higher values indicate better conditions. For example, a higher value of corruption index indicates an environment with stronger anticorruption measures and enforcement.
[e]The democracy index is also known as the political constraint index — a higher value means a more democratic system.
[f]A higher value for government fractionalization means a more fractionalized government.
[g]The *de jure* KA openness variable ranges between −1.8 and +2.6 (Chinn and Ito, 2006). A higher value indicates a more open capital account.

Table 3.A.3 List of economies in the Asian and Latin American samples.

The Asian sample	The Latin American sample
Australia	Argentina
Bangladesh	Bolivia
Bhutan	Brazil
Cambodia	Chile
China	Colombia
Fiji	Costa Rica
Hong Kong	Dominican Republic
India	Ecuador
Indonesia	El Salvador
Japan	Guatemala
Korea	Haiti
Lao PDR	Honduras
Malaysia	Mexico
Maldives	Nicaragua
New Zealand	Panama
Pakistan	Paraguay
Papua New Guinea	Peru
Philippines	Uruguay
Samoa	Venezuela, RB
Singapore	Antigua and Barbuda
Solomon Islands	Dominica
Sri Lanka	Grenada
Thailand	Guyana
Tonga	Jamaica
Vietnam	St Kitts and Nevis
	St Lucia
	St Wincent and the Grenadines
	Suriname

References

Aizenman, J, Y Lee and Y Rhee (2007). International reserves management and capital mobility in a volatile world: Policy considerations and a case study of Korea. *Journal of the Japanese and International Economies*, 21, 1–15.

Aizenman, J and N Marion (2003). The high demand for international reserves in the far east: What's going on? *Journal of the Japanese and International Economies*, 17, 370–400.

Aizenman, J and N Marion (2004). International reserve holdings with sovereign risk and costly tax collection. *The Economic Journal*, 114, 569–591.

Alfaro, L, S Kalemli-Ozcan and V Volosovych (2003). Why doesn't capital flow from rich to poor countries? An empirical investigation. Manuscript, University of Houston.

Baumol, WJ (1952). The transactions demand for cash: An inventory theoretic approach. *Quarterly Journal of Economics*, 66, 545–556.

Beck, T, G Clarke, A Groff, P Keefer and P Walsh (2001). New tools in comparative political economy: The database of political institutions. *The World Bank Economic Review*, 15, 165–176.

Beck, T, A Demirgüc-Kunt and R Levine (2001). A new database on financial development and structure. In *Financial Structure and Economic Growth: A Cross-Country Comparison of Banks, Markets, and Development*, A Demirgüc-Kunt and R Levine (eds.). Cambridge, MA: MIT Press.

Caballero, RJ and S Panageas (2004). Insurance and international reserves management in a model of sudden stops. Manuscript, MIT.

Caprio, G and D Klingebiel (2003). Episodes of systematic and borderline financial crises. Manuscript, The World Bank.

Chang, R and A Velasco (1999). Financial fragility and the exchange rate regime. NBER Working Paper 7272.

Cheung, Y-W and H Ito (2007). A cross-country empirical analysis of international reserves. Mimeo.

Chinn, DM and H Ito (2006). What matters for financial development? Capital controls, institutions, and interactions. *Journal of Development Economics*, 81, 163–192.

Corsetti, G, P Pesenti and N Roubini (1999). Paper tigers? A model of the Asian crisis. *European Economic Review*, 43, 1211–1236.

Courchene, TJ and GM Youssef (1967). The demand for international reserves. *Journal of Political Economy*, 75, 404–413.

de Beaufort Wijnholds, JO and A Kapteyn (2001). International reserve adequacy in emerging market economies. IMF Working Paper 01/43.

Dooley MP (1997). A model of crises in emerging markets. NBER Working Paper No. 6300.

Dooley, MP, D Folkerts-Landau and P Garber (2005). *International Financial Stability: Asia, Interest Rates, and the Dollar.* Deutsche Bank Global Research.

Edison, H (2003). Are foreign exchange reserves in Asia too high? In *World Economic Outlook*, September, pp. 78–92, Chapter II, IMF.

Edwards, S (2004). Thirty years of current account imbalances, current account reversals and sudden stops. NBER Working Paper No. 10276.

Feldstein, M (1999). A self-help guide for emerging markets. *Foreign Affairs*, 78, 93–109.

Flood, RP and PM Garber (1984). Collapsing exchange rate regimes: Some linear examples. *Journal of International Economics*, 17, 1–13.

Flood, RP and NP Marion (1999). Perspectives on the recent currency crisis literature. *International Journal of Finance and Economics*, 4, 1–26.

Frenkel, JA (1974a). Openness and the demand for international reserves. In *National Monetary Policies and the International Financial System*, RZ Aliber (ed.). Chicago: University of Chicago Press.

Frenkel, JA (1974b). The demand for international reserves by developed and less-developed countries. *Economica*, 41, 14–24.

Frenkel, JA and B Jovanovic (1981). Optimal international reserves: A stochastic framework. *Economic Journal*, 91, 507–514.

Greenspan, A (1999). Currency international reserves and debt. Remarks made before the *World Bank Conference on Recent Trends in International Reserves Management*, Washington, DC, April 29, http://www.federalinternational reserve.gov/BoardDocs/Speeches/1999/19990429.htm.

Heller, HR (1966). Optimal international reserves. *Economic Journal*, 76, 296–311.

Jeanne, O and R Ranciere (2006). The optimal level of international reserves for emerging market economies: Formulas and applications. IMF Working Paper No. WP/06/229.

Johnson, HG (1958). *International Trade and Economic Growth: Studies in Pure Theory*. Cambridge: Harvard University Press.

Kelly, MG (1970). The demand for international reserves. *American Economic Review*, 59, 655–667.

Krugman, P (1979). A model of balance of payment crises. *Journal of Money, Credit and Banking*, 11, 311–325.

Krugman, P (1999). Balance sheets, the transfer problem, and financial crises. In *International Finance and International Crises*, P Isard, A Razin and AK Rose (eds.). Washington DC: International Monetary Fund.

Lane, PR and D Burke (2001). The empirics of foreign international reserves. *Open Economies Review*, 12, 423–434.

Lane, PR and GM Milesi-Ferretti (2006). The external wealth of nations mark II: Revised and extended estimates of foreign assets and liabilities, 1970–2004. IMF Working Paper No. 06/69.

Obstfeld, M (1995). The logic of currency crises. In *Monetary and Fiscal Policy in an Integrated Europe*, B Eichengreen, J Frieden and J von Hagen (eds.). London: Springer Verlag.

Obstfeld, M (1996). Models of currency crisis with self-fulfilling features. *European Economic Review*, 40, 1037–1047.

Reinhart, C and K Rogoff (2002). The modern history of exchange rate arrangements: A reinterpretation. NBER Working Paper 8963.

Rodrik, D (2006). The social cost of foreign exchange reserves. NBER Working Paper 11952.

Roubini, N and JD Sachs (1989). Government spending and budget deficits in the industrial countries. *Economic Policy*, 8, 99–132.

Willett, TD (2003). Fear of floating need not imply fixed exchange rates. *Open Economies Review*, 14, 77–91.

CHAPTER 4

THE DOMESTIC FINANCIAL CONSEQUENCES OF RESERVE ACCUMULATION: SOME EVIDENCE FROM ASIA[1]

Corrinne Ho and Robert N McCauley

4.1. Introduction

Since 2002, Asia's official reserves have grown rapidly, as the authorities in the region have sought to resist or to slow down currency appreciation. This is not the first time that such an effort to counter large capital inflows by accumulating reserves has come under international scrutiny. There were earlier bouts of rapid reserve growth in Asia in the late 1980s and in the early 1990s (Figure 4.1). The episode in the early 1990s has particular resonance with the situation since 2002: at the time, international capital returned full force to emerging markets after the crises of the 1980s against the backdrop of low U.S. dollar interest rates.

The apparent similarities with past episodes of large capital inflows, coupled with the much larger magnitude of reserve growth this time around, prompted many prophecies that Asia's resistance to currency appreciation could not be sustained. Although the *technical* capacity to accumulate reserves is in principle unlimited, critics warn that prolonged periods of large reserve accumulation risk running up against *economic* limits, which in turn would force an abandonment of the policies driving the accumulation. Indeed, at least since Calvo (1991), many have warned of the "perils" (i.e., unintended adverse domestic consequences) of handling capital inflows

[1]This is an abridged version of a BIS Working Paper (forthcoming in 2008) on the same topic. The authors thank Eric Chan and Michela Scatigna for support with tables and figures. Views expressed in this chapter are those of the authors and not necessarily those of the Bank for International Settlements.

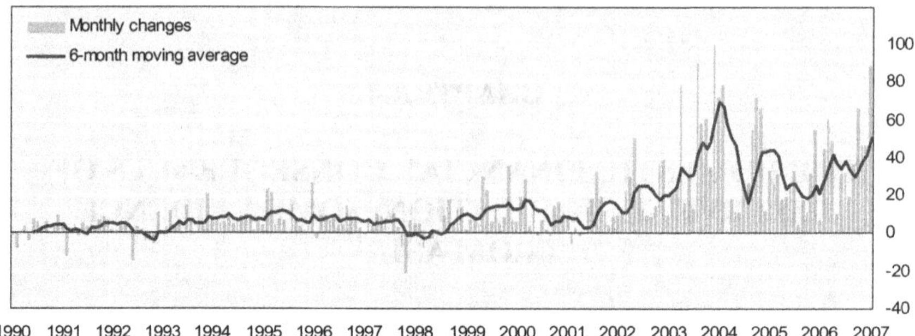

Fig. 4.1. Foreign exchange reserve growth in 13 Asia-Pacific economies (in billions of U.S. dollars).
Sources: IMF; National Data.

with sterilized intervention, quite apart from any concerns over external adjustment or international political repercussions.[2]

So, which economies in Asia are the most in peril? Judging by the increase in the headline reserve figures over 2002–2006, China and Japan, followed at the distance by Taiwan (China),[3] Korea, and India, would appear to be the prime candidates (Figure 4.2).[4]

However, the exposure to economic or financial consequences is perhaps better gauged in relation to the size of the economy or of the banking system.[5] Relative to GDP, China's reserve accumulation in 2002–2006 in fact only ranked fourth in Asia, behind that of Singapore, Taiwan, and

[2]Other earlier works on this topic include, among others, Fernandez-Arias and Montiel (1995), Frankel (1994), Goldstein (1995), and Spiegel (1995).

[3]Hereafter, Taiwan.

[4]These comparisons are distorted to the extent that the currency allocation of reserves differs across economies. Given the trend of U.S. dollar depreciation since 2002, reserve portfolios with considerable euro or sterling investments would show stronger growth in dollar terms. Of the economies that disclose their currency compositions, Hong Kong's non-dollar share is low, and those of Australia and New Zealand are high, relative to the (partial) global average reported by the IMF. However, the effect of the low non-dollar share of Hong Kong's reserves is offset by its unusual weight on equities, which performed very well in the sample period.

[5]The comparisons of reserve growth relative to GDP or to the size of the domestic banking system are also distorted by the different extent of currency appreciation. Appreciation of the won and the baht, for instance, against the U.S. dollar understates Korean and Thai reserves in domestic currency terms.

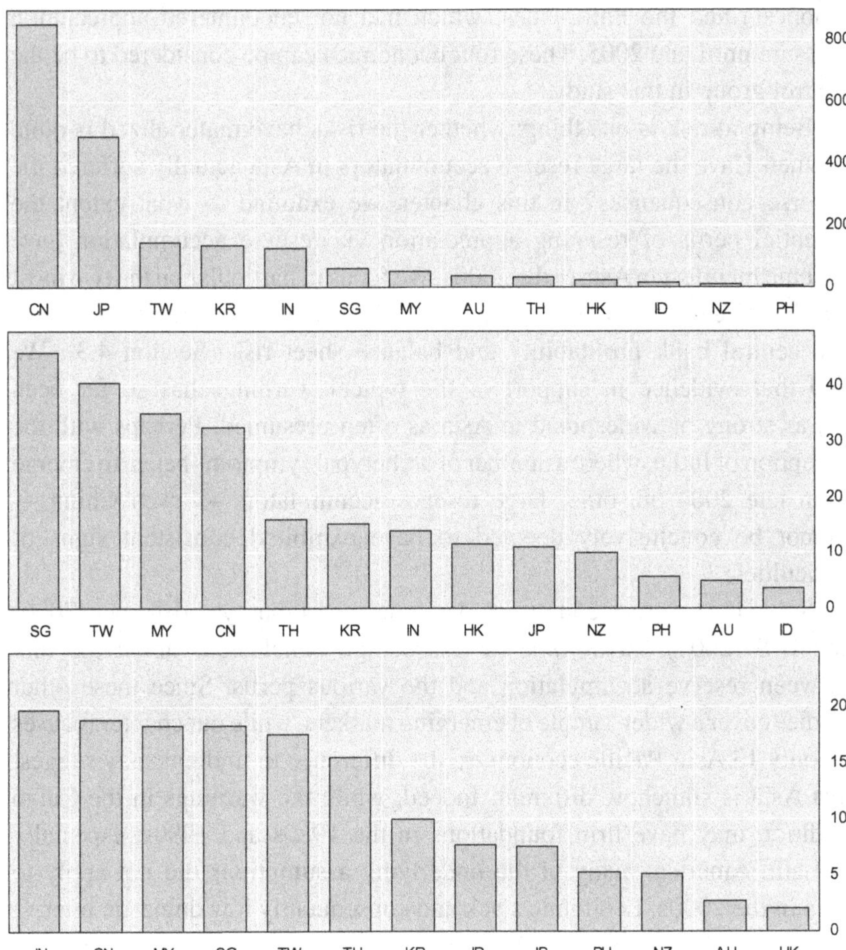

Fig. 4.2. Changes in foreign reserves (top panel), relative to GDP (middle panel) and relative to size of banking system (bottom panel), end-2001 to end-2006. Changes in foreign exchange reserves between December 2001 and December 2006, in billions of U.S. dollars, as a percentage of GDP and as a percentage of total assets in the banking system, respectively. (In billions of U.S. dollars (top panel) and in percent (middle and bottom panels))
Sources: CEIC; IMF; WEO; National Data.

Malaysia. Relative to the size of the domestic banking system, however, India's reserve accumulation bulks larger than that of all others. On the opposite end of the reserve accumulation spectrum are Australia and New Zealand, which have not actively resisted currency appreciation, and

Indonesia and the Philippines, which had not encountered appreciation pressure until late 2005. These four economies can be considered to be the control group in this study.

Being at risk is one thing; whether the risks have materialized is quite another. Have the large reserve accumulators in Asia actually suffered the adverse consequences? In this chapter, we examine to what extent the potential perils of resisting appreciation via reserve accumulation have become manifest in Asia in the 2000s. We focus in particular on the two most familiar categories of consequences, namely, monetary control (Section 4.2) and central bank profitability and balance sheet risk (Section 4.3). We find that evidence in support of the typical warnings has so far been not as strong or widespread in Asia as often presumed. Perhaps with the exception of India, where a number of archetypal symptoms began to emerge from late 2004 on, other large reserve accumulators — even China — cannot be conclusively deemed to have exhibited consistent signs of difficulties.

Some recent cross-country studies, such as Mohanty and Turner (2006) and BIS (2007), have come to less benign conclusions about the link between reserve accumulation and the various perils. Since these other studies cover a wider sample of emerging markets, while our chapter focuses on only 13 Asia-Pacific economies, the difference in findings may suggest that Asia is somehow different. Indeed, while the warnings in the Calvo tradition may have firm foundations in the 1980s and 1990s, especially in Latin America, many of the underlying assumptions did not apply to Asia in the 2000s. Economic slack and consequently low domestic interest rates in Asia contributed to the weak manifestation of the conventionally argued side-effects. Rather than speaking of reserve accumulation as if it were an exogenous policy with consequences, we suggest that reserve accumulation might be better seen as a consequence of the economic circumstances. The efforts to resist currency appreciation in Asia can be seen as a response to the weak post-crisis recovery of real investment and, in China, corporate savings outpacing real investment, in the early 2000s.

Before proceeding, the limits of this chapter deserve emphasis. It covers only the recent episode of reserve accumulation (2002–2006) in Asia. It is interested in reserve accumulation only in the sense of being a by-product of countering appreciation pressure, not an end in itself (e.g., post-crisis rebuilding of reserves).[6] And it examines only the main adverse domestic financial consequences thereof for which we can present tangible evidence.[7] Since the external and political consequences[8] as well as the benefits of holding reserves and of exchange rate management are not discussed here, this chapter should not be read as a full cost-benefit analysis of the policy course of the Asian authorities.

4.2. Monetary Control

A classic potential adverse consequence of central bank foreign exchange purchases is that the associated injection of base money could ultimately prove inflationary. Indeed, some critics argue that even if *nominal* exchange rate appreciation is successfully resisted, the real exchange rate would still appreciate as a result of rising inflation. This argument follows from the classic adjustment mechanism under a fixed nominal exchange rate: external surpluses expand the domestic money supply, increase spending, and drive up prices until the surpluses disappear. However, this mechanism's inflationary consequences may not manifest themselves in situations of chronic demand deficiency — and in any case the mechanism only operates over the long term.

This classic mechanism may also be short-circuited if the central bank offsets the money supply effects of intervention by undoing ("sterilizing") the injection of base money via domestic liquidity management operations. But even so, some critics contend that the authorities could find their ability to sterilize impaired in the face of large-scale and prolonged intervention,

[6] See Chapter 3 of this volume.

[7] Macroeconomic effects, such as potential misallocations between domestic capital stock and foreign assets, or between the traded and nontraded sectors, are not considered in this chapter. The broader financial stability consequences are also not covered here, but are discussed in the longer BIS Working Paper version of this chapter.

[8] Political consequences may result at home if large holdings of reserves create the appearance of a "wealthy" government, enabling it to finance certain "worthy" projects (e.g., bank recapitalization in China, infrastructure in India, or investment in Taiwan) without resorting to the ordinary budgetary procedures or checks and balances. International political consequences can include pressure to reverse what are regarded as mercantilist policies of exporting unemployment. Such pressures could be accentuated in the event of weak growth abroad or job losses in particular sectors, which might also nurture protectionist sentiments.

like that in Asia, thereby foiling the implementation of the desired monetary policy. This might be called the "technical" sterilization problem. A more subtle problem could arise if the adverse consequences induce the authorities to adopt a more accommodative monetary policy stance than that required by their inflation objective. This might be called the "compromise of goals" problem.

This section first considers whether Asian central banks have met the technical sterilization challenge. It then examines whether these central banks have evidently compromised their inflation goals. Finally, it looks at a broader aspect of monetary control: credit growth. Even if the effect of intervention on the monetary base is neutralized, it is possible that a financial system flooded with safe sterilization debt might be emboldened to extend credit at a faster rate. Thus, the question, regardless of the interest rate or monetary aggregate outcome, is whether credit growth has been excessive against the backdrop of foreign exchange reserve buildup.

4.2.1. *The Technical Sterilization Problem*

Foreign exchange intervention causes a technical problem when it interferes with a central bank's ability to achieve its day-to-day operating target. Operating targets can be framed in terms of quantity or price. Many central banks used to target some measure of money over which they had direct control, typically base money or bank reserves. In this case, a technical problem arises if the injection of liquidity associated with intervention is not adequately sterilized via domestic operations, resulting in an expansion of base money that exceeds its targeted path.[9] In current practice, however, many

[9]The typical textbook portrayal of sterilized intervention suggests an intentional, simultaneous, one-for-one offset (so as to keep "money" constant). In practice, however, the mapping between foreign exchange and domestic liquidity operations is not so mechanically precise. The two types of operations are typically implemented in separate departments, each functioning according to its own mandate. The domestic operations department would treat the injection of domestic currency liquidity during foreign exchange intervention as only one out of several autonomous factors it faces. How much liquidity it would eventually withdraw would depend on (1) the net liquidity position of the system after taking into account all autonomous factors and (2) its operating objective. Thus, "sterilization" is in practice more an interpretation rather than a separate policy: sterilized intervention can be said to have occurred if the surplus liquidity that is being mopped up originates predominantly from foreign exchange purchases. That monetary control at the operational level does not require "fully" sterilizing each unit of foreign exchange purchase is illustrated by the

central banks define their operating targets in terms of a short-term interest rate, leaving quantities endogenous. In this case, a technical problem arises if inadequate sterilization leaves the relevant market interest rate to fall and stay below the targeted level. Much of the discussion of sterilized intervention suffers from anachronism, since it applies measures consistent with quantity targeting to assess the behavior of interest rate targeting central banks.

The evidence on interest rates and central bank balance sheets suggest that technically successful sterilization was the norm in most of Asia during the recent period of active foreign exchange purchases. Central banks with explicit short-term interest rate operating targets or official rate corridors (e.g., India, Indonesia, Korea, Malaysia, the Philippines, and Thailand) were able to manage money market liquidity such that the relevant interest rates did not fall and stay below their announced targets or their relevant lower bounds (Figure 4.3). Taiwan's case is less clear, since the policy rate in principle only provides a ceiling for the overnight rate.[10] Only in late 2006 and early 2007 in the Philippines and in May to July 2007 in India did overnight rates trade well below the reverse repo rate that would ordinarily be expected to provide a floor for short-term rates (Figure 4.3). On this showing, there have been at most only recent and exceptional signs of technical difficulties in sterilization.[11]

Federal Reserve's operations in 1991. That year, the Federal Reserve acquired 12.6 billion dollars in foreign currency assets while its net liabilities rose by 11.1 billion dollars. It would therefore appear that very little of the foreign exchange acquisition was sterilized. In fact, it just happened that the liquidity drain from additional demand for cash (which varies from year to year but is always positive) nearly matched the injection from foreign exchange purchases, while other factors nearly netted to zero. In the market for overnight bank deposits, federal funds traded normally in relation to the Federal Reserve's targets. Operationally, there was full sterilization, but a naïve juxtaposition of the rise in foreign exchange holdings and the rise in liabilities would conclude the contrary. We are indebted to Dino Kos for pointing out this case.

[10] Nonetheless, the only sizeable deviation from the *de facto* operating target for the overnight rate occurred in June 2007, when the authorities sold U.S. dollars and allowed the overnight rate to rise in order to squeeze short positions in the domestic currency. Similarly, albeit more frequently, the overnight rate in Indonesia at times traded well above the SBI target rate, especially during the period of rupiah weakness in 2005.

[11] However, neither the Indian nor the Philippine case is a clear-cut one of technical difficulty in sterilization: each has some suggestion of the central bank choosing to let market rates fall relative to the stated policy rates. In India, previous technical problems had been evident in

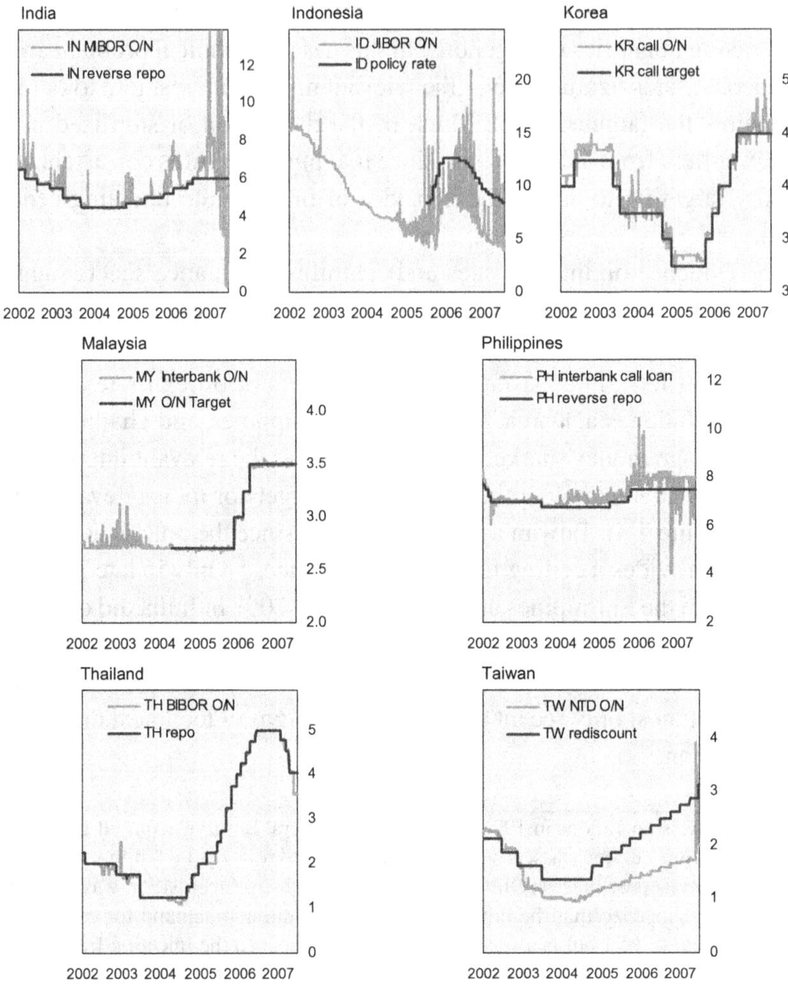

Fig. 4.3. Sterilization: Price interpretation. (Central bank policy rate targets and interbank market overnight rates in percentage points.)
Source: Bloomberg.

---

the injection of liquidity, as Indian overnight rates traded well above the official corridor in 2006 and more so in early 2007. In March 2007, the central bank decided to limit the daily absorption of funds through its reverse repo facility, stating its intention to rely more on sales of government bills and bonds to absorb "structural" excess liquidity under the Monetary

It is also notable that even though quantities are in principle endogenous in interest rate targeting economies such as Korea, Malaysia, Taiwan, and Thailand, liquidity draining operations nonetheless managed to constrain these economies' base money growth. This is evident in the clear gaps between central bank net foreign asset growth and base money growth (Figure 4.4). Thus, in both price and quantity terms, sterilization was technically effective in these economies, and monetary control at the operational level remained intact.

There have been four notable exceptions to the prevalence of interest rate targeting in the region. Under its currency board regime, Hong Kong does not have an active monetary policy. The equivalent of the operating target would be the spot exchange rate. Moreover, the foreign exchange operations undertaken to maintain the spot rate link to the U.S. dollar are as a rule not sterilized. Thus, base money clearly expanded in tandem with foreign reserves during the bout of U.S. dollar-buying that started in September 2003, before reversing in the second half of 2004 (Figure 4.4).[12] Hong Kong dollar interbank interest rates endogenously fell below their U.S. dollar counterparts before gradually reconverging in early 2005, after official U.S. dollar sales in response to market demand had deflated the banking system's bloated aggregate balance back to more normal levels. Given its effective exchange rate based monetary policy framework, Singapore's domestic currency interbank interest rates are also in principle

---

Stabilisation Scheme (RBI, 2007). In the event, as the central bank bought dollars in May–July 2007, its sales of government paper lagged and overnight call interest rates fell toward zero. One interpretation is that the central bank chose for a time not to enforce its interest rate corridor as the rupee strengthened toward 40 to the dollar. In the case of the Philippines, the central bank allowed money-market interest rates, especially the benchmark 91-day Treasury bill yield, to fall below its policy rate corridor by putting in place in November 2006 a tiering system that in effect rationed access to its deposit facility. The stated purpose was to catalyze domestic bank lending, and the decline of the benchmark lending rate to about 3 percent would have increased the attractiveness of borrowing from banks. In mid-2007, the two central banks removed their respective limits on the enforcement of their interest rate corridors, and the unusual configurations of interest rates ended.

[12]Prior to this episode, base money was generally very stable relative to the swings in foreign reserves. However, this is not a result of "sterilization". The institutional peculiarity is that the Exchange Fund's liabilities to the Hong Kong Government and its own accumulated surplus (net worth) have been important counterparts to changes in foreign reserves. Banks and other market participants generally stood ready to offset the effect of changes in Government-held foreign assets on the monetary base, on the basis of the signals of smallish foreign exchange operations.

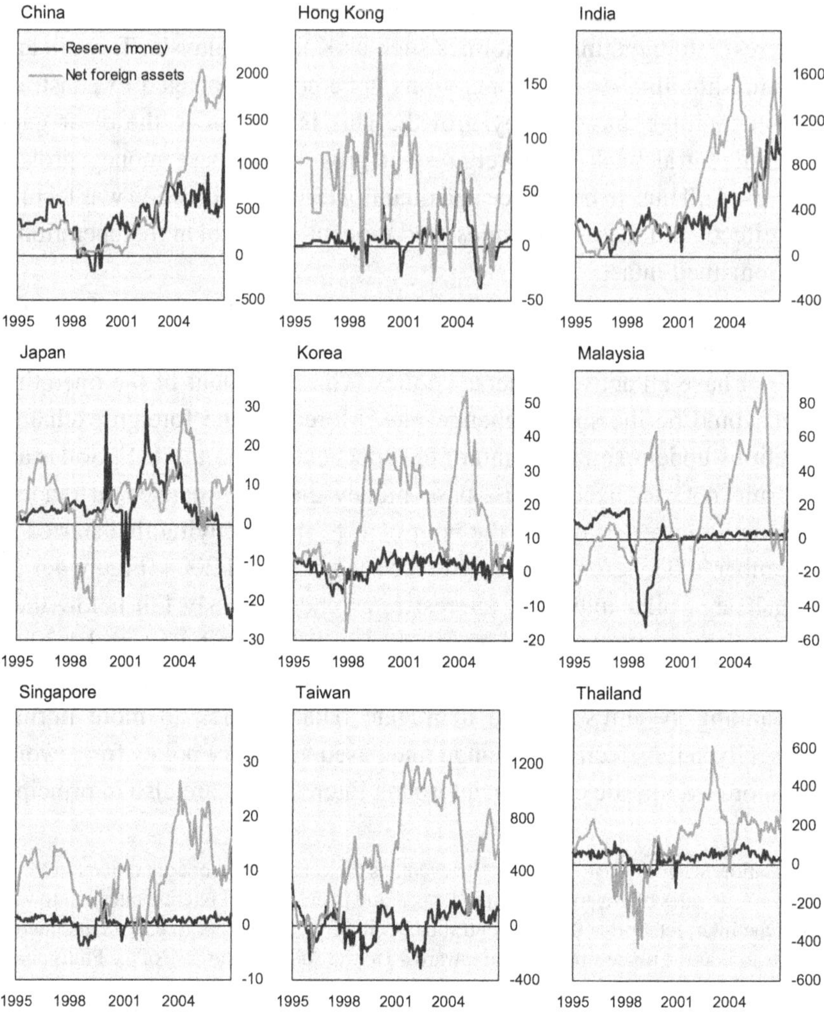

Fig. 4.4. Sterilization: Quantity interpretation. (Annual changes, in billions of local currency; for Japan and Korea, trillions of local currency.)
Sources: IMF; National Data.

endogenous.[13] However, foreign exchange intervention appears to be generally sterilized at the operating horizon. In fact, the gap between the

[13]Over a longer horizon, domestic interest rates should be ultimately constrained by open interest rate parity, via the interaction of the targeted path of the exchange rate and the interest rate levels of trading partners.

monetary authority's net foreign asset growth and the remarkably stable base money growth has been a feature in Singapore even long before the period under investigation (Figure 4.4).

Japan also presents a special case that has inspired conflicting interpretations. With the adoption of "quantitative easing" in March 2001, the Bank of Japan switched from targeting the overnight call rate to targeting the financial system's current account balances held at the central bank. This quantity target was raised in multiple steps between March 2001 and January 2004, driving a rapid expansion of base money, while short-term rates remained close to zero. The very rough parallel between base money growth and foreign exchange reserve accumulation over that period prompted some observers to describe the Japanese authorities' intervention as "*de facto* unsterilized" (Higgins and Klitgaard, 2004). However, one should recall the unique institutional separation in Japan. The Ministry of Finance, not the central bank, is the buyer of foreign exchange at the margin and finances its purchases by issuing bills. Thus, intervention is essentially always sterilized. Moreover, at near-zero interest rates, there is little practical difference between sterilized and unsterilized intervention: private holdings of short-term government paper that in effect paid no interest, and holdings of non-interest bearing central bank current balances are basically perfect substitutes in private portfolios (McCauley, 2004).

China is perhaps the most difficult to interpret of all cases for several reasons. First, the central bank's monetary operation goals are not explicitly stated. Behavior at certain times suggests that the amount of excess reserves in the banking system is an operating target, but there is also an interest rate corridor defined by the interest rate paid on excess reserves at the bottom and the central bank's refinancing rate on the top (Ma and McCauley, 2004). Second, bank reserves (both required and excess) are remunerated, and thus do not carry the same interpretation as the interest-free ones in most other economies. Remuneration, like a deposit facility, helps to keep idle liquidity from pushing money-market rates toward zero, and thus can be seen as a type of passive, automatic sterilization, not easily distinguishable from active sterilization operations. Finally, the multiple hikes in reserve requirements to tighten liquidity since 2003 have increased the demand for reserves and thus permitted rapid base money growth without depressing money market interest rates.[14]

All that said, the profiles of China's base money and foreign reserves expansion look different from the typical pattern observed in other economies (Figure 4.4). Until as recently as early 2003, base money growth had in fact tended to outpace foreign reserve growth. After the first placement of PBC bills in late 2003, base money growth began to lag behind foreign reserve growth, suggestive of a conscious effort to control liquidity. But even so, a clear gap did not take shape until 2004 and, compared to the typical case, China's base money growth is still a relatively large counterpart to foreign reserve growth, somewhat similar to the case of India. Some observers concluded that China was a case of partial sterilization (Higgins and Klitgaard, 2004). However, Yu (2008) holds that the "PBC has been largely successful in mopping up excessive liquidity". Foreign Reserve growth (an 11 trillion renminbi injection over 5 years) was offset by higher reserve requirements (3 trillion), the sale of central bank bills (5 trillion) and the often neglected natural growth of demand for reserves arising from the double-digit nominal growth of the economy even at low to moderate of inflation (an average 600 billion per year for 5 years, or 3 trillion). Likewise, HKMA (2008) shows the monetary base adjusted for reserve requirement hikes to have grown at only around 10%.

In summary, with perhaps the very recent and short-lived exceptions of India and the Philippines, it is difficult to argue that Asian central banks have technical difficulties with sterilization as a result of large-scale foreign exchange purchases. Evidence from interest rate targeting central banks suggests technically effective sterilization.[15] The juxtaposition of foreign reserve growth and base money growth also does not suggest a loss of control. China may be a borderline case, although institutional peculiarities such as reserve remuneration and, more fundamentally, uncertainty

[14]The effect of changes in reserve requirements on the size of reserve demand can be considerable. RBI (2007) notes that reserve money grew 23.7 percent in 2006–2007, but only 18.9 percent if adjusted for the first round effects of the hikes in the reserve requirement. Note also the effect of the cut in required reserves in, say, 1998 in Malaysia or 2002 in Taiwan.

[15]The question of the running cost of sterilization operations will be discussed in Section 4.3.2.

regarding the central bank's operating objectives render a conclusive interpretation difficult.

4.2.2. *Has Sterilized Intervention Compromised Inflation Objectives?*

Notwithstanding the general accuracy of Asian central banks in hitting their interest rate targets, a more subtle and important question is whether the interest rate targets themselves have been set lower than would have been otherwise, in light of heavy intervention, leaving monetary policy looser than warranted. It was tempting for critics to point to, for example, Korea's policy rate cuts in 2004 — a year of heavy intervention on the one hand and upward-creeping core inflation on the other — as evidence of slippage toward pure exchange rate management at the expense of the professed commitment to inflation targeting. However, since core inflation remained within the Bank of Korea's stated target of 2.5–3.5 percent in 2004 and even undershot the target in 2005 and 2006, it was hard to argue that heavy intervention had led the Korean authorities to adopt an overly accommodative policy stance. The rate cuts in 2004 were arguably more consistent with the need to stimulate weak domestic spending than with the desire to resist currency appreciation.[16]

Although Japan is not an inflation targeter, its monetary policy goal during the period of heavy intervention (up until March 2004) was clearly to bring deflation to an end. Accordingly, active efforts to resist yen appreciation were in fact consistent with the easy monetary policy stance adopted then. A similar story applies to other large reserve accumulators such as Taiwan, Malaysia, and Singapore, even in the absence of explicitly quantified inflation goals. The low or even at times negative inflation outcomes in these economies during most of the period under review imply that any efforts to resist currency appreciation were unlikely to have stood in the way of the warranted policy stance.

---

[16]In addition, given the predominance of equity flows (as opposed to fixed-income flows) in Korea's balance of payments, interest rate cuts do not necessarily have the conventional effect of depressing the currency value. By boosting the stock market, rate cuts may in fact encourage portfolio inflows, which in turn exert further upward pressure on the local currency.

As for China and India, the situation was less benign. CPI inflation in China breached the officially flagged 5 percent threshold in the third quarter of 2004, while wholesale price index inflation in India exceeded 8 percent in August 2004. One may infer from both countries' entry into policy rate hiking mode in October 2004 that there was some official discomfort with the price increases.[17] Inflation in both economies retreated subsequently. China's inflation ended up averaging less than 2 percent per year over 2002–2006, but India's averaged over 4 percent. In early 2007, however, inflation climbed again in China and more so in India, prompting more tightening measures. That being said, the absence of explicit inflation targets and the practice of using multiple policy levers[18] in these two economies make it difficult to judge conclusively whether efforts to resist currency appreciation had constrained their monetary policy to be too loose.

All in all, Asia's experience did not provide strong evidence for the well-known argument that large-scale reserve accumulation would be inflationary. The top reserve accumulators, be it in absolute terms (China and Japan) or relative to GDP terms (Singapore, Malaysia, Taiwan, and China), did not experience notably larger rises in inflation over the period 2002–2006 compared to economies that accumulated little reserves (Figure 4.5).[19]

More strikingly, there is in fact an inverse relationship between reserve accumulation and average inflation performance in Asia over the same period (Figure 4.6). The top reserve accumulators all had relatively low inflation or even deflation. In contrast, two economies that saw the least reserve accumulation (Indonesia and the Philippines), given currency weakness through 2005, were the ones that over-shot inflation targets and experienced the highest inflation in the region. This inverse relationship is

[17]China's 5 percent inflation in 2004 was *per se* not very high. However, considering the fact that China just emerged from deflation in 2003, the acceleration was remarkable.

[18]While Chinese policy rate hikes were relatively rare (once in 2004 and twice in 2006), reserve requirements were raised multiple times between 2003 and 2006. The Reserve Bank of India hiked the cash reserve ratio in September 2004 and again in October 2004, but relied more on policy rate hikes subsequently to tighten (once in 2004, twice in 2005, and four times in 2006).

[19]If one considers a broader sample that includes non-Asian emerging markets, a mildly positive relationship emerges. What holds for emerging markets in general does not apply to Asia in particular in this case.

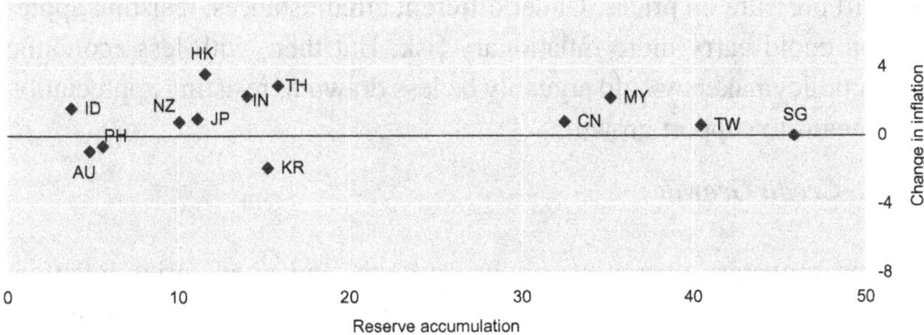

Fig. 4.5. Reserve accumulation and change in CPI inflation (end-2001 to end-2006) as percentage of GDP and in percentage points, respectively.
Sources: IMF; Bloomberg; BIS.

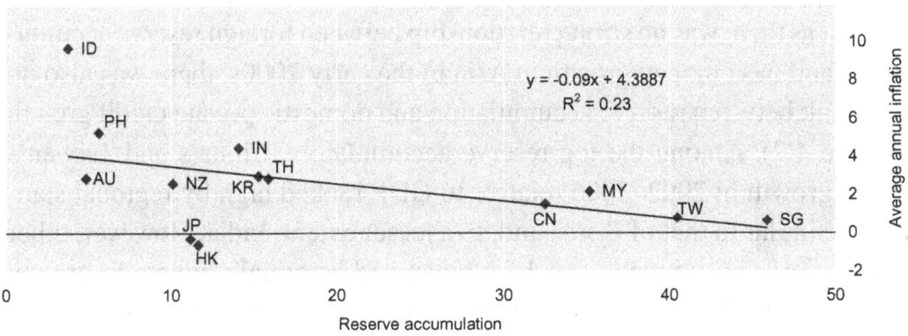

Fig. 4.6. Reserve accumulation and average CPI inflation, 2002–2006 as percentage of GDP and in percent, respectively.
Sources: IMF; Bloomberg; BIS.

even more evident if one juxtaposes the inflation rate in 2001 (i.e., the initial condition) with the subsequent degree of reserve accumulation.

Thus, rather than being an independent policy with supposed inflationary consequences, the heavy intervention in Asia in the early 2000s might be better seen as itself a consequence of the economic circumstances of the time. Macroeconomic slack — related to weak investment expenditure in ex-China Asia and rising enterprise savings in China — was pervasive during the period under review. Even if policy efforts to contain nominal appreciation were successful in supporting external demand, there was still sufficient excess labor and capacity to meet this demand without exerting great upward pressure on prices. Under different circumstances, resisting appreciation could carry more inflationary risk. But then, with less economic slack, policymakers would arguably be less drawn to resisting appreciation as a means to support growth.

4.2.3. *Credit Growth*

Beyond monetary operations, money growth, and goods price inflation, monetary control can also be assessed in a broader sense by examining the growth of credit to the private sector. Some critics would contend that absence of goods price inflation does not necessarily mean that the economy is safe from overheating (White, 2006). If intervention, even if sterilized, created looser-than-otherwise conditions that encouraged excessive credit growth, a kind of "overheating in disguise" would result.

Just as there was no strong relationship between foreign reserve accumulation and base money growth in Asia in the early 2000s, there was also no tight link between reserve accumulation and domestic private credit growth (Figure 4.7). Among the top reserve accumulators, China's and Taiwan's credit growth in 2002–2006 relative to GDP ranked high by regional standards, similar to that of Korea and, to a lesser extent, India. However, other large reserve accumulators such as Japan had essentially no credit growth in excess of GDP growth, while Malaysia and Singapore even saw credit growth being outpaced by GDP growth. In contrast, Australia and New Zealand, two countries that boast freely floating and appreciating currencies,

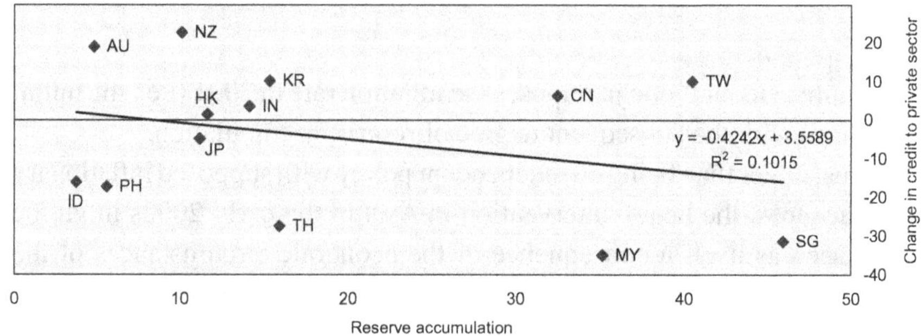

Fig. 4.7. Reserve accumulation and credit deepening (end-2001 to end-2006) as a percentage of GDP.
Sources: IMF; National Data.

had the strongest credit growth relative to GDP in the region. In fact, a negative cross-sectional relationship prevailed.

Feeble credit growth, in light of weak corporate loan demand, was a common phenomenon in post-crisis Asia. Loan-to-deposit ratios declined — most notably in Hong Kong, Indonesia, Singapore, and Thailand — in the wake of the Asian crisis and in most cases remained low through at least 2005. Although China and Taiwan registered relatively strong credit growth in 2002–2006, their loan-to-deposit ratios did not show any increase during this period (Figure 4.8). The only two large reserve accumulators that saw both notable credit growth and a rise in the loan-to-deposit ratio were Korea and India. In these cases, the question that remains is whether any observed rise in credit growth and/or loan-to-deposit ratio is indeed a result of heavy foreign exchange intervention.[20] In any case, as with inflation and credit growth, the change in loan-to-deposit ratio also exhibits a negative relationship vis-à-vis the extent of reserve accumulation among the economies in our sample. Such a relationship suggests that rather than

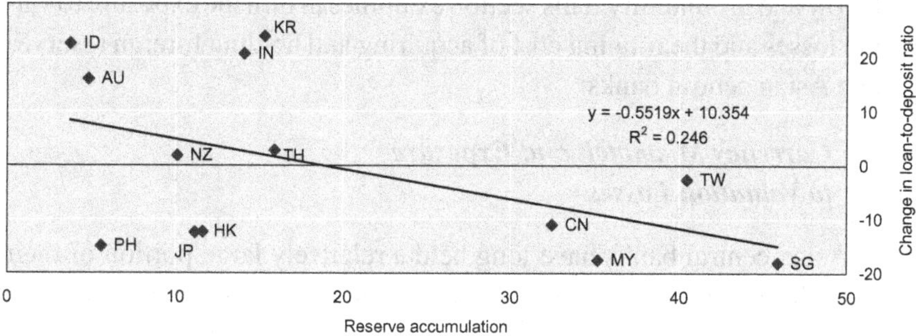

Fig. 4.8. Reserve accumulation and change in loan-to-deposit ratio (end-2001 to end-2006) as a percentage of GDP and in percentage points, respectively.
Sources: Bloomberg; CEIC; Reserve Bank of Australia; Reserve Bank of New Zealand.

[20] In China, for instance, the acceleration in credit growth in 2002 was arguably induced by policy then to spur growth. Credit growth decelerated substantially between mid-2003 and end-2005 in response to a series of restrictive administrative measures to check investment, even as foreign exchange intervention became heavier. Bank lending in Korea recovered relatively quickly after the Asian crisis thanks in part to active policy to encourage lending to households in order to boost consumption. The credit card boom in 2001/2002 was illustrative of this policy-induced lending boom. (See Kang and Ma (2007)).

being an independent policy that has a side-effect of fueling loan growth, the heavy intervention in Asia might have been a response to the lack of loan growth.[21]

4.3. Central Bank Profitability and Balance Sheet Risk

Another familiar category of domestic financial consequences pertains to the risk and cost that reserve accumulation may impose on the balance sheet and cash flow of the central bank itself. Balance sheet risk arises when the counterpart to a central bank's foreign currency assets is mostly domestic currency liabilities.[22] An appreciation of the domestic currency could thus result in valuation losses. Less obvious but also notable is that the benchmark duration for foreign reserves has commonly been extended over time while the duration of interest-bearing liabilities used to finance reserves has generally remained short-term, resulting in an increasing duration mismatch. In addition to these balance sheet risks, the cost of financing the purchase of foreign currency assets by issuing/selling interest-bearing domestic currency liabilities/assets (i.e., sterilization) could undermine a central bank's cash flow and profitability. This section examines in turn the exposure to valuation losses and the running cost of acquiring and holding foreign reserves among Asian central banks.

4.3.1. *Currency Mismatch and Exposure to Valuation Losses*

Most Asian central banks have long held a relatively large portion of their assets in foreign currency assets. They also tend to have little or no foreign currency liabilities, resulting in a potential exposure to foreign exchange valuation changes. The economic significance of such exposure is best gauged by the size of a central bank's net foreign assets in relation to GDP. By this metric, Singapore ranked first with its official foreign assets in excess of

[21]The low and falling loan-to-deposit ratios among the top reserve accumulators could also be interpreted as a sign of sterilization debt "crowding out" the extension of loans by the banking sector.

[22]It is worth noting that, while central banks' reserve management functions are increasingly subject to advanced risk management techniques, different deputy governors often bear responsibility for domestic liabilities and foreign assets. Thus, an integrated asset and liability management perspective cannot always be assumed.

100 percent of GDP, followed by Hong Kong and Taiwan (70–75 percent of GDP). For these economies, every 1 percentage point decline in the value of foreign assets would imply a wealth loss of 0.7–1.0 percent of GDP. In contrast, although the headline official reserve figures of Japan, China, Korea, and India are large, the economic significance of each percentage point decline in value is more modest by comparison — 0.4 percent of GDP for China, as of end-2006, and only 0.2–0.3 percent for the other three economies.

Whatever the extent of mismatch, the actual exposure to exchange valuation is also a function of the currency allocation of the reserve portfolio. Absent detailed public information on currency allocation, Asian authorities are often thought of as holding mostly U.S. dollar assets. Under this assumption, the 30 percent appreciation of the Korean won, for example, against the dollar from 2002 to early 2005 would have eroded Korea's official wealth by some 9 percent of GDP over 3 years, all else being equal.[23] However, if Asian central banks are at all diversified into currencies that have appreciated against the U.S. dollar (e.g., euro, sterling, Australian dollar), valuation losses from domestic currency appreciation would be less than what the all-U.S. dollar assumption indicates.[24] For example, despite a small spot appreciation of the Hong Kong dollar against the U.S. dollar in late 2003, Hong Kong's Exchange Fund in fact recorded valuation gains in 2003, thanks to the even stronger appreciation of the non-U.S. dollar foreign currency component (at least 20 percent) of the portfolio.

How much does exchange valuation really matter in practice? Valuation is only one factor affecting profit and loss — other net cash flows (e.g., net interest earnings, see Section 4.3.2) can sometimes offset any impact of exchange valuation on the headline profit and loss.[25] Moreover, valuation

---

[23]Yetsenga (2007) provides estimates of valuation losses among Asian central banks for the period July 2006–June 2007, apparently under the all-U.S. dollar assumption. Korea's estimated valuation losses are much more modest (0.5 percent of GDP) given the much lower rate of won appreciation in this period.

[24]With a substantial fraction of emerging Asia's reserves not included in the aggregate currency breakdown statistics published by the IMF, it could be that emerging Asia is more diversified than is often presumed.

[25]According to the hypothesis of open interest rate parity, valuation losses should be offset over the long run by interest rate gains.

losses are often charged to provisions or reserves, and not run through the central bank's final profit and loss statement. Such accounting conventions could play a role in muting the fiscal (political) repercussion of valuation losses if central bank profit disposition is based on *reported* and not *actual* profits.[26] In Asia, such accounting conventions are practiced in at least Taiwan and Japan.[27] One known counterexample is Hong Kong, where assets are valued at market prices and the announced investment income is inclusive of foreign exchange valuation effects.

Regardless of whether there are visible fiscal repercussions down the road, exchange valuation losses may still have a near-term impact on the central bank's capital. How much of an effective appreciation a central bank can withstand depends on the size of its capital or reserve fund relative to the size of its net foreign assets. But even if capital is eaten up by losses, there is in principle the option of recapitalization. The perceived seriousness of shortfalls in capital thus depends on how averse the central bank might be to seeking such recapitalization from its government owner. The risk is that the legislation that restores positive capital may carry some political baggage for the central bank. The case studies discussed in Appendix A illustrate how central bank losses could play out in practice.

4.3.2. *The Quasi-fiscal Cost of Financing and Holding Reserves*

Apart from the exposure to foreign exchange valuation changes, the running financial (quasi-fiscal) cost associated with sterilized intervention is another — perhaps more frequent — complaint against such operations. Experience from past decades has led to the view that sterilization is costly because it essentially amounts to exchanging high-yielding domestic assets (government bonds, central bank deposits or paper) for safe but low-yielding

[26]However, a risk behind this apparent convenience is that the central bank may still be transferring notional profits to the fiscal authorities even as the market value of its assets falls short of that of its liabilities.

[27]In Japan, since the Ministry of Finance holds most of the foreign exchange reserves, one might expect a more direct fiscal impact. However, this expectation is only partially borne out. Valuation losses on the foreign reserves are, although publicly reported, not counted as fiscal spending. Thus, the fiscal impact of a stronger yen is institutionally at least muted.

ones (e.g., U.S. Treasuries). Conventional wisdom also warns that sterilization will get costlier over time, as the interest rates on sterilization debt are driven up. This would in turn attract more inflows, fueling a vicious cycle that renders sterilization more difficult and expensive over time. In addition to the flow cost of sterilization operations, there is also a stock opportunity cost to contend with. By accumulating and holding on to a large stock of foreign currency assets, a central bank may be first forgoing then paying potentially higher yields on domestic assets.

These conventional arguments have their roots in episodes of large capital inflows into emerging markets in the 1970s, 1980s, and 1990s. The Latin American experience, in particular, contributed much to the formation of these views. There and then, heavy intervention and sterilization typically occurred in the context of exchange rate based stabilization programs, with high inflation, high (often double-digit) domestic interest rates, and shallow domestic bond markets. These characteristics, however, were not evident in Asia in the 2000s.

For a quick diagnosis, one can look at the difference between short-term domestic interest rates (proxy for gross cost of sterilization operations) and medium-term U.S. Treasury yields (proxy for gross return on foreign reserves). In 2002–2003, the differentials for Japan, Taiwan, China, Singapore, Hong Kong, and Thailand were on average negative (Figure 4.9). This suggests that, rather than being cash-flow costly, reserve accumulation in these economies was in fact potentially cash-flow remunerative. Among economies with positive interest rate differentials, only

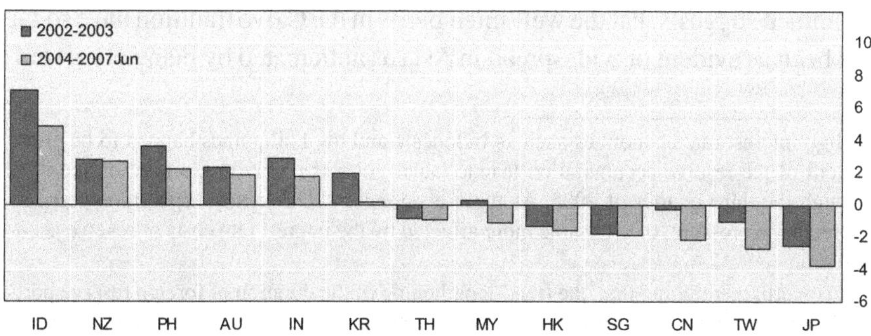

Fig. 4.9. Quasi-fiscal cost: Quick diagnosis (yield of three-month domestic government bill minus average yield of U.S. Treasury 1–5 years).
Sources: Bloomberg; Morgan Stanley.

Korea and India engaged in sizeable sterilized foreign currency purchases during this period, making them the only clear cases of costly reserve accumulation.[28] Even so, with U.S. medium-term rates on net rising faster than most Asian rates in 2004–2006, the running cost of sterilization in fact subsequently decreased.[29]

Appendix B presents the detailed cost calculations for India and Korea. To summarize, estimates for the incremental net flow cost in a 12-month period were in the range 0.10–0.20 percent of GDP for Korea and 0.06–0.10 percent of GDP for India, depending upon the intensity of intervention and the levels of relevant interest rates. For Korea, the "perfect storm" episode was the 12 months to March 2004, when the 12-month increase in central bank foreign assets was the largest and the assumed relevant interest rate differentials were the widest. For India, there was no such clear "perfect storm" episode. June 2004 and July 2006 saw the largest 12-month increase in net foreign assets, but the local peak in interest rate differentials during that period occurred at around November 2004. As for the stock cost, estimates were in the range 0.01–0.50 percent of GDP per annum for Korea and 0.40–0.60 percent of GDP for India, depending on the size of foreign reserve holdings and interest rate differentials. The question here is whether these costs are in fact seen as too large to be justifiable.

4.4. Concluding Remarks

This chapter has assessed whether the large reserve accumulators in Asia over the period 2002–2006 have experienced the predicted adverse domestic consequences of large-scale intervention and sterilization. The evidence examined suggests that the well-cited perils in the Calvo tradition have so far not been as evident or widespread in Asia as anticipated by many observers.

---

[28]High interest rate economies such as Indonesia and the Philippines happen to be at the bottom of the reserve accumulation league table, given the lack of appreciation pressure through the third quarter of 2005. As these economies subsequently began to experience appreciation pressure, they became more affected by the interest rate costs of reserve accumulation.

[29]It is worth mentioning that, the trend-lengthening of the duration of foreign reserve portfolios over the past decades may have in practice helped to mitigate the carry cost of foreign reserves. As longer-dated foreign reserve assets (e.g., five-year U.S. Treasury securities) tend to yield more than shorter-dated reserve assets (e.g., three-month Treasury bills), the carry cost is limited accordingly (see McCauley and Fung, 2003).

With respect to monetary control, be it in terms of liquidity operations, inflation performance, and credit growth, India is the only top reserve accumulator clearly showing multiple symptoms consistent with the perils. The evidence to date on China has been mixed, with its current upsurge in inflation largely driven by food prices. Regarding central bank income and balance sheet risks, while it is true that the carrying cost is significantly positive only for India among the large reserve holders, the exposure to exchange valuation losses applies more widely across the region. Diversified currency allocation and net private sector foreign currency debt are only partial mitigating factors.[30] All in all, although China has been more often implicated in the dire prophesies associated with reserve accumulation, it is in fact India that has exhibited more of the classic symptoms.

Why then has Asia — ex-India — been able to weather 5 years of intervention and over 1.5 trillion U.S. dollars of reserve accumulation without showing conclusive signs of the predicted adverse consequences? The key may lie in Asia's specific economic circumstances in the early 2000s. Large banking systems with weak corporate loan demand against the backdrop of weak corporate investment and macroeconomic slack characterized much of the region, and in China, there was ample corporate savings in relation to investment. These conditions may have helped to weaken any inflationary consequences that reserve accumulation could have brought otherwise. As a corollary, the relatively low domestic interest rates in most of Asia have allowed sustained sterilization operations at little or no carry cost. By contrast, conditions in India have been less favorable: a smaller banking system, and, in recent years, strong loan demand by a corporate sector running a financial deficit (associated with a current account deficit) have kept domestic interest rates high and have made the classic risks recognizable.

Even if the conclusion is so far, surprisingly, so good, there remain grounds for concern. Possible response lags may mean that the adverse consequences are still on their way. While evidence to date suggests no strong relationship between credit growth and the extent of reserve accumulation, the latter's relationship to asset prices merits further investigation,

[30]As discussed in Appendix A, Taiwan's experience in the 1980s suggests that the government may have to forego a decade's seignorage income to make good the sizeable official valuation losses on foreign reserves. In Korea, central bank losses might in time require legislative recapitalization, the political ramifications of which would remain to be seen.

especially in light of the surge in Chinese equity prices in 2006 and 2007. While Indonesia and the Philippines have been spared from appreciation pressure for most of the sample period, their reserve growth has picked up since mid-2006 and mid-2005, respectively. The smaller banking systems and higher interest rates in these two economies might make large-scale reserve accumulation more risky and costly for them than for most of their Asian neighbours. In short, the domestic financial consequences of resisting appreciation and accumulating reserves may remain a topic of policy discussion for some time to come.

Appendix A
Case-studies of Exchange Rate Valuation Changes of Reserves

A.1. Taiwan in the Late 1980s

Taiwan in the second half of the 1980s provides a useful case study of how a large domestic currency appreciation plays out in an economy with large foreign reserves. At the time, Taiwan's foreign exchange reserves were at levels in relation to GDP reached recently by several other Asian economies; so the comparison is quite apt.[31]

In the wake of the period of yen appreciation after the 1985 Plaza Accord, pressure for appreciation focused on the New Taiwan dollar and the Korean won. The Taiwanese authorities resisted appreciation all the way from around TWD 40 to the U.S. dollar at end-1985 to below TWD 29 by end-1987 — an appreciation of almost 40 percent in just 2 years. By 1989, the currency had settled in the range TWD 25–27 per U.S. dollar. As a result of the authorities' continued resistance, foreign reserves grew from just over 22.5 billion U.S. dollars at end-1985 to around 76.7 billion U.S. dollars by end-1987 (i.e., from 36 percent to 75 percent of GDP). Outstanding certificates of deposit (NCDs) issued by the central bank for sterilizing such inflows expanded over 30-fold from a nominal amount of TWD

[31] See Chu (2004) for a reflection on similarities and differences between the situation in Asia in the 2000s and the Taiwanese experience with appreciation pressure in the 1980s.

26.7 billion at end-1985 to TWD 946.1 billion (about 33 billion U.S. dollars) at end-1987.

Against this background, the central bank's foreign exchange valuation losses mounted. By June 1987, losses reportedly exceeded TWD 300 billion, equivalent to 9 percent of GDP and about half a year's fiscal budget (Wang, 1999). With a further 8 percent appreciation in the second half of 1987, the unrealized losses could have reached TWD 450 billion by the end of the year (about 13 percent of GDP). CBC (2006) reports that unrealized exchange valuation losses were "as high as NT634.9 billion at the end of April 1989" (evaluated at TWD 25.55 to the U.S. dollar), amounting to 16 percent of 1989 GDP. Such valuation losses appear to have taken years of seigniorage income to work off. Reported central bank net income fell from 1¼ percent of GDP in fiscal year 1985 to negligible levels in 1987–1990 and did not return to the 1985 level until after the 1997–1998 Asian crisis (Figure 4.A.1).[32]

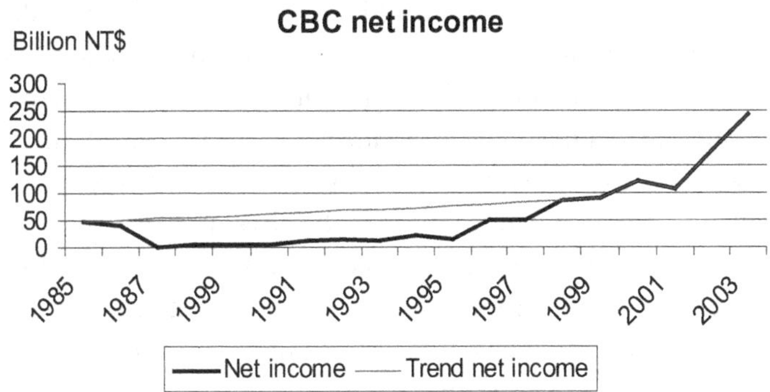

Fig. 4.A.1. CBC net income.
Source: National Data.

[32]The Central Bank of China Act, Article 43 (first introduced in first amendment in 1979) reads "The gain or loss from the Bank's assets or liabilities denominated in gold, silver, foreign currencies, and other forms of international reserve, due to changes in parity of the national currency, or changes in the value, parity or exchange rate of these assets and liabilities relative to the national currency, shall not be listed as the Bank's annual profit or loss. Any gain from the above changes shall be entered into an Exchange Reserve Account, and any loss shall be offset in the balance of that Account."

With regards to the fiscal impact, the decline in central bank net income would have meant lower transferred profits to the government.[33] In fact, CBC (2006) reports that no funds were transferred in 1986–1990. In theory, the gradual recognition of this wealth loss in the fiscal budget could have hurt aggregate demand if government expenditure was cut or taxes were raised in response to the interrupted flow of central bank profits to the budget. However, the observed rise of government debt outstanding between 1986 and 1995, from 3.5 percent to 22.6 percent of GDP (CBC, 1995, p. 30), leaves room for the interpretation that the wealth loss simply resulted in higher government debt rather than pressure on expenditure.

Further illustrating why it could be a fallacy to equate the government wealth loss to a national wealth loss is the sharp rise in private sector external debt during this episode. Given the central bank's preference for a gradual appreciation (instead of a step revaluation, as preferred by the U.S.), the private sector offloaded its foreign currency holdings and even borrowed foreign funds to invest in domestic currency assets. In doing so, while the central bank resisted appreciation, the private sector was in effect transferring its long-dollar position to the official sector. Thus, the counterpart to much of the official sector loss was a private sector gain (or at least a smaller private loss). One could even stretch and regard this transfer as an indiscriminately disseminated adjustment assistance to the private sector. In any case, some of this private profit was presumably captured by corporate taxation.

Overall, the lesson would appear to be that, in practice, the central bank's recovery from losses or even technical insolvency resulting from large reserves and sharp currency appreciation is stretched out over time. Both this gradualism and locus of the risk in the government balance sheet probably attenuate the macroeconomic effects of the wealth loss, as compared to the experience of the same loss in the private sector. Yu Guo-hua, former CBC governor (1969–1984) and the president of the Executive Yuan during the appreciation episode, interpreted the central bank's losses as simply a price to pay for protecting local enterprises' profits from the

---

[33]The profit-sharing rule between the CBC and the government is stated in CBC Act Article 42: at the close of each fiscal year, the CBC is to set aside 50 percent of its net profit as legal retained earnings (can set aside less if the accumulated legal retained earnings are already as large as the central bank's current capital). The rest can be transferred to the government.

presumably more unpleasant alternative of a sharp appreciation (Wang, 1999). Central bank losses in this case were not really seen as a weakness, but as a means to a presumably more important public purpose. Moreover, with local consumers benefiting from the improved terms-of-trade, public perception may have found it difficult to connect a "strong" currency with a "weak" central bank.[34]

A.2. Korea in 2003–2006

The stress on the Bank of Korea's income and capital arising from the appreciation of the won from around 1200 per dollar toward 900 per dollar in 2004–2006 led to initial policy responses similar to those observed in Taiwan in the late 1980s. In 2003, the Bank of Korea recorded a pre-tax profit of KRW 3.175 trillion and paid KRW 1 trillion in income taxes. However, by 2005, with a loss of KRW 1.878 trillion, income taxes fell to zero. At end-2006 the exchange valuation losses stood at KRW 26.1 trillion, well in excess of capital of KRW 2.0 trillion (BOK, 2007, p. 66). The unrealized losses were thus about 3 percent of GDP.

However, if further losses are realized in the income account at the same rate as 2005–2006 and capital is exhausted in a year or two, the Korean approach will change gears. In particular, under the 1999 Bank of Korea law, the government is committed to making good any capital deficiency. This may imply that, rather than just foregoing income, the government will have to seek appropriations from the legislature. It is possible that appropriations associated with this keep-well arrangement will add to the political salience of the wealth loss and make it more likely that fiscal spending or taxes are affected.

Once again, government losses here cannot be taken as a proxy for national losses. The Korean corporate sector is thought to be structurally short the dollar, owing to external debt denominated in U.S. dollars. Broad evidence for this can be seen in Table 4.A.1, which shows that the official

[34] A similar case can be found in Germany, where the appreciation of the Deutsche mark against the U.S. dollar in the early 1970s put the Bundesbank into a position in which its assets fell short of its measured liabilities. And yet, neither the central bank's standing as a counterparty, nor the German public's trust in it, seemed to diminish as a result.

Table 4.A.1. Currency composition of the Korean net international investment position, end-2003.

	Billion U.S. dollar	Percent of GDP
Total	−86	−14
Won	−186[a]	−31
Foreign currency	100[b]	17
Memo: Reserve assets	155	26

Notes:
[a]Sums portfolio equity investment in Korea and direct foreign investment into Korea.
[b]Total less won. This treats foreign-currency bonds that are convertible into Korean equity as foreign-currency.
Source: BOK; author's estimates.

sector's reserve assets exceeded the nation's long position in foreign currency. The difference can be interpreted as the corporate sector's short-dollar position, which can be seen not as a currency mismatch but rather as a hedge against the operating exposure of Korean exporters to won strength. Accordingly, the corporate sector's balance sheet gains from won appreciation would to some extent represent a counterpart to the official sector's balance sheet losses. Even from the strictly fiscal standpoint, the government's tax share of the corporate valuation gains from a strong won should offset to some extent the government's losses from a strong won.

Appendix B
Estimating the Costs of Reserve Accumulation

Cost estimation has been the subject of many pervious studies, and yet there seems to be little agreement on how to define, much less estimate, such costs.[35] We find that there are at least two kinds of financial costs associated with reserve accumulation through sterilized intervention. One is the cost of sterilization operations over a period of time (flow cost). Another is the

[35]For recent examples of cost estimation for Asia by private sector market analysts, see Mathur (2003), Anderson (2004 a,b), Le Mesurier (2004), Ogus (2003 and 2005), and Yetsenga (2007).

financial opportunity cost of holding a given stock of reserves at a point in time (stock cost).[36]

There are some subtle but important differences between the two concepts. A stock (holding) cost in principle exists for any central bank that holds any amount of foreign assets, regardless of whether the acquisition of such assets involved sterilization or not. A flow (sterilization) cost, however, applies only when the acquisition of foreign assets is complemented with interest-costing sterilization operations. The stock cost seems to be the most widely studied by economists, but the flow cost seems to be of more practical and budgetary relevance to the authorities. Confusingly, the term "cost of sterilization" is sometimes loosely applied to mean "the opportunity cost of holding reserves."

In this Appendix, we estimate both flow and stock costs for the period of strong capital inflows and heavy sterilized intervention in 2002–2006. Our approach is to focus on the two most challenged candidates — namely, Korea and India, owing to their relatively high domestic interest rates — under relatively conservative assumptions. The costs so estimated would represent a maximum: costs can only be lower for the other economies facing more favorable conditions.

B.1. Flow Cost: The Cost of Sterilization Operations Over a Period of Time

We need three main ingredients to estimate the flow cost of sterilization operations over a period of time:

(i) *How much sterilization is done?* Since foreign reserves are held at the central bank in most Asian economies (Japan is a clear exception), we proxy the sterilization amount with the difference between the change in central bank foreign assets and the change in base money, expressed as a percentage of GDP. This measure essentially assumes that whatever foreign asset growth that does not have a counterpart

---

[36]We concede that we also do not have the definitive way of estimating costs (if such a way exists). In practice, the definition of costs depends on how the problem is framed in political terms, which varies across economies. For example, the "local" concept of costs in India is based only on the amount of new government securities issued under the Monetary Stabilization Scheme adopted in April 2004.

in base money growth has been actively sterilized. This ignores the possible contribution of other autonomous factors (e.g., government deposits) and also does not cover "passive sterilization" via reserve remuneration or a hike in reserve requirements. However, this measure allows for the possibility of using more than one sterilization instrument and is thus more inclusive than the commonly used approach of proxying sterilization with just the net change in central bank domestic assets or the net change in central bank paper outstanding.[37]

(ii) *What do the authorities pay on the sterilization instrument(s) used?* Existing studies typically apply a short-term domestic rate or domestic government bond yield across the board, without any reference to the sterilization instrument(s) used. We find it more appropriate to relate cost to the instrument(s) actually used or likely to have been used. For Korea, since both the central bank and the Ministry of Finance and the Economy (MOFE) contribute to financing sterilized interventions, we use both the BOK's Monetary Stabilisation Bonds (MSBs) and the MOFE's own bonds and assume average maturities of 1 year and 5 years, respectively. For India, we assume the instrument in question to be five-year Indian government bonds.[38]

(iii) *What do the authorities earn from the acquired foreign assets?* We assume foreign reserves earn the equivalent of medium-term U.S. Treasury notes (average two- to five-year maturity). This is a relatively conservative assumption, though not as conservative as studies that just apply a very short-term (less than 1 year) U.S. T-bill rate. However, the medium-term T-notes assumption is probably more realistic. When foreign reserves are sufficiently large, there is no need to keep all reserves in short-dated but low-yielding instruments.[39]

[37]These two common alternatives, though convenient, are less than ideal also because they do not make any reference to the change in foreign assets and thus do not necessarily have anything to do with intervention. They could be capturing liquidity management operations for reasons other than foreign exchange intervention.

[38]Medium-term Indian government securities could be a plausible assumption before the inception of the Market Stabilisation Scheme (MSS) in April 2004. In practice, the MSS has involved mostly the issuance of short-term securities.

[39]Also, with the possibility of doing repurchase agreements (repos), the nominal maturity of the security becomes a less relevant constraint on liquidity.

Reserve managers can — and do — diversify their foreign reserve portfolios in more lucrative ways.

Tables 4.B.1 and 4.B.2 show the flow cost estimates for Korea and India for selected periods over 2003 and 2006. Overall, the estimates do not appear large. For Korea, the net flow cost for the 12-month period ending March 2004 totalled about 0.2 percent of GDP. This period was arguably a "perfect storm" episode: the increase in central bank foreign assets was the largest and the assumed relevant interest rate differentials were the widest. Interest differentials for Korea narrowed subsequently, helping to lower the

Table 4.B.1. Estimated flow cost of sterilization operations over 12 months: Korea.

	Dec 2003	Mar 2004	Sep 2004
Quantities (% of GDP[a]):			
ΔFA less ΔRM[b]	4.93	8.45	6.43
ΔNFA less ΔRM[b]	3.34	4.11	1.64
ΔMSBs	2.93	3.07	3.02
ΔFL[b]	1.60	4.34	4.79
Interest paid on MSBs 1-year (%)[c]	4.42	4.35	3.18
Interest paid on Gov bonds 5-year (%)[c]	4.75	4.78	4.70
Interest earned, U.S.T ave. 2-5 year (%)[c]	2.28	2.30	2.71
Interest differential MSB-U.S.T(%)[c]	2.14	2.06	1.48
Interest differential Gov bonds-U.S.T(%)[c]	2.47	2.48	1.99
Cost to BOK (% of GDP[a]):			
based on ΔNFA-ΔRM	0.07	0.09	0.02
based on ΔMSBs	0.06	0.06	0.05
Cost to MOFE (% of GDP[a]):			
based on ΔFL	0.04	0.11	0.10

Notes:
[a]2003 GDP for the Dec 2003 calculation, 2004 GDP for the others.
[b]FA = foreign assets at central bank, NFA = net foreign assets at central bank, RM = reserve or base money, FL = Foreign liabilities at central bank (proxy for MOFE's share of foreign reserves).
[c] Average over the period.

Table 4.B.2. Estimated flow cost of sterilization operations over 12 months: India.

	Dec 2003	June 2004	July 2006
Quantities (% of GDP[a]):			
ΔFA less ΔRM[b]	2.67	3.77	2.70
ΔGovernment securities	2.19	(MSS)	(MSS)
Interest forgone/paid, govt bonds 5–year (%)[c]	5.31	5.06	7.02
Interest earned, U.S.T average 2–5 year (%)[c]	2.28	2.54	4.58
Interest differential (%)[c]	3.03	2.52	2.38
Cost to RBI (% of GDP[a]):			
based on ΔFA-ΔRM	0.08	0.10	0.07
based on Δsecurities	0.07		

Notes:
[a]2003 GDP for the Dec 2003 calculation, 2004 GDP for the others.
[b] FA = foreign assets, NFA = net foreign assets, RM = reserve or base money.
[c] Average over the period.

net cost.[40] For India, there was no clear "perfect storm" episode. The two 12-month periods with the largest increase in net foreign assets are the period ending June 2004 and that ending July 2006. In both episodes, the estimated flow cost was at most 0.1 percent of GDP. However, with Indian interest rates rising since 2004, the cost was kept high, despite the small-scale operations, compared to Korea.

B.2. Stock Cost: The Financial Opportunity Cost of Holding a Stock of Foreign Reserves

What are the foregone opportunities of holding safe but low-yielding foreign reserve assets? If the central bank (or the ministry) were to cease holding foreign assets, what would it hold instead? And how much of a gain would this alternative bring?

[40]However, the differential facing of the MOFE did not narrow as much as did that facing the BOK. This together with the bigger share of foreign reserves financing attributable to the MOFE after 2003 contributed to the larger cost incurred to the MOFE.

Generally, instead of holding a unit of foreign assets (earning x percent), the authorities could have held more domestic asset (earning y percent), or pay off costly liabilities (saving z percent), or done a combination of the two. However, the alternative(s) chosen ought to respect the balance sheet composition and institutional constraints. One could run into difficult cases in figuring out the alternatives. For instance, if a central bank is not able or allowed to purchase all the domestic government paper it needs to replace foreign reserves, what other domestic assets can it plausibly hold? Apart from domestic government paper, there are potentially many other domestic assets, some of them possibly very high-yielding (e.g., equities). However, not all can serve as institutionally plausible alternatives. Not respecting the implausibility of certain alternatives could grossly over- or under-estimate the opportunity cost.[41]

We estimate the stock opportunity costs for Korea and India at selected points in 2002–2006. We make the following assumptions regarding the alternatives to holding foreign reserves.[42] For Korea, the MOFE's alternative is to redeem the corresponding amount of bonds outstanding, while the BOK's alternative is first to pay off all outstanding MSBs and then exhaust the remainder on acquiring the benchmark three-year government bond. For India, we assume that the alternative to foreign reserves is five-year domestic government securities.[43]

Tables 4.B.3 and 4.B.4 show that the estimated stock costs are well under 1 percent of GDP per year. For Korea, the total cost was no more than 0.7 percent of GDP at the height of reserve accumulation in Q1 2004,

[41]For example, is it reasonable to think that Hong Kong's next best plausible option after paying off all Exchange Fund paper is to hold more shares in the Hang Seng Index (the only domestic currency financial asset the Exchange Fund currently holds)? Can the People's Bank of China be expected to consider holding more nonperforming bank assets as an alternative to foreign reserves?

[42]The assumptions are based on institutional plausibility rather than on optimality (in the sense of achieving the highest possible gain). In theory, the first next-best option is always the highest-interest alternative available. If the first alternative somehow cannot accommodate the entire stock of foreign reserves to be disposed of, then the next-most-costly alternative should be adopted, and so on.

[43]Up to March 2004, the central bank would bear the opportunity cost. Thereafter, the government, instead of the central bank, would bear the marginal opportunity cost under the Market Stabilization Scheme.

Table 4.B.3. Estimated cost (per annum) of holding foreign reserves: Korea.

	Dec 2002	Mar 2003	Dec 2003	Mar 2004	Dec 2005
Net foreign assets, BOK (% of GDP[a])	16.01	17.88	21.32	20.82	21.27
Yield diff. over U.S.T 2–5 year (%)[b]:					
MSB 1-year	2.02	2.27	2.14	2.06	0.03
Korean government bond 3-year	2.61	2.66	2.27	2.23	0.32
Korean government bond 5-year	2.41	2.47	2.47	2.48	0.58
BOK's gains from alternatives (% of GDP[a]):					
Pay off MSBs, then buy 3-year bonds	0.36	0.42	0.47	0.44	0.01
Switch all NFA to 3-year bonds	0.42	0.47	0.48	0.47	0.07
MOFE's gains from alternatives:					
Pay off 5-year bonds	0.10	0.11	0.14	0.21	0.05

Notes:
[a]2003 GDP for Dec 2002, Mar 2003, and Dec 2003 calculations; 2004 GDP for others.
[b]Average over the previous 12 months.

with the BOK and the MOFE bearing about two-thirds and one-third of this total, respectively.[44] As mentioned above, the decline in Korean interest rates through 2004 at a time when U.S. rates began to rise helped to

[44]In October 2003, a Citigroup study reportedly estimated the holding cost for Korea at 1.5 percent of GDP. Since the study was said to take the reserve stock to be 27 percent GDP, Citigroup's estimate implied a cost factor of over 5 percent. However, it is not immediately clear from the citing reference whether this refers to a gross or net cost. Using our assumptions, a gross cost (not yet net of yield on foreign assets) estimate for March and December 2003 is 1.22 percent and 1.25 percent of GDP, respectively.

Table 4.B.4. Estimated cost (per annum) of holding foreign reserves: India (central bank).

	Dec 2002	Mar 2003	Dec 2003	Mar 2004	Nov 2004	Dec 2005
Net foreign assets (% of GDP[a])	12.23	12.89	16.61	15.52	18.12	20.72
Yield diff. over U.S.T 2–5 year (%)[b]:						
Indian government bonds 5–year	3.46	3.62	3.03	2.80	2.81	2.65
Gains from alternatives (% of GDP[a]):						
Switch all NFA to 5-year bonds	0.42	0.47	0.50	0.43	0.51	0.55

Notes:
[a]2003 GDP for Dec 2002, Mar 2003, and Dec 2003 calculations; 2004 GDP for others.
[b]Average over the previous 12 months.

contain the cost. For India, the stock cost was just under 0.5 percent of GDP in March 2004, just before the Monetary Stabilisation Scheme was launched, but tended to rise subsequently in light of rising domestic interest rates.

Certainly, the "no foreign reserve" alternative assumption underlying these estimates is unrealistic, as it ignores the penalty the economy would incur in the eyes of rating agencies and the international financial markets. But this assumption represents a kind of worst-case scenario. If the "appropriate" level of reserves is higher than zero, then the more realistic estimate of the opportunity cost of holding the current level of reserves ought to be less than that indicated by our baseline calculation. For example, if we consider the "appropriate" or "warranted" level of reserves for Korea in March 2004 to be 123 billion U.S. dollars (3 months imports plus short-term external debt), then the opportunity cost of holding the "excess" 40 billion U.S. dollars of reserves would be only about 0.30 percent of GDP (Genberg *et al.*, 2005, p. 26).

References

Anderson, J (2004a). The Asian liquidity primer. *Asian Economic Perspectives*, 29 March. UBS Investment Research.

Anderson, J (2004b). Asia sterilization update. *Asian Economic Comment*, 1 November. UBS Investment Research.

BIS (2007). 77th *Annual Report*.

Bank of Korea (BOK) (2007). *Annual Report 2006*.

Calvo, GA (1991). The perils of sterilization. *IMF Staff Papers*, 38, 921–926.

Central Bank of China (CBC) (1995). *Annual Report*.

Central Bank of China (CBC) (2006). Central bank profits characterized by a high degree of uncertainty. Press release, 25 December.

Chu, KH (2004). Reflections on the new Taiwan dollar appreciation in the mid 1980's. *HKCER Letters*, Vol. 79. Hong Kong.

Fernandez-Arias, E and P Montiel (1995). The surge in capital inflows to developing countries: Prospects and policy response. *Policy Research Working Paper* No. 1473. World Bank.

Frankel, JA (1994). Sterilization of money inflows: Difficult (Calvo) or easy (Reisen). IMF Working Paper, WP/94/159.

Genberg, H, R McCauley, YC Park and A Persaud (2005). Official reserves and currency management in Asia: Myth, reality and the future. *Geneva Reports on the World Economy*, No. 7. International Center for Monetary and Banking Studies.

Goldstein, M (1995). Coping with too much of a good thing: Policy responses for large capital inflows in developing countries. Policy Research Working Paper No. 1507. World Bank.

Higgins M and T Klitgaard (2004). Reserve accumulation: Implications for global capital flows and financial markets. *Current Issues in Economics and Finance*, 10. Federal Reserve Bank of New York.

Ho, C and RN McCauley (2008). Resisting appreciation and accumulating reserves in Asia: Examining the domestic financial consequences. Forthcoming as BIS Working Paper.

Hong Kong Monetary Authority (2008). Half-yearly monetary and financial stability report, June.

Kang, TS and G Ma (2007). Recent episodes of credit card distress in Asia. *BIS Quarterly Review*, June, 55–68.

Le Mesurier, A (2004). The rising costs of Asian sterilization. *Asia-Pacific Economic Analyst*, 25 June. Goldman Sachs.

Ma, G and RN McCauley (2004). Reining in growth in China. Paper presented to the *Euro 50 2004 Roundtable "Asia in the International Monetary System,"* Beijing, 24–25 June. www.euro50.org/2004/beijing04/chinapolicy.pdf.

Mathur, S (2003). Why are central banks sterilising? *Asian Economic Perspectives*, 7 August. UBS Investment Research.

McCauley, RN (2004). Comments on Ito's "Inflation Targeting and Japan." In *The Future of Inflation Targeting*, C Kent and S Guttman (eds.). Sydney: Reserve Bank of Australia.

McCauley, RN and B Fung (2003). Choosing instruments in managing dollar foreign exchange reserves. *BIS Quarterly Review*, March, 39–46.

Mohanty, M and P Turner (2006). The domestic implications of foreign exchange reserve accumulation in emerging markets. *BIS Quarterly Review*, September, 39–52.

Ogus, S (2003). The limits of sterilisation. *DSGAsia*, 26 May.

Ogus, S (2005). The limits of sterilisation revisited. *DSGAsia*, 12 January.

Reserve Bank of India (RBI) (2007). *Macroeconomic and Monetary Developments*, 23 April.

Spiegel, MM (1995). Sterilization of capital inflows through the banking sector: Evidence from Asia. *FRBSF Economic Review*, No. 3.

Wang, J (1999). 財經巨擘: 俞國華生涯行腳/ 俞國華口述, 王駿執筆, 商智文化出版, 臺北市 (*The Financial Authority: The Life Journey of Yu Guo-hua*, narrated by Yu Guo-hua, written by Wang Jun. Taipei: Sunbright Publishing.)

White, WR (2006). Is price stability enough? BIS Working Paper No. 205.

Yetsenga, R (2007). Asian FX special: The response to currency appreciation matures. HSBC Global Research, June.

Yu, Y (2008). Managing capital flows: The case of the People's Republic of China, *Asian Development Bank Institute*, Discussion Paper No. 96, 13 March.

PART III

CAPITAL FLOWS, SPILLOVERS, AND INTERDEPENDENCE

CHAPTER 5

MACROECONOMIC CONDITIONS AND CAPITAL FLOWS IN EMERGING EAST ASIAN ECONOMIES

Alex Mandilaras and Helen Popper

5.1. Introduction

Many small, East Asian economies have yet to recover the investment rates that prevailed prior to the 1997 crisis.[1] Nevertheless, their savings have been high. The substantial surfeit of savings over investment has meant that the last decade has seen large net outflows of capital from East Asia. Overall, for the last decade, East Asian savings have financed investment elsewhere.

This chapter examines the region's net capital outflows in the context of some of the macroeconomic conditions that may be contributing to them. A country's own macroeconomic conditions form the natural starting point for examining the fluctuations in its overall capital flows. At the same time, the conditions in the greater region also may be important, as may be the conditions in some of the large economies elsewhere in the world. This chapter therefore discusses the empirical links between East Asian capital flows and both internal and external macroeconomic conditions. In discussing the internal conditions of a country, we are interested in such things as the growth of the overall economy and that of investment, as well as in the country's domestic financial conditions and the openness of its financial markets to international capital flows. In terms of the external macroeconomic conditions, we are interested in exploring the influences of regional conditions as well as the importance of macroeconomic conditions outside the region, such as in Europe, and in the largest single recipient of the outflows, the U.S.

---

[1] Kramer (2006) describes the protracted nature of the investment slump, and some of the factors that may be contributing to it.

The chapter's broad geographic sweep is intended to allow us to consider a number of prevalent arguments about the underlying causes of East Asia's recent capital outflows. Of particular interest at present is the argument that it is the policies and conditions of the U.S. that have been and continue to drive the region's capital outflows.[2] In this view, the region's capital outflows are attributed to low U.S. saving rates, either as an outcome of sheer profligacy or as an outcome of substantial improvements in the prospects for U.S. growth.[3] While the evidence on this front is mixed, we discuss some new work in this area that seems to suggest that the U.S. is not the driver of the region's capital flow behavior.

We also discuss some of the more general explanations of the larger puzzle of reverse capital flows — that is, why capital is sent so often from emerging economies to richer ones instead of the reverse. Where capital is scarce, it should earn a high return. Rich economies are more capital-abundant than are emerging economies; so capital should earn a lower return in rich economies than in emerging ones. At least by some measures, this appears to be the case: IMF estimates of the return to capital for the decade from 1994 to 2003 were less than 8 percent in the U.K., just under 10 percent in the U.S., and less than 8 percent in the G-7 economies as a whole; over the same period, the estimated return was about 15 percent in emerging Asia, about 13 percent in Latin America, and about 11 percent in other emerging markets.[4] One expects capital to flow to where its return is

[2]See, for example, the comments of Fitoussi (2007), who writes (with regard to developments in Asia): "Today's global imbalances turn around the increasing current account deficit of the United States .... The only way to assure a smooth absorption of the current global imbalances, at least in the short run, is sustained growth in Europe and in Japan, together with a more cautious fiscal policy in the US .... This ambitious change of perspective is the only hope for avoiding a potentially devastating crisis."

[3]Obstfeld and Rogoff (2004) and Roubini and Setser (2004), emphasize low U.S. saving. Engel and Rogers (2006) examine the implications of high U.S. growth prospects relative to the rest of the world. Bems *et al.* (2007) compare the role of U.S. productivity improvements with changes in U.S. macroeconomic policies.

[4]See IMF (2004), but note that the estimates are controversial. Caselli and Feyrer (forthcoming) roughly equate marginal products across the countries. Of course, even with roughly equal marginal products, the net flows from emerging to mature economies remain puzzling, if somewhat less so.

highest.[5] So, on the face of it, it is puzzling why there is now so much sustained lending from emerging economies, such as many of those in East Asia, to richer ones, such as the U.S. and the U.K.

One intriguing answer to the "reverse" capital flows puzzle relies on the relative efficiency of financial markets. This answer has been formalized in distinct ways by Caballero *et al.* (2006) and by Mendoza *et al.* (2007).[6] Essentially, they suggest that when emerging economies lack the sufficient financial infrastructure for matching borrowers and lenders efficiently in their own countries, savers in those countries send their assets abroad despite high domestic returns to capital. International differences in domestic financial access, along with growth explain the direction of net capital flows; and, countries like the U.S. and the U.K. implicitly export financial services. In this regard, the approach contrasts with other explanations that rely on an absence of fundamental investment opportunities in the emerging markets. Such explanations also address the recent low real interest rates prevailing globally, pointing as their source to developments in the emerging economies' (including those in East Asia) rates of investment and saving. See, for example, Bernanke's (2005) comments on the "global saving glut." The veracity of this view has important implications for policy and for forecasting. Other things being equal, this view implies that as East Asian financial markets deepen, more of their savings will be retained. In that case, we will see diminished capital outflows; and, correspondingly, we will see renewed investment within the region.

The next section of this chapter describes in more detail the behavior of the capital flows in some of the region's economies. Some of their key macroeconomic conditions, including the conditions of their financial markets are described in Section 5.3. Section 5.4 presents some of the recent econometric approaches to understanding the data's underlying links; and, the evidence from those studies is discussed. The chapter ends with a brief summary of some of the key empirical findings and their implications.

---

[5]Of course, as noted by Lucas (1990), other factors that are complementary to capital also affect its return. Acemoglu *et al.* (2001, 2002) and Alfaro *et al.* (forthcoming), among many others, emphasize the role of institutions.

[6]The approach that is formalized in these two papers is also suggested by arguments and empirical work of Prasad *et al.* (2007), whose careful empirical work highlights the financial sector impediments and limited absorptive capacity of emerging economies.

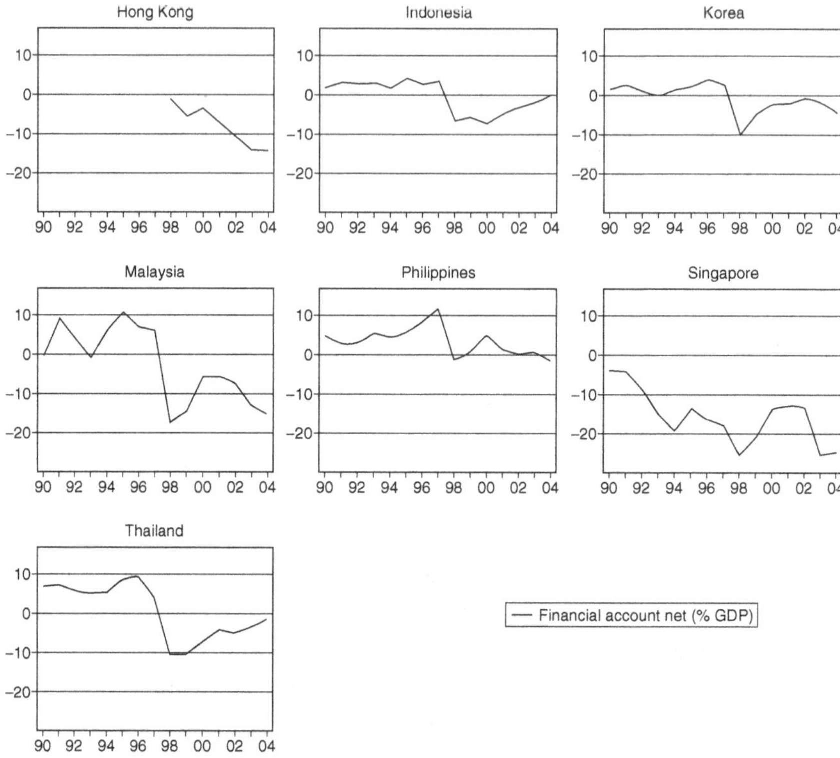

Fig. 5.1. Net capital inflows.
Source: IMF's Balance of Payments Statistics.

5.2. Recent Capital Flows

Figure 5.1 provides a picture of the recent behavior of net capital inflows into some of the economies within the region. Specifically, it gives the annual net flows from 1990 through 2004 for Hong Kong, Indonesia, Korea, Malaysia, the Philippines, Singapore, and Thailand. This list includes all of the emerging market economies represented in the Executives' Meeting of East Asia-Pacific Central Banks (EMEAP), except China.[7] Capital flow data are taken from the IMF's Balance of Payments Statistics and include

[7]The other EMEAP members are Australia, New Zealand, and Japan. These economies, along with China, are excluded because in one way or another they are out of step with the countries that are the focus here: either their size, their pace of investment, or their level of

both private and public flows.[8] The figure gives each economy's net capital inflows as a fraction of its GDP. (Positive values represent net inflows into the country, and negative values represent net outflows.) The largest flows relative to GDP belong to Hong Kong, Malaysia, and Singapore. All three countries now have very large net outflows relative to GDP, with Singapore's outflows exceeding one quarter of its GDP. Indonesia has had the smallest overall flows relative to its GDP; and, in the most recent period, the Philippines and Korea have had limited flows as well. Despite the large differences across these economies, there are some obvious similarities. In most of the countries depicted, total net capital inflows fell precipitously during the Asian crisis. Net capital inflows turned into net outflows after the crisis in Indonesia, Korea, Malaysia, and Thailand. For the most part, total net inflows remained well below their pre-crisis levels.

Figure 5.2 allows us to see how the components of these countries' flows have fared over the same period. The compositional breakdown is particularly interesting in light of the implications of the different theoretical approaches to understanding the region's net capital outflows. At least some of the different theoretical approaches suggest distinctive patterns of financial flows across their categories.[9] For example, the financial

---

industrialization makes them very different from the economies that are the focus of interest here. Also see Chapter 9 of this volume.

[8]Lane and Milesi-Ferretti (2006) have compiled data on the size and composition of external assets and liabilities of over 100 countries for more than three decades, through 2004. Their dataset provides an alternative source for constructing international capital flows. The most important difference between their data and that used in Figure 5.1 is that their evaluation of assets and liabilities explicitly accounts for valuation effects. That is, when a country's exchange rate appreciates, the valuation of its foreign assets falls, and the valuation of its liabilities rises. Thus, when capital flows (the changes in assets and liabilities) are calculated using their data, their value reflects a combination of the underlying, active flows and the exchange rate valuation effect. Inclusion of the valuation effects changes the interpretation of the measured flows: with valuation effects, the measured flows include "passive," paper gains and losses. While inclusion of the passive flows is important in many applications, it can be distracting here because of the variability of the valuation effect. Essentially, the valuation of gains and losses are so large that they swamp the behavior of the underlying flows.

[9]A number of empirical studies also have found the composition of total flows to be important. For example, Campion and Neumann (2004) link the composition of inflows into Latin America with official barriers to international financial flows. While they do not control for output, they find that capital controls affect the composition, but not the volume

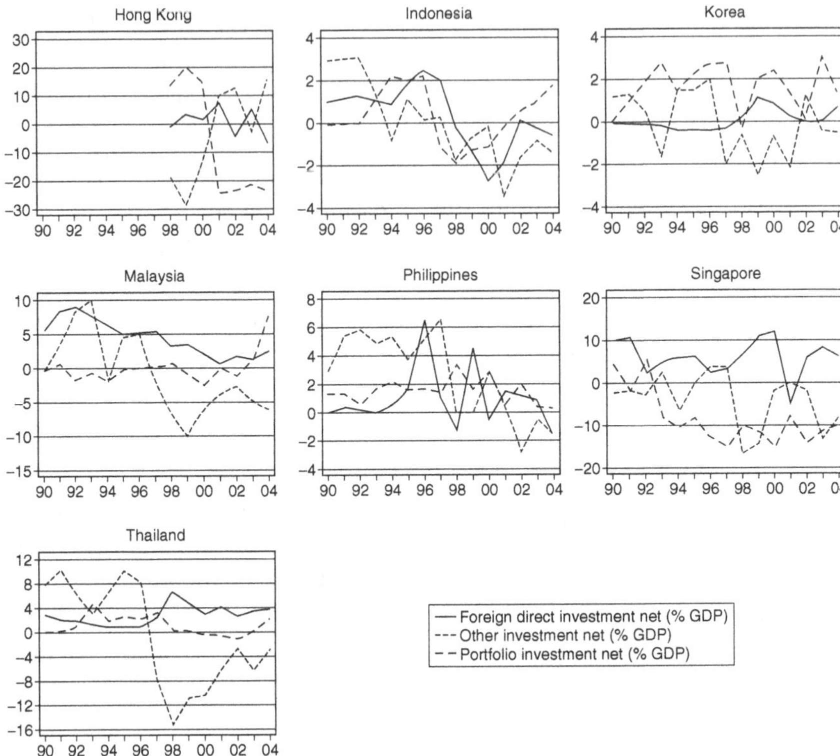

Fig. 5.2. Net capital inflow composition.
Source: IMF's Balance of Payments Statistics.

efficiency and financial development approaches of Caballero *et al.* (2006) and of Mendoza *et al.* (2007) might be interpreted as suggesting one thing for portfolio flows, and quite another for FDI. Specifically, it might be in keeping with their approaches to find that international portfolio flows moving from the emerging economies with little domestic financial development or stability to the mature economies with correspondingly mature financial markets. FDI, on the other hand, might flow in the opposite direction. In contrast, some of the other explanations of the outflows by themselves do not suggest any obvious differences across the types of flows.

of flows, implying that the various categories are substitutes, rather than complements. Likewise, Neumann, *et al.* (2006) have used panel approaches to explore the links between the volatility of various flows and financial liberalization. See also Sula and Willett (2007), Fernandez-Arias and Hausmann (2000), and Chuhan *et al.* (1996).

In particular, substantial net inflows of FDI would be somewhat more difficult to reconcile with either the "savings glut" explanation, which relies on low investment opportunities in Asia, or with the explanations that rely solely on U.S. factors, such as high U.S. growth and productivity or expansionary U.S. fiscal policy.

Included in Figure 5.2 are portfolio investment, FDI, and other investments (which include trade credits, loans, and other assets and liabilities). Portfolio investment flows are given by long-dashed line. As shown, portfolio flows behaved very much like total flows around the time of the Asian crisis in Indonesia, Korea, and the Philippines, which were already among the economies with the smallest shares of portfolio investment relative to GDP. Like total inflows, portfolio inflows in these countries declined sharply at the time of the Asian crisis. But, unlike total flows, portfolio flows in these countries have largely recovered since the crisis. The portfolio flows of Malaysia and Thailand have likewise returned to their earlier levels. It is only Hong Kong and Singapore that continue to see substantial net outflows in the form of portfolio investment.

The category of other investment, which includes trade credits and bank lending, given by the short-dashed line, fell sharply whenever total flows fell sharply. By and large, the category of other investments tends to move with total flows. Hong Kong is the only exception. Hong Kong's other investment inflows have risen substantially since 1999, despite fairly steady increases in total outflows.

Net FDI inflows are shown by the solid line. Overall, net FDI flows have fluctuated less than either portfolio flows or total flows. This is particularly apparent during the crisis period, when declines in net FDI flows were either more attenuated or asynchronous with the timing of the crisis. None of the countries experienced the same precipitous declines in net direct investment that they experienced in total inflows. In fact, FDI continued to flow into Korea, the Philippines, and Thailand during the crisis.

While these observations about the behavior of the component flows do not constitute a test of any of the main explanations proffered above, they are at least in keeping with the ideas suggested by the theoretical work of Caballero *et al.* (2006), and of Mendoza *et al.* (2007). At the very least, the inflows of FDI seem to suggest that the total outflows are not due to a dearth of real investment opportunities in the region.

5.3. Macroeconomic Conditions

We now turn to the macroeconomic conditions within these East Asian emerging economies. The macroeconomic data we examine are taken primarily from the World Bank's *World Development Indicators*. Figure 5.3 gives us some feeling for the economies' recent overall macroeconomic conditions by providing information about GDP and investment. Here, growth in real GDP per capita is shown by the solid line, and the change in gross fixed capital formation is shown by the dashed line. As is well known, everyone of these economies experienced a sharp decline in per capita real GDP growth following the Asian crisis. A few of these economies are once again experiencing or surpassing the rapid rates of growth of the pre-crisis

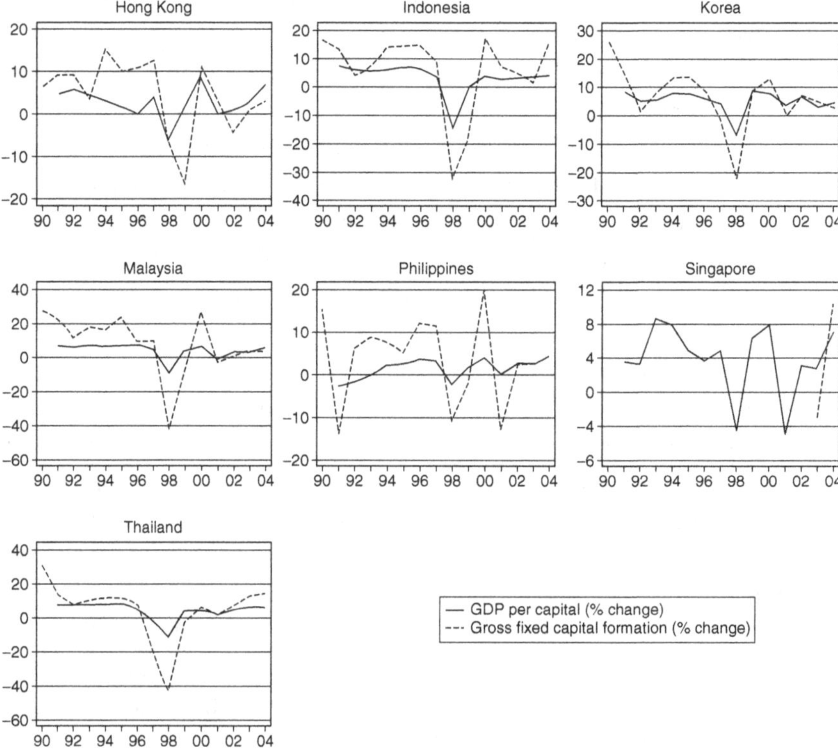

Fig. 5.3. Growth of GDP and capital formation.
Source: World Bank's *World Development Indicators*.

period: the growth rates in Hong Kong, the Philippines, and Singapore are all at or above their earlier rates; and none of the economies examined here continues to languish overall. For investment, the sharp decline and rebound has been, on the whole, even more dramatic. Malaysia and Thailand saw their gross fixed capital formation decline by more than 40 percent during the crisis, and then surged sharply afterward. All of the economies for which we have data saw sharp declines in their investment rates, which have not, overall, quite recovered.

Also important are these countries' financial conditions. Figure 5.4 focuses on two aspects of these conditions: financial market capitalization and international financial market openness. The figure's solid lines provide indicators of the international financial market openness of these economies. The indicators used here rely on a *de facto* measure of openness, the

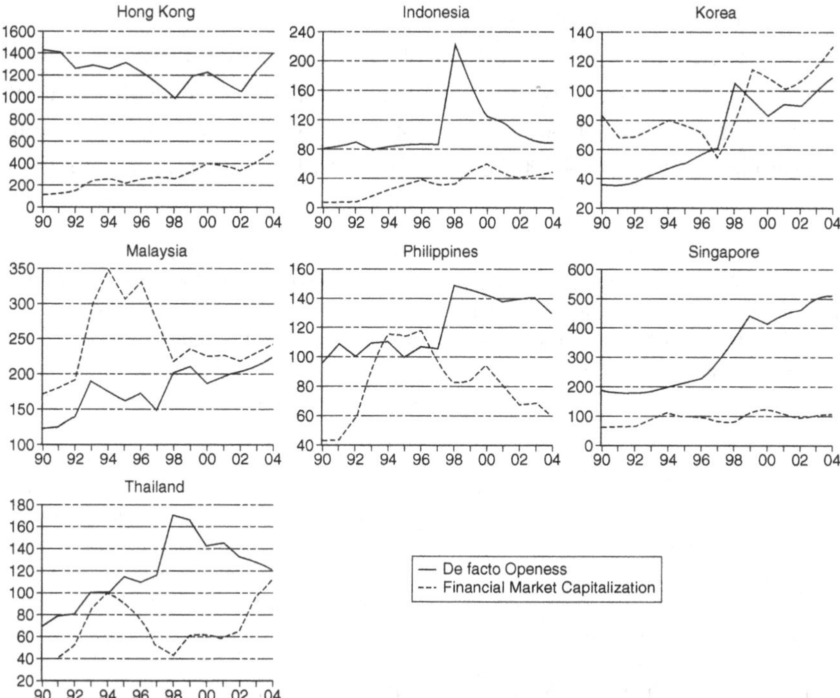

Fig. 5.4. Financial market capitalization and financial openness.
Sources: Lane and Milesi-Ferretti (2006), Beck *et al.* (2006), and Mandilaras and Popper (2008).

sum of gross stocks of foreign assets and liabilities as a ratio to GDP.[10] The measures rely on the data compiled by Lane and Milesi-Ferretti (2006). Note that the scales differ across the graphs in this figure. By the *de facto* measure of financial market openness used here, Hong Kong was and continues to have the most internationally open financial markets. Singapore's *de facto* openness has steadily risen over the period, and its financial markets are also very internationally open by this measure. The other economies fall in a distant pack. Korea and Malaysia both have more open financial markets than those prior to the crisis; while — by this measure — Indonesia, the Philippines, and Thailand have left their peak levels of openness behind. (For Indonesia, the decline roughly coincides with a sharp decline indicated by the Chinn and Ito Index (2007b), a principal components-based measure, though their measure does not indicate the earlier rise.) By 2004, Indonesia had the lowest level of *de facto* capital market openness in the set of economies that we examine.

The dashed lines give measures of each economy's financial market capitalization as a share of its GDP. The capitalization measure includes the capitalized value of both an economy's equity market and its private and public bond markets. These data are taken from Beck *et al.* (2006).[11]

[10]Other measures of financial openness tend to rely on summary statistics of regulatory indicators. While often useful, such measures have their own drawbacks. Most importantly, it is difficult for such measures to capture the *effectiveness* of controls, and — relatedly — it is difficult to know how best to consolidate information about different types of *de jure* barriers to financial flows. Of course, the *de facto* indicator is not without its problems. Some countries with large flows will be characterized as being open, despite perhaps having significant policy barriers to capital mobility. (China is a telling example.) Moreover, as a summary measure neither the *de facto* nor the *de jure* measure does a good job of capturing and consolidating the barriers to financial market openness that are not uniform in nature. In the case of the measure used here, barriers to capital inflows and to outflows are implicitly treated the same manner. Likewise, this measure does not capture compositional distinctions. Despite these limitations, the *de facto* measure is a reasonable starting point in that it reflects both explicit and implicit barriers. It is the analog of the standard measure of trade openness, the sum of exports and imports relative to GDP; and it shares much of its usefulness and many of its limitations.

[11]Like the measure of financial market openness described above, the capitalization measure is only one of a possible range of indicators that one might examine. Demirgüç-Kunt and Levine (1995) provide an important, early assessment of many of the measures and how they are related. Alternative measures of financial development that have been important in the literature include the ratio of M2 relative to GDP and the ratio of private credit to GDP.

Note again that the scales are different, with Hong Kong having the highest bond and stock market capitalization, with its combined capitalization now exceeding four times its GDP, while Indonesia is at the low end of this group, with capitalization closer to half of its GDP. As shown in the figure, market capitalization, while fluctuating, has increased overall during the period in Hong Kong, Indonesia, Korea, and Singapore. However, in Malaysia, the Philippines, and Thailand, market capitalization dropped substantially around the time of the Asian crisis; and, in Malaysia and the Philippines, capitalization remains well below its previous levels.

One typically expects financial market maturity to reflect institutional changes that develop only slowly over time.[12] Thus, the fluctuations in the bond and stock market capitalizations that we observe here may not be entirely indicative of the kind of deep changes that go hand in hand with the maturation of financial markets. Nevertheless, since the ability to use financial markets also fluctuates with conditions that change over just a few years, these measures do give some kind of indication of changes in the accessibility of financing in each of these domestic markets. To the extent that significant declines in bond and equity market capitalization reflect diminished available opportunities for financial intermediation in some of these economies, they may be suggestive of a deterioration in the functioning of their financial markets. This capitalization measure perhaps may be most relevant when considering the financial market episodes described in the approach of Caballero *et al.* (2006): "episodes when it cannot generate 'enough' reliable savings instruments." These may be just the problems faced by Malaysia and the Philippines. Of course, the data in all of these graphs are by themselves only suggestive of the links that may underlie them. Moreover, the experiences of Malaysia and the Philippines are in a sense belied by that of Hong Kong, which has at once the highest capitalization ratio and the largest of capital outflows relative to its GDP. A more thorough consideration of the relationships among these variables is in order. Section 5.4 discusses some of the works that more carefully assess the links between capital flows and their potential determinants.

[12]Some argue that the key institutional arrangements reflect developments that are centuries old. See, for example, Acemoglu *et al.* (2001 and 2002).

5.4. Econometric Approaches and Evidence

The theoretical approaches discussed above suggest that, conditional on sufficient growth, greater financial development or financial accessibility within a country should be expected to go hand in hand with greater financial inflows into that country. The empirical evidence of ties between financial inflows and financial development has been more nuanced. Recent work suggests that while there is evidence that the posited, positive relationship exists, there are important threshold effects in nearly every facet of it. For example, in two panel studies, Chinn and Ito (2005 and 2007a) find support for a positive relationship between financial development and capital inflows only for countries that have reached a certain stage of industrialization.[13] For less developed and emerging market countries, their findings are reversed: for the non-industrialized countries, greater financial development is linked to higher savings. In the absence of correspondingly higher investment, this has meant that greater financial development has led to greater capital outflows for these countries. Moreover, the authors find that a positive association between inflows and financial development occurs only when highly developed legal systems and open financial markets are in place. Relatedly, they also find that foreign financing itself leads to equity market development, but once again there is a threshold effect. This finding only holds if there is sufficiently high institutional development. Their findings are in keeping with those of Kose *et al.* (2006), who also find that threshold effects are important: it appears that countries need to have stable policies and institutions in place to clearly benefit from financial globalization.

Much of the empirical work in this area has relied on panel estimation. While the panel approach is useful, it implicitly constrains the dynamic interactions among the variables of interest. It would be desirable to allow for dynamic interactions among financial flows, financial development, financial openness, and growth. It would likewise be instructive to allow for interactions across countries. This would make it possible to explicitly test for whether the conditions outside a country have a hand in determining its capital flows.

---

[13] Chinn and Ito (2007a) use a panel study of 19 industrialized and 70 developing countries between 1986 and 2005.

An alternative estimation approach would be to use a vector autoregression (VAR) framework. The framework of the VAR makes the relationships among the included variables explicit, and it allows for very general dynamic interactions among the variables. Of course, the VAR's appealing dynamic specification comes at a cost. Feasible estimation requires stringent limitations on the number of variables that can be included in the analysis. In many cases, this renders the VAR particularly susceptible to omitted variable bias. For this reason, VARs have not been heavily relied on in these studies until very recently. The most recent work using a VAR framework in this area builds on the pioneering work of Stock and Watson (2002). Stock and Watson have developed a data-rich technique to address this particular limitation of the VAR framework.[14] Their approach adds to VAR the ability to address the omitted variable problem by conditioning on the key information contained in a large number of variables. Mandilaras and Popper (2008) use this approach (a factor-augmented VAR, or FAVAR) to enrich the VAR and allow for dynamic interactions across both variables and countries.

Using FAVAR to examine the capital flows of small, East Asian emerging markets, Mandilaras and Popper (2008) find that changes in capital flows do indeed appear to respond to financial market capitalization. The flows, however, do not appear to respond much to the changes that have been observed in the *de facto* openness of these economies. Changes in financial market openness seem to matter very little for any of the major components of the region's international capital flows. The FAVAR approach also allows the authors to explicitly examine the role of U.S. macroeconomic conditions in determining the flows within the region. Overall, they find that while U.S. macroeconomic conditions seem to matter (very much) for growth within the region, U.S. macroeconomic conditions on their own have played no obvious role in the behavior of East Asian capital flows over the period.[15]

[14] Stock and Watson (2002) initially demonstrate the usefulness of the approach in forecasting. Its application to monetary policy issues is illustrated most notably by Bernanke *et al.* (2005). The technique has also been applied by Lagana and Mountford (2005) to examine U.K. monetary policy and to a study of the term structure by Mönch (2006). Smith and Zoega (2005) were the first, to our knowledge, to apply the approach to international panel data.

[15] Specifically, Mandilaras and Popper (2008) examine the same eight economies discussed here, over the period 1990–2004. They explicitly test and repeatedly reject the hypothesis that U.S. macroeconomic conditions Granger cause changes in the total and component flows

Their results simply do not support the argument that it has been primarily the macroeconomic conditions in the U.S. that have driven the capital out of the small, emerging East Asian economies.

5.5. Concluding Remarks

The capital outflows from East Asia are one piece in the larger picture of global imbalances. Outflows from East Asia must correspond to inflows elsewhere, and inflows to the U.S. are large indeed. Nevertheless, we cannot substantiate the claim that it is the policies and macroeconomic conditions of the U.S. that lie at the root of the East Asian outflows. The U.S. policies and conditions do, however, play a role in these economies. The U.S. conditions have been found to be significant, independent determinants of growth in the region. It is through this route — through an influence on growth rates, rather than through a direct influence on the behavior of capital flows — that we should expect the policies and macroeconomic conditions of the U.S. to continue to affect the economies of the region.

Within the region's individual economies, investment rates overall remain substantially lower than they were in the heyday of the mid-1990s. The theoretical approaches discussed in this chapter have suggested that problems with financial intermediation may be limiting the deployment of saving in the savers' own domestic economies. Improving the climate for investment by, for example, improving financial infrastructure and corporate governance, would be likely to increase investment. However, the development of good financial intermediation should be viewed as an important objective for the sake of a well-functioning domestic economy. As important as improved financial intermediation is a policy objective in its own right, the empirical studies that we have reviewed here remind us that it should not be viewed as an instrument for increasing net capital

---

of the East Asian economies they examine. In contrast, they cannot reject the hypothesis that in these countries, U.S. conditions do Granger cause growth. The U.S. macroeconomic conditions do, indeed appear to be important determinants of growth, above and beyond the influence both of each country's own lagged growth and of the broader conditions in the region. The authors also provide an empirical interpretation of Caballero *et al.* (2006). They cannot reject the empirical interpretation, but they note that their result rests largely on the importance of financial market capitalization in general, and it derives little from the international differences in growth that are also important to the Caballero *et al's* framework.

inflows (or reducing outflows) in emerging economies. Financial institutions do seem to matter, but increases in measures of their accessibility or maturation do not seem to be linked to increased capital inflows into developing or emerging economies. On the contrary, increased financial development seems to be linked more closely to increased capital outflows — at least until threshold levels of institutional and economic development are reached.

References

Acemoglu, D, S Johnson and JA Robinson (2001). The colonial origins of comparative development: An empirical investigation. *American Economic Review*, 91, 13–69.

Acemoglu, D, S Johnson and JA Robinson (2002). Reversal of fortune: Geography and institutions in the making of the modern world income distribution. *The Quarterly Journal of Economics*, 117, 12–31.

Alfaro, L, S Kalemli-Ozcan and V Volosovych (forthcoming). Why doesn't capital flow from rich to poor countries? An empirical investigation. *The Review of Economics and Statistics*.

Beck, T, A Demirgüç-Kunt and R Levine (2000). A new database on financial development and structure. *World Bank Economic Review*, 14, 597–605.

Bems, R, L Dedola and F Smets (2007). U.S. imbalances: The role of technology and fiscal and monetary policy. ECB Working Paper No. 719, January.

Bernanke, B (2005). Remarks at the Sandridge lecture, Virginia Association of Economics (Richmond, VA, March).

Bernanke, B, J Boivin and P Eliasz (2005). Measuring the effects of monetary policy: A factor-augmented vector autoregressive (FAVAR) approach. *The Quarterly Journal of Economics*, 120, 387–422.

Caballero, RJ, E Farhi and P-O Gourinchas (2006). An equilibrium model of "Global Imbalances" and low interest rates. NBER Working Paper No. 11996.

Campion, MK and R Neumann (2004). Compositional effects of capital controls — Evidence from Latin America. *The North American Journal of Economics and Finance*, 15, 161–178.

Caselli, F and J Feyrer (forthcoming). The marginal product of capital. *Quarterly Journal of Economics*.

Chinn, M and H Ito (2005). Current account balances, financial development and institutions: Assaying the world "Savings Glut". NBER Working Paper No. 11761.

Chinn, M and H Ito (2007a). East Asia and global imbalances: Saving, investment, and financial development. NBER Working Paper No. 13364.

Chinn, M and H Ito (2007b). Notes on the calculation of the Chinn–Ito financial openness variable. Working Paper, University of Wisconsin.

Chuhan, P, G Perez-Quiros and H Popper (1996). International capital flows: Do short-term investment and direct investment differ? World Bank Policy Research Working Paper No. 1669.

Demirgüç-Kunt, A and R Levine (1995). Stock market development and financial intermediaries: Stylized facts. World Bank Policy Research Working Paper No. 1462.

Engel, C and JH Rogers (2006). The U.S. current account deficit and the expected share of world output. Working Paper, University of Wisconsin.

Fernandez-Arias, E and R Hausmann (2000). Foreign direct investment: Good cholesterol? IADB, Research Department Working Paper No. 417.

Fitoussi, J-P (2007). Exchange rate policy — Potential global imbalances especially with regard to developments in Asia. European Parliament, Committee for economic and monetary affairs, Briefing Paper, June.

IMF (2004). *World Economic Outlook 2004*. Washington, DC: IMF.

IMF (2006). *World Economic Outlook 2006*. Washington, DC: IMF.

Kose, MA, E Prasad, K Rogoff and S-J Wei (2006). Financial globalization: A reappraisal. IMF Research Department Working Paper No. 06/189.

Kramer, C (2006). Asia's investment puzzle. *Finance and Development*, 43, June.

Lagana, G and A Mountford (2005). Measuring monetary policy in the UK: A factor-augmented vector autoregression model approach. *Manchester School*, 73(s1), 77–98.

Lane, P and GM Milesi-Ferretti (2006). The external wealth of nations mark II: Revised and extended estimates of foreign assets and liabilities, 1970–2004. IIIS Discussion Paper No. 126.

Lucas, R (1990). Why doesn't capital flow from rich to poor countries. *American Economic Review*, 80, 92–96.

Mandilaras, A and H Popper (2008). Capital flows, capitalization, and openness in East Asian emerging economies. Working Paper, Santa Clara University.

Mendoza, E, V Quadrini and J-V Rios-Rull (2007). Financial integration, financial deepness and global imbalances. NBER Working Paper No. 12909.

Mönch, E (2006). Forecasting the yield curve in a data-rich environment: A no-arbitrage factor-augmented VAR approach. Working Paper No. 544, European Central Bank.

Neumann, R, R Penl and A Tanku (2006). Volatility of capital flows and financial liberalization: Do specific flows respond differently? Working Paper, University of Wisconsin, Milwaukee.

Obstfeld, M and K Rogoff (2004). The unsustainable US current account position revisited. NBER Working Paper No. 10869.

Prasad, E, RG Rajan and A Subramanian (2007). Foreign capital and economic growth. *Brookings Papers on Economic Activity*, 1, 153–209.

Roubini, N and B Setser (2004). The U.S. as a net debtor: The sustainability of the U.S. external imbalances. Mimeo, Stern School of Business, NYU.

Smith, R and G Zoega (2005). Unemployment, investment and global expected returns: A panel FAVAR approach. Birbeck Working Papers in Economics and Finance, No. 0524.

Stock, JH and MW Watson (2002). Macroeconomic forecasting using diffusion indexes. *Journal of Business and Economic Statistics*, 20, 147–162.

Sula, O and TD Willett (2007). Reversibility of different types of capital flows to emerging markets. Working Paper, Claremont Graduate University.

CHAPTER 6

MEASURING SPILLOVER AND CONVERGENCE EFFECTS IN THE ASIA-PACIFIC REGION

Andrew Hughes Hallett and Christian Richter[*]

6.1. Introduction

The U.S. has long been regarded as the dominant economy of the Asia-Pacific region, and hence the locomotive of the global economy or the economy of first resort through its consumption and use of intermediates in production, trade in sophisticated manufactures, supply of investment capital, and financial stability. However, the rise of China as a major global trader in cheaper manufactures and intermediates, and of Japan as a provider of sophisticated manufactures and source of finance for regional development, may have changed all that. These two economies may have become just as important as trading partners and locomotive economies for the other Asian economies, and may also now have significant spillovers, by virtue of their size, on the U.S. Moreover, their rapidly expanding stocks of foreign assets, acquired through the large and continuing trade imbalances in the region, gives them a certain influence over monetary conditions and financial stability (even if exchange rates are becoming a little more flexible). In that case the pattern of spillovers may have changed, perhaps even to the point that they have become locomotives for the region, while the U.S. is playing a supporting and possibly beggar-thy-neighbor role.

[*]We are grateful to Richard Burdekin, Sven Arndt, Kishen Rajan, Jürgen Wolters and participants at the Claremont-Bologna-SCAPE workshop for helpful comments. Richter gratefully acknowledges the financial support from the Jubiläumsfond of the Austrian National Bank (project no: 9152). We also gratefully acknowledge financial support from the Leverhulme Trust.

Those are the changes we wish to test for in this chapter. Enhanced trade and financial integration effects come in three parts: an increased convergence (coherence, correlation) between the economies; an increased impact (spillovers) from events in one economy on another; and stronger lead/lag relationships between economies (a lag for those supplying materials, process inputs, consumption goods or services; but a lead for those supplying investment goods, investment parts, FDI or finance, etc.) as shown in Chaplyguin *et al.* (2006). Notice also that the trade in investment goods, FDI and possibly network production will strengthen the correlations between long cycles; while trade in consumption goods, materials and intermediate inputs will imply strength at business cycle frequencies. We examine these cycles in the Asian context, focusing on measures of coherence, gain and phase shifts respectively. We can then ask: to what extent are growth cycles becoming more correlated in the Asia-Pacific region? Is there any evidence of cyclical convergence at the business cycle frequency (the focus for policy purposes) or at other frequencies? Does that imply a common business cycle? Cyclical convergence is an essential pre-condition for the continued success of the current system of pegged exchange rates and the implied dependence on foreign monetary conditions.

In this chapter, we show how spectral analysis can be used to answer such questions, even where data samples are small and structural breaks or changing structures are a part of the story. We need a spectral approach to determine the degree of convergence at different frequencies and cycles. The inconclusive results obtained in the past for business cycle correlations, particularly in the Euro area, may have been the result of using a correlation analysis which averages the degree of convergence across all frequencies. That is problematic because two economies may share a trend or short-term shocks, but show no coherence between their business cycles.

From a theoretical perspective, neoclassical growth models show that every economy approaches a steady-state income level determined by the discount rate, the elasticity of factor substitution, the depreciation rate, capital share, and population growth. Once at the steady state, the economy grows at a constant rate. Thus, to the extent that the determinants of the steady state are similar across economies, convergence is expected. But if these determinants are different, they will not converge. Therefore, in practice, Mankiw *et al.* (1992), Dowrick and Nguyen (1989), Wolff (1991),

Barro and Sala-I-Martin (1991, 1992), and Quah (1993) find evidence of convergence for a sample of OECD countries at similar levels of development over the years 1960–1985. But, they reject convergence in a wider sample of 75 economies whose structures and vulnerability to uncertainty vary a good deal more. Similarly, Chauvet and Potter (2001) report that the U.S. business cycle was in line with the G7 from the mid 1970s, but then diverged thereafter. Likewise Stock and Watson (2002, 2005), Hughes Hallett and Richter (2006) find divergence caused by structural breaks, and argue that cyclical convergence is a global rather than regional phenomenon.

In contrast, Artis and Zhang (1997), Frankel and Rose (1998) and Prasad (1999) have all argued that if exchange rates are successfully pegged, and trade and financial links intensify, business cycles are likely to converge. In practice, Inklaar and de Haan (2000) do not find any evidence for a common business cycle in the Eurozone. Similarly Gerlach (1989), and Baxter and Kouparitsas (2005), find no evidence of greater convergence among the OECD economies as exchange rates have stabilized or trade increased. Doyle and Faust (2003), Kalemli-Ozcan *et al.* (2001), and Peersman and Smets (2005) provide further evidence in the same direction. All these results suggest a time-varying approach is going to be necessary if we are to analyze an emerging convergence among economies.[1]

The studies cited above also make it clear that the results can be sensitive to: (a) the choice of coherence measure; (b) the choice of cyclical measure (classical, deviation or growth cycles); and (c) the detrending measure used (linear, Hodrick–Prescott filter, band pass, etc.). This sensitivity to the detrending technique is a point stressed in particular by Canova (1998). Accordingly, there are a number of advantages of using a time–frequency approach:

(i) It does not depend on any particular detrending technique, so we are free of the lack of robustness found in many recent studies.

[1]Also because structural characteristics and institutional arrangements change. It appears that cyclical correlations typically fall with the degree of industrial specialization, but may rise as trade and financial integration expand with network production, outsourcing and the investments to supply the network inputs (Kalemli-Ozcan *et al.* 2001, 2003). But, market reforms, liberalization, and the extent to which policies are coordinated may have the opposite effect.

(ii) Our methods also do not have an "end-point problem" — no future information is used, implied or required as in band-pass or trend projection methods.
(iii) There is no arbitrary selection of a smoothing parameter, such as in the HP algorithm and equivalent to an arbitrary band-pass selection (Artis *et al.*, 2004).

However, any spectral approach is tied to a model based on a weighted sum of sine and cosine functions. That is not restrictive. Any periodic function may be approximated arbitrarily well by its Fourier expansion (a weighted sum of sine and cosine terms). Hence, once we have time-varying weights, we can get almost any cyclical shape we want. For example, to get long expansions but short recessions, we need only a regular business cycle plus a longer cycle whose weight increases above trend but decreases below trend (i.e., varies with the level of activity). This is important because many observers have commented on how the shape of economic cycles change over time in terms of amplitude, duration, and slope (Harding and Pagan, 2001; Stock and Watson, 2002; Peersman and Smets, 2005), not least in the "great moderation" of output variabilities since 1987. Once again, a time-varying spectral approach which separates out changes at different cyclical frequencies in the economy will be necessary to provide the flexibility to capture these features. It will also be needed if we are to be able to accommodate all the structural breaks which must be expected with China emerging as one of the world's largest economies; with the increasing sophistication of the Japanese economy; and with the Asian crisis in 1997; with the surge in trade, liberalization and trade imbalances since 2003; and with the changes to the supply chain of components/network inputs and FDI between China, Japan and the U.S.

6.2. A Technical Introduction to Time–Frequency Analysis

6.2.1. *Time-Varying Spectra*

Spectral analysis decomposes the variance of a sample of time series data across different frequencies. The power spectrum itself shows the relative importance of the different cyclical components in creating movements in that data, and hence describes the cyclical properties of a particular time series. It is assumed that the fluctuations of the underlying data are produced by a large number of elementary cycles of different frequencies. Furthermore, it is usually assumed that the contribution of each cycle is constant throughout the sample.

However, as Chauvet and Potter (2001) show for the U.S., business cycles cannot be assumed to be constant over time. Hence the spectrum would not be constant over time due to the changing weights associated with each of the elementary cycles. A "traditional" frequency analysis cannot handle that case. But in recent years a time frequency approach has been developed which can do so. It depends on using a Wigner–Ville distribution for the weights (see, for example, Matz and Hlawatsch, 2003).

In this chapter, we use a special case of the Wigner–Ville distribution, namely the "short-time Fourier transform" (STFT). The STFT catches structural changes (here interpreted as changes of the underlying lag structure of output in accordance with Wells (1996)), but assumes local stationarity. We employ the STFT for two reasons: firstly, the time series we analyze are already in log-differenced form (see Eq. (6.1) below) so stationarity may be assumed. Moreover, standard unit root tests performed on our data (specifically ADF and the Phillips–Perron tests, which are available on request) confirm that assumption. Finally, the available results in the literature on similar data (Campbell and Mankiw, 1987; Clark, 1987; Watson, 1986) also confirm that conclusion. Secondly, if the time series is stationary, then the STFT and the Wigner–Ville distribution coincide (Boashash, 2003). Employing the Wigner–Ville distribution directly would not have changed our results.

All the data collected are from the IMF's *International Financial Statistics*, including the real GDP. We use seasonally adjusted quarterly data from 1980:1 to 2005:1. Growth rates are then defined, using GDP data, as follows:

$$y_t = \Delta(\log(Y_t)) = \log\left(\frac{Y_t}{Y_{t-1}}\right). \tag{6.1}$$

Next we employ a two-step procedure. As Evans and Karras (1996) point out, if business cycles are to converge, they have to follow the same AR(p) process. We therefore estimate an AR(p) process for each variable individually. That is, we estimate the data generating process of each of the growth rates separately. Then we estimate the bilateral links between the cycles in those growth rates. In order to allow for the possible changes in the parameters, we employ a time-varying model by applying a Kalman filter to the chosen AR(p) model as follows:

$$y_t = \alpha_{0,t} + \sum_{i=1}^{9} \alpha_{i,t} y_{t-i} + \varepsilon_t, \qquad (6.2)$$

with

$$\alpha_{i,t} = \alpha_{i,t-1} + \eta_{i,t}, \quad \text{for } i = 0, \ldots, 9 \qquad (6.3)$$

and $\varepsilon_t, \eta_{i,t} \sim$ i.i.d. $(0, \sigma^2_{\varepsilon,\eta_i})$, for $i = 0, \ldots, 9$. In order to run the Kalman filter we need to define the initial parameter values. The initial parameter values are obtained by OLS estimation using the entire sample (see also Wells, 1996).[2] Given these starting values, we can then estimate the parameter values using the Kalman filter. We then employ a general to specific approach, eliminating insignificant lags using the strategy specified below. The maximum number of lags is determined by the Akaike Criterion (AIC), and is found to be nine in each case. Each time we run a new regression we use a new set of initial parameter values. Then, for each regression we apply a set of diagnostic tests to confirm the specification found.[3] The final parameter values are filtered estimates, independent of their start values.

Using the above specification implies that we get a set of parameter values for each point in time. Hence, a particular parameter could be significant for all points in time, or at some but not others. or it might never be significant. The parameter changes are at the heart of this chapter as they imply a change of the lag structure and a change in the spectral results. We therefore employ the following testing strategy: if a particular lag is never significant then this lag is dropped from the equation and the model is

[2]Obviously, using the entire sample implies that we neglect possible structural breaks. Therefore, the initial estimates may be biased. The Kalman filter will then correct for this since, as Wells (1996) points out, the Kalman filter will converge to the true parameter value independently of the initial value. But choosing initial values which are "close" to the true value accelerates convergence. Hence we employ an OLS estimate to start. But our start values have no effect on the parameter estimates by the time we get to 1990.

[3]Diagnostic tests are available on request from authors.

estimated again. If the AIC criterion is less than before, then that lag is completely excluded. If a parameter is significant for some periods but not others, it is kept in the equation with a parameter value of zero for those periods in which it is insignificant. This strategy minimizes the AIC criterion, and leads to a parsimonious specification. Finally, we test the residuals in each regression for auto-correlation and heteroscedasticity.

The specifications (6.2)–(6.3) are then validated using two different stability tests. Both tests check for the same null hypothesis (in our case a stable AR(9) specification) against differing temporal instabilities. The first is the fluctuations test of Ploberger *et al.* (1989), which detects *discrete* breaks at any point in time in the coefficients of a (possibly dynamic) regression. The second test is due to LaMotte and McWorther (1978), and is designed specifically to detect *random* parameter variation of a specific unit root form (our specification). We find that the random walk hypothesis for the parameters is justified for each country.[4] Finally, we choose the fluctuations test for detecting structural breaks because the Kalman filter allows structural breaks at any point and the fluctuations test is able to accommodate this.[5] Thus, and in contrast to other tests, the fluctuations test is not restricted to any pre-specified number of breaks.[6]

Once the above regression and tests are completed, it gives us a time-varying AR(p) model. From this AR(p) we can then calculate the STFT, as proposed by Gabor (1946), and from there the time-varying spectrum. The basic idea is to find the spectrum of a signal $x(t)$, at time t, by analyzing a small portion of the signal around that time.

---

[4]Results are available on request from the authors.

[5]Note that all our tests of significance, and significant differences in parameters, are being conducted in the time domain, *before* transferring to the frequency domain. This is because no statistical tests exist for calculated spectra (the transformations are nonlinear and may involve complex arithmetic). Stability tests are important here because our spectra could be sensitive to changes in the underlying parameters. But with the stability and specification tests conducted, we know there is no reason to switch to another model that fails to pass those tests.

[6]The fluctuations test works as follows: one parameter value is taken as the reference value, e.g., the last value of the sample. All other observations are now tested whether they significantly differ from that value. In order to do so, Ploberger *et al.* (1989) have provided critical values which we have used to make the test. If the test value is above the critical value then we have a structural break, i.e., the parameter value differs significantly from the reference value and vice versa.

Boashash and Reilly (1992) and Boashash (2003) show that the STFT can always be expressed as a time-varying discrete fast-Fourier transform calculated for each point in time. This transforms the time series signal into the frequency domain at each point. It also has the convenient property that the "traditional" formulae for the coherence and the gain are still valid, but have to be recalculated at each point in time. The time-varying spectrum of the growth rate series can therefore be calculated as (Lin, 1997):

$$P_t(\omega) = \frac{\sigma^2}{\left|1 + \sum_{i=1}^{9}, \alpha_{i,t} \exp(-j\omega i)\right|^2}, \tag{6.4}$$

where ω is the angular frequency and j is a complex number ($j^2 = -1$). The main advantage of this method is that, at any point in time, a power spectrum can be calculated instantaneously from the updated parameters of the model (see Lin, 1997). Similarly, the power spectrum for any particular time interval can be calculated by averaging the filter parameters over that interval. This would then result in the "traditional" spectra.

6.2.2. *Time-Varying Cross-Spectra*

Moving to the next step in our analysis, we can now estimate the relationships between two variables. We restrict ourselves to bilateral relationships in order to avoid multicollinearity between a series of potentially interrelated cycles. By transferring the time domain results into the frequency domain, we can show how the relationship between two economies has changed in terms of individual frequencies. That is, we are able to investigate whether any convergence took place over time, and, if so, at which frequencies. As a measure of that relationship, we use the coherence test. We then decompose the coherence in order to see whether a change in the coherence is caused by a change in the relationship between the two variables (i.e., in the ADL model below); or by a change in the data generating process itself (i.e., in the AR(p) model itself). With a time-invariant method that decomposition cannot be done. The next section outlines these ideas.

Suppose we are interested in the relationship between two variables, $\{y_t\}$ and $\{x_t\}$ say, where $\{y_t\}$ might be the Chinese growth rate and $\{x_t\}$ the U.S. growth rate for example. We assume that they are related in the following way:

$$V(L)_t y_t = A(L)_t x_t + u_t, \quad u_t \sim \text{i.i.d. } (0, \sigma^2), \tag{6.5}$$

where $A(L)_t$ and $V(L)_t$ are filters, and L is the lag operator such that $Lz_t = z_{t-1}$. Notice that the lag structure, $A(L)_t$, is time-varying, which means that we need to use a state space model (we use the Kalman filter) to estimate the implied lag structure. This is given as

$$\begin{aligned} v_{i,t} &= v_{i,t-1} + \varepsilon_{i,t}, \quad \text{for } i = 1, \ldots, p \text{ and } \varepsilon_{i,t} \sim (0, \sigma^2_{\varepsilon_i}), \\ a_{i,t} &= a_{i,t-1} + \eta_{i,t}, \quad \text{for } i = 0, \ldots, q \text{ and } \eta_{i,t} \sim (0, \sigma^2_{\eta_i}). \end{aligned} \tag{6.6}$$

As before, we test for the random walk property using the LaMotte–McWother test. And for structural breaks, we employ the fluctuations test as suggested by Ploberger *et al.* (1989). Finally, we again use our general to specific approach to estimate Eq. (6.6); starting off with lag lengths of nine and $p = q$, and dropping those lags which are never significant (as before).

Having estimated the coefficients in Eq. (6.6), we can calculate the gain, coherence and cross spectra based on the time-varying spectra just obtained. That allows us to overcome a major difficulty in this kind of analysis, namely that a very large number of observations would usually be necessary to carry out the necessary frequency analysis by direct estimation. This may be a particular problem in the case of structural breaks since the sub-samples would typically be too small to allow the associated spectra to be estimated directly or accurately.

Following Hughes Hallett and Richter (2002, 2004, 2006), we use the fact that the time-varying cross spectrum, $f_{YX}(\omega)_t$, using the STFT is given by

$$f_{YX}(\omega)_t = T(\omega)_t f_{XX}(\omega)_t, \tag{6.7}$$

where $T(\omega)_t$ is the transfer or filter function is defined by Eq. (6.5) and calculated as follows:

$$T(\omega)_t = \left(\frac{\sum_{b=0}^{q} a_{b,t} \exp(-j\omega b)}{1 - \sum_{i=1}^{p} v_{i,t} \exp(-j\omega i)} \right), \quad \text{for } t = 1, \ldots, T. \tag{6.8}$$

The last term in Eq. (6.7), $f_{XX}(\omega)_t$, is the spectrum of pre-determined variable. This spectrum may be time varying as well. However, in this chapter we are interested in the coherence and in the decomposition of the changes to that coherence over time. So we need expressions for the coherence and gain between X_t and Y_t. The spectrum of any dependent variable is defined as (Jenkins and Watts, 1968; Wolters, 1980):

$$f_{YY}(\omega)_t = |T(\omega)_t|^2 f_{XX}(\omega)_t + f_{vv}(\omega)_t. \tag{6.9}$$

From Eq. (6.5) we get the time-varying residual spectrum

$$f_{vv}(\omega)_t = \frac{f_{uu}(\omega)_t}{\left|1 - \sum_{i=1}^{p} v_{i,t} \exp(-j\omega i)\right|^2} \tag{6.10}$$

and the gain as $A(\omega)_t = |T(\omega)_t|^2$.

Finally, given knowledge of $f_{YY}(\omega)_t$, $|T(\omega)_t|^2$, and $f_{XX}(\omega)_t$, we can now *calculate* the coherence between X_t and Y_t as

$$K^2_{YX,t} = \frac{1}{\left\{1 + f_{VV}(\omega)_t / (|T(\omega)_t|^2 f_{XX}(\omega)_t)\right\}}. \tag{6.11}$$

The coherence is equivalent to R^2 in the time domain. The coherence measures, for each frequency, the degree of fit between X and Y, or the R^2 between each of the corresponding cyclical components in X and Y. Hence, the coherence measures the link between two variables at time t. For example, if the coherence has a value of 0.6 at frequency 1.2, then this means that country X's business cycle at a frequency of 1.2 determines country Y's business cycle *at this point in time* by 60 percent. The coherence does not take into account a shift in the business cycle, e.g., if the European business cycle leads the German one by one quarter. In this section, we are concerned only with the coherence, not the gain or phase shift elements.

Last, but not least, a note on the figures shown in the following two sections. We first present the time-varying spectra and then the coherences. One can see from these figures that the spectra change. However, one cannot infer directly from those figures that the changes in the spectra are also statistically significant. The figures for the time-varying spectra have to be accompanied by the fluctuation test results. Once a structural break has been identified by the fluctuation test, the results of that change will show up as significant in the corresponding spectrum or cross-spectrum.

6.3. Single Spectra

In this section and the next, we study the spectra and cross-spectra of output growth in selected Asian economies compared to the U.S., or compared to China or Japan, over the past 20 years. We take the U.S., China and Japan to be the potential leading economies ("economies of first resort") in the Asia-Pacific area, and analyze the changing relations between them since the Asian financial crisis in 1996–1997. Similar results for the U.S. vs. the U.K. and the U.S. vs. the Eurozone can be found in Hughes Hallett and Richter (2006) and may be used as a point of comparison here. We use quarterly, seasonally adjusted data for real GDP in all three economies, as published in the IMF's *International Financial Statistics*. The resulting growth rates are then fitted to an AR(p) model, as described above, and tested for stationarity, statistical significance, and a battery of other diagnostic and specification tests are used to confirm our statistical model.

6.3.1. *Individual Spectra for the Core Asian Economies*

One striking feature of the individual country spectra (Figures 6.1–6.3) is that, in all three economies, the trend growth rate does not play an important role in terms of spectral mass. Indeed, taking into account the vertical scale in each diagram, there is a very little volatility in output growth of any kind in either China or Japan after 1987; except at the business cycle frequency in the Asian crisis period (1998–2002) in Japan, and until the period of especially rapid trade growth (and trade surpluses) in China from 2004 onwards. This is in stark contrast to the U.S. spectrum which shows the declining power of trend growth after 1987, and very mildly increasing volatilities at short or short-to-medium cycle lengths, but a clear persistence in her trend growth rates nonetheless.

In making these points, we are drawing a distinction between persistent trends, meaning those events whose effects on performance last a long time before dying away or being overtaken by subsequent events; and constant growth trends whose effects are persistent and always the same in terms of economic performance. Obviously, the former implies some variance in the outcomes, if only slowly changing, and hence some long cycle power in the associated spectrum. But the latter implies no effective variance in the outcomes, and hence no power in the corresponding spectrum at low

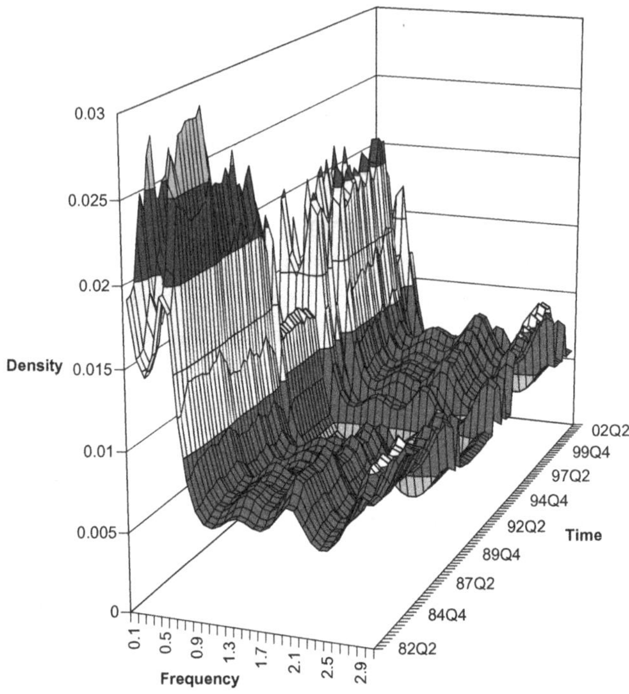

Fig. 6.1. The spectrum of the U.S. growth rate.

frequencies (or anywhere else). So there may have been change in these economies; but it is not a change that has altered the pattern of growth in the U.S. in any significant way, or the growth in Japan and China for that matter (except perhaps in the period 2003–2005). That is not to say that the relationships between these economies have not changed. But if they have, it must have been a change involving factors outside the region; or, more likely, a change that involved a reallocation of production or policy initiatives between the economies of the Asia-Pacific area rather than a change in behavior/dependency as such. The latter appears more likely because the pattern of structural (regime) breaks shows little in common taking each economy separately.[7] Had they been settling into a new regime, there would have been something in common in the structural breaks as each

[7]The detailed fluctuations tests which demonstrate these structural breaks, and those applying to the coherences and gains which follow, are available from the authors on request.

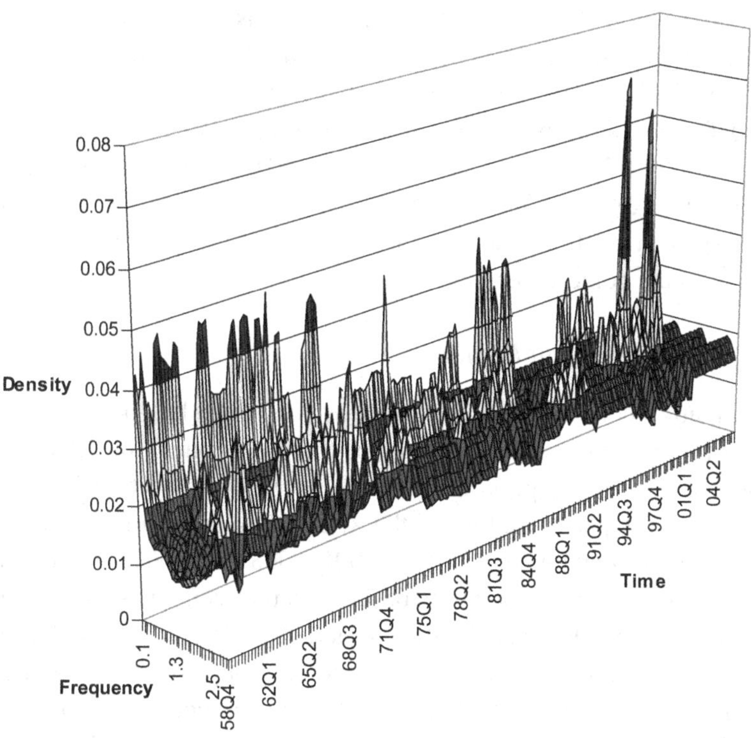

Fig. 6.2. The spectrum of the Japanese growth rate.

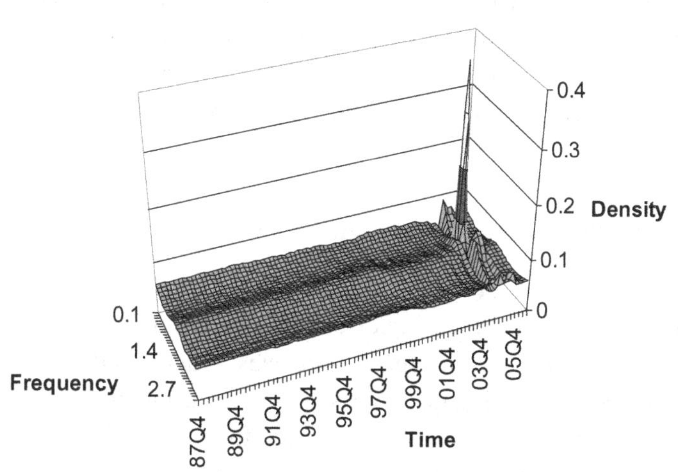

Fig. 6.3. The spectrum of the Chinese growth rate.

economy entered that regime. As it is, the U.S. is only showing structural breaks in 1996 and 2001 (the Clinton–Greenspan boom); while Japan shows breaks in 1977–1980, 1983–1992, and in 1994–2002 (boom times, and then deflation); and China a series of small breaks in 1993, 1995 (internal reforms), 1999–2000 (trade liberalization; WTO membership), 2002 and then a very large one in 2004–2005 (the expansion of trade and curtailing of imports). With a pattern like that, these breaks are far more likely to reflect changes in the domestic economies.

6.3.2. *Commentary on Results*

The tentative conclusion at this stage is that there has been no significant change in the growth patterns of these economies in the past two decades; with the exception of the increase in volatility at business cycle frequencies in Japan at the time of the Asian crisis, and of the liberalization of the Chinese economy and trade in 2001–2003. This makes it hard to see if there is any one emerging group of Asia-Pacific economies with common cyclical behavior. One suspects there is none, although it is possible. But to show that, we need to see whether the within group coherences and gains have increased; and whether those out-of-group, particularly with the U.S., have decreased. If that were true, it would be consistent with Demertzis *et al.* (1998) who find that the "core" and "periphery" economies in Europe had more in common with each other than any of them did with those "out-of-group". Even so, the low spectral power in these two Asian economies implies they are influenced by stable growth rates (in contrast to the U.S). But it is not a new phenomenon. It has been apparent since the end of the 1980s.

6.4. Increasing Coherence between Asian Economic Cycles?

We turn now to the coherence, or correlations, between the economic cycles of our Asian economies at different frequencies — and whether those coherences have been increasing or decreasing. These results will provide a test of the hypothesis that the Asian economies form one coherent economic group, more similar in their performance than with those outside the group, and whether their dependence on the U.S. economy has decreased as the strength of the linkages within Asia has increased. In addition, we can test the proposition that, if exchange rates are pegged, then business cycles will converge as trade and financial links strengthen. This is an important finding as Artis and Zhang (1997), Prasad (1999) and Frankel and Rose (1998, 2002) all argue that this is likely to be observed if the trade and financial links intensify. On the other hand, Kalemli-Ozcan *et al.* (2001, 2003), Hughes Hallett and Piscitelli (2002), Baxter and Kouparitsas (2005), Peersman and Smets (2005) show that it has not happened in practice and may not happen in the Asian case. The advantage of our approach, however, is that China has maintained a pegged exchange rate with the U.S. throughout this period, whereas Japan has not. We can therefore test this hypothesis directly and attribute the results to the exchange rate regime rather than to increased trade and financial flows.

6.4.1. *Coherence and Spillovers between the U.S. and China*

Taking the China–U.S. relationship first (Figure 6.4),[8] we can see that the coherence has been gradually declining from 1987 to 2001, but has remained at a fairly high level of 0.4–0.5 throughout. However, it increased again rather abruptly since 2001, which imply a stronger if somewhat uncertain (there are several interruptions to this increased coherence) association of U.S. growth with China at the short, long, and (most of all) at business cycle frequencies from 2004 to 2006. The gains (Figure 6.5) however show that the impact of variations in U.S. growth on China has been quite small, with multipliers of below 0.08 perunit change in the U.S., and declining, until 2002. But then there is a sudden increase in the U.S. influence at short,

[8]Note that each coherence/gains relationship implies a direction of causality, and hence different degrees of association or spillover effects, depending on whether we are looking at how much the U.S. growth affects growth in China or how much Chinese growth affects the U.S. performance. We therefore get different results, and different implications, depending on whether the underlying regressions specify Chinese growth as a function of U.S. growth rates, or U.S. growth as a function of Chinese growth. Coherences can therefore imply one growth pattern is more closely associated or dependent on another, than will hold in reverse (the dependence/association of the second on the first). Coherence therefore measures the general closeness of fit between two variables x and y, rather than the simple correlation coefficient which is symmetric. Gains likewise measure the impact of growth in one economy on another, and therefore vary with the direction in which the linkage is supposed to run.

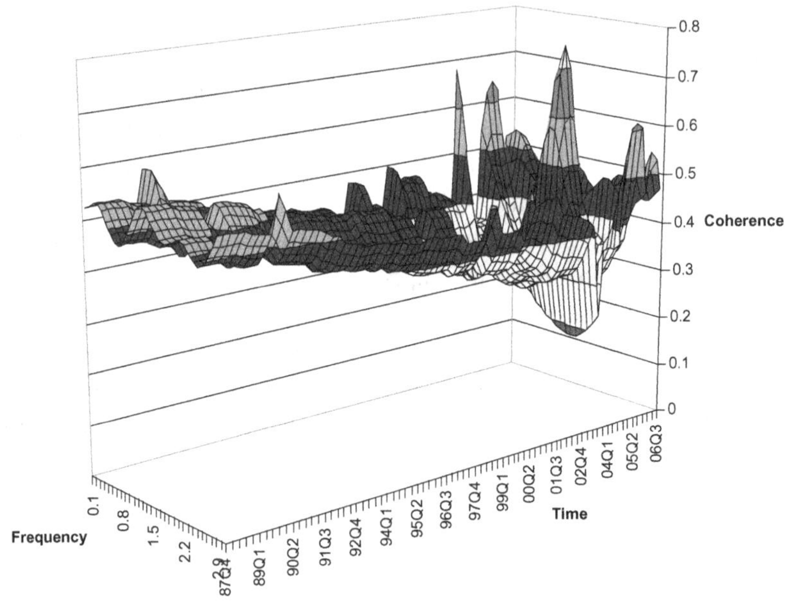

Fig. 6.4. The coherence, China dependent on the U.S. (China–U.S.).

long and business cycle frequencies in 2003–2004 such that, by 2005, the spillovers onto China had settled back to the levels of 1990–1991. So, there is partial support for our first hypothesis, but not quite as expected: U.S. dominance and economy of first resort effects have indeed been declining with respect to China, but only slowly and only up until 2002. The recent surge in trade with the U.S., based as it is on expanding Chinese exports and the domestic substitution of imports,[9] has restored much of the U.S. influence on China although at a fairly low level.

In the light of the above results, it is important to see if the counterpart is true, i.e., whether China's impact on the U.S. economy has also been increasing. We might expect to see the China to U.S. gains and coherence increasing with the expansion of trade and financial flows

[9]It is very clear in the data that Chinese exports and imports have grown at equal speeds since 2000, and at 30 percent annually for the period 2002–2004. But import growth stopped altogether in 2004, and edged slowly back up to 10 percent in 2007, while export growth remained above 20 percent. As a result China's trade surplus tripled in 2005 and doubled again in 2007.

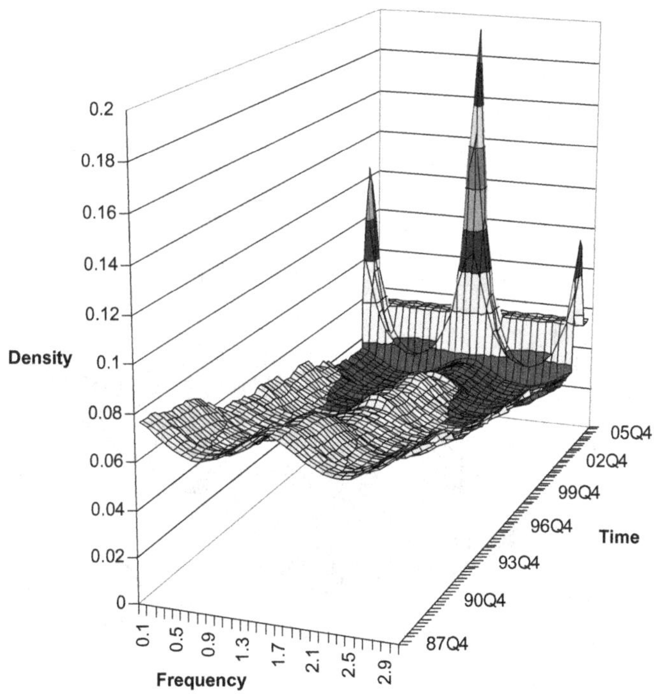

Fig. 6.5. The gains, China from the U.S. (China–U.S.).

between the two, in the same way as the U.S. to China coherence and gains have increased. And to some extent we do observe this. The U.S.–China coherence (Figure 6.6) is rather low, but falls steadily (from 0.1 to 0.05) up until 2001 just as the China–U.S. coherence did. It then jumps back up to 0.1 (and more strongly to 0.3 at the business cycle frequency) and then remains, rather uncertainly, at that level. In the same way, the U.S.–China gain (Figure 6.7) is high but falls steadily until 2001, and then recovers sharply thereafter to values similar to those of the early 1990s — again similarly to the China–U.S. case.[10]

[10]We observe this more in the long and short cycles than in business cycles. That suggests a change in the phase relationship. If there is such a change, then the strength of coherence or gain must increase at some frequency and decrease at another, while the change itself takes place. Since we are not interested in the size of the leads/lags, only their changes, we limit our tests for changing phase shifts and changes in the product mix (proportion of consumption goods, process inputs, components, and investment goods) to such events.

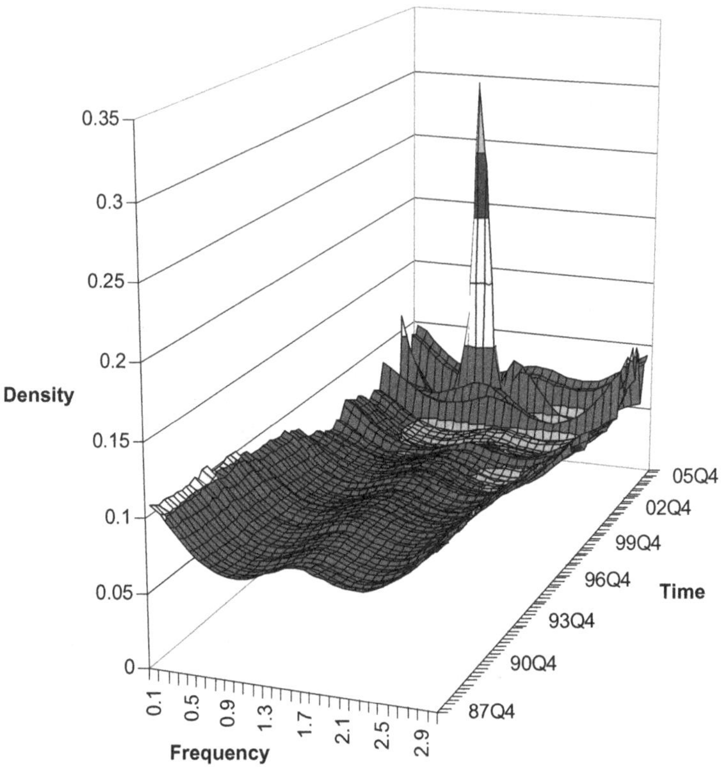

Fig. 6.6. The coherence, the U.S. dependent on China (U.S.–China).

Those results might therefore suggest a mutual dependence between China and the U.S., similar to the assumed leadership of the U.S. economy in the 1980s and 1990s. However this would be wrong due to the asymmetries in the linkage: the U.S. to China linkage has a high coherence but a low gain, while China to U.S. linkage has low coherence but a high gain. Such asymmetries give us the pattern of dependency or leadership. In this case, it appears that the U.S. has the power to *shape* the cycle in China — this is the coherence part — through her control of monetary and financial conditions (interest rates, supply of capital, exchange rates), while China has the power to influence spillover effects onto the U.S., and hence the *size* of the cycle (this is the gain effect) through the "outsourcing" of manufactures and cheap components or intermediates for the U.S. economy. This fits neatly with the

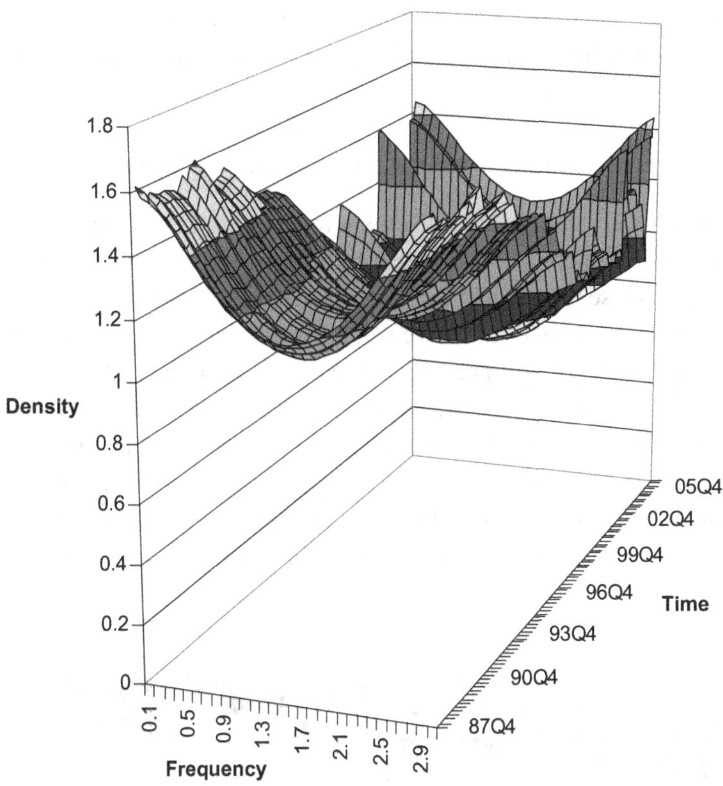

Fig. 6.7. The gains, the U.S. from China.

facts. Chinese imports of process goods, intermediates and components now account for 42 percent of total imports; those from the U.S. having risen by a factor of eight since 1992 (and by three times since 2001), and those from Japan by 12 times since 1992 (and $2\,\frac{1}{2}$ times since 2001). Similarly, Chinese process exports, components, etc. are now 53 percent of total exports, with those going to the U.S. up by a factor of $4\,\frac{3}{4}$, and those going to Japan up 15 times, since 1992.

These results give a more complex view than the usual of the relationship between the U.S. and China, where they dominate and where they are vulnerable. It is consistent with the idea that China has gained greater influence through it expansion of trade, but at the cost of a dependence on foreign monetary conditions (risking thereby inflation, excess liquidity, asset bubbles). However, the key point is that this relationship is not new. It has been in this form since the 1980s; and has become distinctly stronger, if more uncertain, since 2000.

6.4.2. *Coherence and Gains between the U.S. and Japan*

The Japan–U.S. relationship presents a much simpler picture (Figures 6.8 and 6.9). The coherence shows a steady but surprisingly strong linkage between Japanese growth and U.S. growth. That association may be stronger at long cycles, and may have weakened in the past five years, but those changes are very small. The gain, however, the impact of U.S. income movements on Japanese growth, shows larger changes: those spillovers fall from around 0.3 in the 1970s and 1980s, especially in the persistence of long cycles and short-term volatility, to about 0.15 now. But that is still twice as large as the corresponding impact of the U.S. on China. And, at the business cycle frequencies, the spillovers are at twice that strength again

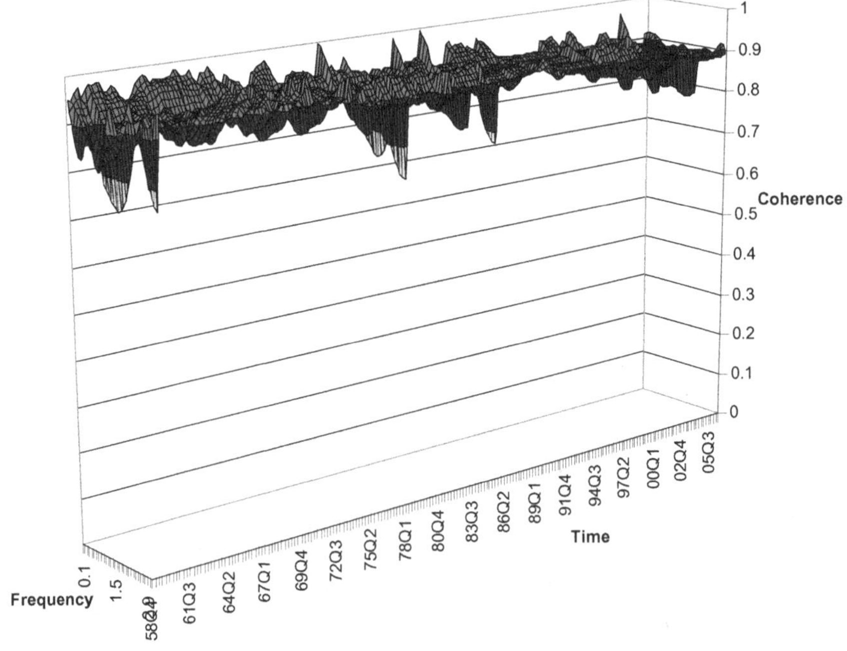

Fig. 6.8. The coherence between Japan and the U.S. (Japan–U.S.).

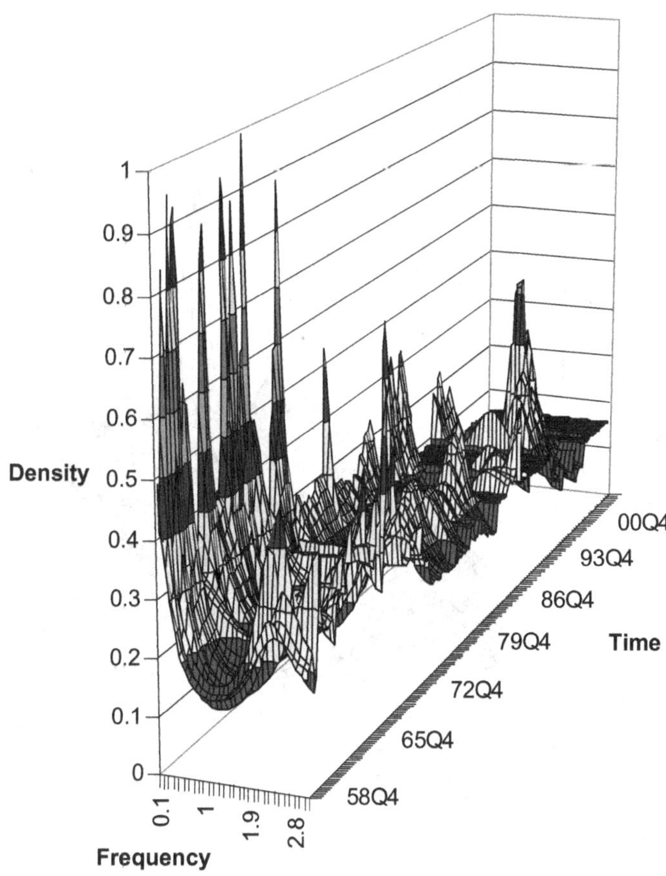

Fig. 6.9. The gains, Japan–U.S.

after 2001. These results therefore also support our original hypothesis, but only weakly because the linkage between U.S.–Japanese business cycles is increasing (if anything) at the end of the sample, and because the constant coherence means there will be correspondingly few changes in the Japan to U.S. relationship. (Therefore, we do not report that relationship separately).

6.4.3. *Coherences and Gains between China and Japan*

The Japan–China (China influences Japan) coherence (Figure 6.10) is very low through-out, at 0.1, but shows distinct increases in 1997 and in 2003 where the relationship starts to show a significant increase in volatility. At

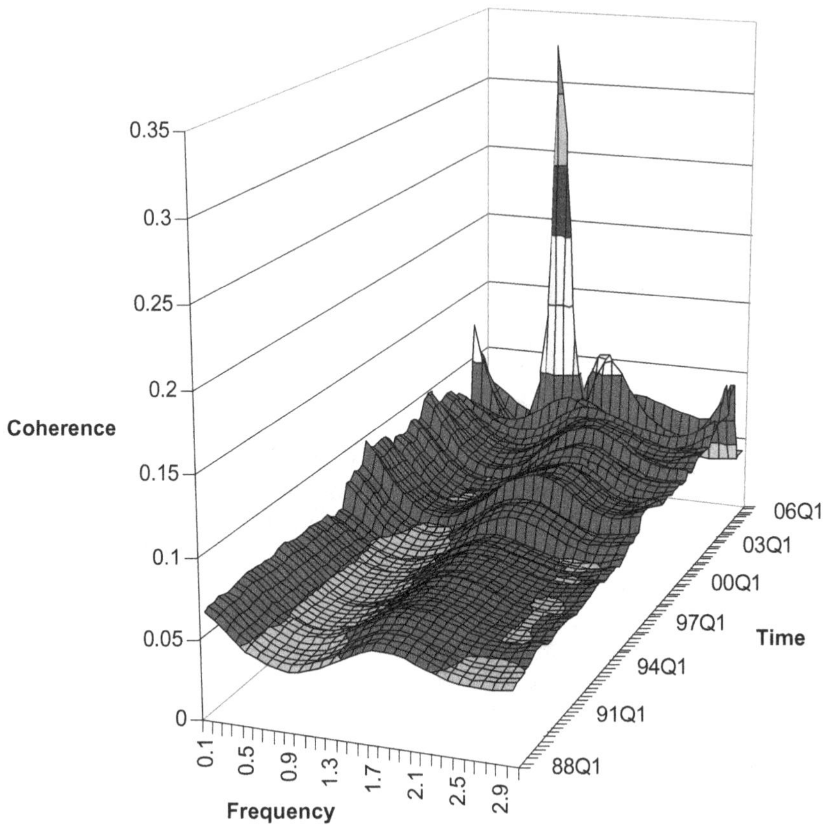

Fig. 6.10. The coherence, Japan dependent on China (Japan–China).

that point, the transmissions from China are mainly to the business cycle frequencies in Japan. However, the coherence remains small, in fact no more than for China influencing the U.S., and smaller (by factors of 5–6) than the U.S.'s coherence with China or Japan. The gains (Figure 6.11) are smaller again at 0.02–0.03, although they too show a clear increase in 1997 at the short and long frequencies before tailing off again after 2003. This is consistent with a Japan trading bloc developing separately from a China bloc, even though one might have expected more linkage between the two as Chinese components are increasingly used, and manufactures consumed, in Japan; and as more Japanese equipment or investment goes to China. However, the fact that the same thing is also happening in the U.S. means

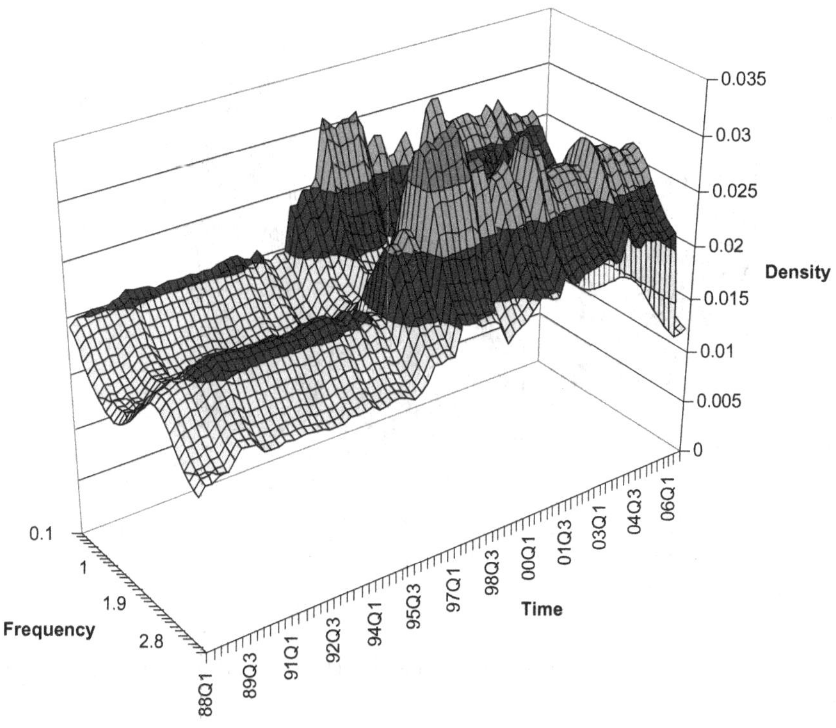

Fig. 6.11. The gains, Japan–China.

that Japan and the U.S. continue to behave in the same way with respect to each other despite their, and China's, changing roles in the Asian economy. Since China's role in either partner's economy is the thing that has been changing, it is her relationship with the U.S. and Japan that has changed; not those elsewhere in the region.

Together with the above, the reverse relationship (Figures 6.12 and 6.13) shows something of the same pattern as the China–U.S. relationships, although much less clearly marked because of the decade of depression in Japan. Like in the U.S. comparisons, Japan's influence on China shows low coherence and high gains, but China's influence on Japan (as above) has a high coherence and low gains. However, these linkages are weaker: the ratio of coherence to gain is 4:1 for China–Japan and 1:8 (1:2 in the 90s) for Japan–China, compared to 10:1 and 1:12 for their China/U.S. counterparts. And the picture has been confused by the loss of any form

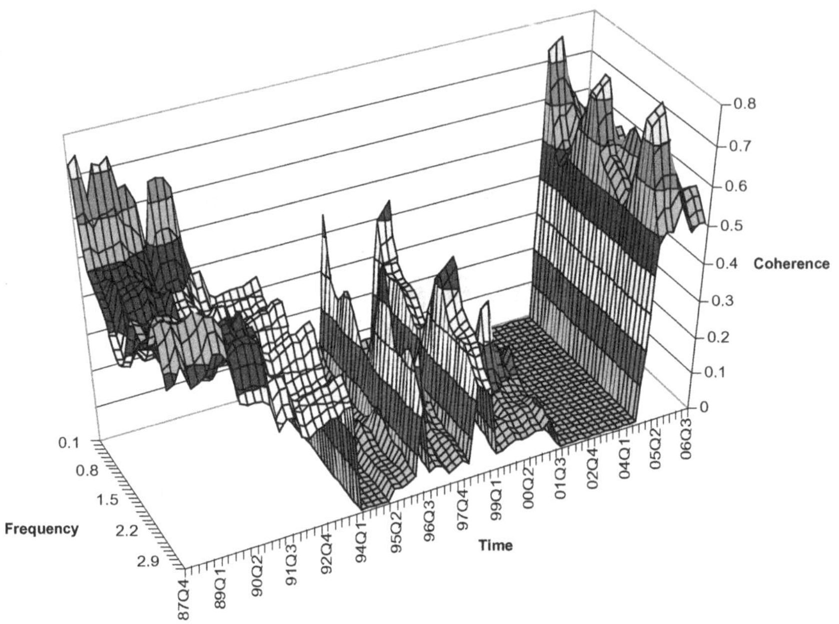

Fig. 6.12. The coherence, China dependent on Japan (China–Japan).

of (statistically significant) linkage during Japan's decade of depression (1993–2004). As one might expect, as Japan sank into depression her influence on China vanished, even if China's weak but strengthening influence on Japan did not. Consequently, the China–Japan linkage shows a lot of uncertainty, especially with the Japanese attempts at revival in 1996 and 1999, while the Japan–China one does not. But the successful revival in 2004 restores more than the status quo ante, and fairly evenly so across most frequencies. In summary, we draw the same conclusions as we did in the China/U.S. case: China can influence the size of the cycle in Japan, but Japan exerts some influence over the shape (existence) of the cycle in China, though the effects are more limited than in the U.S. linkage. And, evidently, Japan's influence on China is spread over the long (investment), short (monetary financing), and business (network production and consumables) cycles, whereas China's influence over Japan is mostly at business cycle frequencies (out-sourced production and components).

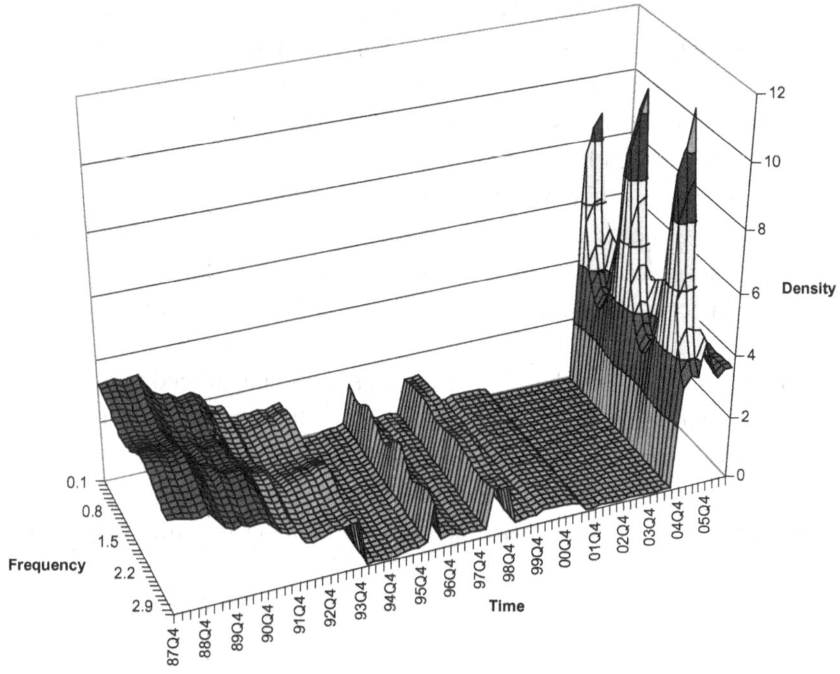

Fig. 6.13. The gains, China–Japan.

6.5. Concluding Remarks

The contribution of this chapter has been to examine the hypothesis that the economic links and leadership-dependency relationships in the Asia-Pacific area have changed over the past 20 years. Has this changed the size or direction of the spillovers between economies, and reduced U.S. hegemony in the region by strengthening the links between Asian economies? Does Asia now influence the U.S. economy, and can one speak of a common Asian bloc? We have used time-varying spectral methods to decompose the growth rates, and linkages between them, of the two largest Asian economies and the U.S. to study the coherence, spillover effects, and leads/lags or product composition, at each cycle length.

The empirical findings of this chapter can be summarized as follows:

1. The economic links with the U.S. have indeed weakened, and those elsewhere may have strengthened. However, this is not new. It has been

happening steadily since the mid-1980s, and it has now been partly (but not completely) reversed by the unbalanced expansion of Pacific trade.

2. The linkage with the U.S. is more complex than usually supposed. It appears that the U.S. still influences the shape and existence of cycles elsewhere through her control of monetary conditions where exchange rates are pegged (China); but China has some control of the size of the cycles at home and elsewhere through the strength of her trade in consumption, components and intermediate goods. Since the changes with respect to Japan are very similar, the Japan–U.S. relationship is largely unchanged.
3. There is no evidence that fixed exchange rates encouraged convergence despite increasing trade and financial links. In fact, the opposite seems to be true here; most likely because of the capacity of misaligned (undervalued) exchange rates to generate excess liquidity, easy credit, and domestic asset bubbles — as Japan found to her cost in the early 1990s.

References

Artis, M, M Marcellino and T Priorietti (2004). Dating the Euro area business cycle. In *The Euro Area Business Cycle: Stylised Facts and Measurement Issues*, L Reichlin (ed.). London: Centre for Economic Policy Research.

Artis, M and W Zhang (1997). International business cycles and the ERM: Is there a European business cycle? *International Journal of Finance and Economics*, 2, 1–16.

Barro, RJ and X Sala-I-Martin (1991). Convergence across states and regions. *Brookings Papers on Economic Activity*, 1, 107–182.

Barro, RJ and X Sala-I-Martin (1992). Convergence. *Journal of Political Economy*, 100, 223–251.

Baxter, M and MA Kouparitsas (2005). Determinants of business cycle comovement: A robust analysis. *Journal of Monetary Economics*, 52, 113–158.

Boashash, B (2003). *Time Frequency Signal Analysis and Processing*. Oxford: Elsevier.

Boashash, B and A Reilly (1992). Algorithms for time-frequency signal analysis. In *Time-Frequency Signal Analysis — Methods and Applications*, B Boashash (ed.), pp. 163–181. Melbourne: Longman-Cheshire.

Campbell, JY and NG Mankiw (1987). Permanent and transitory components in macroeconomic fluctuations. *American Economic Review*, 77, 111–117.

Canova, F (1998). Detrending and business cycle facts. *Journal of Monetary Economics*, 41, 475–512.

Chaplyguin, V, A Hughes Hallett and CR Richter (2006). Monetary re-integration in the ex-Soviet Union: A union of four? *Economics of Transition*, 14, 47–68.

Chauvet, M and S Potter (2001). *Recent Changes in the U.S. Business Cycle.* Mimeo, University of California.

Clark, PK (1987). The Cyclical Component of the U.S. Economic Activity. *Quarterly Journal of Economics*, 102, 797–814.

Demertzis, M, A Hughes Hallett and O Rummel (1998). Is a 2-speed system in Europe the answer to the conflict between the German and the Anglo-Saxon models of monetary control? In *Competition and Convergence in Financial Markets*, S Black and M Moersch (eds.). New York: Elsevier North Holland.

Dowrick, S and D-T Nguyen (1989). OECD comparative economic growth 1950–1985. *American Economic Review*, 79, 1010–1030.

Doyle, B and J Faust (2003). Breaks in the variability and comovement of G7 economic growth. International Finance Discussion Paper, No. 786, Board of Governors, Federal Reserve System, Washington, DC.

Evans, P and G Karras (1996). Convergence revisited. *Journal of Monetary Economics*, 37, 249–265.

Frankel, J and A Rose (1998). The endogeneity of the optimal currency area criteria. *Economic Journal*, 108, 1009–1025.

Frankel, J and A Rose (2002). An estimate of the effect of a common currency on trade and income. *Quarterly Journal of Economics*, 117, 437–466.

Gabor, D (1946). Theory of communication. *Journal of the Institute of Electrical Engineering*, 93, 429–457.

Gerlach, S (1989). Information, persistence, and real business cycles. *Journal of Economic Dynamics and Control*, 13, 187–199.

Harding, D and A Pagan (2001). *Extracting, Analysing and Using Cyclical Information.* Mimeo, Australian National University.

Hughes Hallett, A and L Piscitelli (2002). Does trade cause convergence? *Economics Letters*, 75, 165–170.

Hughes Hallett, A and C Richter (2002). Are capital markets efficient? Evidence from the term structure of interest rates in Europe. *Economic and Social Review*, 33, 333–356.

Hughes Hallett, A and C Richter (2004). Spectral analysis as a tool for financial policy: An analysis of the short end of the British term structure. *Computational Economics*, 23, 271–288.

Hughes Hallett, A and C Richter (2006). Is the convergence of business cycles a global or a regional Issue? The UK, U.S. and Euroland. *International Journal of Finance and Economics*, 11, 77–94.

Inklaar, R and J de Haan (2000). Is there really a European business cycle? Working Paper No. 268, CESifo, Munich.

Jenkins, GM and DG Watts (1968). *Spectral Analysis and its Applications*. San Francisco: Holden-Day.

Kalemli-Ozcan, S, B Sorenson and O Yosha (2001). Economic integration, industrial specialization, and the asymmetry of macroeconomic fluctuations. *Journal of International Economics*, 55, 107–137.

Kalemi-Ozcan, S, B Sorensen and O Yosha (2003). Risk sharing and industrial specialization: Regional and international evidence. *American Economic Review*, 93, 903–918.

LaMotte, LR and AJ McWorther (1978). An exact test for the presence of random walk coefficients in a linear regression. *Journal of the American Statistical Association*, 73, 816–820.

Lin, Z (1997). An introduction to time-frequency signal analysis. *Sensor Review*, 17, 46–53.

Mankiw, NG, D Romer and D Weil (1992). A contribution to the empirics of economic growth. *Quarterly Journal of Economics*, 107, 407–437.

Matz, G and F Hlawatsch (2003). Time-varying power spectra of nonstationary random processes. In *Time Frequency Signal Analysis and Processing*, B Boashash (ed.). Amsterdam: Elsevier.

Peersman, G and F Smets (2005). Industry effects of monetary policy in the Euro area. *Economic Journal*, 115, 319–342.

Ploberger, W, W Krämer and K Kontrus (1989). A new test for structural stability in the linear regression model. *Journal of Econometrics*, 40, 307–318.

Prasad, ES (1999). International trade and the business cycle. *Economic Journal*, 109, 588–606.

Quah, DT (1993). Galton's fallacy and tests of the convergence hypothesis. *Scandinavian Journal of Economics*, 95, 427–443.

Stock, JH and MW Watson (2002). Has the business cycle changed and why? NBER Working Paper No. 9127. Cambridge.

Stock, JH and MW Watson (2005). Understanding changes in the international business cycles. *Journal of the European Economic Association*, 3, 966–1006.

Watson, MW (1986). Univariate detrending methods with stochastic trends. *Journal of Monetary Economics*, 18, 49–75.

Wells, C (1996). *The Kalman Filter in Finance*. Dordrecht: Kluwer Academic Publishers.

Wolff, EN (1991). Capital formation and productivity convergence over the long term. *American Economic Review*, 81, 565–579.

Wolters, J (1980). *Stochastic Dynamic Properties of Linear Econometric Models*. Berlin: Springer Verlag.

CHAPTER 7

TRADE INTERDEPENDENCE AND EXCHANGE RATE COORDINATION IN EAST ASIA

*Willem Thorbecke**

7.1. Introduction

East Asia is characterized by intricate production and distribution relationships, constituting part of a global trading network. Generally speaking, Japan, Korea, Taiwan, and multinational corporations (MNCs) located in ASEAN produce sophisticated technology-intensive intermediate goods and capital goods and ship them to China and ASEAN for assembly by lower-skilled workers. The finished products are then exported to the U.S., Europe, and the rest of the world. These production and distribution networks have promoted economic efficiency and helped to make East Asia as a whole (not just China) the manufacturing center of the world.

FDI flows and MNCs have played an important part in these triangular trading patterns. As Gaulier *et al.* (2005) discuss, FDI flows and MNC activities have reduced costs in host countries, transferred technological and managerial know how, increased local procurement, multiplied trade in intermediate goods, and strengthened distribution networks.

While networks are common in other parts of the world (e.g., parts and components exported from the U.S. for assembly in Mexico), fragmentation in East Asia is particularly sophisticated and well developed. It involves

*This manuscript draws on work the author has done at the Research Institute of Economy, Trade, and Industry. He thanks RIETI for providing an excellent and stimulating research environment. He also thanks participants at the 2007 Claremont-Bologna-SCAPE Policy Forum for helpful comments.

complicated combinations of intra-firm trade, arms-length transactions, and outsourcing (Kimura and Ando, 2005). One definition of these production networks has been provided by Borrus *et al.* (2000, p. 2):

> By a lead firm's "cross-border production network" (CPN) we mean the inter- and intra-firm relationships through which the firm organizes the entire range of its business activities: from research and development, product definition and design, to supply of inputs, manufacturing (or production of a service), distribution, and support services. We thus include the entire network of cross-border relationships between a lead firm and its own affiliates and subsidiaries, but also its subcontractors, suppliers, service providers, or other firms participating in cooperative relationships, such as standard setting or R&D [research and development] analysis (p. 2).[1]

These networks have allowed firms to exploit comparative advantage by slicing up long production processes and allocating the production blocks created in this way throughout Asia. The trade–FDI linkages have led to production–distribution networks in East Asia that can be characterized as vertical intra-industry trade (VIIT).

This VIIT differs both from the exchange of final goods emphasized by traditional trade theory for vertical inter-industry trade between the North and the South (e.g., between capital goods and apparel) and for horizontal intra-industry trade between the North and the North (e.g., between two differentiated types of automobiles). As Fukao *et al.* (2002) discuss, the production processes of an industry (e.g., the electronics industry) has been split into fragmented production blocks that can be located in different countries and the new VIIT is essentially based on differences in factor endowments in the fragmented production blocks between developing, emerging, and developed economies in the region.

The rapid development of the value-added chain in the region has been accompanied by massive flows of exports from East Asia (particularly China) to the rest of the world and by growing trade imbalances. The trade imbalances are particularly large for East Asian trade with the U.S. The East Asian surplus with the U.S. equaled $300 billion in 2004, $350 billion in

[1]Also quoted in Yusuf *et al.* (2003).

2005, and $385 billion in 2006. The overall U.S. deficit in these years was $650 billion, $770 billion, and $818 billion, respectively.[2]

Many questions follow from these considerations. How dependent are East Asian production networks on the rest of the world for final goods demand? How would exchange rate changes affect arms-length and intra-firm trade within these networks? How would an appreciation of the Chinese Renminbi (RMB) and other East Asian exchange rates affect exports to the rest of the world? What type of exchange rate regime would facilitate the flow of trade within these networks?

This chapter investigates these questions. The next section presents an analytical description of the triangular trading patterns. Section 7.3 considers the factors affecting China's processed exports. Section 7.4 examines the effects of exchange rate changes on triangular trade. Section 7.5 draws policy implications and concludes.

7.2. Global Triangular Trading Patterns in East Asia[3]

7.2.1. *Intermediate Goods Trade in East Asia*

Triangular trading patterns involve Japan, South Korea, Taiwan, and MNCs in ASEAN shipping sophisticated intermediate goods to China and ASEAN for processing and re-exporting of the final products all over the world. Examining the flow of intermediate goods can shed light on the evolution of production networks in Asia.

Figure 7.1 (and Table 7.1) shows Japan's exports of intermediate goods to East Asia. China received 38 percent of Japan's exports for processing. Large quantities also flowed to ASEAN countries and the East Asian newly industrializing economies (NIEs, i.e., South Korea and Taiwan). Figure 7.2 shows the level of technological intensity of Japanese exports to East Asia.[4]

[2]More than half of this surplus was recorded as being with China. If exports were measured on a value-added basis rather than on a gross basis, however, the deficit with China would have been far less and the deficit with the rest of Asia far more.

[3]This section draws on Thorbecke and Yoshitomi (2006).

[4]Technological intensity is calculated by the Centre D'Etudes Prospectives et D'Information Internationale (CEPII) based on the type of goods exported measured at the HS 6 digit level. For instance, 252 products at the HS 6 digit level are classified as high-tech. See Gaulier *et al.* (2005).

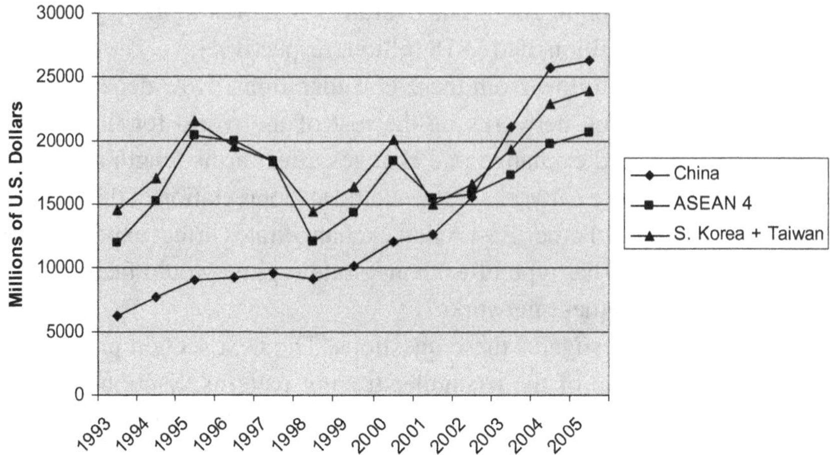

Fig. 7.1. Japanese intermediate goods exports to East Asia.
Source: CEPII-CHELEM Database.

Table 7.1. Japanese intermediate goods exports to East Asia (billions of U.S. dollars).

Regions	1993	1996	1999	2000	2001	2002	2003	2004	2005
China	6.2	9.2	10.1	12.1	12.6	15.6	21.1	25.7	26.3
ASEAN 4	12.0	20.0	14.3	18.4	15.5	15.8	17.3	19.7	19.7
Korea + Taiwan	14.5	19.5	16.3	20.1	15.0	16.6	19.3	22.9	23.9

Source: CEPII-CHELEM Database.

Not surprisingly, over 75 percent of these exports are either high-tech or medium high-tech goods. In addition, almost none of these exports are low-tech goods.

Figure 7.3 (and Table 7.2) shows the NIEs' exports of intermediate goods to East Asia. China receives 57 percent of the NIEs' exports of intermediate goods to the region. Figure 7.4 shows that 46 percent of the NIEs' exports to the region are high-tech goods and 70 percent are either high-tech or medium high-tech goods. Ten percent of these exports are low-tech goods.

Figure 7.5 (and Table 7.3) reports results for East Asia aggregated together. They indicate that intermediate goods imports into China from East Asia exploded after 2001. Imports into ASEAN 4 and the NIEs from

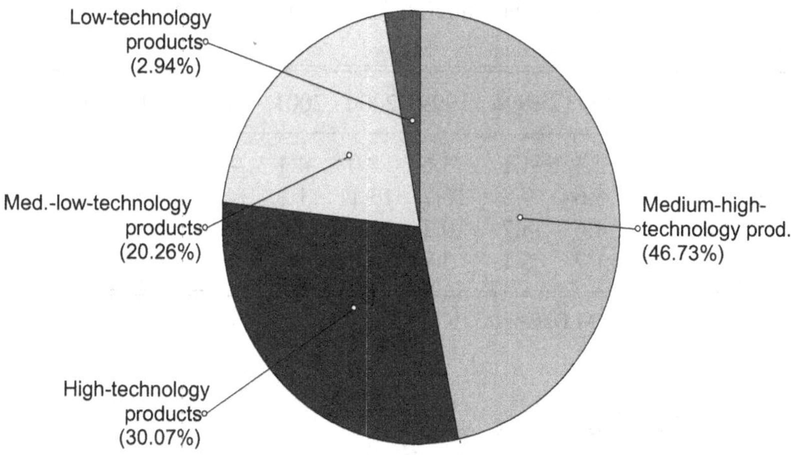

Fig. 7.2. Exports from Japan to East Asia by technological intensity.
Note: Technological intensity is calculated based on the type of goods exported measured at the HS 6 digit level. For instance, 252 products at the HS 6 digit level are classified as high-tech. See Gaulier *et al.* (2005).
Source: CEPII-CHELEM Database.

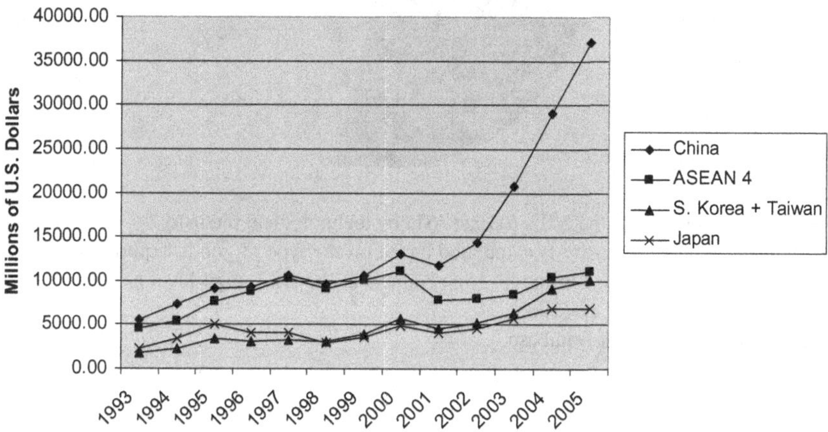

Fig. 7.3. S. Korea and Taiwan's intermediate goods exports to East Asia.
Source: CEPII-CHELEM Database.

East Asia nevertheless remained strong. As would be expected, intermediate goods imports into Japan from East Asia were the smallest.

Given the multiplication of intermediate goods exports from East Asia to China, the next section considers Chinese processing trade in more detail.

Table 7.2. Korea's and Taiwan's intermediate goods exports to East Asia (billions of U.S. dollars).

Regions	1993	1996	1999	2000	2001	2002	2003	2004	2005
Japan	2.3	4.1	3.6	5.0	4.1	4.6	5.7	6.8	6.9
China	5.6	9.3	10.7	13.1	11.8	14.4	20.7	29.1	37.1
ASEAN 4	4.6	8.7	10.1	11.2	7.8	8.0	8.6	10.5	11.2
Korea + Taiwan	1.7	3.1	3.9	5.8	4.6	5.2	6.4	9.2	10.1

Source: CEPII-CHELEM Database.

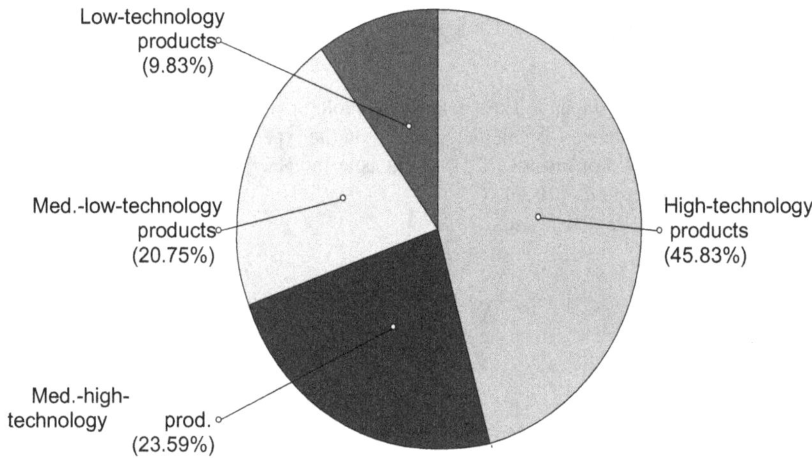

Fig. 7.4. Exports from the NIEs to East Asia by technological intensity.
Note: Technological intensity is calculated based on the type of goods exported measured at the HS 6 digit level. For instance, 252 products at the HS 6 digit level are classified as high-tech. See Gaulier *et al.* (2005).
Source: CEPII-CHELEM Database.

7.2.2. China's Role in the Global Triangular Trading Patterns

Figures 7.6–7.8 (and Tables 7.4–7.7) show China's role in this triangular trading structure. The data are taken from China's Customs Statistics, which distinguish between imports and exports linked to processing trade and ordinary imports and exports. Imports for processing are goods that are

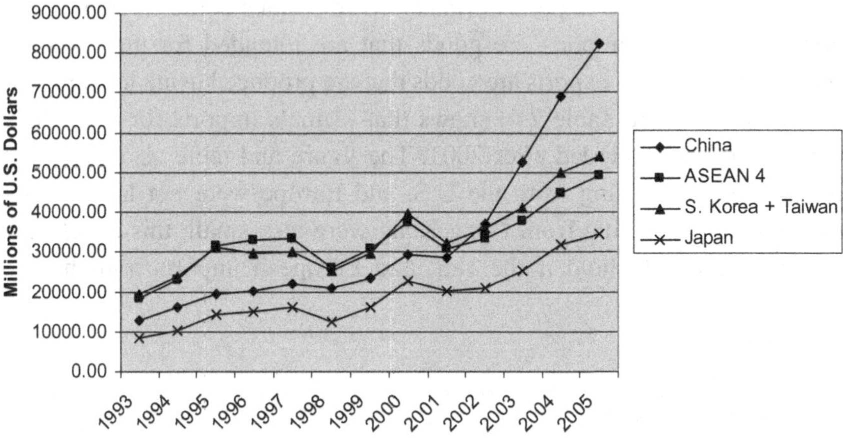

Fig. 7.5. Intermediate goods imports of individual East Asian countries and regions from East Asia as a whole.
Source: CEPII-CHELEM Database.

Table 7.3. Intermediate goods imports of individual East Asian countries and regions from East Asia as a whole (billions of U.S. dollars).

Regions	1993	1996	1999	2000	2001	2002	2003	2004	2005
Japan	8.3	15.2	16.2	22.8	20.2	21.0	25.2	31.9	34.7
China	12.8	20.2	23.7	29.3	28.8	37.0	52.6	69.1	82.1
ASEAN 4	18.4	33.2	30.9	37.6	30.9	33.4	37.8	44.9	49.4
S. Korea + Taiwan	19.6	29.7	29.8	39.8	32.2	36.0	41.0	49.9	53.9

Source: CEPII-CHELEM Database.

brought into China for processing and subsequent re-export. Processed exports, as classified by Chinese customs authorities, are goods that are produced in this way. Imports for processing are primarily intermediate goods but also include some primary goods and some final goods.[5] They are imported duty-free and neither these imports nor the finished goods

[5]In 2003, 36% of imports for processing were semi-finished goods, 42% were parts and components, 3% were primary goods, 5% were consumption goods, and 13% were capital goods. I am indebted to Deniz Unal-Kesenci of CEPII for this information.

produced using these imports normally enter China's domestic market. By contrast, ordinary imports are goods that are intended for the domestic market and ordinary exports are goods that are produced using local inputs.

Figure 7.6 (and Table 7.4) shows that China's imports for processing from East Asia exploded after 2001. The figure and table also show that imports for processing from the U.S. and Europe were not large. Since imports for processing from Hong Kong were also small, this conclusion would continue to hold if the U.S. and European imports transshipped

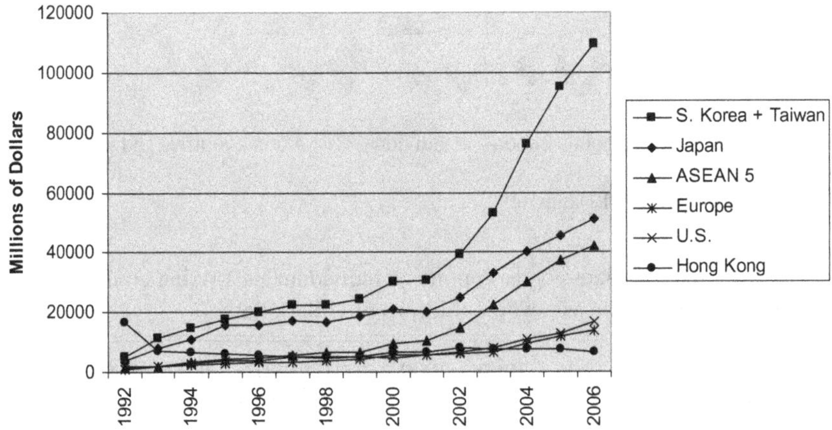

Fig. 7.6. China's Imports for processing by country and region.
Source: China Customs Statistics (2007).

Table 7.4. China's imports for processing by country and region (billions of U.S. dollars).

Regions	1992	1995	1998	2001	2002	2003	2004	2005	2006
Japan	3.9	15.6	16.7	19.9	25.0	32.8	40.2	45.2	51.1
S. Korea + Taiwan	5.0	17.9	22.7	30.4	39.3	53.3	75.9	94.9	109.7
ASEAN 5	1.3	4.2	6.7	10.4	14.9	22.6	30.0	37.4	42.3
U.S.	2.0	3.7	4.9	5.5	6.9	8.1	11.0	12.8	16.8
Europe	1.1	2.9	3.6	5.9	6.3	6.9	9.8	12.1	14.0
Hong Kong	16.6	6.3	5.2	6.6	8.0	7.7	7.8	7.7	6.8

Source: China Customs Statistics (2007).

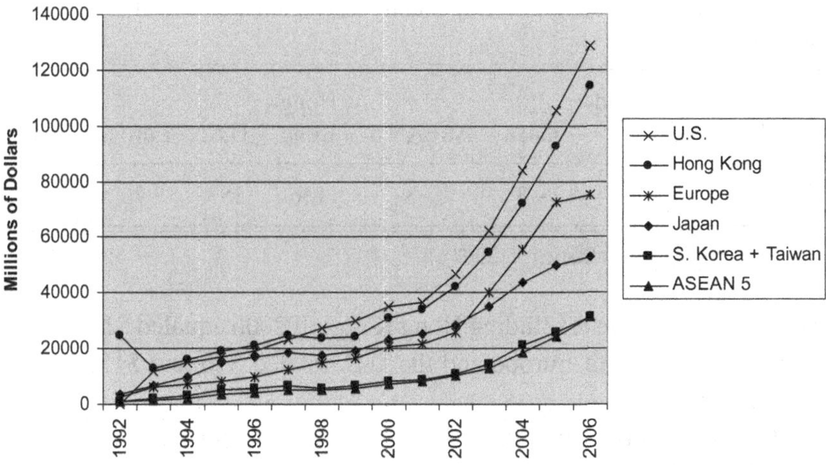

Fig. 7.7. China's processed exports by country and region.
Source: China Customs Statistics (2007).

Table 7.5. China's processed exports by country and region (billions of U.S. dollars).

Regions	1992	1995	1998	2001	2002	2003	2004	2005	2006
Japan	3.5	14.8	17.5	25.3	28.2	35.1	43.5	49.7	52.9
S. Korea + Taiwan	0.8	5.0	5.9	8.7	10.9	14.5	21.0	25.7	31.4
ASEAN 5	0.9	3.4	5.1	8.0	10.2	12.8	18.4	24.1	31.5
U.S.	27.1	17.2	23.4	36.3	46.8	62.4	83.7	105.7	128.7
Europe	2.4	8.5	12.2	21.9	25.5	39.9	55.5	72.6	75.2
Hong Kong	24.9	18.9	24.8	34.2	42.3	54.6	72.2	92.7	114.0

Source: China Customs Statistics (2007).

through Hong Kong were included. Figure 7.7 (and Table 7.5) shows China's processed exports. Processed exports to the U.S. and Europe also surged after 2001.

Because intermediate inputs are imported primarily from East Asia but not from Europe and the U.S. and because processed exports are exported throughout the world, China tends to run trade deficits with Asia but trade surpluses with Europe and the U.S. As Table 7.6 shows, China's

Table 7.6. China's trade balance by country and region in 2006 (billions of U.S. dollars).

World	S. Korea and Taiwan	Japan	ASEAN 5	Hong Kong	U.S.	Europe	ROW
178	−89	−3	−8	136	153	76	−88

Source: China Customs Statistics (2007).

deficit with East Asia (excluding Hong Kong) in 2006 equaled $100 billion and its surpluses with Europe and the U.S. totaled $76 and $153 billion, respectively.

China's surplus with the U.S. was actually larger than the official statistics indicate because of the distortionary effects of entrepôt trade through Hong Kong. Kwan (2006) argues that, because of entrepôt trade, import data are much more accurate than export data. When Chinese firms transship goods through Hong Kong, the Chinese government often does not know the final destination of the goods. They thus record these goods as being exported to Hong Kong. On the other hand, when the goods arrive at their ultimate destination the importing country records the goods as coming from China. Kwan (2006) thus advocates using import data from both trading partners to calculate bilateral trade balances. Figure 7.8 shows

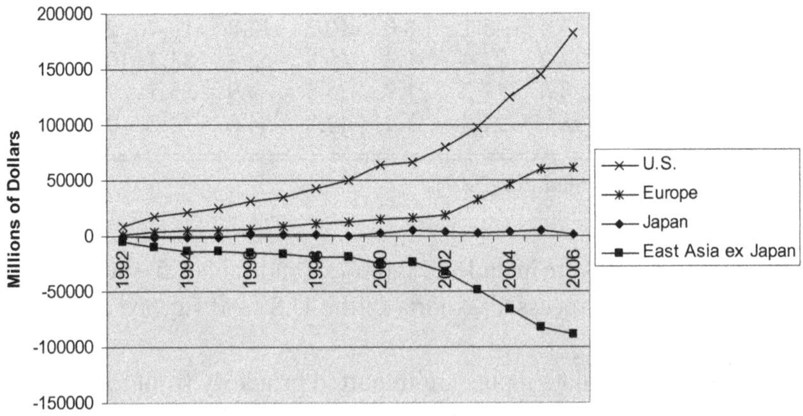

Fig. 7.8. China's trade balance in processed goods by country and region.
Source: China Customs Statistics (2007).

Table 7.7. China's trade balance in processed goods by country and region (billions of U.S. dollars).

Regions	1992	1995	1998	2001	2002	2003	2004	2005	2006
Japan	−0.4	−0.7	0.9	5.3	3.1	2.4	3.3	4.5	1.8
East Asia ex Japan	−4.6	−13.7	−18.4	−24.1	−33.1	−48.6	−66.6	−82.6	−89.0
U.S.	9.3	24.5	42.6	65.8	79.7	97.5	124.4	145.3	182.0
Europe	1.4	5.6	11.5	15.9	19.2	33.0	45.7	60.4	61.1

Source: China Customs Statistics (2007).

China's balance in processing trade with the U.S. data corrected using Kwan's approach. The figure indicates that the U.S. plays a disproportionate role as an engine of growth for processed goods.

The next section investigates the determinants of processing trade. One of the goals is to determine how exposed East Asian processing trade is to a slowdown in the rest of the world (especially the U.S.).

7.3. The Effect of Changes in Income in the Rest of the World on China's Exports[6]

7.3.1. *Data and Methodology*

According to the imperfect substitutes model of Goldstein and Khan (1985), the quantity of China's exports *demanded* by other countries depends on income in the other countries and the price of China's exports relative to the price of domestically produced goods in those countries. The quantity of exports *supplied* by China depends on the export price relative to China's price level. By equating demand and supply one can derive an export function (for instance, see Chinn, 2005):

$$\mathrm{ex}_t = \alpha_{10} + \alpha_{11}\mathrm{rer}_t + \alpha_{12}\mathrm{rgdp}_t * + \varepsilon_{1t}, \tag{7.1}$$

[6]This section focuses on the effects of changes in income in the rest of the world on China's exports. Thorbecke and Smith (2007) focus on the effects of exchange rate changes in China and the countries supplying intermediate inputs on China's exports.

where ex_t represents real exports, rer_t represents the real exchange rate, and $rgdp_t*$ represents foreign real income.

To control for any changes in the supply of exports we include the Chinese capital stock in manufacturing. Cheung *et al.* (2006) employ this variable as a proxy for China's supply capacity.[7]

We thus model the individual export equations using the following specification:

$$ex_{it} = \beta_0 + \beta_1 rgdp_{it} + \beta_2 rer_{it} + \beta_3 K_t + \beta_4 Time + \mu_i + \nu_{it}, \qquad (7.2)$$
$$t = 1, \ldots, T; \quad i = 1, \ldots, N.$$

where ex_{it} represents real processed exports from China to country i, $rgdp_{it}$ equals real income in the importing country, rer_{it} represents the bilateral real exchange rate between China and country i, K_t denotes the Chinese capital stock in manufacturing, *Time* is a time trend, and μ_i is a country i fixed effect. The variables are measured in natural logs.[8]

Data on processed exports are obtained from China's Customs Statistics. They are deflated using (1) the U.S. Bureau of Labor Statistics (BLS) price deflator for imports from non-industrial countries, (2) the Hong Kong export price deflator, and (3) the U.S. consumer price index. The first approach follows Cheung *et al.* (2006), the second may be useful since many of Hong Kong's exports are re-exports from China, and the third follows Eichengreen *et al.* (2004). The results reported below are insensitive to the choice of deflator.

Data on real GDP and the real exchange rate are obtained from the CEPII-CHELEM database.[9] Real GDP is measured in millions of PPP dollars. The real exchange rate is calculated using PPP standards and represents the bilateral real exchange rate between China and the importing country measured in levels.

[7]The series on China's capital stock in manufacturing was constructed by Bai *et al.* (2006).
[8]Rahman and Thorbecke (2007) report the results of Levin–Lin–Chu (2002) panel unit root tests that indicate the real exports and real gross domestic product are trend stationary series and the exchange rate variables are I(0) stationary series.
[9]For a description of CHELEM, see www.cepii.fr/anglaisgraph/bdd/chelem.htm.

The panel is composed of processed exports from China to 33 countries over the 1994–2005 period.[10] The variables ex_{it}, rer_{it}, and $rgdp_{it}$ vary both over time and across countries, while K_t only varies across time.

7.3.2. *Results*

Table 7.8 presents the results. Results are presented using all three deflators and both including and excluding the capital stock and the time trend.

The focus here is on the income elasticity. It is positive and statistically significant in every case. The values range from 2.46 to 2.63. The results are robust to the choice of deflator or to whether the capital stock or the time trend variable is included. Thus, the income elasticity for processed exports is high. The coefficient on the bilateral exchange rate is of the expected negative sign. It is also statistically significant in every specification. The elasticities range from −0.64 to −0.86.

One problem is that the bilateral RMB exchange rate is very closely correlated with the trade-weighted exchange rate in the rest of East Asia. Since much of the value added for processing trade comes from other East Asian countries, the trade-weighted exchange rate in the rest of Asia may be more important than the bilateral RMB exchange rate in explaining processed exports. Rahman and Thorbecke (2007) and Thorbecke and Smith (2007) present evidence that a generalized appreciation in Asia would have a much larger effect on processed exports than a unilateral appreciation of the RMB.

Either the time variable or the Chinese capital stock is significant when it is included alone. When both are included together, however, neither is significant. This probably reflects the fact that the two variables are highly correlated because both are trending upwards.

The important implication of the results presented here is that a decrease in foreign income could cause a large decrease in processed exports. This in turn could reduce output and employment throughout the region. Thus,

[10] The countries are Argentina, Australia, Austria, Belgium, Brazil, Canada, Denmark, Finland, France, Germany, Greece, Hong Kong, Indonesia, Iceland, Ireland, Italy, Japan, Luxembourg, Malaysia, Mexico, the Netherlands, New Zealand, the Philippines, Portugal, Russian Federation, Singapore, South Korea, Spain, Sweden, Taiwan, Thailand, the U.K., and the U.S.

Table 7.8. Panel OLS estimates of China's processed exports to 33 countries over the 1994–2005 period.

	Exports deflated by:								
Independent variables	BLS manu-facturing price deflator	BLS manu-facturing price deflator	BLS manu-facturing Price deflator	Hong Kong export price deflator	Hong Kong export price deflator	Hong Kong export price deflator	U.S. CPI	U.S. CPI	U.S. CPI
Real GDP	2.57***	2.65***	2.46***	2.57***	2.63***	2.46***	2.61***	2.53***	2.47***
	(0.64)	(0.57)	(0.59)	(0.64)	(0.56)	(0.59)	(0.64)	(0.56)	(0.59)
Bilateral RER	−0.69***	−0.64***	−0.83***	−0.69***	−0.65***	−0.85***	−0.66***	−0.71***	−0.86***
	(0.16)	(0.18)	(0.16)	(0.16)	(0.18)	(0.16)	(0.16)	(0.17)	(0.16)
Capital stock	1.36	1.84***		1.51*	1.88***		1.93***	1.46***	
	(0.86)	(0.16)		(0.86)	(0.15)		(0.86)	(0.15)	
Time	0.04		0.16***	0.03		0.16***	−0.04		0.12***
	(0.08)		(0.01)	(0.08)		(0.01)	(0.08)		(0.01)
Adjusted R-squared	0.98	0.98	0.98	0.98	0.98	0.98	0.98	0.98	0.97
No. of observations	396	396	396	396	396	396	396	396	396

Notes: Heteroskedasticity-consistent standard errors are in parentheses.
*** (**) [*] denotes significance at the 1% (5%) [10%] level.

East Asian countries involved in processing trade are exposed to the risk of a slowdown among the countries purchasing the assembled final products.

The next section considers how exchange rate changes affect the flow of goods within East Asian production networks.

7.4. Estimating the Effects of Exchange Rate Changes on Triangular Trading Patterns[11]

7.4.1. *Data and methodology*

We use a gravity model to estimate the effect of exchange rate changes on triangular trading patterns in Asia. Gravity models posit that bilateral trade between two countries is directly proportional to GDP in the two countries and inversely proportional to the distance between them. In addition to GDP and distance, these models typically include other factors affecting bilateral trade such as whether trading partners share a common language or a common border.[12]

Bénassy-Quéré and Lahrèche-Révil (2003) estimate a gravity model using panel data techniques for total exports from East Asian countries to other East Asian countries and to the rest of the world. Their model includes variables measuring how exports are affected by changes in the level and volatility of exchange rates and by changes in the exporting country's competitiveness relative to other East Asian countries.

We modify Bénassy-Quéré and Lahrèche-Révil's (2003) model by disaggregating exports into intermediate goods and capital goods. Disaggregating by stages of production should shed light on how exchange rate changes affect trade within Asia, given the importance of fragmented production blocks in the region. To do this we use the CHELEM database constructed by the Centre D'Etudes Prospectives et D'Information Internationale (CEPII). CHELEM disaggregates international trade into stages of production. The data are harmonized to reconcile discrepancies between exports reported by a country and imports of the same goods reported by its trading partner.

[11] This section draws on Thorbecke (2006a).

[12] Leamer and Levinsohn (1995, p. 1384) have stated that gravity models yield "some of the clearest and most robust findings in economics."

The baseline model estimated here has the form:

$$\begin{aligned}\ln Ex_{ijt} = {} & \beta_0 + \beta_1 \ln Y_{it} + \beta_2 \ln Y_{jt} + \beta_3 \ln DIST_{ij} + \beta_4 Asia * \ln RER_{ijt} \\ & + \beta_5(1 - Asia) * \ln RER_{ijt} + \beta_6 * VOL_{ijt} + \beta_7 LANG \\ & + \partial_i + \Omega_j + \pi_t + \varepsilon_{ijt},\end{aligned} \tag{7.3}$$

where Ex_{ijt} represents real exports from East Asian country i to country j (either in East Asia or in the rest of the world), t represents time, Y represents real GDP, *DIST* represents the distance between the two countries, *ASIA* is a dummy variable equaling 1 if the country is in East Asia and 0 otherwise, RER_{ijt} is the bilateral real exchange rate between country i and country j, *VOL* represents exchange rate volatility (the annual coefficient of variation calculated using quarterly data), *LANG* is a dummy variables equaling 1 if the countries share a common language and 0 otherwise, and ∂_i, Ω_j, and π_t are country i, country j, and time fixed effects, respectively.[13] East Asia includes China, Hong Kong, Indonesia, Japan, Malaysia, Singapore, South Korea, Taiwan, and Thailand. Non-East Asian countries include the OECD countries[14] and Argentina, Brazil, Mexico, and India. The focus here is on the export of capital goods and intermediate goods from Japan, South Korea, and Taiwan to the rest of Asia.[15]

Data on exports disaggregated into intermediate goods and capital goods; real income, and the real exchange rate are obtained from the CEPII-CHELEM database. Export and import data are measured in current dollars and deflated by the U.S. CPI. Real GDP is measured in millions of PPP dollars. The real exchange rate is calculated using PPP standards and represents the bilateral real exchange rate between the exporting and importing countries measured in levels. The export, import, exchange rate, income, and relative competitiveness variables are measured in natural logs. Data on distance and common language are obtained from www.cepii.fr. Distance is measured in kilometers and represents the distance between economic centers.

[13]Because of multicollinearity problems the common border dummy variable is dropped.

[14]The OECD countries used are Australia, Austria, Belgium-Luxembourg, Canada, Germany, Denmark, Spain, Finland, France, the United Kingdom, Greece, Ireland, Italy, the Netherlands, New Zealand, Portugal, Sweden, and the United States.

[15]Thorbecke (2007) looks at capital and intermediate goods exports from Japan alone.

The gravity model is estimated as a panel using annual data for the 30 countries over the 1982–2003 sample period. Fixed effects are included for the exporting and importing countries and for time. The maximum possible number of observations is 5742.

7.4.2. *Results*

Table 7.9 presents the results for capital goods. The model performs well. All of the variables are of the theoretically expected sign and many are statistically significant. The results indicate that a 10 percent appreciation of the bilateral exchange rate on average reduces capital goods exports from Japan, South Korea, and Taiwan to the rest of East Asia by 15.9 percent and to the rest of the world by 15.2 percent. The exchange rate volatility variable is not statistically significant.

Table 7.10 presents the results for intermediate goods. Again the model performs well. The results now indicate that a 10 percent appreciation of the bilateral exchange rate on average reduces intermediate goods exports from Japan, South Korea, and Taiwan to the rest of East Asia by 6.2 percent and to the rest of the world by 3.8 percent. The exchange rate volatility variable is now negative and statistically significant, indicating that an increase in volatility reduces intermediate goods exports.

These findings indicate that the level of the exchange rate is more important for capital goods exports within Asia but the volatility of the exchange rate is more important for intermediate goods exports. Capital goods exports from Japan and the NIEs are often part of arms–length exchanges. Japan and the NIEs are the major suppliers of sophisticated capital goods to firms in the rest of Asia. An appreciation in developed Asia would make it harder for firms in the rest of Asia to obtain these vital inputs that are difficult to procure elsewhere.

Intermediate goods exports, especially parts and components, are often part of intra-firm trade. When firms are deciding on the optimal degree of fragmentation they weigh the benefits and costs along several dimensions (Kimura and Ando, 2005). One such dimension is location. Exchange rate volatility, by increasing uncertainty, reduces the locational benefits of cross-border fragmentation. It thus reduces intermediate goods exports.

There are two important implications of these findings. One implication is that capital goods exports within Asia are sensitive to bilateral

Table 7.9. Determinants of capital goods exports from developed Asia.

Explanatory Variables							
For Exports from Developed Asia		For Exports from all East Asian Countries[a]					
Bilateral RER (for exports to other East Asian countries)	Bilateral RER (for exports to countries in the ROW)	Income (Importer)	Income (Exporter)	Distance	Quarterly volatility	Common language	Constant term
−1.59***	−1.52***	0.45**	0.01	−0.65***	0.10	0.37***	−1.12
(−8.46)	(−8.68)	(2.99)	(0.02)	(−7.51)	(0.63)	(2.71)	(−0.55)
Number of observations	5587						
Adjusted R-squared	0.83						
S.E of regression	1.04						
F-statistics	401.6						
Prob (F-statistic)	0.000000						

Notes: Developed Asia is defined as Japan, South Korea, and Taiwan. East Asia is defined as China, Hong Kong, Indonesia, Japan, Malaysia, Singapore, South Korea, Taiwan, and Thailand. ROW is defined as the OECD countries plus Argentina, Brazil, Mexico, and India. The model is estimated as a panel with 9 East Asian countries exporting to each other and to 21 non-East Asian countries over the 1982–2003 period. Because the data are pooled, developed Asia's RER elasticity for exports to East Asia represents the average of the RER elasticities for exports to each of the other East Asian countries. Similarly, developed Asia's RER elasticity for exports to the ROW represents the average of the RER elasticities for exports to each of the 21 non-East Asian countries. White's (1980) standard errors are employed. t-statistics are in parentheses. *** (**) denotes significance at the 1% (5%) level.

[a]The exchange rate coefficient for exports from East Asian countries other than Japan was −2.01 with a t-statistic of 12.97.

Table 7.10. Determinants of intermediate goods exports from developed Asia.

Explanatory Variables							
For Exports from Developed Asia		For Exports from all East Asian Countries[a]					
Bilateral RER (for exports to other East Asian countries)	Bilateral RER (for exports to countries in the ROW)	Income (Importer)	Income (Exporter)	Distance	Quarterly volatility	Common language	Constant term
−0.62***	−0.38***	0.30**	−0.03*	−0.56***	−0.44**	0.44***	0.51
(−3.87)	(−2.39)	(2.40)	(−1.71)	(−7.51)	(−2.18)	(2.39)	(0.28)
Number of observations	5677						
Adjusted R-squared	0.86						
S.E of regression	0.82						
F-statistics	527.9						
Prob(F-statistic)	0.000000						

Notes: Developed Asia is defined as Japan, South Korea, and Taiwan. East Asia is defined as China, Hong Kong, Indonesia, Japan, Malaysia, Singapore, South Korea, Taiwan, and Thailand. ROW is defined as the OECD countries plus Argentina, Brazil, Mexico, and India. The model is estimated as a panel with 9 East Asian countries exporting to each other and to 21 non-East Asian countries over the 1982–2003 period. Because the data are pooled, developed Asia's RER elasticity for exports to East Asia represents the average of the RER elasticities for exports to each of the other East Asian countries. Similarly, developed Asia's RER elasticity for exports to the ROW represents the average of the RER elasticities for exports to each of the 21 non-East Asian countries. White's (1980) standard errors are employed. t-statistics are in parentheses. *** (**) denotes significance at the 1% (5%) level.

[a]The exchange rate coefficient for exports from East Asian countries other than Japan was −1.04 with a t-statistic of −8.62.

exchange rate changes. Since there is essentially a complimentary relationship between developed East Asian countries on the one hand and developing Asia on the other hand in sophisticated intermediate and capital goods trade, these results imply that exchange rate appreciations in developed Asia relative to developing Asia would reduce intra-regional gains from trade. Firms in developed Asia would be harmed because their exports to the rest of Asia would fall and firms in developing Asia would be harmed because they would be less able to procure vital inputs that are difficult to obtain elsewhere. The second implication is that exchange rate volatility deters the flow of intermediate goods and thus the slicing up of the value-added chain. By extension, exchange rate stability should provide a stable backdrop for East Asian production networks.

7.5. Concluding Remarks

Multinational corporations have split up production processes in East Asia into fragmented blocks that can be allocated across countries based on differences in capital, skill, labor, and infrastructure. The resulting efficiency gains have been enormous. The rapid development of the value-added chain in the region has been accompanied by massive flows of exports from East Asia to the rest of the world and by growing trade imbalances. Large surpluses in East Asian countries coupled with a variety of exchange rates in the region threaten to create exchange rate instability. This in turn could disrupt regional production networks.

The results presented here and other work provide some guidance for policymakers in the area of exchange rate policy. First, exchange rate stability might provide a stable backdrop for East Asian production networks. Second, an appreciation in Japan, South Korea, and Taiwan relative to the rest of East Asia would disrupt the complimentary relationship that exists between Japan and developed Asia in sophisticated capital goods trade. Third, elements of competition exist in any international trading market and hence fear of losing competitiveness relative to other Asian economies may prevent them from allowing their currencies to strengthen alone. This may explain the unwillingness of some countries in the region to allow unilateral appreciations of their currencies. Fourth, since intra-regional trade accounts for more than 50 percent of total trade in Asia, a multilateral appreciation against the dollar would increase effective exchange rates in Asia by less than half as much. Fifth, exchange rate appreciations throughout Asia would affect the relative foreign currency costs not just of China's value-added in processed exports but also that of the entire output of processed exports (see Yoshitomi, 2007; Thorbecke and Smith, 2007). They would thus have a much larger effect on China's processed exports than a unilateral RMB appreciation.

An RMB appreciation alone would primarily affect ordinary (non-processed) exports.[16] These tend to be simple, labor-intensive goods such as toys and textiles. If the goal of an RMB appreciation is to help resolve imbalances between China and the rest of the world (especially the U.S.), a reduction in ordinary exports might not be helpful. A reduction in ordinary exports from China to the rest of the world would probably be replaced by an increase in labor-intensive exports from other countries occupying lower rungs on the ladder of comparative advantage. A generalized appreciation in East Asia, on the other hand, would cause a larger decline in the export of capital-intensive, technologically sophisticated processed exports. A generalized appreciation would thus be more likely to switch expenditures towards the U.S. goods and help to rebalance the world trade.

It might thus be desirable to have stable exchange rates within Asia that appreciate together in response to large surpluses with the rest of the world. This would preserve the flow of capital and intermediate goods within production networks. It may also help to resolve potentially unsustainable global imbalances. However, as Yoshitomi (2007) and Kawai (2006) discuss, global imbalances could disrupt exchange rate stability within the region.

There are currently a variety of exchange rate systems in Asia. Japan and South Korea have essentially free floating regimes; Thailand and Indonesia have managed floats; and China has a *de facto* fixed exchange rate regime (see Chapter 2 of this volume). Under the current system, if trade imbalances triggered appreciations in the region, currencies in developed Asia would appreciate relative to currencies in developing Asia. This problem could be mitigated if China and other countries in the region with less flexible

---

[16]While Thorbecke (2006b) reports that an RMB appreciation would reduce China's exports, Thorbecke and Smith (2007) find that ordinary exports would be affected much more than processed exports.

exchange rates adopted more flexible regimes. In this case the large surpluses that East Asia is running in processing trade would allow currencies in the region to appreciate together. If market forces led to joint appreciations in this way, they would help to maintain relatively stable intra-regional exchange rates in the face of the current global imbalances.

For China and other developing Asian countries more flexible regimes could be characterized by (1) multiple currency basket-based reference rates instead of a dollar-based central rate, and (2) wider bands around the reference rate. Greater exchange rate flexibility in the context of a multiple currency basket-based reference rate would probably be preferable to a free floating regime for Asian countries with underdeveloped financial institutions. It would allow their currencies to appreciate in response to global imbalances but still enable policymakers to limit excessive volatility.

Stable intra-regional exchange rates, in turn, would provide a steady backdrop for the production and distribution networks that have helped to make East Asia the manufacturing center of the world.

References

Bai, C, C Hsieh, and Q Qian (2006). Returns to Capital in China. *Brookings Papers on Economic Activity*, 2, 1–60.

Bénassy-Quéré, A and A Lahrèche-Révil (2003). Trade linkages and exchange rates. In *Asia: The Role of China*. CEPII Working Paper No. 21. Paris: Centre D'Etudes Prospectives et D'Information Internationales.

Borrus, J, D Ernst and S Haggard (2000). *International Production Networks in Asia*. London and New York: Routledge.

Cheung, Y, M Chinn and E Fujii (2006). China's current account and exchange rate. Paper presented at NBER Conference on China's Growing Role in World Trade, Cambridge, MA (December 14).

Chinn, M (2005). Doomed to deficits? Aggregate U.S. trade flows re-visited. *Review of World Economics*, 141, 460–85.

Eichengreen, B, Y Rhee and H Tong (2004). The impact of China on the exports of other Asian countries. NBER Working Paper No. 10768.

Fukao, K, H Ishido, K Ito and Y Yoshiike (2002). Vertical intra-industry trade and foreign direct investment in East Asia. Asian Development Bank Institute Research Paper No. 51.

Gaulier, G, F Lemoine and D Unal-Kesenci (2005). China's integration in East Asia: Production sharing, FDI, and high-tech trade. CEPII Working Paper No. 2005–2009. Paris: Centre D'Etudes Prospectives et D'Information Internationales.

Goldstein, M and MS Khan (1985). Income and price effects in foreign trade. In *Handbook of International Economics*, Vol. 2, RW Jones and PB Kenen (eds.). Elsevier Science Publishers.

Kawai, M (2006). The role of an Asian currency unit. Paper presented at the RIETI International Conference on Regional Monetary Coordination and Regional Monetary Unit (December 23).

Kimura, F and M Ando (2005). Two-dimensional fragmentation in East Asia: Conceptual framework and empirics. *International Review of Economics and Finance*, 14, 317–348.

Kwan, CH (2006). *The Actual State of the United States and Japan's Trade Imbalances with China—Taking into Consideration Transit Trade through Hong Kong*. Tokyo: Research Institute of Economy, Trade, and Industry. Available at: http://www.rieti.go.jp/en/china/06022402.html.

Leamer, E and J Levinsohn (1995). International trade theory: The evidence. In *The Handbook of International Economics*, Vol. III, Grossman G and K Rogoff, (eds.). Amsterdam: North Holland.

Levin, A, CF Lin and C Chu (2002). Unit root tests in panel data: Asymptotic and Finite-sample properties. *Journal of Econometrics*, 108, 1–24.

Rahman, M and W Thorbecke (2007). How would China's exports be affected by a unilateral appreciation of the RMB and a joint appreciation of countries supply in intermediate imports? *RIETI Discussion Paper 2007/03 07-E-012*. Tokyo: RIETI. Available at: http://www.rieti.go.jp/en/publications/summary/07030015.html

Thorbecke, W (2006a). The effect of exchange rate changes on trade in East Asia. *RIETI Discussion Paper 2006/03 06-E-009*. Tokyo: RIETI. Available at: http://www.rieti.go.jp/en/publications/summary/06030003.html.

Thorbecke, W (2006b). How would an appreciation of the RMB affect the U.S. trade deficit with China? *The B.E. Journal in Macroeconomics*, 6, 1–15.

Thorbecke, W (2007). Global imbalances, triangular trading patterns, and the Yen/Dollar exchange rate. *Journal of the Japanese and International Economies*, forthcoming.

Thorbecke, W and G Smith (2007). The effect of an appreciation in China and other East Asian countries on China's ordinary and processed exports. *Review of International Economics*, forthcoming.

Thorbecke, W and M Yoshitomi (2006). Trade-FDI-technology linkages in East Asia. Prepared for the NEAT Working Group Meeting in Tokyo, 7 July 2006. Available at: http://www.rieti.go.jp/users/neat/en/pdf/finalreport.pdf.

White, H (1980). A heteroscedasity-consistent covariance matrix estimator and a direct test for heteroscedasity. *Econometrica*, 48, 817–838.

Yoshitomi, M (2007). Global imbalances and East Asian monetary cooperation. In *Toward an East Asian Exchange Rate Regime*, D-K Chung and B Eichengreen (eds.). Washington, DC: Brookings Institution Press.

Yusuf, S, A Altaf, B Eichengreen, S Gooptu, K Nabeshima, C Kenny, D Perkins and M Shotten (2003). Redrawing the international boundary of the firm in East Asia: The evolution of international production networks. In *Innovative East Asia: The Future of Growth*, Yusuf *et al.*, (eds.). Washington, DC: World Bank.

PART IV

REGIONAL EXCHANGE RATE, MONETARY AND FINANCIAL COOPERATION

CHAPTER 8

REGIONAL MONETARY COORDINATION IN EAST ASIA

Eiji Ogawa

8.1. Introduction

The Asian Currency Crisis has given the monetary authorities of East Asian countries strong incentive to launch a regional monetary cooperation in the last 10 years. The ASEAN (Association of Southeast Asian Nations) plus Three (ASEAN plus Three) countries (Japan, China, and Korea) have been strengthening their regional monetary cooperation since 2000 under the Chiang Mai Initiative (CMI). Under the CMI, they established a network of bilateral swap arrangements for managing currency crises among the member countries. The regional monetary authorities have also established a surveillance process for preventing currency crises under the CMI. Further, the ASEAN plus Three Finance Ministers' Meeting has set up a research group to study the feasibility of creating a Regional Monetary Unit (RMU) for a surveillance process under the CMI and a possibility of a coordinated exchange rate policy in the future.

This chapter considers recent linkages among East Asian currencies with three major world currencies (i.e., the U.S. dollar, the euro, and the Japanese yen) and examines recent movements of Asian exchange rates with the aim of ascertaining the extent of divergence in the regional exchange rate policies. Using a synthetic Asian Monetary Unit (AMU) and AMU Deviation Indicators,[1] Section 8.2 finds that there has been widening deviation among the East Asian currencies. The deviation of the

[1] See Ogawa and Shimizu (2005) for detailed explanation. Data of AMU and AMU Deviation Indicators are available at a website of the Research Institute of Economy, Trade, and Industry (http://www.rieti.go.jp/users/amu/en/index.html).

East Asian currencies is argued to be mainly due to a coordination failure in exchange rate policy among the monetary authorities of East Asian countries. Section 8.3 emphasizes the importance of regional monetary coordination, and in particular, recommends the creation of a RMU to coordinate exchange rate policy among the monetary authorities of East Asian countries. It recommends a multi-step approach to regional monetary coordination in East Asia. The final section offers a few concluding remarks. Appendix A elaborates on how a RMU for Asia (the so-called AMU) might be computed and can be used as a basis for coordination of the exchange rate policy.

8.2. Coordination Failure in Exchange Rate Policy among APT Countries

One would logically have expected the growing current accounts deficits in the United States (U.S.) to have caused the U.S. dollar to depreciate against currencies of the rest of the world, including those in East Asia. However, when we examine the movements of the East Asian currencies, we find that East Asian economies have experienced asymmetric reactions to the U.S. dollar depreciation in the last several years (Ogawa and Kudo, 2007). The Korean won, the Thai baht, and the Singapore dollar have appreciated against the U.S. dollar since 2002. The Japanese yen also appreciated before 2006 although it has been fluctuating a great deal more recently. The Chinese yuan and the Malaysian ringgit were pegged to the U.S. dollar before July 21, 2005, after which the Chinese and Malaysian governments announced that they were moving to a managed floating exchange rate systems with reference to a currency basket. However, the Chinese yuan still has very strong linkages with the U.S. dollar in a sense that over the years it has experienced a gradual appreciation against the U.S. dollar at an almost constant rate (Ogawa and Sakane, 2006). Since the rate of appreciation of the Chinese yuan against the U.S. dollar is slower than that of the other Asian currencies, the Chinese yuan has effectively been depreciating against the other Asian currencies.

The East Asian currencies have experienced asymmetric reaction to the depreciation of the U.S. dollar under a variety of exchange rate systems as pointed out in Ogawa (2004). The asymmetric reaction of the East Asian currencies to the depreciation of the U.S. dollar has deviated among the East Asian currencies and has given a bias to relative prices among products made in the East Asian countries. In particular, as discussed by other chapters in this volume (see Chapter 2 by Cavoli and Rajan and Chapter 10 by Genberg and He), we can classify the East Asian countries' exchange rate systems into three groups: a floating group, a managed floating group, and a fixed (dollar pegging) group. The group of the countries that adopts the floating or managed floating exchange rate systems has seen their home currencies appreciate against the U.S. dollar since 2002. This group includes Japan, Korea, Thailand, and Singapore. The other group consists of countries that have fixed their home currencies to the U.S. dollar. This group includes China, Cambodia, and Vietnam as well as Malaysia before July 21, 2005.

It would be useful to examine the extent of deviation of each East Asian currency from "the weighted average" of East Asian currencies or "AMU" for East Asia (Ogawa and Shimizu, 2005, 2006). The AMU is basically a weighted average of the ASEAN plus Three currencies. The weights of the currencies in the currency basket are based on arithmetic averages of the countries' respective shares of GDP measured at Purchasing Power Parity (PPP) and trade volumes (the sum of exports and imports) in the total of sampled countries for the relevant country. In Appendix A, the countries' shares of GDP measured at PPP and their trade volumes are calculated as the average for the most recent 3 years (from 2002 to 2004) for which data are available. In addition, an AMU Deviation Indicator is created in order to measure the extent of deviation of each currency from the AMU. The AMU Deviation Indicators are set to zero during their benchmark period of 2 years in 2000 and 2001 when trade imbalances of East Asian countries were the smallest during the recent decade (see Appendix A for details).

Figure 8.1 shows the recent trends of nominal exchange rate of the AMU in terms of a currency basket of the U.S. dollar and the euro as well as in terms of the U.S. dollar and the euro individually. The currency basket of the U.S. dollar and the euro is composed of the U.S. dollar with 65 percent of share and the euro with 35 percent of share based on trade shares of East Asian economy respectively, with the U.S. and the euro area in years of 2002–2004 in order to reflect the value of the AMU in terms of the major trading partners' currencies. Figure 8.1 shows that the AMU has been gradually depreciating against the currency basket of the U.S. dollar and

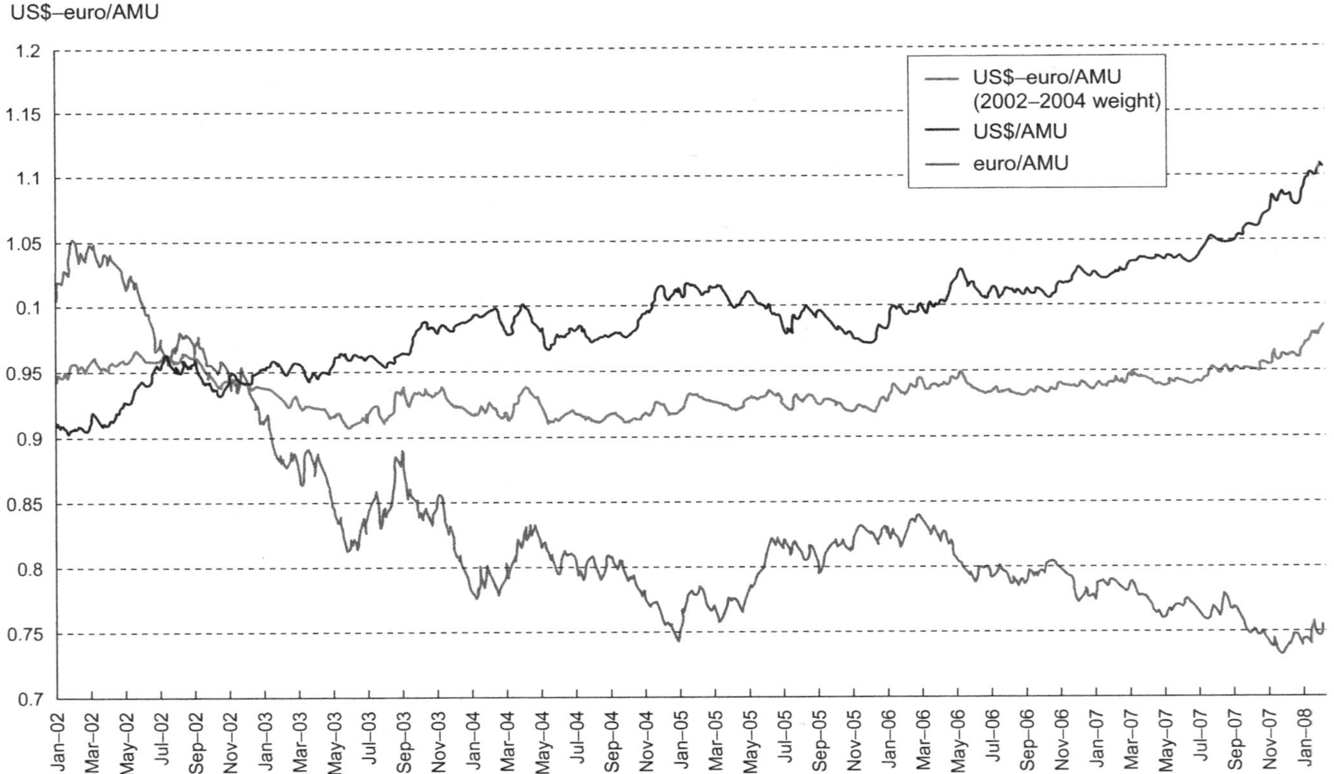

Fig. 8.1. AMU in terms of the US$-euro (benchmark year = 2000/2001, basket weight = 2003–2005).
Source: http://www. rieti.go.jp/users/amu/en/index.html.

the euro. It has depreciated against the currency basket by about 5 percent in May 2007 as compared with the benchmark years of 2000–2001. The AMU has been gradually appreciating against the U.S. dollar, while it has been gradually depreciating against the euro.

Figure 8.2 shows the movements in deviations of East Asian currencies against the AMU. The AMU Deviation Indicators of East Asian currencies had been limited within ±10 percent during the period from 2001 to the end of 2004 except for the Philippine peso. The Korean won appreciated against the AMU in 2005. It was overvalued by more than 20 percent when compared to the benchmark years. The Thai baht appreciated very quickly from the end of 2005 to mid-2006. It was overvalued by more than 20 percent as compared with the benchmark years. On the other hand, the Philippine peso had been undervalued by more than 10 percent from 2003 to 2006. The Laos kip was devalued by 25 percent in April 2004, though it has been relatively stable after the devaluation although it is undervalued vis-à-vis the AMU. The Vietnamese don has been gradually depreciating and is undervalued by 20 percent as compared with the benchmark years. In summary, the AMU or a weighted average of East Asian currencies has been appreciating against the U.S. dollar in the recent years while it has been depreciating against the currency basket of the U.S. dollar and the euro. In addition, deviations among the East Asian currencies have been widening in recent years (also see Ogawa and Yoshimi, 2007).

Ogawa and Ito (2002) point out the possibility of coordination failure in choosing exchange rate system and exchange rate policy in a game theoretical framework as long as one country's choice of the dollar peg system has an adverse effect on others' choice of their own exchange rate system through relative price effects. Ogawa (2007) conducts an empirical analysis on whether the dollar pegging currencies led to adverse effects on other East Asian countries' choice of exchange rate system and exchange rate policy. It was found that regional countries chose a *de facto* dollar peg system because the dollar pegging countries keep adopting official or *de facto* dollar peg systems. In other words, the monetary authorities in East Asian countries appear to face coordination failure in choosing a desirable exchange rate system among East Asian countries. It appears that the regional coordination of exchange rate may be a desirable way forward as opposed to the *de facto* dollar peg system that still largely operates in East Asia.

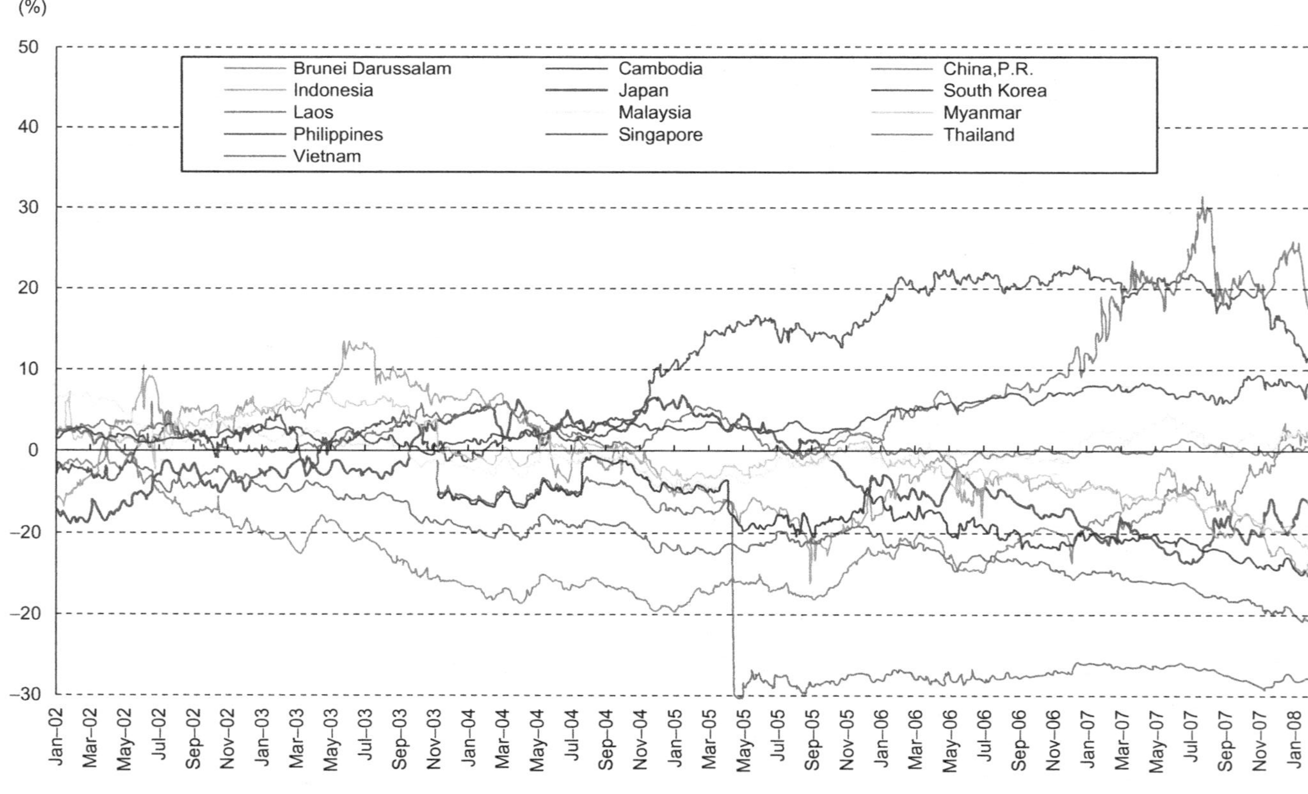

Fig. 8.2. Nominal AMU deviation indicators (benchmark year = 2000/2001, basket weight = 2003–2005, daily).
Source: http://www. rieti.go.jp/users/amu/en/index.html.

8.3. Monetary Cooperation in East Asia: Current Situation and Way Forward

8.3.1. *Current Situation: Need for Cooperation*

As noted, the monetary authorities of ASEAN plus Three have been strengthening their regional monetary cooperation since the Asian Currency Crisis in 1997 through the CMI, which is basically a network of bilateral swap arrangements (BSAs) for managing a currency crisis in the member countries. Under the CMI, the monetary authorities are supposed to conduct a surveillance process for preventing a currency crisis in the future. However, the monetary authorities do not have any working institutions to carry out any surveillance processes in East Asia. Instead, they regularly meet in an event called the Economic Review and Policy Dialogue during the ASEAN plus Three Deputy Finance Ministers' Meeting for surveillance over their macroeconomic performance although they focus on only domestic macroeconomic variables which include GDP, inflation, and the soundness of financial sector.

It is important that the East Asian monetary authorities prevent biased changes in the relative prices caused by the U.S. dollar depreciation under the different exchange rate systems in East Asian countries. To do so, they may need to coordinate their exchange rate policies and systems. Kawai *et al.* (2004) emphasize that the monetary authorities of the ASEAN plus Three should discuss the exchange rate issue as a part of the surveillance process. They argue that the regional authorities should focus on the exchange rate issue in addition to domestic macroeconomic policies and on the soundness of financial sector.

Indeed, each country in the East Asia region has strong economic relationships with the other intra-regional countries as well as vis-à-vis the U.S. and European countries. Exchange rates among the intra-regional currencies affect economic activities in each country of East Asia through intra-regional trade, investments, and finance. The monetary authorities should not only look at the movements of the exchange rates but also their deviations from the regional averages and, in turn, their exchange rate policies *per se*. The surveillance process in itself might not be sufficiently effective to preserve the regional policy coordination in the long run because the monetary authorities from each country are not committed to the policy coordination.

They may make a limited contribution to the policy coordination. It is necessary to have a mechanism that is able to preserve the regional coordination in the long run by compelling the monetary authorities to be committed to the regional policy coordination.

8.3.2. *Way Forward: Multi-Step Approach to Regional Monetary Cooperation*

Regarding regional policy coordination, it may be desirable to create a regional common unit of account to which monetary authorities of East Asian countries should target in conducting their exchange rate policies. To do so, consideration should be given to the possible introduction of a RMU to be used as a regional common unit of account into East Asia. For this purpose, a common currency basket that includes regional currencies of the ASEAN plus Three countries could be created. In fact, as noted, the ASEAN plus Three Finance Ministers' Meeting has launched a research group study a RMU for the surveillance and possible coordinated exchange rate policy, while the Asian Development Bank (ADB) also has been studying about a regional common unit of account that is called as an Asian Currency Unit (ACU).[2]

Ogawa and Shimizu (2007) suggest that a common currency basket system in the region will be gradually developed if each East Asian country adopts an individual currency basket. We suggest below a multi-step approach to regional monetary coordination in East Asia.

First, the ASEAN plus Three monetary authorities should launch policy dialogue on exchange rates and exchange rate policies for coordinated exchange rate policies among them. At the time, an RMU and deviation indicators of regional currencies should be used (see Section 8.4) to conduct surveillance over the exchange rates and exchange rate policies as well as domestic macroeconomic situation at the Economic Review and Policy Dialogue of ASEAN plus Three Deputy Finance Ministers' Meeting. The surveillance process based on the RMU should include Japan because it is a leading country in the surveillance process. Accordingly, the Japanese yen should be included in the RMU because the RMU is used as a deviation

[2]Also see Rajan (2008).

indicator at the surveillance process of the Economic Review and Policy Dialogue.

In the second step, the monetary authorities of ASEAN plus Two countries (China and Korea) should adopt a managed floating exchange rate system with reference to its own individual G3 currency (the U.S. dollar, the euro, and the Japanese yen) basket for managed floating countries. On the one hand, at the same time, the monetary authorities of ASEAN plus Three (including Japan) should keep conducting the surveillance process using the RMU and the deviation indicators of regional currencies from the RMU.

In the third step, the monetary authorities of ASEAN plus Two should shift to a managed floating exchange rate system with reference to a common G3 currency basket for managed floating countries.[3]

In the fourth step, some ASEAN plus Three countries (the so-called "core countries") would peg to a common regional currency basket (i.e., the RMU), in order to stabilize intra-regional exchange rates among the core countries. They should conduct coordinated monetary policies in order to stabilize intra-regional exchange rates. At the time, the core countries should be limited to those that adopt the RMU peg system.

In the fifth step, some of ASEAN plus Three economies would introduce a bilateral grid method based on the RMU to conduct some intervention in foreign exchange markets of the relevant intra-regional exchange rates. An Asian Exchange Rate Mechanism should be established for their coordinated intervention, which could be similar to the mechanism under the European Monetary System (EMS) before introducing the euro into the euro area.[4]

---

[3]At the second and third steps, the Japanese yen should be one of the G3 currencies that the monetary authorities of ASEAN plus Two targeted in conducting their exchange rate policies.

[4]At the fourth and fifth steps, the core countries should include Japan as an anchor country. In this case, the Japanese yen should be a regional key currency in terms of keeping its value appreciating against the U.S. dollar and the euro and maintaining disinflationary stance of monetary policy. East Asian currencies should be linked with the Japanese yen so as to ensure that the regional currencies are stable vis-à-vis on another. This might be significant in the prevention of future currency crises.

8.4. Concluding Remarks

This chapter argues that the monetary authorities in East Asia do not have coordinated exchange rate policies. However, regional monetary authorities have begun to consider how to coordinate their exchange rate policies among themselves to ensure stability of intra-regional exchange rates in a situation of developing production networks and supply chains in East Asia (also see Chapter 8 in this volume). The ASEAN plus Three Finance Ministers' Meeting has been established, and there has been a strengthening of the currency swap arrangements under the CMI. The regional policy makers are also undertaking surveillance over domestic macroeconomic variables at the Economic Review and Policy Dialogue under the CMI. The ASEAN plus Three Finance Ministers' Meeting created a research group to study the feasibility of creating an RMU for coordinated exchange rate policy as well as private uses (which might include currency denomination of Asian bonds). This chapter has emphasized the importance of creating such an RMU and has outlined a multi-step approach to regional monetary coordination in East Asia.

Appendix A

Creating an Asian Monetary Unit (AMU) and AMU Deviation Indicators

As emphasized, it is important for East Asian countries to take the first step toward regional monetary coordination by introducing a Regional Monetary Unit (RMU) into the region. How would such a unit for Asia (i.e., Asian Monetary Unit or AMU) be computed and how would it be used?

The AMU is calculated as a weighted average of East Asian currencies. The AMU Deviation Indicators for each East Asian currency are measured to show the degree of deviation from the benchmark rate for each of the East Asian currencies in terms of the AMU. Real AMU Deviation Indicators can be created by adjusting for differences in inflation, on a monthly basis as well as the Nominal AMU Deviation Indicators on a daily basis (see Ogawa and Shimizu, 2005, 2006). The real AMU Deviation Indicators are more appropriate for conducting surveillance on the effects of changes in exchange rates on the real economy, while the nominal AMU Deviation Indicators are more useful for monitoring their day-to-day deviations from the AMU.

The weight of each currency in the currency basket is based on the arithmetic averages of both the countries' respective shares of GDP measured at PPP, and trade volumes (the sum of exports and imports) in the total of sampled countries for the relevant country. We calculate the countries' shares of GDP measured at PPP and their trade volumes for 2001–2003 as the currency shares of the AMU. The average for the past 3 years on the basis of available data is used to calculate the currency shares in order to reflect the most recent trade relationships and economic conditions of the 13 East Asian countries for the calculation of the AMU. Table 8.A.1 shows the AMU weights as well as trade volume share, share of GDP measured at PPP, arithmetic shares of both the shares, and the benchmark exchange rates.

A benchmark period is chosen in order to calculate AMU Deviation Indicators. The benchmark period is defined as the following: The total trade balance of member countries, the total trade balance of member countries (excluding Japan) with Japan, and the total trade balance of member countries with the rest of world should be relatively close to zero. Data on trade accounts of the 13 East Asian countries from 1990 to 2003 indicates that the trade accounts were the closest to balance in 2001. If we assume that a one-year time lag before changes in exchange rates affect trade volumes, we should choose 2000 and 2001 as a benchmark period.

Regarding currencies with higher inflation rates, inflation rate differentials should be taken into account to calculate an AMU Deviation Indicator in real terms. Real AMU Deviation Indicators are calculated according to the following equation:

$$\text{Real deviation indicator}_i = \text{Nominal deviation indicator}_i - (\dot{P}_{\text{AMU}} - \dot{P}_i), \qquad \text{(A.1)}$$

where $\dot{P}_{\text{AMU}}$ is the inflation rate in the AMU area and $\dot{P}_i$ is the inflation rate in country i.

The Consumer Price Index (CPI) is used as the price index in calculating the real AMU Deviation Indicator because there are data constraints for

Table 8.A.1 AMU shares and weights of East Asian currencies.

	Trade volume[a] %	GDP measured at PPP[b] %	Arithmetic average shares % (a)	Benchmark exchange rate[c] (b)	AMU weights[d] (a)/(b)
Brunei	0.33	0.33	0.33	0.589114	0.0056
Cambodia	0.19	0.23	0.21	0.000270	7.6219
China	23.99	51.70	37.85	0.125109	3.0251
Indonesia	6.47	5.31	5.89	0.000113	522.9228
Japan	24.79	25.72	25.04	0.009065	27.6235
South Korea	13.01	6.66	9.83	0.000859	114.4362
Laos	0.08	0.08	0.08	0.000136	5.7474
Malaysia	8.10	1.72	4.91	0.272534	0.1801
Myanmar	0.32	0.32	0.32	0.159215	0.0202
Philippines	2.66	2.56	2.61	0.021903	1.1926
Singapore	11.71	0.81	6.26	0.589160	0.1603
Thailand	6.36	3.46	4.91	0.024543	2.0005
Vietnam	1.98	1.55	1.76	0.000072	246.5203

[a]The trade volume is calculated as the average of sum of exports and imports in 2002, 2003, and 2004 taken from the DOTS (IMF).
[b]GDP measured at PPP reflects the average of that data in 2002, 2003, and 2004 taken from the *World Development Report* (The World Bank). For Brunei and Myanmar, we use the same share of trade volume since no GDP data are available for these countries.
[c]The benchmark exchange rate is the average of the daily exchange rate in terms of a currency basket of the U.S. dollar and the euro with shares of 65 percent: 35 percent, respectively in 2000–2001.
[d]The AMU shares and weights were revised in September 2007.
Source: http://www.rieti.go.jp/users/amu/en/detail.html.

some of the sampled countries where we have no alternative data but to use the CPI data as a price index. As the CPI data are only available on a monthly basis, we calculate the real AMU Deviation Indicator per month. As for the inflation rates in the AMU area, we calculate a weighted average of the CPI for the AMU area by using the AMU shares, which is the combination of shares in terms of trade volumes and GDP measured at PPP.

Figure 8.A.1 shows movements in the nominal AMU Deviation Indicators on a monthly basis for each of the East Asian currencies, while Figure 8.A.2 shows movements in the real AMU Deviation Indicators on a monthly basis for comparison. It is easy to find some differences between the nominal and real AMU Deviation Indicators by comparing Figures 8.A.1 and 8.A.2. In the case of Indonesia rupiah, the real AMU Deviation Indicator has been rather appreciating since July 2003, while the nominal AMU Deviation Indicator has been depreciating from July 2003 onwards. The differences reflect a higher inflation rate in Indonesia. Higher inflation tends to cause the real appreciation of home currency even though it is depreciating in nominal terms. The Lao kip has been appreciating in terms of the real AMU Deviation Indicator although it has been depreciating in terms of nominal AMU Deviation Indicator. In contrast, both the Korean won and the Thai baht have been appreciating in terms of Real AMU Deviation Indicators by reflecting the appreciation in terms of Nominal AMU Deviation Indicators. Moreover, the Japanese yen has depreciated in terms of real exchange rates but not in terms of the nominal exchange rate.

Thus, the monetary authorities should monitor the real AMU Deviation Indicators rather than the nominal AMU Deviation Indicators in order to consider the effects of exchange rates on real economic variables such as trade volumes and real GDP. On the other hand, the nominal AMU Deviation Indicators are more useful than the real AMU Deviation Indicators when we consider both frequency and time lags as important for monitoring these measures. Accordingly, we should use the nominal and real AMU Deviation Indicators as complementary measures for scrutinizing the exchange rate policies and related macroeconomic variables and, in turn, for devising coordinated exchange rate policies among the East Asian currencies.

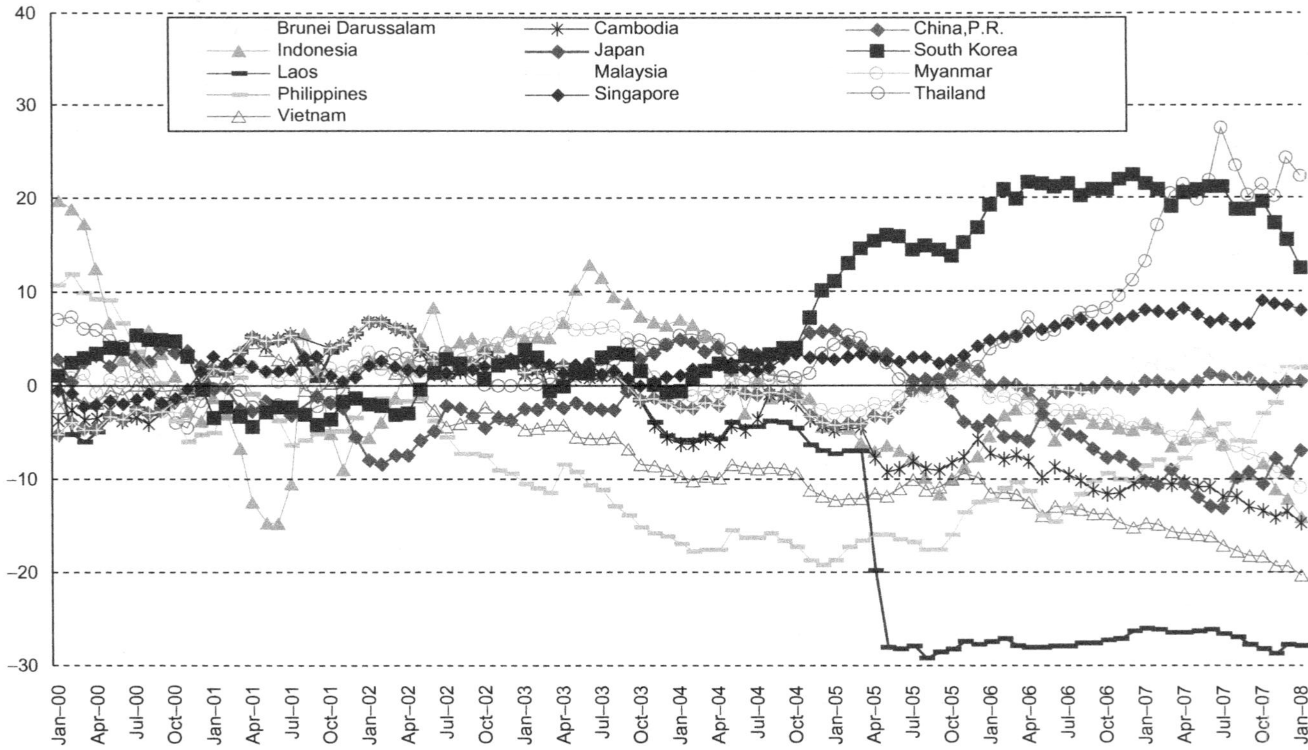

Fig. 8.A.1 Nominal AMU deviation indicators (monthly) (benchmark year = 2000/2001, basket weight = 2003–2005, monthly).
Source: http://www.rieti.go.jp/users/amu/en/index.html.

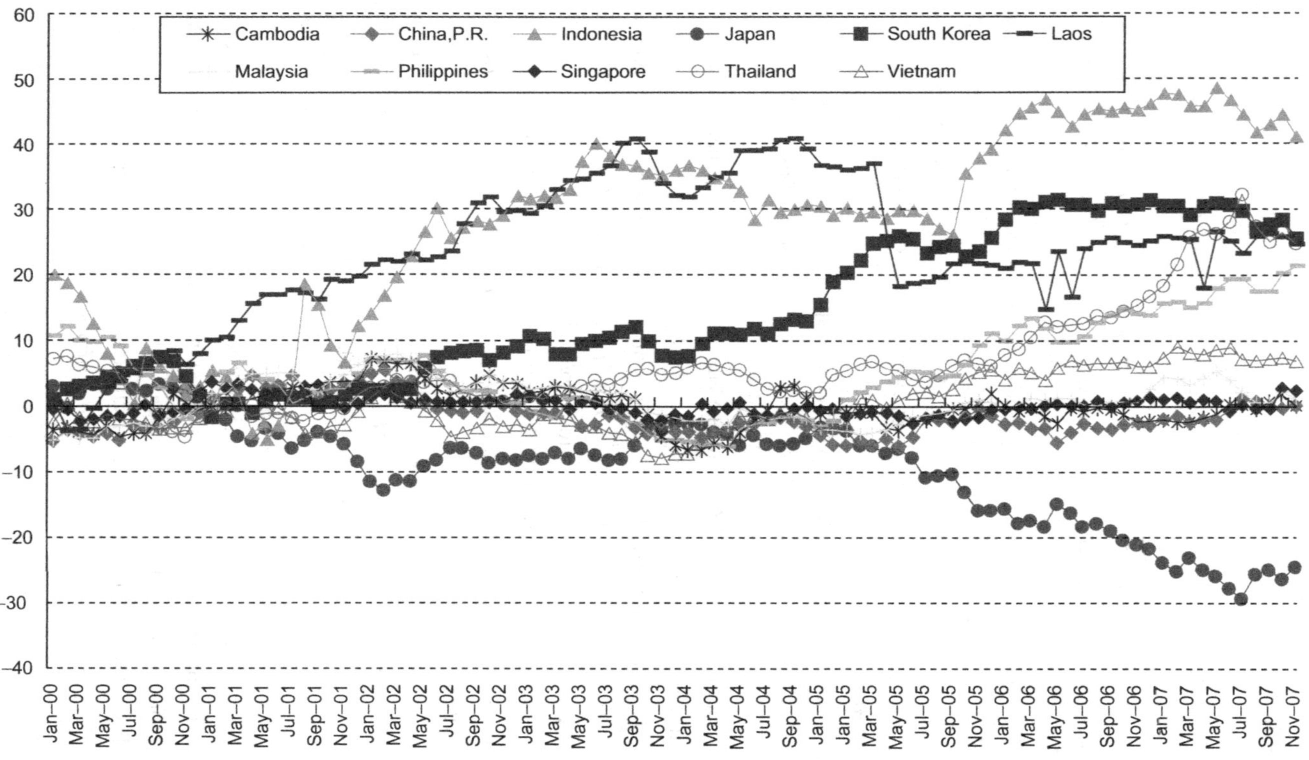

Fig. 8.A.2 Real AMU deviation indicators (monthly) (benchmark year = 2000/2001, basket weight = 2002–2004, monthly).
Source: http://www.rieti.go.jp/users/amu/en/index.html.

References

Kawai, M, E Ogawa and T Ito (2004). *Developing New Regional Financial Architecture: A Proposal*. Mimeo.

Ogawa, E (2004). Regional Monetary Cooperation in East Asia against asymmetric responses to the U.S. dollar depreciation. *Journal of Korean Economy*, 5, 43–72.

Ogawa, E (2007). Economic interdependence and international coordination in East Asia. In *A Basket Currency for Asia*, T. Ho (ed.), Routledge, pp. 99–123.

Ogawa, E and T Ito (2002). On the desirability of a regional basket currency arrangement. *Journal of the Japanese and International Economies*, 16, 317–334.

Ogawa, E and T Kudo (2007). Asymmetric responses of East Asian currencies to the U.S. dollar depreciation for reducing the U.S. current account deficits. *Journal of Asian Economics*, 18, 175–194.

Ogawa, E and M Sakane (2006). Chinese Yuan after Chinese exchange rate system reform. *China and World Economy*, 14, 39–57.

Ogawa, E and J Shimizu (2005). A deviation measurement for coordinated exchange rate policies in East Asia. *RIETI Discussion Paper Series*, 05-E-017 (http://www.rieti.go.jp/jp/publications/dp/05e017.pdf).

Ogawa, E and J Shimizu (2006). Stabilization of effective exchange rates under common currency basket systems. *Journal of the Japanese and International Economies*, 20, 590–611.

Ogawa, E and J Shimizu (2007). Progress toward a common currency basket system in East Asia. *RIETI Discussion Paper Series*, 06-E-038 (http://www.rieti.go.jp/jp/publications/dp/06e038.pdf).

Ogawa, E and T Yoshimi (2007). Exchange rate regimes in East Asia — recent trends. A paper prepared for the International Conference on "Ten Years After the Crisis: Evolving East Asian Financial System and Challenged Ahead" that is held by the Ministry of Finance, the Asian Development Bank, and the Asian Development Bank Institute on 12 June 2007.

Rajan, RS (2008). Monetary and financial cooperation in Asia: Taking stock of recent ongoings. *International Relations of the Asia-Pacific*, 8, 31–45.

CHAPTER 9

MONETARY AND FINANCIAL COOPERATION AMONG CENTRAL BANKS IN EAST ASIA AND THE PACIFIC

Hans Genberg and Dong He

9.1. Introduction

In the past decade, the issue of monetary and financial cooperation in Asia has been the subject of many research studies, academic conferences, and meetings of officials.[1] One motivation behind these initiatives is the belief that closer regional cooperation may help reduce the probability of another crisis like the one that shook the region 10 years ago and make the economies better able to react to external shocks. Concrete examples of cooperative arrangements are the Chiang Mai Initiative (CMI) on bilateral credit lines with subsequent extensions toward limited reserve pooling and the Asian Bond Fund (ABF) initiatives aiming to expand the market for local currency bonds. A number of proposals have also been made, mainly but not exclusively from academic circles, regarding cooperation on exchange rate policy.[2] No agreements have been reached in this area, however.

In parallel with discussions about monetary and financial cooperation, there have been developments in the conduct of monetary policy by regional central banks that point toward more emphasis on domestic objectives rather than international coordination. Following a trend that has influenced many central banks worldwide, several regional central banks have adopted domestic inflation control as their overriding policy objective and exchange rates have consequently become more flexible.

[1] Kenen and Meade (2007) provide a comprehensive survey of the subject.

[2] See, for example, Ogawa and Ito (2002) and Ogawa in Chapter 8 of this volume.

Against this background, this chapter analyzes what scope, if any, there is for extending regional cooperation, particularly in the areas of monetary and exchange rate policies and financial market development. We start by documenting that most regional central banks have adopted policy strategies in which domestic price stability is the principal objective of monetary policy while monetary policy instruments remain rather heterogeneous. We then argue that in this environment it is undesirable to focus regional cooperation on exchange rate policies because of the risk of creating conflicts with domestic objectives that would lead to loss of central bank credibility and possibly speculative attacks. We also show that the case for a coordinated exchange rate policies is in fact weak, even after taking into account the region's traditional emphasis on export performance and the emergence of a regional supply chain with Mainland China in the center of such a network.[3]

Rather than focusing cooperation on the setting of policy instruments, we suggest an alternative that centers on developing more liquid financial markets in the region in the foreseeable future, and on harmonizing the objectives of monetary policy and designing institutions that could form the basis of deeper forms of cooperation in the longer-term future.

This chapter is organized as follows. Section 9.2 describes the revealed preferences for monetary policy frameworks among the EMEAP central banks.[4] Section 9.3 discusses the pitfalls with exchange rate coordination. Section 9.4 analyzes the implications of export-led growth strategies for monetary and exchange rate policies. Section 9.5 concludes the chapter by sketching an approach to regional monetary and financial cooperation that is consistent with monetary policy frameworks with a focus on domestic objectives.

---

[3]For instance, see Thorbecke in Chapter 7 of this volume.

[4]EMEAP stands for the Executives' Meeting of East Asia-Pacific Central Banks. Founded in 1991, EMEAP is a cooperative organization of central banks and monetary authorities in the East Asia and Pacific region. Its primary objective is to strengthen the cooperative relationship among its members. It comprises the central banks and monetary authorities of the following 11 economies: Australia, Mainland China, Hong Kong SAR, Indonesia, Japan, Korea, Malaysia, New Zealand, Philippines, Singapore, and Thailand.

9.2. Revealed Preferences for Monetary Policy Objectives

In this section, we will argue that the primary objectives of monetary policy by EMEAP central banks, with the exception of the Hong Kong Monetary Authority and Bank Negara Malaysia, are defined in terms of domestic variables rather than in terms of the level of the exchange rate. For some central banks, this represents an important change from the situation prevailing before the financial crisis that hit the region in 1997–1998. We document the current focus of monetary policy in three different ways, viz. by statements of the central banks themselves, by characterizing movements in nominal exchange rates, and by investigating the nature of central bank policy reaction functions.

9.2.1. *Central Bank Statements*

Each central bank in the group maintains a website which contains information on its monetary policy.[5] Some websites are more transparent than others in revealing the objective of monetary policy, but after some search it is possible to find explicit statements. Table 9.1 contains relevant quotes.

It is noteworthy that in seven of the 11 economies price stability is the principal policy objective, and out of the remaining four the somewhat ambiguous notion of stability of the value of the currency is mentioned by three central banks: the People's Bank of China, Bank Indonesia, and Bank Negara Malaysia. The value of the currency can, of course, mean either domestic price stability or exchange rate stability. Only one central bank, the Hong Kong Monetary Authority, has exchange rate stability as the overriding objective.

Probing further reveals that Bank Indonesia has a numerical target for the domestic inflation rate which suggests that it too is focusing importantly on an internal target for its monetary policy. Likewise for the Reserve Bank of Australia, the Bank of Korea, the Reserve Bank of New Zealand, the Bangko Sentral Ng Pilipinas, and the Bank of Thailand all of which refer to their

[5] See Cavoli and Rajan (Chapter 2 of this volume) for a compilation of announced exchange rate regimes in various Asian economies.

Table 9.1. Central bank statements about their policy objectives.

Jurisdiction	Central Bank	Policy objective	
Australia	Reserve Bank of Australia	Price stability	…. to focus on price (currency) stability while taking account of the implications of monetary policy for activity and, therefore, employment in the short term.
China, Mainland	The People's Bank of China	Value of the currency	The objective of the monetary policy is to maintain the stability of the value of the currency and thereby promote economic growth.
Hong Kong SAR	Hong Kong Monetary Authority	Exchange rate stability	The primary monetary policy objective of the Hong Kong Monetary Authority (HKMA) is to maintain exchange rate stability.
Indonesia	Bank Indonesia	Price stability and exchange rate stability	In its capacity as central bank, Bank Indonesia has one single objective of achieving and maintaining stability of the Rupiah value. The stability of the value of the Rupiah comprises two aspects, one is stability of Rupiah value against goods and services and the other is the stability of the exchange rate of the Rupiah against other currencies.

(*Continued*)

Table 9.1. (*Continued*)

Jurisdiction	Central Bank	Policy objective	
Japan	Bank of Japan	Price stability	The Bank of Japan Law states that the Bank's monetary policy should be "aimed at, through the pursuit of price stability, contributing to the sound development of the national economy."
South Korea	The Bank of Korea	Price stability	Like other central banks, the Bank of Korea takes price stability as the most important objective of its monetary policy. The Bank of Korea Act, which came into effect in April 1998 following its revision at the end of 1997, stipulates price stability as the purpose of the Bank of Korea.
Malaysia	Bank Negara Malaysia	Price stability and exchange rate stability	To issue currency and keep reserves safeguarding the value of the currency; To promote monetary stability and a sound financial structure; To influence the credit situation to the advantage of the country.
New Zealand	Reserve Bank of New Zealand	Price stability	The Reserve Bank of New Zealand Act 1989 specifies that the primary function of the Reserve Bank shall be to deliver "stability in the general level of prices."
Philippines	Bangko Sentral Ng Pilipinas	Price stability	The primary objective of BSP's monetary policy is to promote a low and stable inflation conducive to a balanced and sustainable economic growth.

(*Continued*)

Table 9.1. (*Continued*)

Jurisdiction	Central Bank	Policy objective	
Singapore	The Monetary Authority of Singapore	Price stability	The primary objective of monetary policy in Singapore is to promote price stability as a sound basis for sustainable economic growth.
Thailand	Bank of Thailand	Price stability	Setting the monetary policy direction which is consistent with the nation's economic conditions, with the ultimate objective of maintaining price stability and sustainable economic growth.

Source: Authors' compilation based on Central Banks' websites.

monetary policy strategies as "Inflation Targeting". Concerning the Peoples Bank of China, it is widely believed, although not stated explicitly that an inflation rate of less than 3 percent per annum is an important objective of central bank policy.

From this brief review we may conclude that, judged by their own words, nine or the 11 EMEAP central banks have domestic price stability as their main policy objective, the two exceptions being Bank Negara Malaysia and the Hong Kong Monetary Authority. This is an important conclusion because, as we shall argue below, it restricts the scope of cooperation between central banks to areas that will not come in conflict with the domestic objectives they have chosen. In particular, it is likely to make joint exchange rate commitments incredible in the eyes of private sector market participants.

9.2.2. *Characterization of Exchange Rate Movements*

The behavior of exchange rates of EMEAP currencies is consistent with the view that domestic variables, rather than exchange rate levels, are predominant objectives of monetary policies. Before the 1997–1998 crisis, there was a relatively widespread tendency among central banks in the region to stabilize the values of their currencies with respect to the U.S. dollar. Seven of the 11 central banks allowed only limited movements of their U.S. dollar exchange rates in the years immediately prior to the financial turmoil unleashed by the attack on the baht in July 1997.[6] This gave rise to the notion that the region was on a dollar standard, a belief that has continued even though recent evidence shows that U.S. dollar exchange rates now are significantly more flexible than before.[7]

Ho *et al.* (2005) argue that movements in Asian currencies are increasingly related to those of a wider group of trading partners than just the U.S. dollar. They illustrate this point in two ways: by calculating the ratio of U.S. dollar exchange rate volatility to effective exchange rate volatility, and by regressing, following Frankel and Wei (1994), movements of individual dollar exchange rates on dollar exchange rates of major local trading partners/competitors.

If Asia were on a dollar standard, the volatility of U.S. dollar exchange rates should be very small relative to the volatility to effective exchange rates. Conversely, for a country that stabilizes the effective exchange rate, the ratio would be large. Ho *et al.* (2005) show that — with the notable exception of Hong Kong, Mainland China, and Malaysia — the volatility ratio is far from zero and has typically increased over time. In other words, currencies are increasingly priced relative to all their trading partners rather than only to the U.S.

Ho *et al.* (2005) (and Genberg (2006) for a longer sample and using weekly rather than daily data) present additional evidence counter to the dollar standard hypothesis by estimating regressions of the following form:

$$\Delta S_{i,t} = \alpha_0 + \sum_j \alpha_j \Delta S_{j,t} + u_{i,t} \quad j \neq i, \tag{9.1}$$

where S_k represents the U.S. dollar exchange rate of currency k. If results show that coefficient α_j is equal to unity and $u_{i,t}$ is "small" for all t then currency i is pegged to currency j. On the other hand, if all α's are zero and the $u_{i,t}$'s are small, then the currency is pegged to the U.S. dollar. When some α's are non-zero, then currency i is systematically related to the currencies

[6]China, Hong Kong, Indonesia, Malaysia, Philippines, South Korea, and Thailand.

[7]The following discussion refers to EMEAP economies other than Mainland China, Hong Kong, and Malaysia.

corresponding to the non-zero coefficients. Such relationship could come about either because the central bank is actively managing the currency or simply because the behavior of currency traders/investors in the market generates a correlation between particular currencies.[8]

From his results, Genberg (2006) concludes that the evolution of the Singapore dollar and the Thai baht depends quite strongly on movements in the euro, the Japanese yen, and the South Korean won. The won reacts systematically to the yen, and changes in the yen correlate positively with those of the euro. Movements in the Indonesian rupiah and the Philippines peso on the other hand are quite idiosyncratic.[9] In addition, comparison of the regression coefficients across different sample periods reveals instability over time, suggesting that central banks (with the possible exception of the Monetary Authority of Singapore (MAS)) do not systematically target the exchange rate. Finally, it is noteworthy that there are considerable differences across countries in the way their currencies relate to movements in the euro, yen, and the won. Different trade patterns or differences in economic structure which translates into differences in the reaction to common shocks are potential explanations.

9.2.3. *Evidence from Policy Reaction Functions*

Direct estimates of policy reaction functions give a third piece of evidence that domestic objectives are predominant for regional central banks. When the policy instrument of a central bank reacts systematically to deviations of the domestic inflation rate from a target level or the output gap, this almost certainly indicates that the central bank is attempting to use monetary policy to control domestic inflation. It may also indicate that it is trying to limit deviations of output from its full-employment level. If the central bank also reacts systematically to the exchange rate or to external interest rates, it may be tempting to conclude that it is targeting these variables as well. This does not necessarily follow, however, since such variables may well be included

[8]An example might be the relationship between the Swiss frank and the euro. In a regression of movements of the former on the latter is likely to show a dependence of the CHF/U.S.$ rate on the EUR/U.S.$ rate even though the Swiss National Bank does not engage in systematic exchange rate management.

[9]Pegging to the U.S. dollar can be ruled out by visual inspection.

in the policy reaction function simply because they carry information about the future rate of inflation in the economy, and it is therefore appropriate to react to them. For example, a depreciation of the domestic currency may elicit a contractionary monetary policy not because the central bank targets a particular level of the exchange rate, but simply because currency depreciation may lead to domestic inflation. Similarly, if an increase in the U.S. policy interest rate reflects a reaction to rapid demand growth in the U.S., it may elicit an analogous defensive interest rate increase in a country that has a similar cyclical pattern as the U.S. This would again be appropriate even if the interest rate differential did not itself constitute a policy goal of the domestic policymaker. However, if a central bank reacted *only* to the exchange rate or to foreign interest rates, there would be a prima facie case that the central bank actually has an exchange rate target.

What is known about the policy reaction functions of EMEAP central banks? We concentrate our discussion on central banks whose monetary policy strategies may not be generally understood. We take these to be the People's Bank of China, Bank Indonesia, the Bank of Korea, Bangko Sentral Ng Pilipinas, the Monetary Authority of Singapore, and the Bank of Thailand.[10] The recently published proceedings of the BIS/HKIMR conference on "Monetary policy in Asia: approaches and implementation" contains papers that present estimates of policy reaction functions for Singapore, South Korea, and Thailand.[11] The conclusions from these studies can be summarized as follows:

- The MAS implements its monetary policy by means of steering a nominal effective exchange rate (with undisclosed weights). Gerlach and Gerlach-Kirsten (2006) find that the rate of change in their measure of the Nominal Effective Exchange Rate (NEER) responds significantly to both inflation

[10]Of the remaining central banks, we take it as resolved that the Bank of Japan and the Reserve Banks of Australia and New Zealand set their policy instruments to control domestic inflation with little, if any, concern for the level of the exchange rate. For the Hong Kong Monetary Authority the notion of a policy reaction function is not applicable since it is operating an automatic exchange rate target zone. We are not aware of studies that have tried to estimate monetary policy reaction functions for the Bank Negara Malaysia.

[11]See respectively the papers by Gerlach and Gerlach-Kirsten (2006), Kim and Park (2006), and McCauley (2006) in BIS (2006).

and the output gap in Singapore, consistent with the stated objective to maintain price stability.

- Kim and Park (2006) find that the Bank of Korea adjusts its policy interest rate in response to both inflation and the output gap. The size of the response to inflation implies that the real short-term interest rate increases when inflation is above target, a condition that is necessary for the policy to be stabilizing.
- McCauley (2006) estimates a policy reaction function of the Bank of Thailand and concludes:

> First, no specification found a response of the policy rate to the exchange rate. This does not necessarily imply that the authorities are unconcerned with the exchange rate; it could imply that another instrument is assigned to it. Second, the estimates suggest that the policy rate is responding to forward-looking measures of inflation. (p. 182).

Available studies for Mainland China, Indonesia, and the Philippines reach broadly similar conclusions. He and Pauwels (2008) show that the People's Bank of China reacted systematically to domestic price developments in the past 10 years. Affandi (2004) presents evidence consistent with the hypothesis that Bank Indonesia has reacted in a stabilizing manner to domestic inflation since (but not before) the financial crisis. For the Philippines, Salas (2004) finds that the central bank has reacted strongly and significantly to deviations of inflation from a target but neither to the output gap nor to a real effective exchange rate index. This is the case in particular for the period 2000:01 to 2003:09 which, he argues, corresponds to the period of implicit (during 2000 and 2001) and explicit (since January 2002) inflation targeting.

We conclude from the evidence in this section that all EMEAP central banks, with the exception of the Hong Kong Monetary Authority and Bank Negara Malaysia, now have demonstrated strong commitments to domestic inflation as their principal monetary policy objective. Bank Negara may also have domestic price stability as an important goal, but it is more difficult to prove this using the measures that we have utilized.

While we are suggesting that domestic objectives dominate for these central banks, we are not arguing that it is the only objective. As McCauley (2006) notes for the case of the Bank of Thailand, even if empirical evidence fails to detect any effect of the exchange rate on the policy interest rate, it is possible that other instruments, e.g., foreign exchange market intervention, are used to influence it. If capital controls are in place and/or if domestic and foreign assets are sufficiently weak substitutes, it may be possible for a central bank to exercise some independent control over both the short-term interest rate and the exchange rate. As we argue in the next section, however, this does not eliminate the danger associated with exchange rate coordination between central banks.

9.3. Pitfalls with Exchange Rate Coordination

When monetary policy coordination is brought up in the East Asian context, it often focuses on intra-regional exchange rates. It is frequently argued, at least outside central banks, that East Asian central banks should coordinate exchange rate policies in order to prevent intra-regional misalignments in the process of adjustment of global imbalances and capital flows, and as a strategy to create deeper monetary integration. With respect to the former, it is argued that exchange rate stability vis-à-vis the renminbi has become an important policy concern, given the increasing degree of vertical integration of regional trade and the central role that China plays in this process. It is further asserted that sufficient exchange rate adjustments are not forthcoming because of a type of co-ordination failure: no central bank will allow its currency to adjust lest the economy will lose competitiveness if other central banks do not follow suit.

In this section, we argue that proposals for exchange rate coordination pay insufficient attention to two related issues, viz. the source of the nominal anchor in a system based on exchange rate coordination, and the credibility of exchange rate commitments in the East Asian context and the risk of currency crises. We therefore conclude that it would be counter-productive to build monetary and financial cooperation in the region on some exchange rate coordination scheme.

9.3.1. *What is the Nominal Anchor in a System Based on Coordinated Exchange Rate Policies?*

Consider first a group of economies between which capital mobility is high enough that interest parity holds. In this case there can only be one interest rate among the countries that maintain mutually fixed exchange rates. Which central bank will determine that rate? If the currency basket, which forms the basis of the coordination, contains currencies external to the region, the U.S. dollar and the euro say, then the common interest rate in the region will be determined by the monetary policies of the U.S. Federal Reserve and the European Central Bank. In other words, the countries that coordinate their exchange rate policies will loose control of their own monetary conditions.

If, on the other hand, the currency basket that forms the basis of the common exchange rate policy is exclusively made up of currencies of the coordinating group, then the well-known $n - 1$ problem implies that some mechanism must be found to determine the monetary policy for the group as a whole. For example, when Europe created the European Exchange Rate Mechanism (ERM), the German Bundesbank provided the *de facto* anchor for the participating economies. It is difficult to imagine that a similar arrangement could emerge for the entire EMEAP group, although some subset of countries may decide that a solution of this kind is worth considering in the future.

What if capital is not sufficiently mobile for the interest parity relationship to tie down interest rates? In this case, it is in principle possible for a central bank to influence both the domestic interest rate and the exchange rate, as the two would no longer be rigidly linked. Traditional open market operation could be used to focus on domestic interest rates, and interventions in the foreign exchange market could be targeted on the exchange rate. In other words, the central bank would have two instruments with which it could pursue two targets, for example, domestic inflation rate and the level of the exchange rate. In this context, the issue of coordination of exchange rate policies would be relevant, as it would be important for central banks not to intervene at cross purposes.

While imperfect capital mobility technically implies that central banks do have two policy instruments, there are several reasons why monetary authorities in the region may not want to exploit this additional degree of freedom. First, there is the issue of the quantitative importance. This depends in part on the degree of substitutability among assets denominated in different currencies and in part on the *de facto* severity of capital controls. Empirical evidence on these issues is emerging. Ouyang *et al.* (2007b) estimate offset coefficient for seven countries in emerging Asia and find that while *de facto* capital mobility declined substantially after the 1997–1998 crisis, it has recently increased to pre-crisis levels which can be characterized as reflecting a high, although not perfect, degree of capital mobility.[12] Conducting a similar analysis for Mainland China, Ouyang *et al.* (2007a) find a significantly lower degree of capital mobility in that economy. This is consistent with the results in Ma and McCauley (2007), which presents evidence that capital controls in China do bind to a significant degree.

Second, an important goal among EMEAP central banks is to further financial development and integration in the region. Therefore, even if capital mobility is not complete in some jurisdiction at present, it is likely to increase over time, which implies that the ability to pursue both interest rate and exchange rate targets independently of each other will be significantly circumscribed as time passes.

Third, and most importantly, if we are right that the overriding objective of monetary policy is domestic price stability, then the simultaneous pursuit of both an exchange rate goal and an interest rate objective is not likely to be viewed as credible by the market, even if it is technically, or at least partially, feasible. An imperfectly credible exchange rate commitment is an invitation to trouble as we argue in the following section.

9.3.2. *Will Exchange Rate Coordination Increase the Risk of Speculative Attacks?*

The answer to this question is, we believe, quite simply "yes". Theoretical models of stress on fixed exchange rate systems as well as practical experience support this conclusion. It has long been known that an economy cannot have two independent nominal anchors. If interest rate policy is used to target domestic price stability, it is potentially dangerous to use foreign exchange market intervention to target the exchange rate. The reason is, of course, the possibility that the two policies are not consistent. This insight was used by the "first generation" models of speculative attacks on currencies to show that a central bank may be forced to let go of either the domestic policy objective or the exchange rate objective.

---

[12] The countries covered in the study are Indonesia, Korea, Malaysia, Philippines, Singapore, and Thailand. The econometric approach did not allow for differences between countries in the offset coefficients, so the estimated coefficient reflects an average across the countries.

When international capital flows are possible, the resolution to inconsistencies between domestic monetary policy and exchange rate policy will be "resolved" by a speculative attack on the currency.

Subsequent models of currency crises introduced the possibility of multiple equilibria and self-fulfilling speculative crises. The argument was based on the principle that a central bank weighs the benefits from honoring the exchange rate commitment against the costs of doing so, which are typically related to the departures from domestic policy objectives implied by defending the fixed exchange rate. In this environment, it may happen that the mere expectations that the monetary authority may have to abandon the exchange rate target will bring about changes in macroeconomic conditions that will make this decision optimal. In other words, speculations of the demise of the central bank's exchange rate objective may be self-fulfilling.[13]

The implication of these arguments is that coordinated exchange rate policies are potentially destabilizing, at least if they take the form of commitments regarding the level of the exchange rate. The reason is that it is very difficult to design a cooperative common exchange rate arrangement that is consistent with the domestic monetary policy objectives of each member economy. Eventually, an idiosyncratic shock would present a member of the group with a choice between the domestic policy objective and the international commitment. Our analysis in the previous section implies that maintaining the domestic objective would have higher priority and, knowing this, market participants would speculate on the demise of the exchange rate commitment. In fact, such speculation could happen simply in the anticipation that such shocks would eventually materialize, and it would therefore be likely that the exchange rate system would be subject to sporadic bouts of instability.

9.4. Exchange Rate Policy and the Export Sector

One reaction to our argument so far might be that policymakers in the region need to retain some control over the exchange rate in order to support their

[13]The Linked Exchange Rate system of the Hong Kong dollar has been considered by market participants as credible because the Hong Kong Monetary Authority has stated consistently that maintaining the exchange rate peg with the U.S. dollar is the *only* monetary policy objective in Hong Kong, and its deeds have matched its words.

export sectors. One form of this reaction usually involves an assertion that Asian economies need to maintain undervalued exchange rates in order to support their export-led growth strategies. It is sometimes accompanied with the suggestion that it would be better if the economies switched to a model based on domestic-demand led growth. Another form of the reaction builds on the idea that increasing intra-regional trade requires that the rest of the EMEAP economies maintain a competitive exchange rate vis-à-vis the renminbi lest they lose market share to China. A third reaction is that the export sector in the economies is politically powerful and will use its power to lobby the government for favors including a weak exchange rate. We will argue that the first of these arguments is fundamentally flawed, and that the second is not well supported by the emerging structure of regional trade integration, and the third can be addressed at least partially by the development of means by which the exchange rate risk can be hedged.

9.4.1. *Exchange Rate Policy, Openness, and Economic Growth*[14]

The link between exchange rate policy on the one hand and export dependence, export-led versus domestic-demand led growth, on the other is very weak. Our assertion is that while the smaller Asian countries are highly dependent on exports in the sense that they are very open to international trade, the degree of openness is not out of line with small economies in other continents. Furthermore, the openness is beneficial for economic growth and does not require the need for undervalued exchange rates. As a basis for an explanation or argument for exchange rate coordination, the export dependence hypothesis is inadequate.

It is indeed true that Asian economies are very open to international trade, but this is not surprising as we would expect small economies to have large international exposure. The degree of openness in Asia is also not out of line with that of small European economies (see Figure 9.1).

A large body of empirical evidence provides support for the view that a high degree of openness to imports and concentration in production on exports is entirely appropriate for small economies, as this is associated

[14]This discussion draws on He *et al.* (2007).

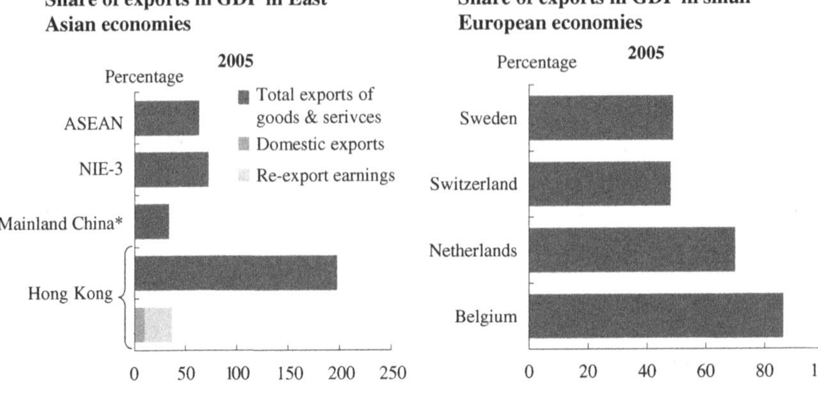

Fig. 9.1. Share of exports in GDP.
Source: He *et al.* (2007).

with higher rates of economic growth than otherwise would be the case. The reason is that openness to trade stimulates competition and technological progress which in turn boosts economic growth. Note also that the stimulus to competition and technological progress can occur either through the export sector or the import-competing sector, so there is no case to be made for trying to achieve an under- or over-valued exchange rate on these grounds. It bears emphasizing (if only because it seems to be misunderstood in the recent discussion of global imbalances) that it is, of course, the degree of *openness* and not trade surpluses and deficits that is related to economic growth, and outward orientation by itself implies neither a tendency toward current account surpluses or deficits. For example, economies in the region generally had balance of trade deficits in the years immediately before the financial crisis in 1997–1998 and they were as "export-dependent" then as they are now.

So why are East Asian economies being characterized as too dependent on exports for their growth and should rely on domestic demand? We believe it is due to mixing of two arguments. One is the incorrect proposition according to which sustained economic growth can be influenced by aggregate demand, and that growth can therefore be driven by either domestic or external demand. According to modern theories of economic growth, however, growth is instead determined by the accumulation of factors of production and technical progress, and this view has been backed up by a large body of empirical analysis. As already noted, according to this view, openness is likely to foster technical progress and growth, and it should therefore be encouraged.

The second argument related to East Asian export dependence is the correct statement that, to reduce current account surpluses, domestic absorption (demand) must increase relative to income. However, this refers only to a cyclical adjustment phase and has no implication for the medium- to long-term growth rates of those two variables. Balanced growth requires that output, domestic demand, and external demand all grow at the same rate. Indeed, if domestic absorption systematically grew faster than domestic output, the economy would be on a path with increasing trade deficits over time, a clearly unsustainable situation.

In summary, these arguments imply that: (i) openness is beneficial for economic growth, (ii) current account surpluses are not the necessary consequence of openness and "export dependence", (iii) correcting current account imbalances does not require reducing openness or switching to "domestic demand-led growth", and (iv) reaping the benefits from trade and openness does not require keeping the exchange rate "undervalued".

9.4.2. *Implications of Regional Trade Integration for Exchange Rate Policy*

Relating to the belief that a competitive exchange rate is important for export-led growth, it has also been argued that exchange rate stability vis-à-vis the renminbi has become an important policy concern, given the increasing degree of vertical integration of regional trade and the central role that China plays in this process (for instance, see Chapter 7 of this volume). However, this argument is based on the assumption that China is a major competitor of the rest of the EMEAP economies. In fact, there is little evidence overall that increases in China's exports reduce exports of other emerging Asian economies. Indeed, it appears that China's exports and exports of other economies are positively correlated, largely driven by common shocks such as trading partner income (Ahearne *et al.*, 2003). The trade structure among the EMEAP economies is diverse, including trade that is oriented for domestic use within the region, processing trade through China, as well as trade with economies outside the region. Thus, appreciation and depreciation against the renminbi would have different consequences for these different forms of trade.

In any case, changes in the exchange rates have not been the primary determinant of export growth for the major Asian exporters; a more important determinant has been the income growth in the major trading partners (Ahearne *et al.*, 2003). The "Great Moderation" observed in the last decade indicates that monetary policies that focus on stabilizing inflation have also succeeded in bringing about a tangible reduction in output volatility, and therefore a stable income demand for exports. For the growth of Asian economies such stability of external demand is likely to outweigh the effects of any increased fluctuations in export prices as a result of nominal exchange rate volatility. This is borne out by the phenomenal growth in world trade despite the high volatility in the exchange rates of the major currencies. Therefore, monetary policy can best promote export-led growth by providing a stable domestic macroeconomic environment. It is thus difficult to make a convincing case that exchange rate stability vis-à-vis the renminbi should be an important consideration for facilitating intra-regional trade.

9.4.3. *Political Pressure and Exchange Rate Policy*

Even if the central bank considers domestic price stability rather than exchange rate stability as the principal objective of monetary policy, pressure may be brought to bear on the authorities to support politically powerful sectors of the economy by means of a targeted exchange rate policy. This potential conflict between the objectives of the central banks and other policy authorities is likely to bring about greater instability in financial markets as investors assess the relative political strength of different policy institutions. If monetary policy is to be successful in targeting internal price stability without undue constraints imposed by volatile foreign exchange markets, and if monetary policy is to avoid being "captured" by the vested interest of the export sector, it is important that the private sector be given the possibility to learn how to live with and protect itself against more variable and unpredictable exchange rate fluctuations. This involves developments of financial markets where exporters and importers can hedge currency exposures. Thus, developing more sophisticated financial products for risk management and more liquid and integrated regional financial markets should facilitate meeting price stability targets by central banks. Regional cooperation in developing such markets could play a positive role in this process.

9.5. Concluding Remarks: Implications for Cooperation

9.5.1. *Setting of Policy Instruments Need Not Be Coordinated*

In the foreseeable future it is likely that the majority of EMEAP central banks will continue to practice an approach to monetary policy that focuses on domestic macroeconomic stabilization. As we have seen, the specific goal is typically defined in terms of price stability with, in some cases, additional references to real economic growth and employment. The pursuit of this type of monetary policy does not require explicit coordination between monetary authorities. There are plenty of examples of central banks with a long history of following such a strategy without coordination with neighbors. Examples that come to mind are the monetary authorities in countries such as Canada, Norway, Sweden, and Switzerland to mention just four. All of these countries have small highly open economies, and the independent pursuit of domestic price stability together with a floating exchange rate has been very successful. Although the exchange rates have fluctuated relative to competitors, there have not been any calls for policy consultations as a result. Possibly a contributing factor to the lack of conflict is that the policy objectives have been expressed clearly and transparently, with little doubt that domestic price stability is the principal goal. Exchange rate fluctuations have been recognized as a by-product of a monetary policy focused on domestic price stability and not as a result of attempts to gain competitive advantages.

Critics of the unilateral pursuit of domestic policy objectives have expressed two types of concern that need to be addressed. One argument is that without explicit coordination of policies, exchange rates will be excessively volatile to the detriment of economic growth. There are several responses to this concern. First, judging by existing empirical evidence, there does not seem to be any clear evidence that greater exchange rate volatility is damaging for economic growth (Rogoff *et al.*, 2004). Second, there is nothing in principle that prevents a central bank targeting domestic price stability from intervening in the foreign exchange market to reduce excessive exchange rate volatility. Of course, it may be difficult to determine what constitutes "excessive", but this is an issue that each central bank would have to grapple with on its own. Third, if volatility of bilateral exchange rates is the result of idiosyncratic shocks, then coordinated policies designed to limit such movements would shift the burden of adjustment onto domestic prices and income, and hence conflict with the domestic objectives of monetary policy. The credibility of the central bank would hence be affected.

A second objection to uncoordinated monetary policy strategies is that they would make regional exchange rates relative to the U.S. dollar too rigid thereby preventing international adjustment. This is the coordination failure argument mentioned before, and we would argue that it is fraught with two significant shortcomings. First, it is counterfactual in that it does not recognize that there has been significant inter- as well as intra-regional exchange rate adjustments in the recent past (Table 9.2). It is, of course, possible to argue that adjustments should have been even larger in view of the remaining global current account imbalances, but this presumes that nominal exchange rate adjustments are the most appropriate vehicle with which to deal with such imbalances. This presumption is the second shortcoming of the coordination failure argument. While *real* exchange

Table 9.2. Exchange rate adjustments relative to the U.S. dollar (percent change, January 2005–July 2007).

Japan	17.22
Hong Kong	0.26
Indonesia	−1.54
Average	**−7.32**
Singapore	−7.52
Mainland China	−8.61
Malaysia	−9.43
New Zealand	−10.14
Korea	−10.47
Australia	−11.21
Philippines	−16.90
Thailand	−22.21

Source: Authors' own calculations.

rate adjustments typically accompany current account adjustments, it is generally believed that changes in *nominal* exchange rates can influence real exchange rates only temporarily.

9.5.2. *Harmonization of Goals and Consultation on Institution Building*

Having argued that regional coordination of the setting of policy instruments is not required for central banks to be able to carry out a successful monetary policy, we now want to suggest that in the foreseeable future, the focus of regional cooperation should be on promoting further financial integration. In the longer term, with a high level of both trade and financial integration, business cycles in the region will be more synchronized; in such a scenario, consultation and coordination in defining policy goals and institution building can be beneficial.

We take it for granted that central banks in the region aim to create a fully integrated regional financial market as well as an environment of monetary stability in which trade and economic growth can thrive. Any approach with these aims must be compatible with the constraint of the so-called impossible trinity, which in this case implies that participating central banks must chose between having an independent monetary policy or effectively outsourcing it to an external institution, be it another central bank or a separate regional monetary authority. In view of central banks' current emphasis on the independent pursuit of domestic policy goals, these constraints imply that any acceptable approach to regional monetary cooperation must be evolutionary so that initially each central bank is able to implement its own monetary policy independently of external constraints. In the longer term, there could be collaboration on agreeing on a consistent objective to be pursued by all participants in the arrangement.[15]

To be compatible with the liberalization of international capital flows, there should be no commitment toward maintaining a particular exchange rate level. Of course, this does not mean that the exchange rate should be ignored in the implementation of the monetary policy strategy. Indeed, there is a presumption that attention should be paid to the information

[15]Note that unless such an agreement can be achieved, there is no point in trying to achieve monetary unification in the first place.

contained in exchange rate movements when the inflation targeting strategy is implemented.[16]

As financial markets become fully integrated, and if inflation objectives of the regional central banks are sufficiently similar, interest rates are likely to become highly correlated across the economies. The reason is simply that with common objectives and similarity of cyclical developments, the interest rate decisions of each central bank will be substantially similar.[17]

How stable bilateral exchange rates will be depend on a number of factors? As already noted, in highly open economies a monetary policy strategy that targets inflation will pay attention to exchange rate movements. This will tend to dampen exchange rate fluctuations. However, even if objectives of central banks are similar, it is possible that financial markets will not evaluate economies identically, and therefore it is possible that exchange rates will show some fluctuations. The credibility of each central bank's commitment to the announced objective and its ability to implement the policy are important considerations in this regard, as is the consistency of other macroeconomic policies with the monetary policy objective. Taking these considerations into account, one should expect exchange rates to be subjected to some short run fluctuations. For example, Switzerland is highly integrated with economies in the Euro area and the Swiss National Bank has much the same objectives as the European Central Bank, yet the exchange rate between the Swiss frank and the euro does display a non-trivial degree of volatility.

If complete monetary unification is desired by some subset of central banks, they can formally agree to centralize monetary policy decisions in a common central bank, which has been established in the intervening period, or they can decide to delegate it to an existing central bank.[18] In the first case the delegation of monetary policy will be carried out simultaneously with

[16]It is also quite possible to use the exchange rate rather than some short-term interest rate as the operating target. This is indeed the approach of the Monetary Authority of Singapore (MAS).

[17]Some differences may still be observed if the monetary policy transmission mechanism is not exactly the same across countries, because in this case the timing of changes in policy interest rates may vary across jurisdictions. However, even in this case long-term interest rates should still evolve in a rather similar pattern.

[18]Wyplosz (2004) emphasizes the role of institution building in the process of monetary integration process in Europe, as does Salvatore (Chapter 10 of this volume).

the introduction of a new common currency, and in the second case with making the currency of the chosen central bank the common currency in the group. Of course, there is no requirement that the last step of the approach — that of adopting a common currency — be implemented by all countries in the region. The benefits from financial integration and monetary stability will be forthcoming anyway even if those of a common currency will not.

The advantages of the approach to monetary integration that we have sketched here are that: (a) it is compatible with increasing integration of financial markets; (b) it naturally evolves from a system where central banks pursue similar objectives in their own self-interest which makes it incentive compatible; and (c) it allows for a "variable geometry" of the final area that adopts a common currency.

References

Affandi, Y (2004). *Estimating Monetary Policy Rule in Post Crisis Indonesia.* Mimeo.

Ahearne, AG, JG Fernald, P Loungani and JW Schindler (2003). *China and Emerging Asia: Comrades* or *Competitors?* Federal Reserve Bank of Chicago, WP 2003–27.

BIS (2006). *Monetary Policy in Asia: Approaches and Implementation.* BIS Papers No. 31.

Frankel, JA and S Wei (1994). Yen block or Dollar bloc? Exchange rate policies of the East Asian economies. In *Macroeconomic Linkage: Savings, Exchange Rates, and Capital Flows*, T Ito and A Krueger (eds.). Chicago: University of Chicago Press, pp. 295–333.

Genberg, H (2006). Exchange-rate arrangements and financial integration in East Asia: On a collision course? *International Economics and Economic Policy*, 3, 359–377.

Gerlach, S and P Gerlach-Kirsten (2006). Monetary policy regimes and macroeconomic outcomes: Hong Kong and Singapore. In BIS (2006).

He, D, L Cheung and J Chang (2007). Sense and nonsense on Asia's export dependency and the decoupling thesis. HKMA Working Paper 03/2007.

He, D and L Pauwels (2008). What prompts the People's Bank of China to change its monetary policy stance — Evidence from a discrete choice model. HKMA Working Paper 06/2008.

Ho, C, G Ma and RN McCauley (2005). Trading Asian currencies. *BIS Quarterly Review*, 49–58.

Kenen, P and EE Meade (2007). *Regional Monetary Integration*. Cambridge University Press.

Kim, S and YC Park (2006). Inflation targeting in Korea: A model of success? In BIS (2006).

Ma, G and RN McCauley (2007). Do China's capital controls still bind? — Implications for monetary autonomy and capital liberalization. Bank for International Settlements, Working Papers No. 233.

McCauley, RN (2006). Understanding monetary policy in Malaysia and Thailand: Objectives, instruments, and independence. In BIS (2006).

Ogawa, E and T Ito (2002). On the desirability of a regional basket currency arrangement. *Journal of the Japanese and International Economies*, 16, 317–334.

Ouyang, A, R Rajan and T Willett (2007a). China as a reserve sink: The evidence from offset and sterilization coefficients. Hong Kong Institute for Monetary Research. Working Paper No. 10/2007.

Ouyang, A, R Rajan and T Willett (2007b). Managing the monetary consequences of reserve accumulation in emerging Asia. Hong Kong Institute for Monetary Research. Working Paper No. 20/2007.

Rogoff, K, AM Husain, A Mody, R Brooks and N Oomes (2004). Evolution and performance of exchange rate regimes. IMF Occasional Paper 229. Washington: International Monetary Fund.

Salas, JMI (2004). The Philippine Central Bank's monetary policy reaction function from 1992 to 2003. Master's paper, School of Economics, University of Philippines.

Wyplosz, C (2004). Regional exchange rate arrangements: Lessons from Europe for East Asia. In *Monetary and Financial Integration in East Asia, The Way Ahead*, Asian Development Bank (ed.), Vol. 2. Palgrave Macmillan, pp. 241–284.

CHAPTER 10

ECONOMIC AND FINANCIAL INTEGRATION IN EAST ASIA: LESSONS FROM THE EUROPEAN MONETARY UNION

Dominick Salvatore

10.1. Introduction

During the past decade, there has been an increasing interest and debate on the need and benefits of economic and monetary integration in East Asia so as to achieve greater monetary and financial stability and avoid future financial crises, such as the very painful one that afflicted most of the region in the late 1990s. To some extent this interest has also been stimulated by the success of the European Monetary Union (EMU) in creating a common central bank (the ECB) and adopting a common currency (the euro) as a necessary stepping stone to ultimately achieving full economic integration, characterized also by a common fiscal policy and eventual political union. This chapter reviews the process of economic, monetary, and financial integration in Europe, as well as the benefits and costs of the EMU, in order to draw conclusions as to their relevance and the lessons that we can learn from them for economic integration in East Asia.

10.2. Economic and Monetary Integration in Europe before the Euro

The impetus that gave rise to the long process of economic integration in Europe more than 50 years ago was clearly political. That is, to eventually link European economies so closely together as to make future conflicts among them practically impossible. The process started in 1950 by merging French and German steel and coal production. It continued with the creation of a customs union in 1957 and a common market in 1993, and it culminated with the creation of the euro in 1999 in order to "bind Germany irrevocably into a United Europe." Never before had a group of large sovereign nations voluntarily given up their own currency for a common currency without first achieving full economic and political union. In fact, an important reason for the creation of the euro was to encourage the process toward full economic and political union in Europe.[1]

10.2.1. *The Creation and Expansion of the European Union*

The European Union (EU) was founded by the Treaty of Rome, signed in March 1957 by West Germany, France, Italy, Belgium, the Netherlands, and Luxembourg, and came into being on January 1, 1958. The common external tariff was set at the average of the 1957 tariffs of the six nations. Free trade in industrial goods within the EU and a common price for agricultural products were achieved in 1968; restrictions on the free movement of labor and capital were reduced by 1970. Membership increased to 15 after the United Kingdom, Denmark, and Ireland joined in 1973, Greece in 1981, Spain and Portugal in 1986, and Austria, Finland, and Sweden in 1995. On January 1, 1993, the EU removed all the remaining restrictions on the free flow of goods, services, and resources (including labor) among its members, thus becoming a single unified market. The expanded Union became the largest trading block in the world. Intra-EU trade has been estimated to be double what it would have been in the absence of integration.

The formation of the EU significantly expanded trade in industrial goods with non-members. This was due to (1) the very rapid growth of the EU, which increased its demand for imports of industrial products from outside the Union; and (2) the reduction to very low levels of the average tariff on imports of industrial products as a result of the Kennedy and Tokyo Rounds (initiated by the United States, which feared trade diversion). On the other hand, the formation of the EU resulted in trade diversion in agricultural commodities, particularly in temperate products such as grain. The high

[1] For a more in-depth analysis of the process of economic integration in Europe see Salvatore (1996, 1997, 2002a,b, 2005).

farm support price level led to huge agricultural surpluses within the EU, high storage costs, and subsidized exports. This farm policy was a major obstacle to British entry into the EU because Britain kept agricultural prices low and instead aided its farmers by "deficiency payments" to raise their income to desired levels. It was also responsible for some of the sharpest trade disputes with the U.S. and at the Uruguay Round and it was major cause of the collapse of the Doha Round in 2006. The overall net gains from the formation of the EU have been estimated at about 5 percent of GDP of the EU and arose from the removal of production and trade barriers, economies of scale, intensified competition, and increased FDI inflows into the EU (out of fear of increased protectionism against outsiders).

In May 2004, 10 more countries, mostly from the former communist bloc in Central and Eastern Europe, became members of the EU (Poland, Hungary, Czech Republic, Slovak Republic, Slovenia, Estonia, Lithuania, Latvia, Malta, and Cyprus). Bulgaria and Romania joined at the beginning of 2007 and Albania, Bosnia-Herzegovina, Croatia, Macedonia, Serbia, Montenegro, and Turkey are negotiating accession. With the admission of the 10 new members in 2004 and two more members in 2007, the 27-nation EU has 485 million people, exceeding Japan's 128 million, NAFTA's 430 million, but it is much smaller than China's 1.3 billion population.

10.2.2. *The Move Toward Monetary Integration: The European Monetary System*

In March 1979, the EU announced the formation of the European Monetary System (EMS) as part of its aim toward greater monetary integration among its members, including the ultimate goal of creating a common currency and a community-wide central bank. The EMS operated from 1979 until 1998. Its main features were: (1) the creation of the European Currency Unit (ECU), defined as the weighted average of the currencies of the member nations; (2) The creation of the Exchange Rate Mechanism (ERM) which allowed the currency of each EU member to fluctuate by a maximum of 2.25 percent on either side of its central rate or parity (6 percent for the British pound and the Spanish peseta; Greece and Portugal joined later). The EMS was thus created as a fixed but adjustable exchange rate system and with the currencies of member countries floating jointly against the dollar; and (3) The establishment of the European Monetary Cooperation

Fund (EMCF) to provide short- and medium-term balance-of-payments assistance to its members.

From March 1979 to September 1992, there were a total of 11 currency realignments within the EMS. In general, high-inflation countries such as Italy and France (until 1987) needed to periodically devalue their currency with respect to the ECU in order to maintain competitiveness in relation to a low-inflation country such as Germany. Starting in September 1992, the EMS came under attack (the U.K. and Italy, facing deepening recession and high unemployment, and unable to lower interest rates in the face of high interest rates in Germany, were forced to devalue their currencies). This was followed by the devaluation of the Spanish peseta, the Portuguese escudo, and the Irish pound between September 1992 and May 1993. After renewed speculative attacks (this time against the French franc), the range of allowed fluctuation was increased from 2.25 percent to 15 percent in August 1993. These point to the fundamental weakness of the EMS in attempting to keep exchange rates among member nations within narrowly defined limits without at the same time integrating their monetary, fiscal, tax, and other policies.

Member nations were assigned a quota into the EMCF, 20 percent to be paid in gold (valued at the market price) and the remainder in dollars, in exchange for ECUs. The amount of ECUs grew rapidly as member nations converted more and more of their dollars and gold into ECUs. Indeed, ECUs became an important international asset and intervention currency. One advantage of the ECU was its greater stability in value with respect to any one national currency. It was anticipated that the EMCF would eventually evolve into an EU central bank. By the beginning of 1998, the total reserve pool of the EMCF was over US$50 billion and the value of the ECU was US$1.1042.

10.3. The Transition to Monetary Union and the Creation of the Euro

In June 1989, a committee headed by Jacques Delors, the president of the European Commission, recommended a three-stage transition to the goal of monetary union. The first stage, which started in July 1990, called for convergence of economic performance and cooperation in monetary and fiscal policy, as well as the removal of all restrictions to intra-community capital movements. The second stage, approved at a meeting in the Dutch city of Maastricht in December 1991, called for the creation of a European Monetary Institute (EMI) as the forerunner of a European Central Bank (ECB) to further centralize members' macroeconomic policies and reduce exchange rate margins by January 1994. The third stage was to involve the completion of the monetary union by either 1997 or 1999 with the establishment of a single currency and an ECB that would engage in foreign exchange market interventions and open market operations. This meant that member nations relinquished their sovereign power over their money supply and monetary policy. In addition, they would no longer have full freedom over their budget policies. With a common union-wide central bank, the central bank of each nation would assume functions not unlike those of Federal Reserve banks in the U.S.

10.3.1. *The Maastricht Treaty*

The Maastricht Treaty set several conditions before a nation could join the monetary union: (1) The inflation rate must not exceed by more than 1.5 percentage points the average rate of the three Community nations with the lowest rate; (2) its budget deficit must not exceed 3 percent of its GDP; (3) its overall government debt must not exceed 60 percent of its GDP; (4) long-term interest rates must not exceed by more than two points the average interest rate of the three countries with the lowest inflation rates; and (5) its average exchange rate must not fall by more than 2.25 percent of the average of the EMS for the two years before joining. By 1991, only France and Luxembourg had met all of these criteria. Because the cost of reunification pushed its budget deficit to 5 percent of its GDP, Germany did not meet all conditions for joining in 1991. Italy, with its budget deficit of 10 percent of GDP and overall debt of more than 100 percent of GDP, did not meet any of the conditions. By 1998, however, most member countries of the EU had met most of the Maastricht criteria, and the stage was set for true monetary union.

In 1997, the Stability and Growth Pact (SGP) was negotiated to further tighten the fiscal constraint under which countries participating in the monetary union would operate. The SGP required member countries to aim at budget deficits smaller than 3 percent of GDP, so that in case of recession the nation could conduct expansionary fiscal policy and still remain below the 3 percent guideline. Nations that violated the fiscal indicator would be subject to heavy fines. Germany demanded the Pact as a condition for proceeding toward monetary union in order to make sure that fiscal discipline would prevail in the monetary union and avoid excessive money creation, inflation, and a weak euro.

Throughout the negotiations, the U.K. tried consistently to slow the EU's moves toward greater economic and political union for fear of losing more of its sovereignty. The U.K. refused to promise that it would give up the pound sterling as its national currency or that it would accept community-wide labor legislation. Differences in culture, language, and national temperament made progress toward monetary union difficult, and the future admission of the new democracies of Eastern and Central Europe was expected to greatly complicate matters. Nevertheless, the Maastricht Treaty operated as the bridge that led to true monetary union in Europe at the beginning of 1999, when the ECB (created in 1998) began to operate and the euro came into existence.

10.3.2. *The Creation of the Euro*

At the beginning of 1999, the EMS became the EMU with the introduction of the euro and a common monetary policy by the ECB. On January 1, 1999 the euro (€) came into existence as the common currency of 11 countries of the euro area or euroland (Austria, Belgium, Germany, Finland, France, Ireland, Italy, Luxembourg, Spain, Portugal, and the Netherlands). Greece was admitted on January 1, 2001, Slovenia on January 1, 2007, and Malta and Cyprus at the beginning of 2008. Britain, Sweden and Denmark chose not to participate.

In order to avoid excessive volatility and possible misalignments between the currencies of the U.K., Sweden, Denmark vis-à-vis the euro, the Exchange Rate Mechanism II (ERM II) was set up, similar to the one operating under to the EMS. But, as experience with the 1992–1993 ERM crisis showed, such a system is unstable and crisis prone.

The euro was introduced on January 1, 1999, at the exchange rate of €1 = U.S. $1.17 but, contrary to most experts' opinion, it fluctuated downward to just below parity (i.e., €1 = U.S. $1) by the end of 1999. It fell to a low of U.S. $0.82 at the end of October 2000 before returning to near parity with the dollar by the middle of 2002. It then rose to a high of U.S. $1.36 in December 2004, it fell to a low of U.S. $1.17 in November 2005, and then it rose to U.S. $1.38 in July 2007 (see Figure 10.1).

The adoption of the euro as the common currency of the euro-area countries conferred major benefits on the participating countries, but it also led to significant costs. The benefits are: (1) elimination of the need to exchange currencies among euro-area members (this has been estimated to save as much as U.S.$30 billion per year); (2) elimination of exchange rate volatility among the currencies of participating countries; (3) more rapid economic and financial integration of participating nations; (4) the ability of the ECB to conduct a more expansionary monetary policy than the one practically imposed by the German Bundesbank on other members of the EU in the past; (5) greater economic discipline for countries such as Belgium, Greece, and Italy, which seemed unwilling or unable to put their houses in order without externally imposed conditions; (6) seignorage from the use of the euro as an international currency; (7) reduced cost of borrowing in international financial markets; and (8) increased economic and political importance for the EU in international affairs. The greatest

Fig. 10.1. The U.S. dollar exchange rate from 1999 to 2007.
Source: Federal Reserve Statistical Release — Foreign Exchange Rates Historical Data, 2007.

benefits of the euro in the long run, may be political, however, by having brought together nations that were once bitter enemies and making armed conflicts among them practically impossible in the future. It also brought political stability in some member countries and security to central and Eastern Europe.

The most serious problem created by the adoption of the euro for the participating countries arises when only one or a few of them face a recession or some other asymmetric shock. The reason is that the nation or nations so affected can use neither exchange rate nor monetary policy to overcome the problem and fiscal policy is also severely constrained. In such a situation, the nation or nations must then wait for the problem to be resolved by itself, gradually, over time. In a more fully integrated economy, such as the U.S., if a region is in a recession, some labor will immediately move out and the region will also benefit from a great deal of fiscal redistribution (such as greater unemployment insurance receipts). In Europe, however, labor mobility is much lower than in the U.S. and so is fiscal redistribution. It is true that economic integration will encourage intra-EMU labor mobility, but this is a slow process that is likely to take years to complete. Capital mobility can to some extent substitute for inadequate labor mobility in overcoming the problem but it can also limit needed labor market adjustments.

10.3.3. *The European Central Bank and the Common Monetary Policy*

In 1998, ECB was established as the operating arm of the European System of Central Banks (ESCB), a federal structure of the national central banks of the EU. Since January 1999, the ECB assumed responsibility for the common EMU monetary policy. ECB's monetary decisions are made by a majority vote of the governing council, composed of a six-member executive board (including the President of the ECB) and the heads of the participating national central banks.

The Maastricht Treaty entrusted the ECB with the sole goal of pursuing price stability and made it almost entirely independent of political influences. The ECB is only required to brief regularly the European Parliament on its activities, but the European Parliament has no power to influence ECBs decisions. For example, while the U.S. Congress could pass laws reducing the independence of the Federal Reserve Board, The Maastricht

Treaty itself would have to be amended by the legislatures or voters in every member country for the ECB's statute to be changed. The almost total independence of the ECB from political influences was deliberate so as to shield it from political influences that might force it to provide excessive monetary stimulus, and thus lead to inflation. But this also led to the criticism that the ECB is distant and undemocratic, and not responsive to the economic needs of the citizens.

What is strange is that the exchange rate policy of the euro is ultimately in the hands of politicians, rather than of the ECB. This is puzzling because monetary and exchange rate policies are closely related, and it is impossible to conduct a truly independent policy in one without the other. Be that as it may, the first year of operation of the EMU in 1999 was somewhat turbulent, with politicians demanding lower interest rates to stimulate growth and overcome the weakness of the euro, and with the ECB resisting for the most part (at least in its official pronouncements) for fear of resurgent inflation. The conflict in the conduct of a union-wide monetary policy also became evident during 1999, when nations such as Ireland and Spain faced excessive growth and the danger of inflation and hence requiring a more restrictive monetary policy, while other nations (such as Germany and Italy) faced anemic growth (and hence requiring lower interest rates).

As is it was, the ECB adopted and intermediate monetary policy, with interest rates possibly being too low for Ireland and Spain and too high for Germany and Italy. From 2000 to 2002, the ECB conducted a fairly tight monetary policy (certainly much tighter than the one pursued by the U.S. Fed during 2001 and 2002) for fear of resurgent inflation and in order to establish its credibility. Since then, however, the ECB has conducted a fairly easy monetary policy as evidenced by the fact that the real interest rate (the nominal interest rate minus the rate of price inflation) has been only about 1 percent.

10.4. Effect of the Euro on Stability and Growth of the EMU

We can also draw lessons from the EMU for Asia by examining the effect of the EMU on growth and stability of the Euro Area. Specifically, we need to examine the effect of the EMU on (1) smoothing the business cycle, (2) long-run growth, and (3) monetary and financial stability for the countries of the euro area. Conceptually, the best way of doing this would be by counterfactual simulations. That is, by examining what the short-run and the long-run economic performance of the euro area would have been without the euro and then comparing them with the actual performance with the euro, by constructing a macro model of the euro area nested in a global model of the world economy. Counterfactual simulations involving such a large economic area facing major structural changes in a world economy in great flux are so complex and usually require so much calibration in order to obtain reasonable scenarios, however, as to make the results obtained practically meaningless. Thus, we take the safer and ultimately more useful route of evaluating the effect of the EMU by more traditional partial-equilibrium analysis. "It is better to be broadly correct than precisely wrong" as famously stated by the great Alfred Marshall at the end of the 19th century.

10.4.1. *The Relative Growth of the EMU*

Table 10.1 provides data on the economic performance of the EMU as compared with other leading advanced countries. The first column of the table shows that the average growth of the major EMU countries (Germany, France, and Italy), with the exception of Spain, as well as for the EMU as a whole, was smaller than for the other large advanced countries, except Japan, from 1999 (the year the euro came into existence) to 2006. Only the small members of the EMU, on average, grew faster. While growth could certainly could have been lower without the EMU, the fact remains that large EMU members grew more slowly than the other large advanced non-member nations (with the exception of Japan). The small members, on the other hand, grew faster than the large EMU member and non-member countries. However, so did other small advanced non-member nations such as Norway, New Zealand, and Australia (which belong neither to the euro area nor to the European Community (EC)) or Sweden and Denmark (which do belong to the second grouping, but not to in the first). Thus, a "prima facie" case can be made that the creation of the EMU did not seem to have substantially affected the growth of member countries directly.

Table 10.1. Economic performance of the Euro area and other major advanced nations, 1999–2006.

Nation/ region	Growth of real GDP (Avg. annual %)	Inflation rate (Avg. annual %)	Interest rate (Avg. annual %)	Budget deficit (Avg. % GDP)	Exports growth (2000–2005)
Germany	1.4	1.5	3.1	−2.4	5.5
France	2.0	1.8	3.1	−2.7	1.7
Italy	1.4	2.3	3.1	−3.1	−0.8
Spain	3.7	3.2	3.1	0.0	2.8
Smaller EMU	3.7	2.7	3.1	0.5	3.4
EMU	**2.1**	**2.1**	**3.1**	**−2.0**	**3.3**
U.K.	2.8	1.5	6.2	−1.1	2.6
U.S.	2.9	2.7	4.9	−2.1	0.3
Canada	3.3	2.3	4.8	0.9	0.0
Japan	1.4	−0.4	0.2	−6.5	6.2

Source: OECD Economic Outlook, June 2007 and World Bank Economic Indicators, 2007.

10.4.2. *EMU Monetary and Fiscal Policies for Stability and Growth*

Did monetary policy smooth the business cycle and stimulate growth of the EMU? The Maastricht Treaty entrusted the ECB with the sole mandate of pursuing price stability, defined as an annual inflation rate of less than 2 percent for the euro area as a whole (Duisenberg, 1999; Issing, 2005). This makes the ECB the world's most independent central bank. The ECB is only required to brief regularly the European Parliament on its activities, but the latter has no power to influence ECB's decisions. This is in sharp contrast to the situation under which the U.S. Fed operates, which is constitutionally required to pursue both price stability (by the Federal reserve Act of 1913) and full employment (by the Employment Act of 1946 and the Employment and Balanced Growth Act of 1978) and this limits somewhat its effectiveness as an inflation fighter when a conflict arises between the two goals. The almost total independence of the ECB from political influences was deliberate so as to build its reputation and shield it from political influences that might force it to provide excessive monetary stimulus, and thus lead to inflation.

The real interest rate (the nominal interest rate minus the rate of inflation) was about 1.5 percent from 1999 to 2001 and less than 1 percent from 2002 to 2006, thus making ECB monetary policy expansionary. However, the one-size-fits-all monetary policy could not help member nations facing a negative asymmetric shock (such as Italy, France, and Germany) in the face of inadequate labor mobility and fiscal transfers. This is much less of a problem for the states of the U.S., where labor mobility and fiscal transfers are much greater than in the EMU. In addition, the monetary policy of the EMU also seemed more restrained in countering cyclical fluctuations than in other large advanced countries, such as the U.S. and the U.K. What it did do was to dampen inflationary pressures in nations such as Italy facing inadequate monetary discipline.

Although fiscal policy remains a national prerogative in the EMU, it was not of much help in smoothing the business cycle and overcoming differences in cyclical or growth conditions among large EMU members because of the constrains imposed by the SGP. The 3 percent budget deficit limit relative to GDP was exceeded, however, by France between 2002 and 2004, Germany from 2002 to 2005, and Italy from 2003 to 2005, forcing a revision of the SGP. Among the other large advanced, only Canada was fiscally virtuous, while Japan the most profligate (even more than Italy). What the SGP did achieve was some fiscal discipline in the EMU members such as Belgium, Greece that Italy and, to that extent, it improved somewhat their long-term growth prospects.

10.4.3. *EMU Trade Openness*

The creation of the European free trade area and customs union increased intra-union trade. The introduction of the euro then eliminated currency volatility among member nations and stimulated trade further by eliminating the need and cost of hedging foreign exchange risks and promoting price convergence within the EMU. Firms, however, have learned how to hedge foreign exchange risks and hedging costs are very small. More effective in expanding within-EMU trade was the price convergence, especially in standardized products. Rose (2004) and Berger and Nitsch (2005) find that the creation of the euro provided a strong stimulus to intra-EMU trade. WTO (2007) data indicates, however, that intra-EU (15) trade has remained at about 62 percent of total EMU trade since the introduction of the euro. The major trade-expansionary effect in the EU seems to have occurred as a result of the creation of the free trade area and the customs union rather than by the introduction of the euro. Nevertheless, intra-EMU trade is higher than in NAFTA and much higher than in Mercosur, which do not have a common currency.

With respect to the extra-EMU trade of member countries, the creation of the euro did not seem to have had a major impact since the euro was as volatile and misaligned as the exchange rates of the member countries before the creation of the euro. Extra-EMU trade expanded only to the extent that the euro stimulated higher growth in the EMU and that some of this spilled over into more trade with the rest of the world.

10.4.4. *Conclusion*

The conclusion that we can draw from the effect of the EMU on the stability and growth of the euro area that can provide lessons for East Asia are as follows:

1. The growth of the EMU was probably not much affected *directly* by the adoption of the euro in the short run.
2. EMU monetary policy was not as responsive as in the United States and Britain; the Stability and Growth Pact imposed some fiscal discipline on EMU nations lacking it; and the one-size-fit-all monetary policy was somewhat problematic.
3. Most increase in intra-EMU trade occurred as a result of the creation of the customs union rather than by the introduction of the euro. By encouraging rapid financial integration, the euro stimulates EMU growth and trade with outsiders.
4. While the single currency brought monetary stability and prevented possible financial crises in some member countries, the euro fluctuated in value as much or more than some of the pre-EMU currencies and faced major misalignments.

10.5. Lessons from the EMU for Asia

The questions now are these: What is it that the major countries of East Asia wish to achieve with economic and monetary integration? Should they pursue these integrating schemes? What lessons can they learn from the EMU experience? It should be clear at the outset that East Asian countries, as contrasted with European countries, do not have full economic and political union as their ultimate aim. And it is not to stimulate long-term growth that they may want to pursue economic and monetary integration since they are already growing very rapidly. It is rather to put growth on a more sustainable basis and achieve monetary and financial stability, both internally and externally (i.e., avoid financial crises).

The rapid growth of the major East Asian economies is today based mostly on export-led growth and this resulted in huge trade surpluses and rapid accumulation of international reserves (mostly U.S. dollars) on their part (see Section 10.2 of this Chapter). This is clearly unsustainable in the long run and may not even be so in the medium run (say, in the next 3–5 years). Unsustainable U.S. trade deficits may lead to a collapse of the U.S. dollar and a sharp increase in interest rates and recession in the U.S., which could then spread worldwide. Although not in their immediate self-interest, the same result could occur if East Asian countries started a major unloading their dollars reserves on foreign exchange markets or even if they sharply reduced their accumulation of dollar reserves.

Unsustainable U.S. trade deficits, however, are part of a world structural problem that cannot be solved, as some economists such as Fred Bergsten (2006) and the Bush Administration believe, by a large depreciation of the Chinese currency, and thus of the yen and of the currencies of the other major Asian surplus countries. This could only bring partial and temporary relief. The solution of the problem requires structural changes in the major economies. Specifically, it requires increasing savings in the U.S., improving financial markets in emerging markets (especially in China) so as to absorb more of their savings domestically, and further economic restructuring in Europe and Japan which would stimulate their growth and imports (and thus contribute to the reduction of the U.S. trade deficits; see Salvatore, 2005). Although it would contribute to internal stability, a single East Asian currency (even if that were now possible) would not resolve the major structural problem facing the world economy today and would probably not even bring exchange rate stability, as the case of the euro clearly indicates. But let us examine the feasibility and possible benefits that East Asia could derive from economic and monetary integration and the best way to achieve it.

10.5.1. *Is East Asia an Optimum Currency Area?*

Monetary integration (a single central bank and a common currency, as in the EMU) that leads to positive net benefits requires first and foremost that the region be an optimum currency area (OCA). The conditions or criteria for an OCA include:

1. free trade or high openness to area members;
2. product, factor and financial market integration;
3. synchronized business cycle and symmetry of shocks in member countries.

The first two conditions for OCA require that the area be a common market, the third condition that they also face similar macroeconomic conditions. Is East Asia an OCA and thus a candidate for beneficial monetary integration? Although market-driven rather than formally negotiated, East Asia is already a nearly *de facto* free trade area. Intra-East Asian trade now exceeds 50 percent of total East Asian trade and is rapidly approaching NAFTA's 56 percent (WTO, 2007). In a decade it is likely to match the 62 percent intra-EC-15 trade and even the 67 percent of intra-EC-25 trade. As pointed out by Kawai and Motonishi (2005), however, intra East Asian trade is not very high without China and Japan, but it becomes 40 percent when China is included and over 50 percent when Japan is also included (up from about 35 percent in 1980). Clearly, trade integration in East Asia is inextricably linked to trade with Japan, but especially to trade with China, and it is now being further encouraged by a proliferation of bilateral and sub-regional free trade agreements (FTAs). Hughes Hallett and Richter (2007) find that although Asia-Pacific trade with the U.S. declined, relatively speaking, it is still very important (also see Chapter 7 of this volume).

With regard to the second condition for being an OCA (product, factor and financial market integration), Kawai and Motonishi (2005) find that capital movements, particularly in the form of financial flows and FDI, are high within most East Asian economies. Labor mobility is as high in

Southeast Asia (particularly in Singapore, Malaysia, and Thailand) as it was in Europe in the early 1990s, but it is still much lower than in the U.S. today, and it remains low in Northeast Asia, including Japan and Korea.

The third condition for being an OCA is that its members also face more or less synchronized business cycles and macroeconomic shocks. Evidence also presented by Kawai and Motonishi (2005) shows strong cross-economy correlation of real economic activities, financial variables and inflation rates, as well as of supply shocks, among Japan, Korea, Taiwan, Singapore, Hong Kong and even Malaysia and Thailand, but not yet with China, Indonesia, and the Philippines. Thus, the former countries are moving closer to being an OCA, but they are not quite there yet. China, Indonesia, and the Philippines need more economic restructuring in order to qualify for an OCA or join the first group. Hughes Hallett and Richter (2007) find that there are, or there may be, two Asian blocs emerging: Japan–Korea being one group and China–Singapore–Taiwan forming the other, with Malaysia as a part-time member of each group. As Frankel and Rose (1998) point out, however, a region need not fully satisfy all of the conditions for being an OCA in order to move forward toward monetary integration since monetary integration endogenously promotes and leads to further intra-area economic integration.

10.5.2. *Could Monetary Integration Work Well in East Asia?*

As pointed out above, for monetary integration to result in net benefits, a region must be an OCA, but East Asia is not yet nearly one (or two) OCA(s). However, as the EMU experience shows, being an OCA is a necessary but not a sufficient condition for beneficial monetary integration to work well. It also requires that member nations:

1. share a similar output–inflation tradeoff;
2. be willing to coordinate other economic policies, including adequate fiscal transfers;
3. create and support appropriate institutions.

Member nations must share similar output–inflation tradeoffs so that no conflicts arise in determining the appropriate common monetary policy for the area. That nations do not always have similar output–inflation tradeoffs

Table 10.2. Economic performance of the major East Asian economies. (average annual percentage, 1999–2006).

Nation/ Region	Growth of real GDP	Inflation rate	Exports growth	Growth in international reserves	Exchange rate in 2006*
China	**9.3**	**0.9**	**25**	**18.1**	**TMF**
Korea	5.7	1.5	11	12.3	IF
Taiwan, PC	4.0	−1.0	5	—	IF
Hong Kong SAR	5.3	−3.4	8	2.9	CB
Singapore	5.7	−0.2	8	6.4	MF
Average NIE	**5.2**	**−0.8**	**8**	—	—
Thailand	4.9	2.2	10	6.9	MF
Indonesia	4.4	10.5	6	4.3	MF
Philippines	4.6	5.4	1	4.0	IF
Malaysia	5.4	2.1	7	11.4	MF
Average ASEAN-4	**4.8**	**5.1**	**6**	**6.7**	—

*TMF = tightly managed floating; IF = independent floating; CB = Currency board; MF = managed floating.

Source: IMF, International Financial Statistics, 2006 & May 2007; World Bank Economic Indicators, 2007.

is shown by the U.S. willingness to accept more inflation in order to achieve higher output growth than Europe. Do the countries of East Asia share a similar inflation–output trade off? From Table 10.2, we see that, aside for Indonesia and the Philippines, the rate of inflation was very similar in East Asia, except for deflation in Taiwan, Hong Kong, Singapore and, of course, in Japan. But by their statements and their policies, the monetary authorities of deflation countries are clearly interested in avoiding deflation and having a mild inflation (in the range of 1–2 percent per year), which seems to be most conducive to economic growth. Thus, one could say that East Asian countries do share a similar output–inflation tradeoff.

Despite the strong cross-economy correlation of real economic activities, financial variables and inflation rates, as well as of supply shocks, across East Asia (except for China, Indonesia, and the Philippines) found by

Kawai and Motonishi (2005) (and Japan–Korea–U.S., on the one hand, and China–Singapore–Taiwan, on the other, according to Hughes Hallett and Richter (2007)), it is inevitable that some of the countries within the area (or each group) will be facing some negative asymmetric shocks or shocks of different dimensions with respect to other area members. This requires adequate fiscal transfers to the member nations so affected in order for monetary integration to work well. The EMU experience shows that lack of such fiscal transfers can create serious problems. De Grauwe (2006) goes as far as believing that this could even cause the collapse of the EMU unless this is remedied and the EMU moves forward toward eventual political union. Would an East Asian OCA(s) be prepared to deal (i.e., avoid) this problem?

Even more importantly, have East Asian nations created, are creating, or are willing to create the institutions necessary for monetary integration to work well? Europe spent decades in building the institutions deemed necessary to move toward monetary integration. These included the EMS (which involved the creation of the ECU), the ERM (to keep exchange rates fluctuating only within narrowly defined limits), the EMCF (to provide short- and medium-term balance-of-payments assistance to its members), and the EMI (as the forerunner of the ECB).

On the political level, the EU created the EC (the executive body of the EU), the Council of Ministers (whose members represent their own national governments), the European Parliament (elected by direct vote in the member nations every 5 years), and the Court of Justice (with power to rule over the constitutionality of the decisions of the Commission and the Council). Even with all of this, only some of the EU members chose to belong to the EMU. Britain, Sweden, Denmark, as well as all the new entrants since 2004 (with the exception of Slovenia, which joined the EMU in January 2007 and Malta and Cyprus joined in 2008), are not yet members of the EMU. Furthermore, despite the will for political integration, even the EMU is not working as well as possible because of inadequate labor mobility, little or no fiscal redistribution, and the stalling of the political unification process. This points to how difficult and how long the road to economic integration in East Asia is likely to be.

In East Asia, the creation of regional economic institutions necessary for monetary integration to work well is only in its infancy. It is limited to

(1) the Chiang Mai Initiative (CMI) established in 2000 by the ASEAN plus Three (Japan, Korea, and China) as a network of bilateral and multilateral swap arrangements aimed at helping member nations facing a currency crisis (and eventually hoping to conduct surveillance to prevent such a crisis from arising in the first place); (2) the Asian Bond Market Initiative (ABMI) and the Asian Bond Fund (ABF I and II) to encourage the development of regional bond markets; and (3) efforts to create an "East Asian Community" to pursue economic and financial cooperation. These initiatives, however, are not very operational or effective. In view of its strong dependence on extra-regional trade, political diversity, capital mobility, and lack of a political unification goal, it may take decades before East Asia could achieve monetary integration following the EMU example. The question is what can East Asian economies do now and what is the best road map to pursue the goal of future monetary integration?

10.5.3. *Moving Toward Monetary Integration in East Asia*

From what has been said above, it is clear that the conditions for monetary integration in the form of a common central bank and a single currency do not exist in East Asia today. The region is not yet an OCA and, more importantly, it does not have the institutions necessary for monetary integration to work well. As the EMU experience clearly shows, it takes time to build the necessary institutions and it requires a degree of political commitment that does not exist in Asia today — and this is not due only to the China–Japan differences. All that there exists is an awareness of the need for economic and monetary cooperation in order to achieve monetary and financial stability in the short run (i.e., avoid financial crises) and to put rapid growth on a more sustainable basis in the long run (by overcoming the serious structural problems facing the world economy today).

The growth of intra-regional trade (especially vertically integrated intra-industry trade) and financial and FDI flows clearly indicates the desirability for maintaining a reasonable degree of intra-regional stability in East Asia. This can be achieved by the adoption of a common G3 currency basket based on the U.S. dollar, the euro, and the Japanese yen against which the various members could more or less stabilize their exchange rate, depending on their specific conditions and preferences.[2] Those economies that are not ready to stabilize their currencies could start by adopting managed floating with inflation targeting. Stabilizing their exchange rates vis-à-vis the common G3 basket, more or less tightly, will also stabilize extra- and intra-regional exchange rates in East Asia. The CMI should also be enhanced or an Asian Monetary Fund (AMF) created to provide financial assistance to member countries facing a currency crisis.

After achieving reasonable regional exchange rate stabilization, the East Asian economies could move to the next level of monetary integration. This involves the creation of an Asian Monetary Unit (AMU), similar to the ECU, and setting up an Asian ERM (similar to the European ERM), requiring each member to tightly stabilize its currency to the AMU. To make the stabilization scheme credible, an AMF or AMU (similar to the EMCF) should be set up to provide adequate short-term liquidity to support all the necessary exchange market interventions to keep currencies fluctuating within the narrowly defined limits (snake) specified. It must be pointed out, however, that this did not prevent the 1992–1993 currency crisis in the EMS and the near collapse of the ERM in Europe.

It is for this reason that Chung and Eichengreen (2007, pp. 18–19) suggest a market-led rather than a political-led approach to the next or intermediate level of monetary integration in East Asia. Instead of a regional currency grid or exchange rate stabilization agreement, Chung and Eichengreen (2007) would start with the creation of a synthetic Asian Currency Unit (ACU) having full legal tender status in the member countries and circulating in parallel with existing regional currencies. There would be no need to limit the variability of East Asian currencies and thus face the danger of a European-style currency crisis. The synthetic ACU would be more stable than the regional currencies in terms of aggregate East Asian trade and financial flows, and thus it would become more attractive over time as a unit of account, medium of exchange, and store of value than the currencies of the individual member countries.

Once the parallel ACU acquires significant market share, the creation of East Asian Central Bank and common currency would be the natural

[2]This may become a four-currency basket with the inclusion of the renminbi.

next step. In the meantime, East Asia should have created the monetary and political institutions necessary for a well-functioning monetary union.[3] As the European experience shows, however, this last step (especially institution building) may take decades. Indeed, the movement toward full monetary integration may take much longer in East Asia than it took in Europe in view of the lack of an underlying political aim of eventual political unification. East Asia is further beyond the position of Europe of the 1950s toward achieving monetary unification. France and Germany have shared the common aim of achieving economic, monetary and, ultimately, full economic integration or union since the 1950s. Japan and China are nowhere near that today.

As pointed out by Kenen and Meade (2006), it may be that the way to proceed toward monetary integration, after its initial steps, would be with two or three East Asian, sub-regional monetary schemes, one revolving around Japan, one around China, and another among the ASEAN-4 countries. China may even have to remain outside any East Asian monetary union, at least at the beginning, because its much faster growth will require significant changes in its real exchange rate vis-à-vis those of other East Asian countries. While this situation could be resolved or accommodated by adequate labor and capital mobility, and price flexibility within a monetary union, it is much easier with nominal exchange rates changes. Genberg (2005) also suggests that renminbi, the yen, and the won remain independent currencies with their central banks following inflation targeting, while some of the other East Asian economies could proceed toward monetary union.

Furthermore, the size of the Chinese economy is so large in relation to other possible members of a monetary union that China may not want to share monetary authority with them. In that case, smaller countries that are highly integrated with China through trade and investments flows may want to dollarize (i.e., unilaterally adopt the renminbi as their currency, as is the case for Panama, which uses the dollar as its domestic currency; see Salvatore *et al.* (2003) and Salvatore (2004)). The only other alternative to

[3]Genberg (2005) would skip all intermediate steps and proposes that independent East Asian central banks start by closely coordinating their monetary policy through the adoption of common objectives and build the appropriate institutional framework, as a less risky road to monetary union in East Asia (recognizing, of course, that monetary unification may take even longer to achieve by this route). Also see Chapter 9 of this volume.

monetary union is for the smaller East Asian economies to follow inflation targeting with managed floating (see Cavoli and Rajan, 2003). Experience has shown that the alternative of pegging their exchange rate to another currency or a basket of currencies may be very dangerous and unsustainable for the smaller economies of East Asia in a world of very high capital flows.

In the final analysis, East Asia can achieve its major goal of some degree of monetary stability and avoid financial crises without trying to achieve full monetary integration. Monetary and financial stability requires, first and foremost, domestic monetary and fiscal discipline and the strengthening the banking sector (i.e., putting the house in order). Even then, some financial crises may not be avoided as they are the inevitable result in a world of high capital mobility.

10.6. Concluding Remarks

In Europe, monetary integration started by creating a customs union and then the institutions necessary eventual monetary unification. The process evolved over five decades in the context of its ultimate goal of political unification. Although not yet fully an OCA or having achieved fiscal unification, the EMU is moving in that direction and this provides increasing benefits to its members in terms of short-run stability and long-run growth.

This is to be contrasted in the situation in East Asia today, which is moving toward trade integration in the face of already large capital mobility without having reached the status of an OCA. Even more importantly, East Asia is still in its infancy in terms of institution building for viable monetary integration and does not have political unification as its ultimate goal. Indeed, differences between China and Japan are so great that monetary unification that includes both nations does not now seem possible.

The desire for economic and monetary integration in East Asia is based on the benefits that it expects to gain in terms of economic and financial stability in the short- and medium-term and of putting rapid growth on a more sustainable level in the long run. The EMU experience leads us to expect that these goals may have to be pursued by various partial integrating monetary schemes. One might involve the renminbi, the yen, and the won remaining independent currencies, with their central banks following inflation targeting and coordinating their policies as much as politically feasible, with some of the other East Asian economies proceeding toward deeper monetary integration.

In the final analysis, East Asia can achieve greater monetary stability and avoid financial crises without full monetary integration. Monetary and financial stability requires, first and foremost, domestic monetary and fiscal discipline and the strengthening the banking sector (i.e., putting the house in order). Even then, some financial crises may not be avoided as they are the inevitable result in a world of high capital mobility. The conclusion that monetary integration in East Asia may take a very long time and may be impossible and even unnecessary, may be too pessimistic. Remember the title an article in *Foreign Affairs* in 1996 by Rudiger Dornbusch (Dornbusch, 1996) "Eurofantasies" and that Paul Samuleson, Robert Solow, Martin Feldstein, Paul Krugman and many other distinguished economists predicted at the eve of the introduction of the euro that it would take place and if it did it would fail!

References

Berger, H and V Nitsch (2005). Zooming out: The trade effects of the Euro in historical perspective. CEFifo Working Paper No. 1435.

Bergsten, F (2006). *Testimony before the Hearing on US–China Economic Relations Revisited Committee on Finance*. United States Senate, March 29.

Cavoli, T and RS Rajan (2003). Exchange rate arrangements for East Asia post-crisis: Examining the case for open economy inflation targeting. CIES Discussion Paper 0310, April.

Chung D-K and B Eichengreen (2007). *Towards an East Asian Exchange Rate Regime*. The Brookings Institution.

De Grauwe, P (2006). Enlargement of the Euro Area. CESifo Forum, December, pp. 3–10.

Dornbusch, R (1996). Euro Fantasies: Common Currency as Panacea. *Foreign Affairs*, September/October, 75, pp. 110–124.

Duisenberg, WF (1999). Economic and Monetary Union in Europe — The challenges ahead. In *New Challenges for Monetary Policy*. Federal Reserve Bank of Kansas City, Symposium Sponsored by the Federal Reserve Bank of Kansas City, Kansas City, pp. 185–194.

Frankel, JA and AK Rose (1998). The endogeneity of the optimum currency area criterion. *Economic Journal*, 108, 1009–1025.

Genberg, H (2005). Exchange rate arrangements and financial integration in East Asia: On a collision course? *International Economics and Economic Policy*, 3, pp. 359–377.

Hughes Hallett and C. Richter (2007). *Measuring Spillover and Convergence Effects in the Asia-Pacific Region: Is the US No Longer the Economy of First Resort*? Mimeo.

Issing, O (2005). The ECB and the Euro — The first 6 years: A view from the ECB. *Journal of Policy Modeling*, 27, 405–420.

Kawai, M and T Motonishi (2005). Is East Asia an optimum currency area? In *Financial Interdependence and Exchange Regimes in East Asia*, M Kawai (ed.), pp. 157–198. Policy Research Institute of the Japan Ministry of Finance.

Kenen, P and E Meade (2006). Monetary integration in East Asia. *Proceedings*, pp. 1–38. Federal Reserve Bank of San Francisco, January.

Rose, A (2004). The effect of common currencies on international trade: A meta-analysis. In *Monetary Unions and Hard Pegs. Effects on Trade, Financial Development and Stability*, V Alexander, J Melitz and GM von Fusternberg (eds.), pp. 101–112. Oxford University Press.

Salvatore, D (1996). The European Monetary System: Crisis and Future. *Open Economies Review*, 7, 593–615.

Salvatore, D (1997). The unresolved problem with the EMS and EMU. *American Economic Review*, 87, 224–226.

Salvatore, D (2002a). The Euro: Expectations and performance. *Eastern Economic Journal*, 28, 121–136. Reprinted in *The Globalization and International Economic Instability*, P Gray and R Dillard (eds.), pp. 415–430. Edward Elgar.

Salvatore, D (2002b). The Euro, The European Central Bank, and the International Monetary System. *The Annals of the American Academy of Political and Social Science*, 579, 153–167.

Salvatore, D (2004). Euroization, dollarization and the international monetary system. In *The Euro and Dollarization Forms of Monetary Union in Integrating Regions*, V Alexander, J Melitz and G von Furstenberg (eds.), pp. 27–40. Oxford University Press.

Salvatore, D (2005). Currency misalignments and trade asymmetries among major economic areas. *Journal of Economic Asymmetries*, 2, pp. 1–25. Reprinted in *Problems in International Trade*, Volbert, A (ed.), pp. 1–19. Edward Elgar.

Salvatore, D, J Dean and T Willett (eds.) (2003). *The Dollarization Debate*. Oxford University Press.

WTO (2007). *International Trade Statistics*. Geneva.

INDEX